Structured Finance

For other titles in the Wiley Finance Series
please see www.wiley.com/finance

Structured Finance

The Object-Oriented Approach

Umberto Cherubini
Giovanni Della Lunga

John Wiley & Sons, Ltd

Other Wiley Editorial Offices

John Wiley & Sons Inc., 111 River Street, Hoboken, NJ 07030, USA

Jossey-Bass, 989 Market Street, San Francisco, CA 94103-1741, USA

Wiley-VCH Verlag GmbH, Boschstr. 12, D-69469 Weinheim, Germany

John Wiley & Sons Australia Ltd, 42 McDougall Street, Milton, Queensland 4064, Australia

John Wiley & Sons (Asia) Pte Ltd, 2 Clementi Loop #02-01, Jin Xing Distripark, Singapore 129809

John Wiley & Sons Canada Ltd, 6045 Freemont Blvd, Mississauga, ONT, L5R 4J3, Canada

Wiley also publishes its books in a variety of electronic formats. Some content that appears in print may not be available in electronic books.

Anniversary Logo Design: Richard J. Pacifico

Library of Congress Cataloging in Publication Data

Cherubini, Umberto.
    Structured finance : the object oriented approach / Umberto Cherubini, Giovanni Della Lunga.
      p. cm. — (Wiley finance series)
    Includes bibliographical references and index.
    ISBN 978-0-470-02638-0 (cloth : alk. paper) 1. Structured notes (Securities) 2. Derivative securities.
    3. Investment analysis—Mathematical models. 4. Financial engineering. I. Della Lunga, Giovanni.
    II. Title.
    HG4651.5.C46 2007
    332.63′27—dc22

                                          2007010265

British Library Cataloguing in Publication Data

A catalogue record for this book is available from the British Library

ISBN 978-0-470-02638-0 (HB)

Typeset in 10/12pt Times by Integra Software Services Pvt. Ltd, Pondicherry, India
Printed and bound in Great Britain by Antony Rowe Ltd, Chippenham, Wiltshire
This book is printed on acid-free paper responsibly manufactured from sustainable forestry
in which at least two trees are planted for each one used for paper production.

Contents

1

Structured Finance: A Primer

1.1 INTRODUCTION

In this chapter we introduce the main, and first, concepts that one has to grasp in order to build, evaluate, purchase and sell financial structured products. Structured finance denotes the art (and science) of designing financial products to satisfy the different needs of investors and borrowers as closely as possible. In this sense, it represents a specific technique and operation of the financial intermediation business. In fact, the traditional banking activity, i.e. designing loans to provide firms with funds and deposits to attract funds from retail investors, along with managing the risk of a gap in their payoffs, was nothing but the most primitive example of a structuring process. Nowadays, the structured finance term has been provided with a more specialized meaning, i.e. that of a set of products involving the presence of derivatives, but most of the basic concepts of the old-fashioned intermediation business carry over to this new paradigm. Building on this basic picture, we will make it more and more involved, in this chapter and throughout the book, adding to these basic demands and needs the questions that professionals in the modern structured finance business address to make the products more and more attractive to investors and borrowers.

The very reason of existence of the structured finance market, as it is conceived today, rests on the same arguments as the old-fashioned banking business. That was motivated as the only way for investors to provide funds to borrowers, just in the same way as any sophisticated structured finance product is nowadays constructed to enable someone to do something that could not be done in any other way (or in a cheaper way) under the regulation. In this sense, massive use of derivatives and financial engineering appears as the most natural development of the old intermediation business.

To explain, take the simplest financial product you may imagine, a zero coupon bond, i.e. a product paying interest and principal in a single shot at the end of the investment. The investor's question is obviously whether it is worth giving up some consumption today for some more at the end of the investment, given the risk that may be involved. The borrower's question is whether it is worth using this instrument as an effective funding solution for his projects. What if the return is too low for the investors or so high that the borrower cannot afford it? That leads straight to the questions typically addressed by the structurer: what's wrong with that structure? Maybe the maturity is too long, so what about designing a different coupon structure? Or maybe investors would prefer a higher expected return, even at the cost of higher risk, so why not make the investment contingent on some risky asset, perhaps the payoff of the project itself? If the borrower finds the promised return too high, what about making the project less risky by asking investors to provide some protection? All of these questions would lead to the definition of a "structure" for the bond as close as possible to those needs, and this structure will probably be much more sophisticated than any traditional banking product.

The production process of a structured finance tool involves individuation of a business idea and the design of the product, the determination and analysis of pricing, and the definition of risk measurement and management procedures. Going back again to the commercial banking example, the basic principles were already there: design of attractive investment and funding products, determination of interest rates consistent with the market, management of the misalignment between asset and liabilities (or asset liability management, ALM). Mostly the same principles apply to modern structured finance products: how should we assemble derivatives and standard products together, how should we price them and manage risk?

The hard part of the job would then be to explain the structure, as effectively as possible, to the investors and borrowers involved, and convince them that it is made up to satisfy their own needs. The difficulty of this task is something we are going to share in this book. What are you actually selling or buying? What are the risks? Could you do any better? We will see that asking the right questions will lead to an answer that will be found to be straightforward, almost self-evident: why did not I get it before? It is the **replicating portfolio**. The bad and good news is that many structured products have their own replicating portfolios, peculiar to them and different from those of any other. Bad news because this makes the design of a taxonomy of these products an impossible task; good news because the analysis of any new product is as surprising and thrilling as a police story.

1.2   ARBITRAGE-FREE VALUATION AND REPLICATING PORTFOLIOS

All of the actors involved in the production process described above, i.e. the structurer, the pricer and the risk manager, share the same working tools: arbitrage-free valuation and the identification of replicating strategies for every product. Each and every product has to be associated to a replicating portfolio, or a dynamic strategy, well suited to deliver the same payoff at some future date, and its value has to be equal to that of its replicating portfolio. The argument goes that, if it were not so, unbounded arbitrage profits could be earned by going long in the cheaper portfolio and going short in the dearer one. This concept is the common fabric of work for structurers, pricers and risk managers. The structurer assembles securities in a replicating portfolio to design the product, the pricer evaluates the products as the sum of the prices of the securities in the replicating portfolio, and the risk manager uses the replicating portfolio to identify the risk factors involved and make the appropriate hedging decisions. Here we will elaborate on this subject to provide a bird's-eye review of the most basic concepts in finance, developed along the replicating portfolio idea. This would require the reader to be well acquainted with them. For intermediate readers, mandatory references for a broad introduction to finance are reported at the end of the chapter.

Under a standard finance textbook model the production process of a structured product would be actually deterministic. In fact, the basic assumption is that each product is endowed with an "exact" replicating strategy (the payoff of each product is "attainable"): this is what we call the "market completeness" hypothesis. Everybody knows that this assumption is miles away from reality. Markets are inherently "incomplete", meaning that no "exact" replicating portfolio exists for many products, and it is particularly so for the complex products in the structured finance business. Actually, market incompleteness makes life particularly difficult in structured finance. In fact, the natural effect is that the production process of these securities involves a set of decisions over stochastic outcomes. The structurer would compare the product being constructed against the cheapest alternative directly available to the customers on the market. The pricer has to select the "closest" replicating portfolio to come up with a reasonable price from both the buyer's and the seller's point of view. Finally, the risk manager has to face the problem of the "hedging error" he would bear under alternative hedging strategies.

1.3 REPLICATING PORTFOLIOS FOR DERIVATIVES

Broadly speaking, designing a structured product means defining a set of payments and a set of rules determining each one of them. These rules define the derivative contracts embedded in the product, and the no-arbitrage argument requires that the overall value of the product has to be equal to the sum of the plain and the derivative part. But we may push our replicating portfolio argument even further. In principle, a derivative may be considered as a structure including a long or short position in a risk factor against debt or investment in the risk-free asset. This is the standard *leverage* feature that is the distinctive mark of a derivative contract.

1.3.1 Linear derivatives

As the simplest example, take a forward contract $CF(S, t; F(0), T)$, that is the value at time t of a contract, stipulated at time 0, for delivery at time T of one unit of the underlying S at the price $F(0)$. The payoff to be settled at time T is linear: $S(T) - F(0)$. By a straightforward no-arbitrage argument, it is easy to check that the same payoff can be attained by buying spot a unit of the underlying and issuing debt with maturity T and nominal value $F(0)$. No-arbitrage requires that the value of the contract has to be equal to that of the replicating portfolio

$$CF(S, t; F(0), T) = S(t) - v(t, T)F(0) \tag{1.1}$$

where $v(t, T)$ is the discount factor function – that is, the value, at time t, of a unit of currency to be due at time T. By market convention, the delivery price is the *forward price* observed at time 0, when the contract is originated. The forward price is technically defined as $F(0) \equiv S(0)/v(0, T)$, so that $CF(S, 0; F(0), T) = 0$ and the value of the forward contract is zero at origin. Notice that the price of a linear contract does not depend on the distribution of the underlying asset. Furthermore, the replicating strategy does not call for a rebalancing of the portfolio as time elapses and the value of the underlying asset changes: it is a *static replication* strategy.

1.3.2 Nonlinear derivatives

Nonlinear products, i.e. options, can be provided with a replicating portfolio by the same line of reasoning. Take a European call contract, payoff $\max(S(T) - K, 0)$, with a K strike price for an exercise time T. By the same argument, we look for a replicating portfolio including a spot position in Δ_c units of the underlying and a debt position for a nominal value W_c. The price of the call option at time t is

$$CALL\,(S, t; K, T) = \Delta_c S(t) - v(t, T)\,W_c \tag{1.2}$$

Notice that replicating portfolio can be equivalently represented in terms of two other elementary financial products. These two products are digital, meaning they yield a fixed payoff is the event of $S(T) \geq K$, and 0 otherwise. The fixed payoff may be defined in terms of units of the asset or in units of currency. In the former case the digital option is called *asset-or-nothing* (AoN), and in the latter case, *cash-or-nothing* (CoN). It is easy to check that going long an AoN$(S, t; K, T)$ for one unit of the underlying and going short CoN$(S, t; K, T)$ options for K units of currency yields a payoff $\max(S(T) - K, 0)$. We then have (see Figure 1.1)

$$\text{CALL}(S, t; K, T) = \text{AoN}(S, t; K, T) - K\text{CoN}(S, t; K, T) \tag{1.3}$$

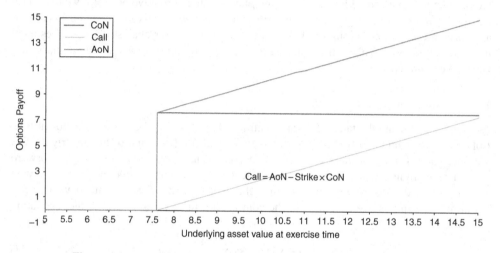

Figure 1.1   Call option payoff decomposition in terms of digital options

Nonlinearity of the payoff implies that the value of the product depends on the probability distribution of $S(T)$. Without getting into the specification of such distribution, notice that for scenarios under which the event $S(T) \geq K$ has measure 0 we have that both the AoN and the CoN products have zero value. For scenarios under which the event has measure 1, the AoN product will have a value of $S(t)$ and the CoN option (with payoff of one unit of currency) will be worth $v(t, T)$. This amounts to stating that $0 \leq \Delta_c \leq 1$ and $0 \leq W_c \leq K$. Accordingly,

$$0 \leq \text{CALL}(S, t; K, T) \leq \text{CF}(S, t; K, T) \tag{1.4}$$

and the value of the call option has to be between zero and the value of a long position in a forward contract. This is the most elementary example of an incomplete market problem. Without further comment on the probability distribution of $S(T)$, beyond the scenarios with probability 0 and 1, all we can state are the *pricing bounds* of the product, and the corresponding replicating portfolios that are technically called its *super-replicating portfolios*. The choice of a specific price then calls for the specification of a particular stochastic dynamic of the underlying asset and a corresponding *dynamic replication* strategy.

Once a specific price is obtained for the call option, the replicating portfolio of the corresponding put option [payoff: $\max(K - S(T), 0)$] can be obtained from the well-known *put–call parity* relationship

$$\text{CALL}(S, t; K, T) - \text{PUT}(S, t; K, T) = \text{CF}(S, t; K, T) \tag{1.5}$$

which can be immediately obtained by looking at the payoffs. Notice that by using the replicating portfolios of the forward contract and the call option above, we have

$$\text{CALL}(S, t; K, T) - \text{PUT}(S, t; K, T) = (\Delta_c - 1) S(t) + v(t, T)(K - W_c) \tag{1.6}$$

Recalling the bounds for the delta and leverage of the call option, it is essential to check that a put option amounts to a short position in the underlying asset and a long position in the risk-free bond. The corresponding pricing bounds will then be zero and the value of a short position in a forward contract.

1.4 NO-ARBITRAGE AND PRICING

Selecting a price within the pricing bound calls for the specification of the stochastic dynamics of the underlying asset. A world famous choice is that of a geometric Brownian motion.

$$dS(t) = \mu S(t) \, dt + \sigma S(t) \, dz(t) \tag{1.7}$$

where $dz(t) \sim \Phi(0, dt)$ is defined a Wiener process and μ and σ are constant parameters (*drift* and *diffusion*, respectively). Technically speaking, the stochastic process is defined with respect to a filtered probability space $\{\Omega, \Im, \Im_t, \mathbf{P}\}$. The filtration determines the dynamics of the information set in the economy, and the probability measure $\mathbf{P}$ describes its stochastic dynamics. It is very easy to check that the transition probability of S at any time $T > t$, conditional on the value $S(t)$ observed at time t, is log-normal. Assuming a constant volatility σ then amounts to assuming Gaussian log-returns.

1.4.1 Univariate claims

To understand how the no-arbitrage argument enters into the picture just remember that the standard *arbitrage pricing theory* (APT) framework requires

$$E\left(\frac{dS(t)}{S(t)}\right) = \mu \, dt = (r + \gamma\sigma) \, dt \tag{1.8}$$

where r is the instantaneous interest rate intensity and γ is the *market price of risk* for the risk factor considered in the economy (the analysis can of course be easily extended to other risk factors). The key point is that the market price of risk (for any source of risk) must be the same across all the financial products. Financial products then differ from one another only in their sensitivity to the risk factors. Based on this basic concept, one can use the Girsanov theorem to derive

$$dS(t) = (r + \gamma\sigma) S(t) \, dt + \sigma S(t) \, dz(t) = rS(t) \, dt + \sigma S(t) \, dz^*(t) \tag{1.9}$$

where $dz^*(t) \equiv dz(t) + \gamma dt$ is a Wiener process in the probability space $\{\Omega, \Im, \Im_t, \mathbf{Q}\}$. The new $\mathbf{Q}$ measure is such that any financial product or contract yields an instantaneous interest rate intensity, without any risk premium. For this reason it is called the *risk-adjusted* measure. To illustrate, consider the call option written on S, described above. We have

$$d\,\text{CALL}\,(S, t; K, T) = \text{CALL}\,(S, t; K, T)\,(rdt + \sigma_{\text{Call}}dz^*(t)) \tag{1.10}$$

where σ_{Call} is the instantaneous volatility that can be immediately obtained by Ito's lemma. Notice that Ito's lemma also yields

$$E_Q\,(d\,\text{Call}) = \left(\frac{\partial \text{Call}}{\partial t} + \frac{\partial \text{Call}}{\partial S} rS\,(t) + \frac{1}{2} \frac{\partial^2 \text{Call}}{\partial S^2} \sigma^2 S\,(t)^2 \right) dt = r\,\text{Call}\,dt \tag{1.11}$$

from which it is immediate to recover the Black–Scholes *fundamental* PDE:

$$\frac{\partial \text{Call}}{\partial t} + \frac{\partial \text{Call}}{\partial S} rS\,(t) + \frac{1}{2} \frac{\partial^2 \text{Call}}{\partial S^2} \sigma^2 S\,(t)^2 - r\,\text{Call} = 0 \tag{1.12}$$

Derivative products must solve the fundamental PDE in order to rule out arbitrage opportunities. The price of specific derivative products (in our case a European call) requires specification of particular boundary solutions (in our case $\text{Call}(T) = \max(S(T) - K, 0)$).

Alternatively the solution may be recovered by computing an expected value under the measure $\mathbf{Q}$. Remember that under such a measure all the financial products yield a risk-free instantaneous rate of return. Assume that in the economy there exists a *money market fund* $B(t)$ yielding the instantaneous rate of return $r(t)$:

$$dB\,(t) = rB\,(t) \tag{1.13}$$

It is important to check that the special property of the measure $\mathbf{Q}$ can be represented as a martingale property for the prices of assets computed using the money market fund as the *numeraire*:

$$E_Q\left[\frac{S\,(T)}{B\,(T)} \right] = \frac{S\,(t)}{B\,(t)} \Rightarrow E_Q\left[\frac{\text{CALL}\,(T)}{B\,(T)} \right] = \frac{\text{CALL}\,(t)}{B\,(t)} \tag{1.14}$$

For this reason, the measure $\mathbf{Q}$ is also called an *equivalent martingale measure* (EMM), where the term *equivalent* refers to the technical requirement that the two measures must assign probability zero to the same events (complying with the super-replication bounds described above).

An alternative way of stating the martingale property is to say that under measure $\mathbf{Q}$ the expected value of each and every product at any future date T has to be equal to its forward price for delivery at time T. So, for example, for our call option under examination we have

$$\text{Call}\,(t) = E_Q\left[\text{Call}\,(T) \frac{B\,(t)}{B\,(T)} \right] = E_Q\left[\exp\left(-\int_t^T r\,(u)\,du \right) \max\,(S\,(T) - K, 0) \right] \tag{1.15}$$

$$= v\,(t, T)\,E_Q[\max\,(S\,(T) - K, 0)]$$

where we have assumed $r(t)$ to be non-stochastic or independent on the underlying asset $S(t)$. It is well known that the same result applies to cases in which this requirement is violated, apart for a further change of measure from the EMM measure $\mathbf{Q}$ to the *forward martingale measure* (FMM) $\mathbf{Q}(T)$: the latter is obtained by directly requiring the forward prices to be martingales, using the risk-free discount bond maturing at time T ($v(t, T)$) instead of the money market fund as the numeraire.

Under the log-normal distribution assumption in the Black–Scholes model we recover a specific solution for the call option price:

$$\text{CALL}\,(S, t;\, K, T) = \Delta_c S\,(t) - v\,(t, T) W_c \tag{1.16}$$

with

$$\Delta_c = \Phi\,(d_1) \qquad W_c = K\Phi\,(d_2)$$

$$d_1 = \frac{\ln(F\,(t)\,/K) + \sigma^2/2\,(T - t)}{\sigma\sqrt{T - t}}$$

$$d_2 = d_1 - \sigma\sqrt{T - t}$$

$$F\,(t) \equiv \frac{S\,(t)}{v\,(t, T)}$$

where $\Phi(.)$ denotes the standard normal cumulative distribution and $F(t)$ is the forward price of $S(t)$ for delivery at time T.

While the standard Black and Scholes approach is based on the assumption of constant volatility, there is vastly documented evidence that *volatility*, measured by whatever statistics, is far from constant. Non-constant volatility gives rise to different implied volatilities for different strikes (*smile effect*) and different exercise dates (*term structure of volatility*). Option traders "ride" the volatility surface betting on changes in skewness and kurtosis much in a same way as fixed income traders try to exploit changes in the interest rate term structure. Allowing for volatility risk paves the way to the need to design a reliable model for the stochastic dynamics of volatility. Unfortunately, no general consensus has as yet been reached on such a model. Alternatively, one could say that asset returns are not normally distributed, but the question of which other distribution could be a good candidate to replace the log-normal distribution of prices (and the corresponding geometric Brownian motion) has not yet found a definite satisfactory answer. This argument brings the concept of *model risk* as a paramount risk management issue for nonlinear derivative and structured products.

1.4.2 Multivariate claims

Evaluation problems are compounded in cases in which a derivative product is exposed to more than one risk factor. Take, for example, a derivative contract whose underlying asset is a function $f(S_1, S_2, \ldots, S_N)$. We may again assume a log-normal multivariate process for each risk factor S_i:

$$dS_i\,(t) = \mu_i S_i\,(t)\,dt + \sigma_i S_i\,(t)\,dz_i\,(t) \tag{1.17}$$

where we assume the shocks to be correlated $E(dz_i(t), dz_j(t)) = \rho_{ij}\,dt$. The correlation structure among the risk factors then enters into the picture.

Parallel to the Black–Scholes model in a univariate world, constant volatilities and correlations lead to the assumption of normality of returns in a multivariate setting. Extending the analysis beyond the Black–Scholes framework calls for a different multivariate probability distribution for the returns. The problem is even more compounded because the joint distribution must be such that the marginal distribution be consistent with the stochastic volatility behaviour analysed for every single risk factor. A particular tool, which will be used extensively throughout this book, enables us to break down the problem of identifying a joint distribution into that of identifying the marginals and the dependence structure independently. The methodology is known as the *copula function* approach. A copula function enables us to write

$$\Pr(S_1 \leq K_1, S_2 \leq K_2, \ldots, S_n \leq K_n) = C\left(\Pr(S_1 \leq K_1), \Pr(S_2 \leq K_2), \ldots, \Pr(S_n \leq K_n)\right)$$
(1.18)

where $C(u_1, u_2, \ldots, u_N)$ is a function satisfying particular requirements.

Alternatively – particularly for derivatives with a limited number of underlying assets – a possibility is to resort to the change of numeraire technique. This could apply to bivariate claims, such as, for example, the option to exchange (OEX), which gives the holder the right to exchange one unit of asset S_1 against K units of asset S_2 at time T. The payoff is then $\text{OEX}(T) = \max(S_1(T) - KS_2(T), 0)$. In this case, using S_2 as the numeraire, we may use the Girsanov theorem to show that the prices of both S_1 and S_2, computed using $S_2(T)$ as numeraire, are martingale. We then have

$$\text{OEX}(t) = S_2(t) E_M \left[\max\left(\frac{S_1(T)}{S_2(T)} - K, 0 \right) \right]$$
(1.19)

with M a new martingale measure such that $E_M(S_1(T)/S_2(T)) = S_1(t)/S_2(t)$. It is easy to check that if S_1 and S_2 are log-normal, it yields the famous Margrabe formula for exchange options.

As a further special case, consider $S_2(t) \equiv v(t, T)$, that is, the discount factor function. As we obviously have $v(T, T) = 1$, we get

$$\text{OEX}(t) = v(t, T) E_M \left[\max\left(S_1(T) - K, 0 \right) \right]$$
(1.20)

and measure M is nothing but the *forward martingale measure* (FMM) $Q(T)$ quoted above. Furthermore, if $Q(T)$ is log-normal, we recover Black's formula

$$\text{CALL}(S, t; K, T) = v(t, T) \left[\Delta_c F(S, t; T) - W_c \right]$$
(1.21)

where the *delta* Δ_c and *leverage* W_c are defined as above.

1.5   THE STRUCTURING PROCESS

We are now in a position to provide a general view of the structuring process, with the main choices to be made in the design phase and the issues involved for the pricing and risk management functions. In a nutshell, the decision boils down to the selection of a set of maturities. For each maturity one has then to design the exposure to the risk factors. Choices are to be made concerning both the nature of the risk factors to be selected (interest rate risk, equity, credit or others) and the specific kind of exposure (linear or nonlinear, long or short). In other words, designing a structure product amounts to assembling derivative contracts to design a specific payoff structure contingent on different realizations of selected risk factors.

1.5.1   The basic objects

Let us start with an abstract description of what structuring a financial product is all about. It seems that it all boils down to the design of three objects. The first is a set of maturity dates representing the due date of cash flow payments:

$$\{t_1, t_2, \ldots, t_i, \ldots, t_n\}$$

The second is a set of cash flows representing the interest payments on the capital

$$\{c_1, c_2, \ldots, c_i, \ldots, c_n\}$$

The third is the repayment plan of the capital

$$\{k_1, k_2, \ldots, k_i, \ldots, k_n\}$$

or (the same concept stated in a different way) a residual debt plan

$$\{w_1, w_2, \ldots, w_i, \ldots, w_n\}$$

Building up a structured finance product amounts to setting rules allowing univocal definition of each one of these objects. Note that all the objects may in principle be deterministic or stochastic. Repayment of capital may be decided deterministically at the beginning of the contract, according to standard amortizing schedules on a predefined set of maturities, and with a fixed coupon payment (as a percentage of residual debt): alternatively, a flat, and again deterministic, payment schedule can be designed to be split into interest and capital payments. Fixed rate bonds, such as the so-called bullet bonds, are the most standard and widespread examples of such structures. It is, however, in the design of the rules for the definition of stochastic payments that most of the creative nature of the structurer function comes into play. Coupon payments may be made contingent on different risk factors, ranging from interest rates to equity and credit indexes, and may be defined in different currencies. The repayment plan may instead feature rules to enable us to postpone (*extendible bonds*) or anticipate (*retractable bonds*) the repayment of capital, or to allow for the repayment to be made in terms of other assets, rather than cash (*convertible bonds*). These choices may be assigned to either the borrower or the lender, and may be made at one, or several dates: notice that this feature also contributes towards making the choice of the set of payment dates stochastic (*early exercise feature*). As one can glean directly from the jargon used, structuring a product means that we introduce derivative contracts in the definition of the coupon and the repayment plans.

1.5.2   Risk factors, moments and dimensions

The core of the structuring process consists of selecting the particular kind of risk exposure characterizing the financial product. With respect to such exposure, a structurer addresses three basic questions. Which are the technical features of the product, or, in other words, which is the risk profile of the product? Is there some class of investors or borrowers that may be interested in such risk profile; that is, which is the demand side for this product? Finally, one should address the question whether investors and borrowers can achieve the same risk profile in an alternative, cheaper way – that is, which are the main competitors of the product?

In this book we are mainly concerned with the first question, i.e. that of the production technology of the structuring process, which is of course a mandatory prerequisite to addressing the other two, which instead are more related to the demand and supply schedules of the structured finance market.

In the definition of the risk profile of the product one has to address three main questions:

- Which kind of risk factors?
- Which moments of risk factors?
- Which dimension of risk factors?

Which kind of risk factors?

One has to decide the very nature of the risk exposure provided in the product. Standard examples are

- interest rates/term structure risk;
- equity risk;
- inflation risk/commodity risk;
- credit risk/country risk;
- foreign exchange risk.

Very often, or should we say always, a single product includes more than one risk factor. For example, interest rate risk is always present in the very nature of the product to provide exchange of funds at different times, and credit risk is almost always present as the issuer of the product often is a *defaultable* entity. Foreign exchange risk enters whenever the risk factor is referred to a different country with respect to that of the investor or borrower. Of course, these kinds of risk are, so to speak, "built-in to" the product, and are, loosely speaking, inherited from standard contractual specification of the product such as the issuer, the currency in which payoffs and risk factors are denominated. Apart from this, of course, some risk factor characterizes the very nature, or the dominant risk exposure of the product, so that, for example, we denote one product equity linked and another one credit linked. More recent products, known as *hybrids*, include two sources of risk as the main feature of the product (such as forex and credit risk in the so-called "*currency risk swap*").

Which moments of risk factors?

The second feature to address is the kind of sensitivity one wants to provide to the risk factors. The usual distinction in this respect is between *linear* and *nonlinear* products. Allowing for linear sensitivity to the risk factor enables us to limit the effect to the first moment. The inclusion of option-like features in the structure introduces a second dimension into the picture: dependence on *volatility*. In the post-Black and Scholes era, *volatility* is far from constant, and represents an important attribute of every risk factor. This means that when evaluating a structured product that includes a nonlinear derivative, one should take into account the possibility that the value of the product could be affected by a change in volatility, even though the first moment of the risk factor stays unchanged.

Which dimension of risk factor?

The *model risk* problem is severely compounded in structured products in which the risk factor is made up of a "*basket*" of many individual risk factors. These products are the very frontier of structured finance and are widespread both in the equity and the credit-linked segments of the market. Using a basket rather than a single source of risk in a structured product is motivated on the obvious ground of providing *diversification* to the product, splitting the risk factor into *systematic* (or *market*) and *idiosyncratic* (or *specific*) parts. From standard finance textbooks we know that the amount of systematic risk in a product is determined by the covariance, or by the correlation between each individual risk factor and the market. But we should also note that, in that approach, volatilities and correlation of asset returns are assumed constant, and this is again clearly at odds with the evidence in financial market data. Correlation then is not constant, and the value of a financial product may be affected by a change in correlation even though neither the value of the risk factor nor its volatility has changed. Again, this paves the way to the need to devise a model for correlation dynamics, a question that has not yet found a unique satisfactory answer.

1.5.3 Risk management

The development of a structured finance market has posed a relevant challenge to the financial risk management practice and spurred the development of new risk measurement techniques. The increasing weight of structured financial products has brought into the balance sheet of the financial intermediaries – both those involved on the buy and the sell side – greater exposure to contingent claims and derivative contracts. Most of these exposures were new to the traditional financial intermediation business, not only for the nature of risk involved (well far beyond term structure risk) but also for the nonlinearity or exotic nature of the payoffs involved.

Optionality

The increased weight of nonlinear payoffs has raised the problem of accuracy of the parametric risk measurement techniques, in favour of simulation-based techniques. The development of exotic products, in particular, has given risk managers a two-fold problem: on the one hand, the need to analyse the pricing process in depth to unravel the risks nested in the product; on the other hand, the need to resort to acceptable pricing approximations in closed form, or at least light enough to be called in simulation routines as many times as necessary. Nonlinear payoffs have also raised the problem of evaluating the sensitivity of the market value of a position to changes in volatility and correlation, as well as the shape of the probability distribution representing the pricing kernel.

Measurement risk

Coping with a specification of volatility and correlation immediately leads to other risks that are brought into the picture. One kind of risk has to do with volatility and correlation estimation. This *measurement risk* problem is common to every statistical application and has to do with how a particular sample may be considered representative of the universe of the events from a statistical inference point of view. Some technical methods can be used to reduce such estimation risk. In financial applications, however, this problem is compounded by the need to choose the proper information source – a choice that is more a matter of art than science and calls for good operating knowledge of the market. What is typical of financial applications is in fact the joint presence of *"implied"* and *"historical"* information and the need to choose between them. So, what is the true volatility figure? Is it the implied volatility backed out from a cross-section analysis of option prices, or is it to be estimated from the time series of prices of the underlying assets? Or do both cross-section prices and time series data include part of the information? And what about correlation?

Model risk

A different kind of risk has to do with the possible misspecification of the statistical model used. Apart from the information source used and the technique applied, the shape of the probability distribution we are using may not be the same as that generating the data. This *model risk* takes us back to the discussion above on possible statistical specifications for volatility and correlation dynamics in a post-Black and Scholes world. As we stated previously, no alternative model has been successful in replacing the Black–Scholes framework. Apart from choosing a specific model, however, one can cope with model risk by asking which is the sign of the position with respect to volatility and correlation and performing *stress testing analysis* using alternative scenarios.

Long-term risk

A particular feature of many structured finance products that compounds the problems of both *measurement* and *model* risk is that typically the contingent claims involved are referred to maturities that are very far in the future. It is not unusual to find embedded options to be exercised in five years or more. The question is then: Which is a reasonable volatility figure for the distribution of the underlying asset in five years? There is no easy way out from this *long-term risk* feature, other than sticking to the standard Black–Scholes constant volatility assumption, or sophisticated models to predict persistent changes in volatility. Again, a robust solution is to resort to extreme scenarios for volatility and correlation.

Counterparty risk

Last, but not least, structured finance has brought to the centre of the scene *counterparty risk*. Not only do these products expose the investor and/or the borrower to the possibility that the counterparty could not face its obligation, but very often these products are *hedged*, resorting to a *back-to-back* strategy on the *over-the-counter* (OTC) market. This is particularly so for products, including complex exotic derivatives, that may be particularly difficult to *delta–gamma hedge* on organized markets. So, to take the example of a very common product, if one is issuing an equity-linked note whose payoff is designed as a basket Asian option, he can consider hedging the embedded option position directly on the market, or can hedge it on the OTC market by buying an option with the same exact features from an investment bank. The cost of the former choice is the need to have sophisticated human resources, and some unavoidable degree of *basis risk* and/or *hedging risk*. The risk with the latter choice is default of the counterparty selling the option, in which case one has to look for a different counterparty and to pay a new premium to keep the position hedged (*substitution cost*). Allowing for counterparty risk causes weird effects on the risk management of derivative products. Not only is it dangerous to overlook this source of risk *per se*, but it may also interfere with market risk inasmuch as counterparty risk is not taken into account in the pricing and hedging activity.

1.6   A TALE OF TWO BONDS

In the spirit of introducing the reader to the methodology of structured products, rather than to a classification, we now provide an example involving two of the easiest cases: an equity-linked and a reverse convertible bond. While these products are probably very well known even to non-professional readers, we think that following them in a sort of "parallel slalom", rather than one by one, would help to summarize and highlight some of the basic methodological aspects discussed above, which are of general interest for the analysis of any other product.

Take a zero coupon bond by which investors provide funding to some borrower. The maturity of the zero coupon bond is T and the nominal amount of principal is L. Define $S(T)$ the value of a risky asset at the date of maturity of the bond.

Consider the two following structures:

- *Equity-linked note*: At time T the note will pay:

  (i) the principal L;
  (ii) a coupon equal to the greater between a guaranteed return r_g (typically low and unattractive) and the rate of appreciation of the risky asset with respect to a given value K: $\max(r_g, S(T)/K - 1)$.

- *Reverse convertible note*: At time T the note will pay:

  (i) the principal L if the value of $S(T)$ is greater than some value K, and an amount of stocks equal to $n = L/K$ otherwise: $\min(L, n^{S(T)})$;
  (ii) a coupon equal to r_g (typically pretty high and attractive).

We will now provide a comparative analysis of these two products, asking which are the similarities and the differences.

1.6.1   Contingent coupons and repayment plans

At a glance, it is immediately clear that both products include nonlinearities, and option-like derivatives. A first difference that emerges from mere description of the payoffs is that in the equity-linked note case the nonlinearity is introduced in the coupon payment, while in the reverse convertible case the derivative component is in the repayment plan.

We may be more precise and discover by straightforward manipulation that the coupon rate of the equity-linked note is given by

$$\text{Coupon} = r_g + \max\left[0, S(T) - (1 + r_g) K\right]/K \qquad (1.22)$$

that is, a constant part **plus** the payoff of a call option. The repayment of the principal L is guaranteed.

In the reverse convertible the coupon payment is guaranteed while it is the repayment of principal that is contingent on the risky asset $S(T)$. We have

$$\text{Repayment} = L - \max\left[0, L - nS\left(T\right)\right] = L - n\max\left[0, K - S\left(T\right)\right]$$

$$= L - L\max\left[0, K - S\left(T\right)\right]/K \tag{1.23}$$

and the principal repaid will consist of the principal **minus** the payoff of a put option.

1.6.2   Exposure to the risky asset

The two products above include a part of the payoff contingent on the value of the risky asset S. The question that immediately follows is their sensitivity to changes in the value of that asset. Does the investor have a long or short position in the asset S? It may be surprising to discover that from this point of view the two products are similar.

Let us start with the equity note. We saw that this product includes a long position in a call option. It is well known that buying a call option is a way to take a long position on the underlying asset for a *delta* ($0 \leq \Delta_c \leq 1$) quantity funded by leverage ($0 \leq W_c \leq strike$). The value of the equity-linked note (ELN) is then

$$\text{ELN} = v\left(t, T\right)\left(1 + r_g\right) + \frac{\text{CALL}\left(S, t; \left(1 + r_g\right)K, T\right)}{K}$$

$$= v\left(t, T\right)\left(1 + r_g\right) + \Delta_c \frac{S\left(t\right)}{K} - v\left(t, T\right)\frac{W_p}{K} \tag{1.24}$$

On the contrary, we know that a put option represents a short position for a *delta* $\Delta_p = \Delta_c - 1(-1 \leq \Delta_p \leq 1)$ and a long position in the risk-free asset, such that $W_p = K - W_c$. Notice, however, that the reverse convertible note (RCN) includes a short position in a put option. Assuming $L = 1$ we then have

$$\text{RCN} = v\left(t, T\right)\left(1 + r_g\right) - \text{PUT}\left(S, t; K, T\right)/K$$

$$= v\left(t, T\right)\left(1 + r_g\right) + \left(1 - \Delta_c\right)\frac{S\left(t\right)}{K} - v\left(t, T\right)\frac{K - W_c}{K} \tag{1.25}$$

We may then check that both the equity-linked and the reverse convertible products share the same feature of a **long** position in the **risky asset** funded by a leverage position.

1.6.3   Exposure to volatility

An increase in the value of the underlying asset would then have a positive effect on both of the structured products. What about a change in volatility? Standard option pricing theory suggests that response of the two products should now be opposite. The equity-linked note in fact embeds a long position in an option, and, unless the option itself is endowed with complex exotic features, that causes the value of the product to be positively affected by a volatility increase. An increase in volatility would also increase the value of the put option in the reverse convertible product, but as in this case the option is sold by the investor to the issuer, that would subtract value from the product. So, recognizing a long or short position in volatility is another question that any investor has to address. Notice that in this case – where we have plain vanilla options – it coincides with being long or short in an option, but that is not a general result. If, for example, as often happens in real world cases, barrier option were used, the sign of exposure to volatility should be measured case by case.

1.6.4 Hedging

The difference between the two products also emerges, in quite a neat form, in a dynamic hedging perspective. Consider a hedging policy in discrete time for both of the products. In both cases, delta hedging would require us to take a short position in the underlying asset. From standard option pricing theory we know that delta hedging is effective against infinitely small changes of the underlying asset, but what about the impact of finite changes in the underlying? This question may be relevant if the hedging portfolio is not frequently rebalanced or the underlying moves a lot between the rebalance dates. It is easy to see that this second-order effect, called *gamma* exposure, has different sign in the two cases. In the equity-linked note case changes of the underlying increase the value of the product, while they correspondingly decrease the value of the reverse convertible note. It should be remembered that as this is a second-order effect, the impact is due to the absolute change in the underlying, rather than its direction: so, a delta-hedged investment position in a reverse convertible note leaves the investor exposed to losses from finite changes of the underlying no matter what their directions, and a *gamma-hedging* strategy would be strongly recommended.

1.7 STRUCTURED FINANCE AND OBJECT-ORIENTED PROGRAMMING

As we saw above, the job of every participant in the structured finance business is to assemble objects. Every product can be decomposed in a stream of cash flows and every cash flow in a set of long and short positions. The term "object" introduces another function that is particularly relevant in the structured finance team, and that is central in this book: IT design and software engineering.

Object-Oriented Programming (OOP) denotes a particular programming technique that is based on the idea of partitioning the programming tasks in elementary units that are then linked together to perform the overall task. The main advantage in favour of OOP is in reusability of the code and updating. In case some adjustment is needed, one has to focus only on the interested part without rewriting the entire code from scratch. Furthermore, the objects are black boxes, including methods and attributes, that can be used without in-depth knowledge of their content. So, when one takes an object called "option", for example, he would take something that would have some methods to compute prices, deltas, leverage, and the like, without any need to know anything about the model used to compute them.

The software engineer and the financial engineer look at the concept of "object" with different attitudes. For software engineers, an object is something in which to hide attributes and methods; it is something to *forget about*. For financial engineers, an object is something to unbundle in order to understand more about its working; it is something to *learn from*. But, curiously enough, in structured finance the objects are the same: they are the basic components of the replicating portfolio. For this reason, both the software and financial engineers very often find themselves designing a system of objects to represent and manage structured products. The result must be consistent with the aims of both of them:

- It must carry the information content with respect to the risk factors as required by the financial engineer.
- It must allow re-usability of code and code update as required by the software engineer.

Complying with the two targets is beneficial for the financial intermediary as a whole, and the benefits are particularly relevant for the risk management process. A well-built object oriented system

- would be able to speak out on the risks involved, the kind of risk, volatility and correlation;
- would allow a consistent update of prices and sensitivities of all the objects involved in the structured products: changes of models are consistently "inherited" by all the products in the portfolio;
- if the structure of the objects is finally shared with the counterparties, that could speed up the transmission of information and could enable automated execution of the deal. This source of execution risk is currently causing much concern to people in the market and to the regulators.

The aim of this book is to reach both the financial engineer and the software engineer, and to lay down a common set of tools for both of them. Our ambition is to make them meet and work together sharing language and concepts. For this reason, we have attempted to address every topic within the common language of the replicating portfolio, and the objects involved, spelled out in the jargon of both the software engineer (OOP) and the financial engineer (*building block approach*). Every topic would be discussed in an object-oriented framework, paying attention to: (i) the global structure of relationships among the objects; (ii) availability of data structures shared by people in the market in that specific instance of XML language called FpML.

Chapter 2 introduces the main concepts of object-oriented programming, and the layout of the basic language that the software engineer would share with the financial engineer. The latter would in turn look for analogies between this language and that of the replicating portfolio that is natural to him. Chapter 3 addresses the main concepts used by the financial engineer to analyse the joint distribution of the risk factors, namely volatility and correlation, both implied and historical.

Chapter 4 moves into the building of a structured financial product: here the software engineer would disclose the problems involved in the construction of a schedule of payments, and these arguments would be merged with the alternatives available to the structurer to design a stream of cash flows (a *leg*, to borrow the wording from swaps) to meet the need of a set of clients. Chapter 5 would address the use of derivative contracts to modify the repayment plan of the product: these are mainly convertible and *reverse* convertible bonds. Chapter 6 will investigate in detail the construction of coupon plans indexed to equity products, both univariate and multivariate. Chapter 7 will introduce credit-linked structured products, limiting the analysis to univariate risks. Multivariate credit-linked products, which represent the bulk of the structured finance market, will be addressed in Chapter 8.

Chapter 9 will finally address what is different about the structured finance business, as far as risk management is concerned. In particular, historical filtered simulation and scenario analysis techniques will be addressed in detail, as well as counterparty risk in derivatives, which is one of the main reasons of concern in the finance world today.

REFERENCES AND FURTHER READING

Black, F. & Scholes, M. (1973) The pricing of options and corporate liabilities, *Journal of Political Economy*, **81**, 637–654.

Brigo, D. & Mercurio, F. (2006) *Interest Rate Models: Theory and Practice* (2nd edition). Springer Verlag, Berlin, Heidelberg, New York.

Cox, J.C. & Rubinstein, M. (1985) *Options Markets*. Prentice-Hall, Englewood Cliffs, NJ.

Cox, J.C., Ingersoll, J.E. & Ross, S.A. (1985) A theory of the term structure of interest rates, *Econometrica*, **53**, 385–407.

Cox, J.C., Ross, S.A. & Rubinstein, M. (1979) Option pricing: A simplified approach, *Journal of Financial Economics*, **7**, 229–263.

Dothan, M.U. (1990) *Prices in Financial Markets*. Oxford University Press, New York.

Duffie, D. (2001) *Dynamic Asset Pricing Theory* (3rd edition). Princeton University Press, Princeton.

Geman, H. (1989) *The importance of the forward risk neutral probability in a stochastic approach to interest rates*. Working Paper, ESSEC.

Harrison, J.M. & Kreps, D.M. (1979) Martingales and arbitrage in multiperiod securities market, *Journal of Economic Theory*, **20**, 381–408.

Harrison, J.M. & Pliska, S.R. (1981) Martingales and stochastic integrals in the theory of continuous trading, *Stochastic Processes Applications*, **11**, 215–260.

Harrison, J.M. & Pliska, S.R. (1983) A stochastic calculus model of continuous trading: Complete markets, *Stochastic Processes Applications*, **15**, 313–316.

Heath, D.C., Jarrow, R.A. & Morton, A. (1990) Bond pricing and the term structure of interest rates: A discrete time approximation, *Journal of Financial and Quantitative Analysis*, **25**, 419–440.

Heath, D.C., Jarrow, R.A. & Morton, A. (1992) Bond pricing and the term structure of interest rates: A new methodology for contingent claim valuation, *Econometrica*, **60**, 77–105.

Hull, J. (2003) *Options, Futures and Other Derivatives*. Prentice Hall, New Jersey.

Jamshidian, F. (1987) *Pricing of contingent claims in the one factor term structure model*. Working Paper, Merrill Lynch Capital Markets.

Jamshidian, F. (1997) The LIBOR and swap market model, *Finance and Stochastics*, **1**, 293–330.

Margrabe, W. (1978) The value of an option to exchange an asset for another, *Journal of Finance*, **33**, 177–186.

Milne, F. (1995) *Finance Theory and Asset Pricing*. Clarendon Press, Oxford.

Musiela, M. & Rutkowski, M. (2005) *Martingale Methods in Financial Modelling* (2nd edition). Springer Verlag, Berlin, Heidelberg, New York.

Ross, S.A. (1976) The arbitrage theory of capital asset pricing, *Journal of Economic Theory*, **13**, 341–360.

Vasicek, O. (1977) An equilibrium characterization of the term structure, *Journal of Financial Economics*, **5**, 177–188.

2
Object-Oriented Programming

2.1 INTRODUCTION

In this chapter we shall introduce the reader to the main ideas of Object-Oriented Programming showing also some tools we can use for software design. It is important to remember, however, that this is not a book about IT details or deep programming techniques, so our main aim is to introduce the reader to a new way of thinking. Many good books are available to those readers who want to go deeper into this fascinating subject.

We have decided to use, as a general programming environment, some tools that are strongly based on the Java world but generally you should be able to read and understand the arguments in this chapter even if you do not have a strong background in the Java programming language.

What you should learn reading this chapter can be summarized as follows:

- The object-oriented way of thinking.
- The benefits of object-oriented software development.
- The basic concept of object orientation.
- Main ideas about UML and object-oriented analysis and design.

2.2 WHAT IS OOP (OBJECT-ORIENTED PROGRAMMING)?

Object-oriented programming (OOP for short) is a particular way of programming that focuses on the *responsibility* of various tasks. The idea behind object-oriented programming is that a computer program is composed of a collection of individual units, or *objects*, as opposed to a traditional view in which a program is a list of instructions to the computer. Each object is capable of receiving messages, processing data, and sending messages to other objects and should be responsible only for a particular task. To give you some idea of what an object is, you can think of it as data and functionality packaged together in some way to form a single unit of well-identified code (examples will be given below).

The peculiar feature of this approach is that special attention is given to creating the appropriate objects as opposed to focusing solely on solving the problem. For this reason OOP is often called a *paradigm* rather than a style or type of programming, to emphasize that OOP can alter the way software is developed by changing the way programmers think about it. A programming paradigm provides (and determines) the view the programmer has of the execution of the program. On the one hand, for instance, in functional programming a program can be thought of as a simple sequence of function evaluations. On the other hand, in object-oriented programming programmers can think of a program as a collection of interacting objects. Therefore the paradigm of OOP is essentially one of design and the challenge in OOP is to design a well-defined object system.

OOP is particularly helpful in coping with complexity and building reusable computer code. By breaking problems down into groups of smaller tasks performed by various objects, complex problems can be managed and solved. This approach emphasizes code reusability, which is extremely valuable to financial quants that are usually under time pressure. The ability to cut and paste objects into new problems dramatically speeds up the development process. This is a particularly important, probably the most important, point when we are dealing with developing computational algorithms for structured finance. As a matter of fact, as we have already introduced in Chapter 1, structurers, pricers and risk managers are already accustomed to thinking in terms of objects because of the no-arbitrage/replicating portfolio arguments.

2.3   ANALYSIS AND DESIGN

Any OOP problem-solving process can be broken down into three main categories: analysis, design and implementation. Analysis refers to identifying the appropriate objects responsible for the various tasks and the way they relate to each other: this exercise is often known as data modelling. Once one has identified an object, it is generalized as a *class* of objects (for the time being just think of Plato's concept of the "ideal" horse that stands for all horses) and defined by the kind of data it contains. Any elaboration of data is performed by means of functions called *methods*. Design refers to the structuring of the solution in terms of appropriate classes. Finally, the design is converted into code in the implementation phase.

2.3.1   A simple example

The best way to explain the methodological approach we are talking about is to give a practical example. We have seen that people in the structured finance market think of financial products in terms of a collection of elementary objects. In a sense they think in an objected-oriented way, even though they may not be aware of it. It is typically in the interaction with a software engineer that they discover they are thinking in the OOP approach: it is like a *"maieutica"* process that one can find in Plato's classical dialogues. For this reason the most effective way to get the ideas across is a dialogue between a software architect (Giovanni) and a financial expert (Umberto) who are building a computer program for structured finance: needless to say, every reference to facts, things or persons is purely casual and involuntary. For the time being, the reader should not worry about understanding every single detail of the conversation since each concept will be defined and described more appropriately in the following paragraphs.

Giovanni: *"Mate, you look puzzled, can I help you in any way?"*
Umberto: *"I am just thinking about this software for structured products. You know, the only way you can define a structured product is as collections of other financial products. It must be something similar to the concept of 'object' you IT guys are using, but I do not know much more about that. Why don't we try to fix ideas on a very simple product, say a zero-coupon bond and an option? Let us focus on the representation of the option, you know, they may be call or put, giving the right to buy or sell some underlying asset at a certain price (strike or exercise price) at a certain date (exercise date)."*
Giovanni: *"Ok, we have an object which we call "option" and another one which is called "underlying asset". The underlying has the following properties: price, a real number,*

and volatility, a real number too. The attributes of an option are: a reference to its underling asset and a flag to specify its payoff (call or put), the exercise price (strike) and the expiry date. Moreover, an option should also have a method in order to compute its fair value. This method will be named "Pricing". According to UML standard we can describe our data in this way . . . "

Umberto: *"So, in general what describes an object? Could you explain this formalism in more detail?"*

Giovanni: *"Option and Asset are two classes. A class is simply a prototype that defines the variables and the methods common to all objects of a certain kind. As you can see in this picture (Figure 2.1), the rectangles are divided into three sections: in the first one I write only the name of the class; the second one contains the list of variables (for each variable a data type and multiplicity are defined) which describe the behaviour of every object of this type; finally in the last section we find the list of methods or operations. The evaluation of an option, for example, is the result of a computational process that I named 'Pricing'. During the implementation of this class, the 'Pricing' method will be designed in order to calculate the option price."*

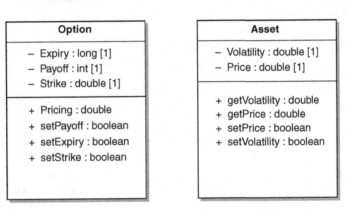

Figure 2.1   Option and Asset classes

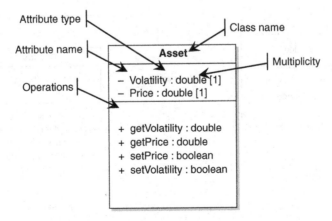

Figure 2.2   Notation elements for classes

Giovanni: *"Now, we introduce the association between the two classes. This is simply a relationship between different objects of the two classes; in our case the relationship is due to the fact that each option has an underlying asset. We represent this association by a single line between the classes, I'll also write a name and a numerical specification, which is called multiplicity, describing how many objects of one side of the association are connected to how many object on the other side. For the time being we may stop to consider univariate options, so this number is one."*

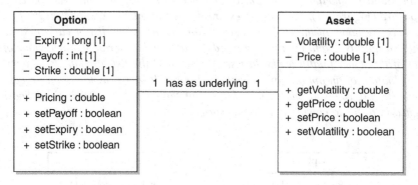

Figure 2.3   Option and Asset classes with their relationship

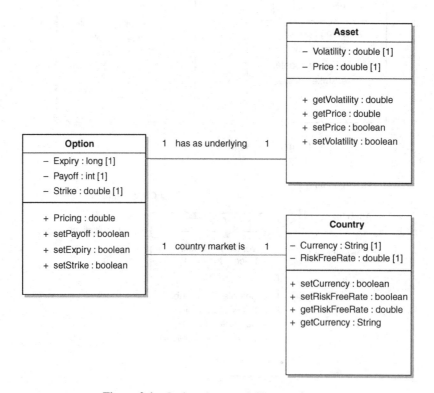

Figure 2.4   Option, Asset and Country classes

Umberto: *"Uhm ... let me think ... actually I may need more data in order to price an option. I need to know the return volatility of the underlying and the risk-free interest rate over the option life time."*

Giovanni: *"You mean that the risk-free rate is not precisely a property of the option?"*

Umberto: *"No, I would say it is a feature of the particular currency area to which the option belongs."*

Giovanni: *"Wow ... finally we have correctly structured data."*

Umberto: *"For the particular application we are looking at, that is fine, but remember that I want to use this class to price and simulate options. ... So, for example, I did not mention that in some structured finance product we will encounter the so-called 'early exercise feature'. Options may be European if they don't allow early exercise or Bermudan/American if they do so."*

Giovanni (just a bit angrier): *"Ok, so we need to add another property which we call* `ExerciseType` *that can assume two different values, European and Early-Exercise ... "*

Umberto: *"Uhm... of course you are surely aware that we must also allow for barriers, they are present in many, many structured products ... "*

Giovanni: *"AAArghhhhh ...."*

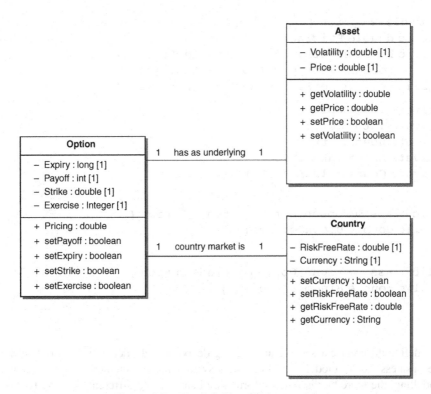

Figure 2.5   The definitive (?) data model

Introduction of barriers must be delayed to a later chapter because of a (hopefully) temporary nervous breakdown of the software engineer. At this point of the process, however, we will have a set of classes which, coded in (simplified) Java looks as follows:

```java
public class Asset {
   public double getVolatility(){}
   public double getPrice(){}
   public boolean setPrice(double newPrice){}
   public boolean setVolatility(double newVolatility){}

   private double Volatility;
   private double Price;
}

public class Country {
   public boolean setCurrency(String newCurrency){}
   public boolean setRiskFreeRate(double newRiskFreeRate){}
   public double getRiskFreeRate(){}
   public String getCurrency(){}

   private double RiskFreeRate;
   private String Currency;
}

public class Option {
   public double Pricing(){}
   public boolean setPayoff(Integer newPayoff){}
   public boolean setExpiry(long newExpiry){}
   public boolean setStrike(double newStrike){}

   private long Expiry;
   private int Payoff;
   private double Strike;
   private Asset lnkAttribute1;
   private Country lnkAttribute2;
}

public class European_Option extends Option {
   public double BlackScholes(){}
}

public class American_Option extends Option {
   public double BinomialTree(){}
}
```

As we define different classes, we are digging deeper and deeper into the problem domain of the business we are modelling. The more a system analyst interacts with the business he is modelling, the more he discovers information belonging to different entities. This is how the process works. We should not be afraid to create new classes. In the analysis phase we need not be concerned about it; the analysis phase is where we test ideas, new questions and eventually evolve towards a solution that is sound, correct and shows the business as it really is (or as we would like it to be). Let us not forget that design time is when it is easiest to structure an application as a collection of self-contained modules or components and this will in turn enable you to reuse code for different applications. Keep in mind that this is the main task: when another application needs the same functionality, the designer should quickly import it. Reusability and modularity of software code are two of the main concepts of modelling, which we will begin to address in the next session.

2.4   MODELLING

In our case, with the word "modelling" we refer to the designing of software applications before coding. Modelling is an essential part of large software projects, and is also helpful to medium and even small projects. In software development, a model plays the analogous role that blueprints and other plans (site maps, elevations, physical models) play in the building of a skyscraper. Using a model, people responsible for a software development project can make sure that business functionality is complete and correct, end-user needs are met, and program design meets the requirements of scalability, robustness, security, extendibility and other characteristics. All of this can be done before the implementation in code renders changes difficult and expensive to make.

There are many different methods to describe the modelling process: one is by means of a modelling language. The UML (Unified Modelling Language) is probably the most widely used language, at least in the field of software engineering. In this book this language will be used extensively, even though it will not be at a professional level, so we need to get at least the flavour of this standard.

2.4.1   The Unified Modelling Language (UML)

The Unified Modelling Language (UML) is the final step of a set of object-oriented analysis and design (OOAD) methods that appeared in the late 1980s and early 1990s. It most directly unifies the methods of Boock, Rumbaugh (OMT) and Jacobson, but its reach is wider than that. The UML went through a standardization process with the OMG (Object Management Group) and is now an OMG standard.

The UML is called a modelling language, not a method. Most methods consist, at least in principle, of both a modelling language and a process. The modelling language is the (mainly graphical) notation that methods use to express designs. In many ways the modelling language is the most important part of the method and is certainly the key part for communication. If you want to discuss your design with someone, it is the modelling language that both of you need to understand, not the process you used to get to that design.

What can you model with UML? UML defines 12 types of diagram, divided into three categories: four diagram types represent static application structures; five represent different aspects of dynamic behaviour; three represent ways you can organize and manage your application modules. Structural Diagrams include the Class Diagram, Object Diagram, Component Diagram, and Deployment Diagram. Behaviour Diagrams include the Use Case Diagram (used by some methodologies during requirements gathering); Sequence Diagram, Activity Diagram, Collaboration Diagram, and State Chart Diagram. Model Management Diagrams include Packages, Subsystems and Models.

A deep understanding of UML constructions in all their varieties requires quite some effort and is beyond the scope of this book. Our treatment will stick to the basic elements. If the reader is interested in further technical details, he is advised to download the UML specification from the OMG website (http://www.omg.org/uml/). It is free, of course, but it is also highly technical, terse and very difficult for beginners to understand. In the following sections we will use, and of course explain, the UML notation as we describe the main ideas of object orientation.

2.4.2   An object-oriented programming language: Java

We have chosen Java as our reference language due to its extremely large diffusion and to the availability of many free tools. As the reader probably already knows, Java is an object-oriented programming language developed by Sun Microsystems in the early 1990s. The main characteristic of Java is that, unlike conventional languages which are generally either designed to be compiled to machine code (like C/C++ for example), or interpreted from source code at runtime (like Microsoft Visual Basic for Application), Java is intended to be compiled to a byte code which is then run by a Java virtual machine. Java is an object-oriented language, this means that the language syntax (largely derived from C++) all the various concept supports that we will find in this chapter. However, unlike C++, which combines the syntax for structured, generic and object oriented programming, Java was built from the ground up to be virtually fully object-oriented: everything in Java is an object with the exceptions of atomic data types (ordinal and real numbers, boolean values, and characters) and everything in Java is written inside a class.

Java Runtime Environment

The Java Runtime Environment (JRE) is the software required to run any application deployed on the Java Platform. End-users commonly use a JRE in software packages and web browser plug-ins. Sun also distributes a superset of the JRE called the Java 2 SDK (more commonly known as the JDK), which includes development tools such as the Java compiler, Javadoc, and debugger.

Sun has defined three platforms targeting different application environments and seg-mented many of its APIs so that they belong to one of the platforms. The platforms are:

- Java Platform, Micro Edition (Java ME) — targeting environments with limited resources,
- Java Platform, Standard Edition (Java SE) — targeting workstation environments, and
- Java Platform, Enterprise Edition (Java EE) — targeting large distributed enterprise or Internet environments.

If you have not already installed a JRE on your computer you can find it at http://java.sun.com/ (actually you can find here almost everything you need - at least for Java beginners). For our needs the Standard Edition is required.

Components

One of the most important characteristics of Java is the enormous quantity of libraries developed. Java libraries are compiled byte codes of source code developed by the JRE implementer to support application development in Java. Many of these are becoming a standard. Examples of these libraries are:

- The core libraries, which include:
  - Collection libraries which implement data structures such as lists, dictionaries, trees and sets
  - XML Parsing libraries.
- The integration libraries, which allow the application writer to communicate with external systems.
- User Interface libraries, which include:
  - The Abstract Windowing Toolkit (AWT), which provides GUI components, the means for laying out those components and the means for handling events from those components
  - The Swing libraries, which are built on AWT but provide (non-native) implementations of AWT widgets.

We will not discuss further details about Java syntax and its architecture, but the reader is referred to a very good tutorial material which can be found at

  http://java.sun.com/docs/books/tutorial/index.html.

2.5   MAIN IDEAS ABOUT OOP

2.5.1   Abstraction

Object orientation is a method that represents things that are part of the real world as objects. A computer is an object in the same way as a car or a financial asset. These objects are in turn composed of other objects, and so on. Real-world objects can have a very complex structure. Obviously in general we do not need to take into consideration every single details of a real-world object; actually one of the main goals of the modelling process is to select only essential aspects of the problem under consideration, neglecting useless information. This particular process is called 'Abstraction'.

Abstraction indicates the ability of a program to ignore some aspects of the information that it is manipulating, i.e. the ability to focus on the essential. Abstraction is implicitly present in everyday life. In a nutshell it means that we work with models of reality. One of the authors is a railroad model fan and is used to playing with railroads, but not with a real railroad of course (that will remain his unreachable dream). Engines, wagons, tracks, crossings and buildings are scaled down representations of reality: it is a model railroad. Software development does essentially the same: objects occurring in reality are reduced to a few features that are relevant in the current situation.

Getting closer to our main application, an exact replicating portfolio for a structured product or a derivative contract is something that emerges from a model of the market in which many other features (e.g., transaction costs, institutional features, micro-structure features, and so on) may bring about the final outcome. Instead of real objects we work with symbols. It could happen that the same object, such as a financial option, could have different representations in different projects. For example, let us think of two different applications, the first oriented to pricing, the other to account management. It is very probable that the two systems require different kind of information and this will be reflected directly on the modelling of our options.

2.5.2   Classes

A class describes the structure and behaviour of a set of similar objects. An object is an instance that is present at runtime, allocates memory for its instance variables and behaves according to the protocol of its class.

In this book classes and objects are represented following the UML notation of rectangles (see Figure 2.2). To differentiate between classes and objects, the names of the objects have been underlined in the figure. If we want to represent the object–class relationship (instance relationship), we draw a dashed arrow from an object in the direction of its class (Figure 2.6)

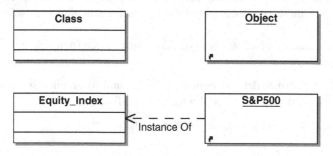

Figure 2.6   Notation of class and object and an example of an instance relationship

2.5.3   Attributes and operations: the Encapsulation principle

The most important properties of a class are *attributes* and *operations* (or *methods*) which are combined make up a single unit (the class itself). Attributes describe the structure of the objects, their components and the information or data contained therein. Methods or operations describe the behaviour of the objects. Attributes are only accessible indirectly via the operations of the class.

Let's get a closer look at the Java-like code produced for the Asset class

```
public class Asset {

    // methods
    public double getVolatility(){}
    public double getPrice(){}
    public boolean setPrice(double newPrice){}
    public boolean setVolatility(double newVolatility){}

    // attributes
    private double Volatility;
    private double Price;
}
```

As you can see, the word `private` is written before the definition of attributes; this is called a "modifier". Another modifier in the class declaration is `public`. These modifiers affect the way in which other objects can access attributes and method of our class. Since the modifier of attributes is `private` this means that no other object can access the data contained in these properties. The only way to get access to these values is by means of the methods `getVolatility()` and `getPrice()` which, on the other hand, are defined as `public`.

For readers who know just a bit of computer programming, this means that the attempt to read/write data from/in our attributes directly with a code like

```
Asset myAsset
myAsset.Volatility = 9.8;
```

or

```
double price = myAsset.Price;
```

will produce an error condition. The correct instructions are instead

```
myAsset.setVolatility(9.8);
double price = myAsset.getPrice();
```

The concept of hiding the inner structure of an object, and that the only way to access the values is by means of well-defined methods, is often called *Encapsulation* or *Hiding*.

2.5.4 Responsibilities

Each class should be responsible for precisely one logical aspect of the total system. The properties located in this area of responsibility should be grouped into a single class and not divided over various classes. Moreover, a class should not contain properties that do not belong to its area of responsibility. This is a very important principle in object-oriented software development. Each responsibility is assigned to a single class. Each class is responsible for one aspect of the total system. This, by the way, is a principle that has already been implemented in previous programming paradigms. It is a sort of modularity requirement: if you have, for example, a general program for computation of option pricing you should design well-separated modules (or classes in our case) to handle data input, computation, output and so on. In turn each of these classes should be divided into further subclasses to handle single operations as elementary as possible.

2.5.5 Inheritance

Classes may represent specializations of other classes, i.e. classes can be arranged hierarchically and assume ("inherit") the properties of the class above them; if required they can specialize ("overwrite") them, but not eliminate them. Subclasses derived from a class automatically have all properties of the superior class: thus, properties are inherited. This principle is the cornerstone of reusability in the contest of OOP. The inheritance relation is represented by an arrow with the subclass always pointing to the superclass. For example it is possible to specialize the option class in order to manage the different exercise type (Figure 2.7).

As we have already stated, in the generalization or specialization process of classes, a subclass inherits the properties of its superclass, but it must also assume its responsibilities and task, at least in principle. Particular features may be specialized – i.e. further developed – and new features may be added. Existing properties, however, should be neither suppressed nor restricted.

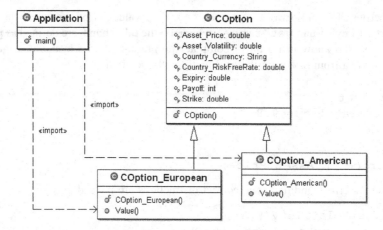

Figure 2.7   Example of inheritance

But how are properties arranged inside an inheritance hierarchy? Fundamentally, properties are situated precisely in those classes where, according to the responsibility assigned to them, they are effectively a property of the class. Conversely classes contain precisely those properties for which they are responsible. Consider, for example, the class COption and its subclasses COption_European and COption_American (see Figure 2.7). A simplified Java code is reported below (for the complete source code see the Java project Ch02_Example_01 on the CD enclosed).

```java
// Class declaration
public class COption {
  // Variables Declaration

  protected double expiry;
  protected double strike;
  protected int payoff;
  protected double asset_Price;
  protected double asset_Volatility;
  protected String country_Currency = "";
  protected double country_RiskFreeRate;

  // Class Constructor

  public COption(){
    expiry               =   0;
    strike               =   0;
    payoff               =   -1;
    asset_Price          =   -1;
    asset_Volatility     =   -1;
    country_Currency     =   ''???'';
    country_RiskFreeRate =   -1;
  }
```

```
// Methods

public double getExpiry() {
  return expiry;
}
public double getStrike() {
  return strike;
}
public int getPayoff() {
  return payoff;
}
public double getAsset_Price() {
  return asset_Price;
}
public double getAsset_Volatility() {
  return asset_Volatility;
}
public String getCountry_Currency() {
  return country_Currency;
}
public double getCountry_RiskFreeRate() {
  return country_RiskFreeRate;
}
public void setExpiry(double expiry) {
  this.expiry = expiry;
}
public void setStrike(double strike) {
  this.strike = strike;
}
public void setPayoff(int payoff) {
  this.payoff = payoff;
}
public void setAsset_Price(double asset_Price) {
  this.asset_Price = asset_Price;
}
public void setAsset_Volatility(double asset_Volatility) {
  this.asset_Volatility = asset_Volatility;
}
public void setCountry_Currency(String country_Currency) {
  this.country_Currency = country_Currency;
}
public void setCountry_RiskFreeRate(double country_
  RiskFreeRate) { this.country_RiskFreeRate = country_
  RiskFreeRate;
}

public Value()
```

```
{
    return 0;
  }
}
```

The *class body* (the area between the curly brackets) contains all the code that provides for the life cycle of the objects created from the class.

The `COption` class declares seven instance variables:

- `expiry` contains the option expiration in years from evaluation date;
- `strike` contains the option strike price;
- `payoff` an integer variable which identifies the type of option payoff (0 stand for a call, 1 for a put);
- `asset_Price` and `asset_Volatility` contain the price and volatility of the underlying asset;
- `country_Currency` is a string indicator for the currency;
- `country_RiskFreeRate` is a double variable that contains the risk-free spot rate used for the option pricing. .

The modifier `protected`, written before each declaration, means that subclasses of `COption` can access directly the value of these variables. Though this is not completely accurate from the point of view of a pure object-oriented way of programming, this choice allows us to write a less complicated code. Of course it is always possible to declare these variables as `private` and use the appropriate methods to set and get their values.

The `COption` class also declares a *constructor* – a subroutine used to initialize new objects created from the class. You can recognize a constructor because it has the same name as the class. The `COption` constructor initializes all seven of the object's variables. Some variables are set to −1, indicating that a generic object `COption` is not usable when the application starts up.

Finally the class declares 14 methods that provide ways for other objects to read and change the value of instance variables without giving other objects access to the actual variables (this is an application of the encapsulation principle mentioned in section 2.5.3) and a method `Value()`.

Let us now consider the two subclasses: `COption_European` and `COption_American`.

```
// Class Declaration

public class COption_European extends COption
{
    public double Value()
    {
        System.out.println("Pricing European Option...");
        return 0;
    }
    public COption_European(double s,
                            double k,
                            double r,
```

```
                      double t,
                      double sigma,
                      int type)
{
   asset_Price              =    s;
   asset_Volatility         =    sigma;
   country_RiskFreeRate     =    r;
   expiry                   =    t;
   strike                   =    k;
   payoff                   =    type;
}
}


// Class Declaration

public class COption_American extends COption
{
   public double Value()
   {
      System.out.println("Pricing American Option...");
      return 0;
   }

   public COption_American(double s,
                           double k,
                           double r,
                           double t,
                           double sigma,
                           int type)
   {
      asset_Price              =    s;
      asset_Volatility         =    sigma;
      country_RiskFreeRate     =    r;
      expiry                   =    t;
      strike                   =    k;
      payoff                   =    type;
   }
}
```

Since they are subclasses of COption, we do not need to define any variable, they simply inherit every variable and every method from their superclass. The extends clause identifies COption as the superclass of the class, thereby setting this class on top of the class hierarchy. Since all the variables were defined as protected, we can assign them directly a new value in the constructor without calling the appropriate "get" methods. Notice that constructors are not members and so are not inherited by subclasses.

An instance method in a subclass with the same signature and return type as an instance method in a superclass *overrides* the superclass's method; in our case the method Value()

overrides the original method of COption. As we will see in the next section, a subclass must always override methods that are declared abstract in the superclass, or the subclass itself must be abstract.

2.5.6 Abstract classes

Classes for which no concrete instances may be created, i.e. which will never become an object, are called *abstract classes*. In our example, there will be objects from the class Option_European, or from the class Option_American, but none from the Option class because Option is merely an abstraction (there are no options without exercise specification!). The class is only included in the model to sensibly abstract the (common) properties of the other classes.

Abstract classes are marked by the property value *abstract* below the class name or by the class name itself in italics. An abstract class can only be subclassed and cannot be instantiated. To declare that your class is an abstract class, use the keyword abstract before the class keyword in your class declaration:

```
abstract class COption
{
    ...
}
```

If you attempt to instantiate an abstract class, the compiler will display an error message. An abstract class can contain *abstract methods* – methods with no implementation. In this way, an abstract class can define a complete programming interface for its subclasses, referring to the subclasses for a complete and detailed implementation of those methods. As an example, the class COption declares a method Value() but the implementation of this method is specialized in the subclasses since different valuation methods are required for European and American options.

2.5.7 Associations

An *association* is a relationship between different objects of one or more classes. A simple example of association is the relationship between an option and its underlying asset.

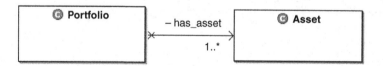

Figure 2.8   Example of an association

In the simplest case an association is represented by a single line between two classes. Usually, however, associations are described in as much detail as possible. The association receives a name and a numerical specification (*multiplicity indication*) of the number of objects on one side of the association that are connected with a number of objects on the other side. Furthermore, names are added which describe in more detail the meaning of the class involved or their objects.

A particular variation of association is *aggregation*. This is again a relationship between two classes, but with the peculiarity that the classes relate to each other as a whole relates to its parts. Aggregation is the composition of an object out of a set of parts. A portfolio, for example, is an aggregation of assets. Aggregation is a *has* relationship (we say that a portfolio *has* different assets).

A special form of aggregation is when the individual parts depend on the aggregate (the whole) for their own existence: this is called a *composition*. With composition any "part" object may belong to only one "whole"; further, the parts are usually expected to live and die with the whole. Usually any deletion of the whole is considered to cascade to the parts.

In an aggregation, the side of the whole is marked by a lozenge, to identify the relationship as an aggregation. Associations are marked with white lozenges while composition are marked by solid lozenges and have always a multiplicity of 1 (or $0 \ldots 1$) on the side of the aggregate, i.e. where the lozenge is located.

The distinction between aggregation and composition is highly relevant for financial applications, because it intervenes in the relationship between a financial product and its replicating portfolio. Take the simplest example of a plain vanilla European option. We know that its payoff is financially equivalent to a composite position in asset-or-nothing digital and cash-or-nothing digital options. So, a way to synthetically construct an option would be to take a suitable position in these digital options. The synthetically constructed option would then be an *aggregation* of digital options: as a result, we could drop a part of the replicating portfolio without closing down the entire position because there is no contractual agreement linking the two obligations together. What about a plain, non-synthetic, option contract? This is a *composition* of digital options, meaning that the contracts in the replicating portfolio disappear as soon as the option contract itself disappears; therefore, in this case, the two obligations are wrapped together in the same contract. The IT representation then makes a fine distinction between the two contracts, synthetic and non-synthetic, that we often overlook in finance. This distinction, however, is of utmost practical relevance, as will be discussed in detail in the chapter on counterparty risk. For the time being, we sketch out the problem by a simple example.

Example 2.1   Assume that you want to buy a call option on 10 000 Generali stocks for the strike price of 20 euros, for three months from now. You can achieve the same result in two different ways:

(a) Buy 10 000 call options on Generali on the Italian derivatives market (IDEM) for a strike of 20 and exercise in three months. According to the organization of the market, the counterparty is going to be the clearing house of the Italian stock exchange (*Cassa di Compensazione e Garanzia*, CCG).
(b) Buy 10 000 asset-or-nothing call options on Generali for strike 20 while selling a cash-or-nothing option for a nominal value of 200 000 euros, with the same strike and exercise. The products will be bought and sold on the over-the-counter (OTC) market – that is, in a bilateral relationship.

Are the products and strategies (a) and (b) the same? No, it is clear that they are markedly different. In the first case, default risk is very low and, if default occurs, all of the option value will be lost. In the second case, default will only affect the asset-or-nothing option that was bought from the counterparty. The difference between these two products of course is expected to show up in a difference in price, and in the chapter on counterparty risk we will see that this is actually the case.

In Figure 2.9 we have described a plain vanilla European option as a *combination* of a cash-or-nothing binary option and an asset-or-nothing binary option. From a general point of view, aggregate objects can consist of objects of the same class. For example, let us consider the aggregation depicted in Figure 2.9. The plain vanilla European option is described as an aggregate object composed by two different options. However, it is very plausible that all the three objects are subclasses of a superclass called COption, so the correct class diagram should be that shown in Figure 2.10.

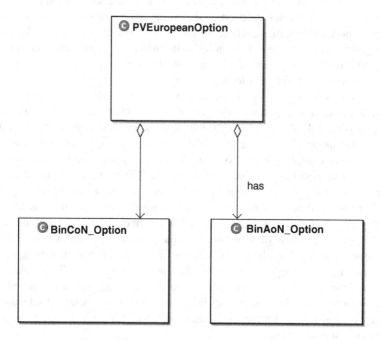

Figure 2.9   A simple example of aggregation

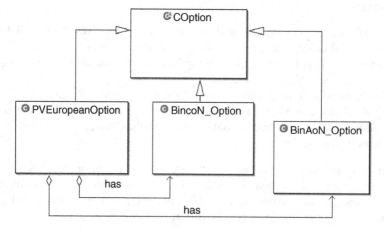

Figure 2.10   Composite objects: combining inheritance and aggregation

2.5.8   Message exchanging

Objects are independent units that cooperate and interact by means of messages they send to each other. These messages lead to the operations, which means that an object may precisely understand those messages for which it has operations. In contrast to conventional programs, operations and data build a unit. An object contains all operations needed for processing its data contents and all of its further behaviour. Facts that are related to each other by their contents are concentrated inside the object. In an object-oriented solution, operations or messages can only be accessed via the object:

```
object.message(arguments)
```

For example, in order to evaluate the price of an option we have to call the method `Value()`, which is defined inside the class `COption`

```
COption myOption;
myOption.Value();
```

Moreover, as has already been stated, object attributes are usually encapsulated and accessible from outside only via appropriate operations (such as `Volatility` of an asset which can only be accessed via the `setVolatility` and `getVolatility` operations).

2.5.9   Collections

Collection classes are usually defined in a standard class library and have in common that they collect and manage sets of objects. Collections are also called container classes. They have all the operations for adding and removing objects, checking whether a given object is contained in the set and determining how many objects are currently contained in the set.

A main distinction can be made between sequential collections and associative collections. In sequential collections, objects are collected in a sequential structure; the best-known example is an array. Associative collections store not only objects but also an additional key for each object through which it can be identified. An example of this is a dictionary.

2.5.10   Polymorphism

Object-oriented programming languages offer a rich set of constructs for modelling runtime[1] behaviour. Understanding polymorphism is key to designing scalable, plug-and-play architectures. Polymorphism means that an operation may behave differently in different instances. This is actually one of the cornerstones that has made object-orientation so powerful.

From a general point of view, polymorphism shows up in multiple methods having the same name.

- In some cases, multiple methods have the same name, but different formal argument lists (*overloaded methods*).
- In other cases, multiple methods have the same name, same return type and same formal argument list (*overridden methods*).

---

[1] Runtime is when a program is running (or being executable) – that is, when you start a program running in a computer, it is the runtime for that program. Programmers distinguish between what happens in a program when it is compiled (compile time) and what happens when it used or at runtime.

Some authors refer to method overloading as a form of *compile-time* or *static* polymorphism, as distinguished from *runtime* or *dynamic* polymorphism. This distinction comes from the fact that, for the invocation of each method, the compiler determines which method (from a group of overloaded methods) will be executed, and this decision is made when the program is compiled. In contrast, the determination of which overridden method to execute is not made until runtime.

Overloading

Let us start our discussion from the polymorphism with method overloading (static), which is the simpler of the two. Static polymorphism is already known from the procedural world, namely in the form of operators such as + or −. These (generic) operators can be applied to both integer and real numbers. Object-oriented programming languages also offer the possibility of using these operators for user-defined data types or classes. Precisely speaking, operators are nothing more than operations with special names. Therefore the same effect can also be achieved for normal operations.

A further aspect of static polymorphism consists in interface variations of operations with the same name (here is a Java example).

```java
public class CDate
{
    public void setDate(int year, int month, int day)
    {
        //....
    }

    public void setDate(String date)
    {
        //...
    }

    public void setDate(int serial)
    {
        //...
    }
}
...
CDate aDate;

aDate.setDate(2006,2,14);
aDate.setDate(''2/14/2006'');
aDate.setDate(38762);
```

In this example there are three operations with the same name but each must be provided with different parameters. Depending on which parameters are specified (year–month–day, date in string format or serial number) one of the operations will be activated.

Overriding

A precondition for dynamic polymorphism is the so-called *late binding*. From a physical point of view, binding is the point in the life of a program at which the caller of an operation is given the memory address of that operation. Usually this happens when the program is compiled and linked. Most of the traditional programming languages have exclusively this form of binding, which is called *early binding*. In late binding the precise memory location of an operation is determined only when the call takes place, i.e. when the corresponding message is sent to the object. Thus the association between message and receiving operation does not occur at compile time but dynamically at runtime of the program. The way in which this kind of polymorphism is implemented in most OO languages is through inheritance and method overriding.

As we have already mentioned, *inheritance* means that a class inherits all the properties of its superclass. Thus, without having to define its own attributes and operations, it can have inherited some. It is, however, free to **redefine** an inherited operation and to overwrite it with the new definition. Which of these operations is to be used at runtime in response to a corresponding message – i.e. which class the called operation comes from – is only decided at runtime.

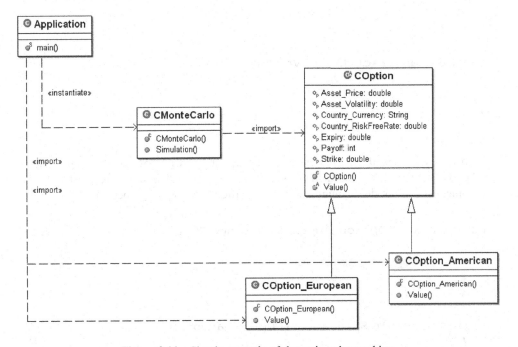

Figure 2.11   Simple example of dynamic polymorphism

Figure 2.11 shows an example in which the classes COption_European and COption_American are both derived from the virtual superclass COption. A feature shared by all the options is that they can be priced according to a precisely defined numerical method. Therefore the superclass already contains a method named Value() although this is abstract and can only be invoked by derived classes. The CMonteCarlo class has a method, `Simulation()`, in which a set of different scenarios are generated and, for each of them, a value of the option has to be calculated. Although the `CMonteCarlo` class cannot know how a particular option must be priced it can nevertheless include this function. When the program is launched (runtime), there is then a point in time in which the `Value()` message (called from the `Simulation()` method) encounters an object. At that moment it will be decided which concrete operation must be called. This is possible because *with runtime polymorphism based on method overriding, the decision of which version of a method will be executed is based on the actual type of object whose reference is stored in the reference variable, and not on the type of the reference variable on which the method is invoked.* As this is a key point that is worth describing more precisely, let us consider the code fragments of interest in the `CMonteCarlo` class and those in the `CApplication` class in which the main function is written.

Here is an operational description of the code:

- We have defined a class named COption which defines a method named `Value()`.

```
public abstract class COption
{
    public COption()
    {
    }

    public abstract double Value();

    //...
}
```

- Two classes named `COption_American` and `COption_European` extend `COption` and override the method named `Value()`(in this very simple example the two methods do not do anything, but simply write what they are expected to do).

```
public class COption_American extends COption
{
    public COption_American()
    {
    }
}
public double Simulation(COption anOption)
{
    for(int i = 0; i < nScenarios; i++)
    {
        // Generate scenario variables
        //...

        // for each scenario call the method value
        // of the generic option
```

```
        double price = anOption.Value();
    }
  }
}
```

Note that the object anOption is declared as an instance of the virtual class COption so at compile time the Simulation() method does not know which concrete Value() method must be called. This is a very important point to grasp. When we write code for the Monte Carlo method we are not concerned with the particular derivative that will be priced with this method; more to the point, our efforts must be concentrated in designing a method that is as general as possible.

• Now assume that in the main procedure a reference to an object of the class named COption_European (subclass) is assigned to a reference variable named anOption of type COption (superclass).

```
// the reference variable anOption is declared of type COption
   COption anOption;

// the invocation of new operator produces the instantiation of an
// object of type COption_European whose reference is stored
   into the
// variable anOption

anOption = new COption_European();
```

• This object is then passed as parameter to the Simulation() method of the CMonteCarlo class

```
CMonteCarlo monte_carlo = new CMonteCarlo();
monte_carlo.Simulation(anOption);
```

• Take a minute to résumé the situation! At this point:
  – we have a reference variable (anOption) whose type is COption;
  – in this variable we include reference to an object whose type is COption_European (also remember that this object is created by the new operator);

so the type of reference variable and the type of object whose reference is stored in the reference variable are different **but** (and this is a very important point) the type of the object (COption_European) is a subclass of the type of reference variable(COption).

• Within the Simulation() method we find the following line of code:

```
double price = genericOption.Value();
```

the version of the method named Value() that will actually be executed is the overridden version in the class named COption_European because the decision of which version of the method to execute is based on the actual type of object whose reference is stored in the reference variable, not on the type of reference variable on which the method is invoked.

- Assume that, after the first call to the Monte Carlo simulation, we write the following code:

```
anOption = new COption_American();
monte_carlo.Simulation(anOption);
```

Now the reference variable `anOption` contains a reference to an object of type `COption_American`. In this case the instruction

```
double price = genericOption.Value();
```

within the `Simulation()` method will result in a call to the `Value()` method of an American option. The same instruction produces two different behaviours!

OK, that's all for the moment! If you have not understood everything, do not worry. We will try to recall as much as possible of this concept in the following chapters. Let us close this chapter with a few references about some useful tools for software programming.

REFERENCES AND FURTHER READING

On object-oriented programming and financial application

For those readers interested in delving into the financial application of object-oriented programming we strongly suggest that you study the following books which, by the way, are full of very interesting examples that are worth the effort by themselves:

Duffy, D.J. (2004) *Financial Instrument Pricing Using C++*. John Wiley & Sons, Chichester.
Duffy, D.J. (2006) *Introduction to C++ for Financial Engineers: An Object-Oriented Approach*. John Wiley & Sons, Chichester.
Joshi, M.S. (2004) *C++ Design Patterns and Derivatives Pricing*. Cambridge University Press.

On the general theory and practice behind object-oriented analysis and designs

Abadi, M. & Cardelli, L. (1996) *A Theory of Objects*. Springer-Verlag, New york, Berlin, Heidelberg.
Abelson, H., Sussman, G.J. & Sussman, J. (1996) *Structure and Interpretation of Computer Programs* (2nd edition). The MIT Press.
Booch, G. (1993) *Object-Oriented Analysis and Design with Applications*. Addison-Wesley.
Eeles, P. & Sims, O. (1998) *Building Business Objects*. John Wiley & Sons, Inc.
Gamma, E., Helm, R., Johnson, R. & Vlissides, J. (1995) *Design Patterns: Elements of Reusable Object-Oriented Software*. Addison-Wesley Longman, Boston, MA.
Harmon, P. & Morrissey, W. (1996) *The Object Technology Casebook – Lessons from Award-Winning Business Applications*, John Wiley & Sons, Inc.
Jacobson, I. (1992) *Object-Oriented Software Engineering: A Use Case-Driven Approach*. Addison-Wesley.
Meyer, B. (1977) *Object-Oriented Software Construction* (2nd edition). Prentice Hall.
Rumbaugh, J., Blaha, M., Premerlani, W., Eddy, F. & Lorensen, W. (1991) *Object-Oriented Modeling and Design*. Prentice Hall.
Taylor, D.A. (1992) *Object-Oriented Information Systems – Planning and Implementation*. John Wiley & Sons, Inc.

On the Unified Modeling Language

The UML bible is:

Booch, G., Rumbaugh, J. & Jacobson, I. (1999) *Unified Modeling Language User Guide* (2nd edition). Addison-Wesley Object Technology Series.

We strongly suggest that the interested reader should visit the official page http://www.uml.org.

About Java

It is impossible to mention a complete list of references on this subject, and the best thing to do is to start with a visit to the sun site: http://java.sun.com/.

3

Volatility and Correlation

3.1 INTRODUCTION

In this chapter we introduce two paramount concepts in structured finance: volatility and correlation. The presence of nonlinear derivatives in almost all the structured finance products induces a second level issue in the valuation of a product. In fact, the value of a product can change even though the underlying risk factors do not change, but simply because the volatility of each risk factor and its co-movements change. Actually a structured finance product could be considered to be synonymous with "volatility product" and "correlation product". Both the structurer and the client pay a lot of attention to the volatility of the risk factors and the way they are wrapped together in a product from an overall point of view, and very often a deal may be directed at exploiting expected changes in volatility and correlation, rather than the direction of the risk factor. When appraising a structured product, then, gauging its sensitivity to each source of risk it is not the end of the story, even though it is a mandatory step. What may be really relevant is to assess the behaviour of the product in scenarios of hectic and very slow movements in the markets and in which the different sources of risk move jointly. The relevant questions are then: Is this product long or short volatility? Is it long or short correlation? To address these questions, a required tool for professionals working in the structured finance market is a broad knowledge of the techniques for modelling and predicting volatility and correlation. Unfortunately, this is not an easy task, particularly because volatility and correlation are not directly observable quantities. A treatment of the subject would certainly require much more space. Here we provide a bird's-eye view over the literature on this subject, the target being to give a broad idea of the issues involved and the strategies available. The reader interested in details is referred to many outstanding books on the subject, such as Rebonato (2000) and Taylor (2005), as well as to the main contribution surveyed here and reported in the "References and Further Reading" section.

3.2 VOLATILITY AND CORRELATION: MODELS AND MEASURES

Volatility and correlation are non-observable quantities. We are interested in these quantities in order to model and understand the structure of another quantity, which represents our final target of interest: the joint probability distribution of future asset returns and risk factor movements in general. Once this problem is solved, simulating scenarios from this distribution would enable us to price the product, to investigate its sensitivity to different events, and to provide a guideline to gauge whether the product is consistent with the "views" of the investor.

This very general issue immediately raises three basic questions. Many of the approaches that will be surveyed in this chapter could be categorized depending on the answers they provide to these questions. Of course, the effectiveness of the answers must be evaluated and confronted with data availability for each market.

- Question 1: Is it more efficient to directly investigate the shape of the distribution or to focus on the specification of its moments? On the one hand, investigating the shape of the distribution is a particularly demanding choice in terms of the amount of data required: a famous example is the "curse of dimension" phenomenon in the non-parametric estimation of multivariate distributions. On the other hand, working on moments amounts to imposing more structure in the *data generating process* (DGP) that is assumed to drive the data: at one extreme, if one is willing to accept that returns are normally distributed, working on the first two moments is exactly analogous to directly working on the probability distribution (technically, the first two moments are *sufficient statistics* for the distribution).
- Question 2: Where can we collect the necessary information? We are of course interested in the future distribution of asset returns conditional on current information. Differently from any other application in statistics, the world of finance provides two different sources of information: (1) historical information recovered from time series of the prices of assets; (2) implied information that may be backed out from cross-section prices of derivative contracts written on the same assets and traded in liquid markets. On one hand, working with historical information is a *backward-looking* choice, and runs into the problem that history rarely repeats itself, and never repeats itself in the same way: structural breaks and "peso problem" effects (major regime changes perceived by the market) represent the major limits to the effectiveness of historical information. On the other hand, working with implied information is a *forward-looking* choice, but runs into the problem that the price formation mechanism may not be fully efficient and may reflect the market risk-aversion along with market expectations: market liquidity and risk premia represent the major limits to the effectiveness of implied information.
- Question 3: How much structure should we impose in the representation of the probability distribution, or volatility and correlation? A famous concept in econometrics and artificial intelligence is that of *parsimony*. The use of an excessive number of parameters and flexible functional forms may induce *overfitting* and a noisy picture of the distribution with low representative power of the future distribution (*estimation risk*), whereas the choice of a model that is too severely specified may easily induce model misspecification and a systematic failure to represent the future distribution (*model risk*).

Based on these questions, one should evaluate different methods to specify the future asset returns distribution. The choice must, of course, be gauged under the constraint of data availability. Broadly speaking, three choices are available:

- Implied information
- Parametric models
- Realized (cross) moments.

3.2.1   Implied information

Implied information is nowadays available for many assets. Depending on the liquidity of the corresponding market, one can choose the amount of structure to be imposed in the estimation procedure, and the amount of parameters involved in the model. In principle, one can choose to estimate

- Implied probability and implied binomial or trinomial trees
- Implied volatility for different strikes ("*smile*") and exercise dates ("*term structure*")
- Implied correlation among exchange rates, stocks and credit risks.

In principle, as we will briefly show, implied probability could be estimated directly in a ideal world in which perfectly liquid option markets would be active for every strike and every maturity on the asset. If this is not the case, we could settle for interpolation of implied volatility and correlation, backing out the probability distribution from that information.

3.2.2   Parametric models

If derivative markets for some assets are not so developed one would have no choice other than to introduce a more structured parametric model. For example, one could postulate the following stochastic process for asset S_i

$$
\begin{aligned}
dS_i(t) &= (r + \lambda \sigma(t)) S_i(t) \, dt + \sigma(t) S_i(t) \, dz_1 \\
dh(t) &= \kappa(\overline{h} - h(t)) \, dt + \xi h^{\alpha}(t) \, dz_2
\end{aligned}
\tag{3.1}
$$

with $h(t) \equiv \sigma^2(t)$ and $E(dz_1, dz_2) = \rho$. The parameter λ denotes the risk premium. The variance process is assumed to be *mean-reverting* and may also embed a risk premium, resulting in changes in the drift parameters (that is the mean reversion coefficient κ and the long-run value mean $\overline{h}$). We could introduce other assets, such as S_j, and specify a dynamic model for their instantaneous correlation ρ_{ij}, such as

$$
d\rho_{ij}(t) = \gamma \left(\overline{\rho_{ij}} - \rho_{ij}(t) \right) dt + \varsigma \left(1 - \rho_{ij}(t) \right) \rho_{ij}(t) \, dz_3
\tag{3.2}
$$

where again the drift parameters may be affected by risk adjustment. Notice that these models can be either estimated from time series data or calibrated from derivative market prices. In principle, the two sources of information could also be used together.

While this choice enables us to save something on the amount of data required, it may raise the problem of systematic model misspecification. For example, assume that the data is generated by a switching regime model, so that both the variance and the correlation conditional distributions could be specified as bimodal quartic-exponential processes. Sticking to the above specification could lead to large misrepresentation of the price of a structured product and its sensitivity to volatility and correlation. The same would happen if either the risk factors or the volatilities were subject to *jump* components.

3.2.3   Realized (cross)moments

As a third option one could resort to the so-called "*realized*" figures. Thus, for example, the realized figure corresponding to a distribution refers to a histogram that may be estimated with non-parametric or semi-parametric techniques. We will see below that non-parametric techniques, which are well known for historical data applications, may also be usefully applied to implied information.

Realized cross(moments) – that is, realized variance and realized correlation – are at the centre of attention in the most recent financial econometrics literature. The idea is very simple. Realized variance is defined as

$$\hat{\sigma}_T^2 = \frac{1}{T-1} \sum_{i=1}^{T} (r_i - \bar{r})^2 \tag{3.3}$$

Similarly, realized covariance is defined as

$$\hat{\sigma}_{jk,T} = \frac{1}{T} \sum_{i=1}^{T} (r_{ij} - \bar{r}_j)(r_{ik} - \bar{r}_k) \tag{3.4}$$

Most of the current research is on the frequency of sampling needed to obtain the best esti-mates. If the data was purely generated by diffusive processes, it would be efficient to sample the data as frequently as possible. The main principle is that while one would have to rely on a very long time series of data to estimate the drift of a process, one would have to rely on a time series sampled at a very high frequency to provide a good estimate of the diffusion parameter. This has spurred research on *high-frequency* data – that is, intraday transactions data sampled at very short time intervals (5 minutes or less). This also comes at a cost, however. In fact, on the one hand, this requires a huge amount of data; on the other, as we get closer and closer to *tick-by-tick* data, we may run into problems raised by the microstructure features of the market. A typical example is the *bid–ask bounce* effect, that is, a spurious auto-correlation induced into the estimate by the sampling of bid and ask quotes. Another typical example, particularly relevant for indices, is the *non-synchronous trading* effect, for which spurious autocorrelation is induced by the fact that not all the constituents of the index are repriced within the sampling frequency. This trade-off has spurred research on the determi-nation of the optimal sampling frequency – a line of research that is still under development.

3.3   IMPLIED PROBABILITY

In an ideal world in which call and put options were traded for each and every strike price, we could extract information about the probability distribution directly from option prices, without any further need to specify the data-generating process of the underlying asset. The idea goes back to Breeden and Litzenberger (1978) and consists in approximating digital option prices by call spreads. We have in fact

$$\lim_{h \to 0} \frac{\text{Call}(S,t;K-h,T) - \text{Call}(S,t;K,T)}{h} = -\frac{\partial \text{ Call}(S,t;K,T)}{\partial K}$$

$$= v(t,T) Q(S(T) > K) \tag{3.5}$$

for call options and

$$\lim_{h \to 0} \frac{\text{Put}(S,t;K,T) - \text{Put}(S,t;K-h,T)}{h} = \frac{\partial \text{ Put}(S,t;K,T)}{\partial K}$$

$$= v(t,T) Q(S(T) \le K) \tag{3.6}$$

for put options. In other words, if, in the limit, we could observe the prices of options for a continuum of strikes, we could actually compute the probability distribution $Q(S(T) \le K)$ for every K. The probability density is obviously obtained by derivation again with respect to the strike. We have then

$$\lim_{h \to 0} \frac{\text{Call}\,(S, t; K - h, T) - 2\,\text{Call}\,(S, t; K, T) + \text{Call}\,(S, t; K + h, T)}{h^2}$$

$$= -\frac{\partial^2 \text{Call}\,(S, t; K, T)}{\partial K^2} = v\,(t, T)\,q\,(K) \tag{3.7}$$

where $q(K)$ is the probability density function.

Of course, in real applications a good approximation of the derivative requires the availability of prices for a wide range of strike prices. This is the case in very few markets for which the corresponding option market is particularly well developed and liquid. For example, in Figure 3.1 we report the probability distribution of the dollar/euro exchange rates recovered from a whole range of options with many strikes. Data was collected on 3 October 2006 for a contract expiring in one month. Of course a problem with this methodology is that the probability distribution is by construction centred around the forward exchange rate. If the analysis is carried out for the purpose of pricing, this would actually be an advantage, while for other applications the distribution ought to be further elaborated to get rid of the risk adjustment.

If the option market is particularly rich, one could also move one step forward to recover the stochastic discrete dynamics over the period. These techniques are known as *implied trees*; the main idea is to build binomial or trinomial trees that could reproduce the prices of a set of actively traded option as accurately as possible. Two main techniques are available:

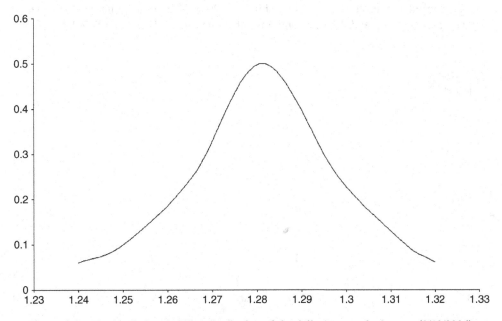

Figure 3.1   The implied probability distribution of the dollar/euro exchange rate (3/10/2006)

- *The Rubinstein model*: Starting from the specification of the implied probability distribution, this model uses *backward induction* to recover the tree.
- *The Derman and Kani model*: Starting from the *at-the-money* option, this model uses *forward induction* to build the tree in a recursive way: for each node the call or put option with the strike on the preceding node is used.

3.4 VOLATILITY MEASURES

3.4.1 Implied volatility

In cases in which the whole spectrum of prices is not available one must resort to some interpolation. A possibility is to interpolate the volatility *"smile"*. The *smile* is the graph of implied volatility plotted against different strike prices. If market data was generated by a geometric Brownian motion, as assumed by Black–Scholes, the plot would be a scatter around the same level, across the whole spectrum of strikes. This is not the case in many markets. In Figure 3.2 we reported the *smile* observed on the dollar/euro exchange rate option market in 3 October 2006 for the contract expiring in one month. The parabolic shape typical of the Forex markets spots excess kurtosis on both sides of the distribution. Other markets, such as the equity option market, are characterized by other typical shapes, such as a decreasing relationship, meaning negative *skew*: downside movements are considered more likely than upside movements of the same size. Thus, modelling and understanding the shape of the *smile* amounts to modelling and understanding the non-normality of returns.

If the number of actively traded options is limited, or if one needs a better definition of the probability distribution, one can resort to interpolation techniques. Three main tools are available:

- Quadratic interpolation of the smile (Shimko, 1994). The smile is interpolated with a quadratic regression and the fitted smile is substituted in the Black and Scholes formula.

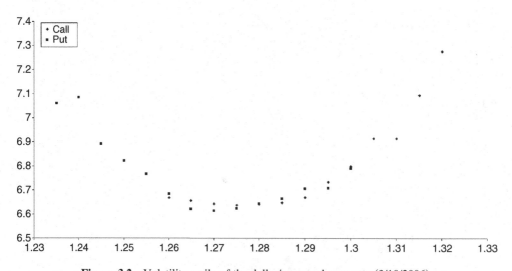

Figure 3.2   Volatility smile of the dollar/euro exchange rate (3/10/2006)

The probability distribution is then recovered by taking derivatives with respect to the strike.

- Polynomial expansion (Jarrow and Rudd, 1982). The probability distribution is approximated by a fourth-degree Hermite polynomial expansion around the Gaussian distribution. The model can be proved to be equivalent to a maximum entropy estimate of the implied probability distribution with constraints on the first four moments.
- Mixtures of shifted log-normal distributions (Marris, 1999; Brigo and Mercurio, 2001). The probability distribution is specified as a weighted geometric average of shifted log-normal distributions in such a way as to fit the smile. The shift term is needed to yield the *volatility skew*.

The dynamics of the volatility could be investigated along a second dimension, which refers to different exercise dates. This is the so-called *volatility term structure*. The plot of volatility against a set of strikes and maturities is called *volatility surface*. Dupire (1993, 1994) proposed a method to back out the volatility surface from market implied volatilities. In a sense, Dupire's idea is to move beyond the representation of the implied volatility smile at a given future time into the dynamics of the volatility smile up to that time. This very closely parallels the way in which *implied trees* techniques provide dynamics to the *implied probability* concept.

3.4.2 Parametric volatility models

In many cases, derivative markets for a risk factor may be very illiquid or may fail to exist at all. In this case, the inclusion of more structure in the model can help to exploit the few data available, and to bridge together cross-section and time series estimation. Of course, this comes at the cost of possible model misspecification.

GARCH Models

The pioneering model in volatility analysis is the AutoRegressive Conditional Heteroskedasticity (ARCH) model, due to Engle (1982) and the Generalize version (GARCH), due to Bollerslev (1986). The idea is to specify the volatility dynamics in discrete time with a standard AutoRegressive Moving Average (ARMA) specification. For example, the model

$$r_t = \varepsilon_t \quad \varepsilon_t \sim \Phi(0, \sigma_t)$$
$$\sigma_t^2 = \omega + \alpha_1 \varepsilon_{t-1}^2 + \beta_1 \sigma_{t-1}^2 \tag{3.8}$$

is read as the GARCH(1, 1), corresponding to the ARMA(1, 1) specification assumed for the variance. The idea is that, conditionally on the volatility observed at time t, the distribution of returns is normal. Volatility, however, depends on past returns, so that the unconditional distribution of returns is not normally distributed. Actually, it may be proved that the dynamics of volatility induces excess kurtosis in the unconditional distribution of returns. The GARCH model has been extensively applied to the modelling of financial time series (see Bollerslev *et al.*, 1992, for a review). It has not been widely used in option pricing (even though Duan, 1995, provides an important exception).

The GARCH family of models has been extended along different lines to enhance the ability of the approach to capture different features of the stochastic behaviour of different markets. Among the main lines of the developments we recall:

- *Volatility asymmetry*: Model specifications have been proposed to generate different volatility impacts of positive and negative shocks to the returns process (GJR model, Glosten *et al.*, 1993; exponential GARCH model, Nelson, 1991).
- *Non-normal conditional distribution*: Sometimes, assuming that conditional returns are normally distributed is not enough to explain the excess kurtosis in the return time series. Model specifications have been proposed in order to allow *fat-tails* in the conditional distribution as well. Bollerslev (1987) proposes to use a Student-t distribution specification for the conditional distribution. Nelson (1991) proposes the Generalized Error Distribution (GED) alternative.
- *Persistence*: The GARCH(1, 1) model is stationary in covariance if the sum $\alpha_1 + \beta_1 < 1$, meaning that after a shock volatility tends to drift back to a time-independent long run value. Actually, there is evidence that shocks to volatility are more persistent. A straightforward modification would be to set $\alpha_1 + \beta_1 = 1$, so that variance is specified as an integrated process (IGARCH, Engle and Bollerslev, 1986). This model can be proved to be equivalent to the Exponentially Weighted Moving Average (EWMA) used by RiskMetrics™ and very well known in the market. Integrated variance means that following a shock in the returns the volatility change lasts forever. Even though the model is very simple to work with, it may be the case that the degree of persistence could look excessive. An alternative is to model volatility as a *fractionally integrated* process (FIEGARCH, Bollerslev and Mikkelsen, 1996): this provides volatility with a long-memory process, so that shocks to the returns decay very slowly in time.

Stochastic volatility models

Even though the GARCH approach to volatility modelling has been largely successful, a quick look at the structure of the model shows that it could be enriched with much further flexibility. In the GARCH family specification, the same shock plays two different roles: it changes the period t return and it changes period $t+1$ volatility. It could be useful to increase the flexibility of the model by introducing a new shock to the variance that may be independent of the shock to the returns. For example, we could specify the model

$$\sigma_t^2 = \omega + \alpha_1 \varepsilon_{t-1}^2 + \beta_1 \sigma_{t-1}^2 + \eta_t \tag{3.9}$$

Models like these are called *stochastic volatility* models, meaning that there is a source of randomness affecting the variance independently of the shocks to the returns. Stochastic volatility models have been much more developed in continuous time for pricing purposes. The first idea that could actually come to mind is to model the instantaneous variance as a geometric Brownian motion independent of the stochastic process followed by the returns. This leads to the Hull & White (1987) model

$$dS_i(t) = (r + \lambda \sigma(t)) S_i(t) dt + \sigma(t) S_i(t) dz_1$$
$$d\sigma(t) = \kappa \sigma(t) dt + \xi \sigma(t) dz_2 \tag{3.10}$$

with $E(dz_1, dz_2) = 0$. This model is very easy to use for pricing purposes. Conditional on volatility, in fact, the pricing formula used is that of Black and Scholes. The unconditional price of an option is then simply obtained by integrating over the volatility scenarios and noticing that by construction these scenarios are generated by a log-normal distribution.

An alternative specification that is widely used in the market, and is the most promising substitute for the Black–Scholes model, is due to Heston (1993):

$$dS_i(t) = (r + \lambda\sigma(t)) S_i(t) dt + \sigma(t) S_i(t) dz_1$$
$$dh(t) = \kappa(\overline{h} - h(t)) dt + \xi\sqrt{h}(t) dz_2 \tag{3.11}$$

with $h(t) \equiv \sigma^2(t)$ and $E(dz_1, dz_2) = \rho$. The instantaneous variance is modelled as a *square root process*. This model is very familiar to the market because it reminds of the Cox, Ingersoll and Ross model of the term structure of interest rates. The nature of the process makes sure that volatility cannot be negative and, for some configuration of the parameters, cannot even reach the zero barrier. The conditional volatility distribution is modelled as a non-central chi-squared distribution, and the stationary distribution is gamma.

Local volatility models

Another class of models, called *local volatility* models, are based on the following specification:

$$dS_i(t) = (r + \lambda\sigma(t)) S_i(t) dt + \sigma(S_i, t) S_i(t) dz \tag{3.12}$$

The diffusion term is specified as a deterministic function of the asset an time. The traditional model in this class is the Constant Elasticity of Variance (CEV) model (Cox, 1975). These

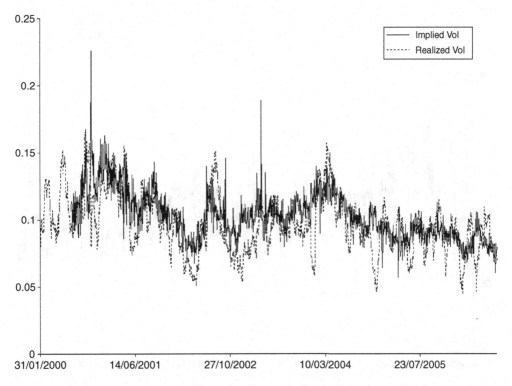

Figure 3.3 Implied volatility and realized volatility; dollar/euro exchange rate

models can be reconstructed to the interpolation techniques of the volatility surface discussed above. (See, e.g., Brigo and Mercurio (2001) for the functional form of the volatility function corresponding to the shifted log-normal distribution model.)

3.4.3 Realized volatility

Recent attention has been devoted to realized volatility. The basic idea is that instead of postulating a model for the dynamics of the returns and their volatility we focus attention on samples of squared returns as representative of the variance. The specification of variance is then model-free, and model risk is avoided. The reduction in model risk is at the expense of an increase in measurement risk. In very liquid markets, one could actually increase the precision of the estimate by increasing the sampling, even at the intraday level (Andersen *et al.*, 2001, 2003). This, however, would encounter the problem that, at the intraday level, market microstructure features and seasonality patterns may eventually increase the noise in the estimates. As an alternative, a long-standing literature suggests the use of information about prices at the beginning and end of the period (open and close) as well as high and low quotes to enhance the efficiency of the estimator. This literature is based on the assumption that the price follows a geometric Brownian motion. As an example of these proposals, we report here the estimator proposed by Parkinson (1980). Under his model, realized variance would be defined as

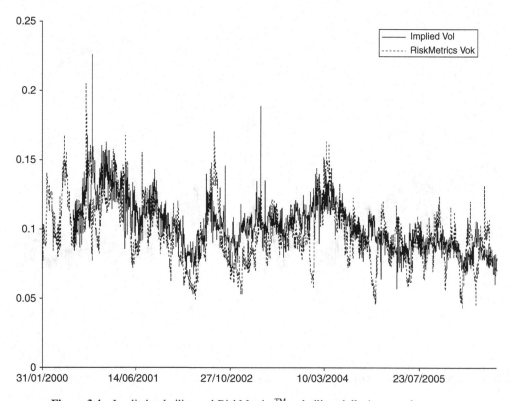

Figure 3.4 Implied volatility and RiskMetrics[TM] volatility; dollar/euro exchange rate

$$\hat{\sigma}_P^2 = \frac{1}{T} \sum_{i=1}^{T} \left[\frac{(H_i - L_i)^2}{4 \ln 2} \right] \tag{3.13}$$

where H and L represent the intra-period highest and lowest prices. Further contributions in this field have been given by Garman & Klass (1980), Rogers & Satchell (1991), Yang & Zhang (2000).

The relative explanatory power of implied and historical volatility remains an important open issue. Figures 3.3 and 3.4 compare implied volatility with realized volatility (monthly average) and RiskMetrics™ volatility. It is the *at-the-money* volatility of the dollar/euro forex option which is a particularly liquid and efficient market. Notice that implied volatility is very volatile, even with respect to the RiskMetrics™ volatility, which, as an integrated process, is much more reactive to market movements.

3.5   IMPLIED CORRELATION

A peculiar feature of financial applications is the distinction between historical and implied information. This duality, which we introduced in the univariate statistics section (section 3.4.2), also shows up, of course, in the multivariate setting. On the one hand, standard time series data from the market enable us to gauge the relevance of market co-movements for investment strategies and risk management issues. On the other hand, some derivative prices are dependent on market correlation: by inverting the prices of such derivatives it is possible to recover the degree of co-movement that investors and financial intermediaries credit to the markets. Of course, recovering implied information is subject to the same flaws the we encountered in the univariate case. First, the possibility of backing out this information in a neat way is limited by the market incompleteness problem, which introduces noise in market prices. Second, the distribution backed out is the risk-neutral one and a market price of risk could be charged by the market to the possibility that correlation could move around. These problems are indeed compounded and, in a sense, magnified in the multivariate setting, in which the uncertainty of the dependence structure among the markets adds to that of the shape of marginal probabilities.

3.5.1   Forex markets implied correlation

The most straightforward case in which implied correlation can be extracted from the market is provided in the Forex market because of the so-called "triangular arbitrage" relationship. Consider the dollar/euro $(e_{\$, €})$, the euro/yen $(e_{€, Y})$ dollar/yen $(e_{\$, Y})$ exchange rates. Triangular arbitrage requires that

$$e_{\$, €} = e_{€, Y} e_{\$, Y} \tag{3.14}$$

taking the logs and denoting $\sigma_{\$, €}$, $\sigma_{€, Y}$ and $\sigma_{\$, Y}$ the corresponding implied volatilities, we have that

$$\sigma_{\$, €}^2 = \sigma_{€, Y}^2 + \sigma_{\$, Y}^2 + 2\rho \sigma_{€, Y} \sigma_{\$, Y} \tag{3.15}$$

from which

$$\rho_{\$,\mathbf{\in}} = \frac{\sigma_{\$,\mathbf{\in}}^2 - \sigma_{\mathbf{\in},Y}^2 - \sigma_{\$,Y}^2}{2\sigma_{\mathbf{\in},Y}\sigma_{\$,Y}} \qquad (3.16)$$

is the implied correlation between the euro/yen and the dollar/yen priced by the market.

3.5.2 Equity "average" implied correlation

A market practice is to recover an "average" measure of correlation from equity market data. Consider the relationship between a market index volatility σ_M, and the corresponding volatility of the constituent assets σ_i, and their correlations $\rho_{i,\,j}$, j, $i = 1, 2, \ldots, N$.

$$\sigma_M^2 = \sum_{i=1}^{N} w_i \sigma_i^2 + \sum_{i=1}^{N}\sum_{j\neq i} \rho_{i,\,j} w_i w_j \sigma_i \sigma_j \qquad (3.17)$$

Notice that, under the assumption that assets are log-normally distributed, the relationship is exact only if the market index is computed using the geometric average. In the standard arithmetic average case, the above relationship postulated by the market can only be considered as an approximation. The market defines the "average correlation" as a number ρ such that

$$\sigma_M^2 = \sum_{i=1}^{N} w_i \sigma_i^2 + \rho \sum_{i=1}^{N}\sum_{j\neq i} w_i w_j \sigma_i \sigma_j \qquad (3.18)$$

Using implied volatility one can compute the "implied average correlation" as

$$\rho = \frac{\sigma_M^2 - \sum_{i=1}^{N} w_i \sigma_i^2}{\sum_{i=1}^{N}\sum_{j\neq i} w_i w_j \sigma_i \sigma_j} \qquad (3.19)$$

For sufficiently large N, we have

$$\rho = \left[\frac{\sigma_M}{\sum_{i=1}^{N} w_i \sigma_i} \right]^2 \qquad (3.20)$$

3.5.3 Credit implied correlation

The most relevant application of implied correlation stems from the credit markets. From the year 2003 a well-known international investment bank launched standard credit derivative contracts referred to the aggregate credit losses (on a given notional amount) out of a set of obligors representative of different markets. Postponing a full discussion of these products to a later chapter of the book, it suffices to say that, by these contracts, agents may buy and sell insurance on "tranches" of these losses (such as losses from 3% to 7% of the notional).

As the value of such insurance for each obligor in the index is quoted and known from the market of univariate credit derivatives (*credit default swaps*, CDSs), the value of insurance on the aggregated losses is a function of correlation among the losses.

In order to grasp the point without getting into the details, assume that for any default in the basket the loss insurance pays 1000 dollars. The expected payment for n losses is then proportional to the joint probability of n defaults, that we denote by $Q(n)$. Denote by Q_i the default probability of each obligor. If default events were independent we would have

$$Q(n) = \prod_{i=0}^{n} Q_i \tag{3.21}$$

On the other hand, if defaults were perfectly dependent we would have instead $Q(n) = \min(Q_1, Q_2, \ldots, Q_N)$, which is the upper Fréchet bound of joint probability. The valuation of this insurance is linked to the dependence structure among the defaults of the obligors in the set, and this clearly emerges if we express such dependence in a measure ranging between -1 and $+1$, such as

$$\rho = \frac{\sum_{i=1}^{n} Q(i) - \sum_{i=1}^{n} \prod_{i=0}^{i} Q_j}{\sum_{i=1}^{n} \min(Q_1, Q_2, \ldots, Q_i) - \sum_{i=1}^{n} \prod_{i=0}^{i} Q_j} \tag{3.22}$$

which is a rank correlation figure.

3.6   HISTORICAL CORRELATION

3.6.1   Multivariate GARCH

Just as in the univariate case, a possible choice to model the non-normal joint distribution of returns is to assume that they could be conditionally normal. A major problem with this approach is that the number of parameters to be estimated can become huge very soon. Furthermore, restrictions are to imposed to ensure that the covariance matrix be symmetric and positive definite. Imposing the latter restriction in particular is not very easy. The most general model of the covariance matrix dynamics is specified by arranging all the coefficients in the matrix in a vector. The most well-known specification is, however, that called BEKK (from the authors). Calling V_t the covariance matrix at time t, this specification reads

$$V_t = \Omega'\Omega + A'\varepsilon_{t-1}\varepsilon_{t-1}A + B'V_{t-1}B \tag{3.23}$$

where Ω, A and B and are n-dimensional matrices of coefficients. Very often special restrictions are imposed to the matrices in order to reduce the dimension of the estimation problem. For example, typical restrictions are to assume that the matrices A and B are either scalar or diagonal, thus limiting the flexibility of the representation to the estimation of the steady-state covariance matrix.

In order to reduce the dimensionality of the problem, the typical recipe used in statistics uses data compression methods: *principal component* analysis and *factor analysis*. Both these approaches have been applied to the multivariate GARCH problem.

Alexander (2001) proposes the so-called *orthogonal GARCH* model. The idea is to use principal component analysis to diagonalize the covariance matrix and estimate a GARCH model on the diagonalized model. Eigen vectors are then used to reconstruct the variance matrix. The maintained assumption under this model is, of course, that the same linear transformation diagonalizes not only the unconditional variance matrix but also the conditional one.

Engle *et al.* (1990) resort instead to a *factor GARCH* representation of the kind

$$r_i = a_i + \sum_{j=1}^{N} \beta_{ij} f_j + \varepsilon_i \tag{3.24}$$

where the dynamics of the common factors f_j are modelled as a multivariate factor model. In this way the dimension of the estimation problem is drastically reduced. Of course, again some risk is left in model misspecification. An alternative computationally effective way to solve the problem would be to separate the specification of the marginal distribution from the dependence structure. This is typically done by means of copula functions, but a similar proposal, within the GARCH family of models, was put forward by Engle. It is the model surveyed below.

3.6.2 Dynamic correlation model

Consider a set of returns generated by univariate GARCH models. The standardized returns $\varepsilon_{j,\,t}$ are distributed according to the standard normal distribution

$$\varepsilon_{j,t} \equiv \frac{r_{j,t}}{\sigma_{j,t}} \approx \Phi(0, 1) \tag{3.25}$$

Notice that the pairwise conditional correlation of asset j with asset k is

$$\rho_{jk,\,t} = \frac{E_t\left(r_{j,\,t} r_{k,\,t}\right)}{\sqrt{E\left(r_{j,\,t}^2\right) E\left(r_{k,\,t}^2\right)}} = E_t\left(\varepsilon_{j,\,t}\varepsilon_{k,\,t}\right) \tag{3.26}$$

Engle (2002) proposes to model such conditional correlations in an autoregressive framework

$$\chi_{jk,\,t} = \overline{\rho}_{jk} + \alpha_\rho\left(\varepsilon_{j,\,t-1}\varepsilon_{k,\,t-1} - \overline{\rho}_{jk}\right) + \beta_\rho\left(\chi_{jk,\,t-1} - \overline{\rho}_{jk}\right) \tag{3.27}$$

which may be rewritten as

$$\chi_{jk,\,t} = \overline{\rho}_{jk} \frac{1 - \alpha_\rho - \beta_\rho}{1 - \beta_\rho} + \alpha_\rho \sum_{i=1}^{\infty} \beta_\rho^{i-1} \varepsilon_{j,\,t-i}\varepsilon_{k,\,t-i} \tag{3.28}$$

It may be verified that the unconditional expectation yields

$$E\left(\chi_{jk,\,t}\right) = \overline{\rho}_{jk} \frac{1 - \alpha_\rho - \beta_\rho}{1 - \beta_\rho} + \alpha_\rho \sum_{i=1}^{\infty} \beta_\rho^{i-1} E\left(\varepsilon_{j,\,t-i}\varepsilon_{k,\,t-i}\right)$$

$$= \overline{\rho}_{jk} \frac{1 - \alpha_\rho - \beta_\rho}{1 - \beta_\rho} + \frac{\alpha_\rho}{1 - \beta_\rho} E\left(\varepsilon_{j,\,t-i}\varepsilon_{k,\,t-i}\right) = \overline{\rho}_{jk} \tag{3.29}$$

The estimator proposed for conditional correlation is

$$\hat{\rho}_{jk,t} = \frac{E_t\left(\chi_{j,t}\chi_{k,t}\right)}{\sqrt{E\left(\chi_{j,t}^2\right)E\left(\chi_{k,t}^2\right)}} \tag{3.30}$$

To express the procedure in matrix form, denote by X_t the matrix whose element in the jth row and kth column is $\chi_{jk,t}$ and denote by ε_t the vector of standardized residuals. We have

$$X_t = \overline{R}\left(1 - \alpha_\rho - \beta_\rho\right) + \alpha_\rho \varepsilon_{.t-1}\varepsilon'_{t-1} + \beta_\rho X_{t-1} \tag{3.31}$$

The model is called *Dynamic Conditional Correlation* (DCC) and generalizes a framework introduced in Bollerslev (1990) in which the correlation was kept constant (CCC). A very appealing feature of the model is that the maximum likelihood estimation enables the use of a two-stage procedure in which the univariate GARCH models are estimated for each univariate series in the first stage and the correlation structure is estimated in the second stage. This feature provides the model with great flexibility and casts a bridge between the family of the parametrically structured multivariate GARCH models and another technique – copula functions – that is widely used in modern finance, and which we are going to address in the following section.

3.7   COPULA FUNCTIONS

Here we give a brief reference to a statistical concept that has been intensively applied to multivariate problems in finance: copula functions. The reader interested in the details of this subject with applications to finance is referred to the book by Cherubini *et al.* (2004) and to the books by Nelsen (1999) and Joe (1997) for an in-depth treatment, albeit limited to the mathematical and statistical formalization. Throughout this book, we will build on these contributions to explore more and further frontier applications in the structured finance field.

3.7.1   Copula functions: the basics

Actually, even at a first sight inspection, copula functions look like tools purposely designed for structured finance applications. Copula functions represent in fact a flexible way to specify marginal distributions and the dependence structure in a separate manner; in structured finance, then they may enable us to neatly disentangle the sensitivity of a product to each risk factor from the sensitivity to the co-movements among them. Typical structured finance questions, such as 'Are we long or short volatility or correlation?' can be answered by in turn assessing the sign of the position with respect to each risk factor and its volatility, and then with respect to risk factors and their co-movements.

The basic technical idea that enables us to disentangle marginal distributions and their dependence structures is the probability integral transformation. Given a random variable X with distribution $H_x(.)$, the integral transform $u = H_x(X)$ is uniformly distributed in the unit interval. This principle is used, for example, in Monte Carlo simulation to generate samples of random variables from the $H_x(.)$ distribution: one generates a uniformly distributed variable u and then computes $H_x^{-1}(u)$ (the inverse is defined in a generalized sense, but we skip such technicalities here). Our task of representing a joint distribution of two variables X and Y in terms of their marginal distributions boils down to the problem of specifying the relationship

$$H(X, Y) = H(H_X^{-1}(u), H_Y^{-1}(z)) = C(u, z) \tag{3.32}$$

The function $C(.,.)$ is called the copula function and fully describes the dependence structure between X and Y. Of course, not every arbitrary function can be well suited to play this role. The requirements that have to met are, however, very easy to explain and absolutely intuitive to grasp.

First of all, the function maps marginal distributions into the joint one, so that the range of the function has to be the unit interval. We must then have

$$C(u, z) : [0, 1]^2 \rightarrow [0, 1] \tag{3.33}$$

The second requirement is that if one of the two events has probability 0, the joint has to be 0 (*groundedness*) and if one of the events has probability 1 the joint probability has to be equal to the marginal probability of the other event.

$$C(u, 0) = C(0, v) = 0 \tag{3.34}$$

$$C(u, 1) = u \quad C(1, z) = z \tag{3.35}$$

The third requirement is that a positive volume cannot have a negative measure (N-increasing property). So, in dimension 2, given that $u_1 > u_2$ and $v_1 > v_2$

$$C(u_1, v_1) - C(u_1, v_2) - C(u_2, v_1) + C(u_2, v_2) \geq 0 \tag{3.36}$$

Alternatively, one could say, to a good degree of approximation, that a joint probability has to be non-decreasing in the marginal probability: if the probability of one of the events increases, the joint probability of the events cannot decrease.

The relationship between copula functions and joint distributions was formally proved by Sklar (1959): *every joint distribution can be written as a copula function taking the marginal distributions as arguments and, conversely, a copula function taking marginal distributions as arguments yields a joint distribution.* It is this result that makes copula functions so useful: they can be used to separately specify marginal distributions and their dependence structure.

3.7.2 Copula functions: examples

As the first exercise in copula function theory, one may easily verify that the product function uv satisfies the above requirements and qualifies as a copula function, the product copula $C_{\perp}(u, z)$. The function $\min(u, z)$ is also a copula, and the maximum value a copula function can achieve. The minimum copula is instead $\max(u + v - 1, 0)$. By taking these basic copulas as building blocks one may prove that their weighted average is again a copula function,

$$C(u, z) = \beta C_{\min}(u, z) + (1 - \alpha - \beta)C_{\perp}(u, z) + \alpha C_{\max}(u, z) \tag{3.37}$$

with $0 \le \alpha$, $\beta \le 1$ and $\alpha + \beta = 1$. This set of copula functions is called the *Fréchet* family.

Extending this family to a general multivariate setting with dimension greater than 2 may be involved, as the number of possible combinations of perfect positive and negative correlation increases exponentially.

Other multivariate copula functions are very easy to recover and are widely used even for large dimension problems. Elliptical distributions are the most famous. Begin with the multivariate normal distribution and simply define

$$C(u_1, u_2, \ldots, u_N) = \Phi(\Phi^{-1}(u_1), \Phi^{-1}(u_2), \ldots, \Phi^{-1}(u_N); R) \quad (3.38)$$

where R is a correlation matrix. This is known as the Gaussian copula, and is one of the few formulas ever recognized as tools to express quotes alternative to prices. As an extension, one may substitute the multivariate Student t distribution to obtain

$$C(u_1, u_2, \ldots, u_N) = T(T^{-1}(u_1), T^{-1}(u_2), \ldots, T^{-1}(u_N); R, v) \quad (3.39)$$

where v is the degree of freedom parameter.

Another well-known family of copulas is that of the so-called Archimedean class. These are recovered from a decreasing generating function $\varphi(.)$ satisfying some conditions, from which one computes

$$C(u_1, u_2, \ldots, u_N) = \varphi^{-1}(\varphi(u_1) + \varphi(u_2), \ldots, +\varphi(u_N)) \quad (3.40)$$

As an example, take $\varphi(t) = (t^{-a} - 1)/a$, which generates the famous Clayton copula

$$C(u_1, u_2, \ldots, u_N) = \max((u_1^{-a} + u_2^{-a} + \cdots + u_N^{-a} - N + 1, 0)^{-1/a} \quad (3.41)$$

3.7.3 Copulas and survival copulas

Copula functions describing joint distributions of events are uniquely linked to copula functions describing the joint distribution of the complement events. The latter are called *survival copulas* (from the use in actuarial science). Take the bivariate case for simplicity: assume that the joint distribution of two events may be represented by $C(u, z)$. Then the joint distribution that neither of the two events takes place has to be

$$\overline{C}(1 - u, 1 - z) = 1 - u - z + C(u, z) \quad (3.42)$$

and $\overline{C}(u, z)$ is called the survival copula of $C(u, z)$.

Example 3.1 *Bivariate digital options.* Assume a digital put option paying one unit of cash if both two stock market indexes S_1 and S_2 are below some given strike levels K_1 and K_2 at exercise time T. Denote by Q_1 and Q_2 the marginal risk-neutral probabilities of S_1 and S_2. Then, the value of the option is

$$DP(S_1, S_2, t; K_1, K_2, T) = v(t, T)C(Q_1(S_1 \le K_1), Q_2(S_2 \le K_2)) \quad (3.43)$$

where $v(t, T)$ is the discount factor from time t to T. The value of the corresponding digital call option – that is, the option paying one unit of cash if both the events $S_1 > K_1$ and $S_2 > K_2$ take place – will be

$$DC(S_1, S_2, t; K_1, K_2, T) = v(t, T) - DP(S_1, t; K_1, T) - DP(S_2, t; K_2, T)$$

$$+ DP(S_1, S_2, t; K_1, K_2, T)$$

$$= v(t, T)\overline{C}(Q_1(S_1 > K_1), Q_2(S_2 > K_2)) \qquad (3.44)$$

where

$$DP(S_i, t; K_i, T) = v(t, T)Q_i(S_i \leqslant K_i) \quad i = 1, 2 \qquad (3.45)$$

is the value of the univariate digital put option written on asset S_i. It may be easily verified that the relationship between copulas and survival copulas enforce no-arbitrage relationships between call and put options. Further examples of multivariate put call parities are reported in Chapter 8 of Cherubini et al. (2004).

3.7.4 Copula dualities

Given a survival copula function $\overline{C}(u, z)$, the function

$$CC(u, z) = 1 - \overline{C}(1 - u, 1 - z) \qquad (3.46)$$

is called the co-copula function of $\overline{C}(u, z)$. Notice that using the relationship between a copula and the corresponding survival one we obtain

$$CC(u, z) = 1 - \overline{C}(1 - u, 1 - z) = u + z - C(u, z) \qquad (3.47)$$

which is called the **dual of copula** function $C(u, z)$.

While copula functions spot the probability of both event A **AND** event B taking place, the dual of the copula, or the co-copula determine the probability that either one event **OR** the other takes place. Notice that since copulas are increasing in correlation, both co-copulas and the dual of copulas are decreasing.

Example 3.2 *First to default swap.* Consider a contingent claim paying one unit of cash if one of a basket of reference obligors defaults by a given time T. The price of this product is clearly a co-copula, and the value is

$$FTD = v(t, T)(1 - \overline{C}(u_1, u_2, \ldots, u_N)) \qquad (3.48)$$

Notice that as the correlation among the risks increases, the value of the long position in the FTD decreases.

Example 3.3 *Rainbow options.* Consider an option written on the minimum of two underlying assets with strike price K. This option will be exercised if both assets S_1 and S_2 are above the strike at the date of exercise. The payoff of this option is

$$\max(\min((S_1, S_2) - K, 0)) \tag{3.49}$$

The probability of exercise under the risk-neutral measure is then

$$\Pr(\min(S_1, S_2) > K) = \Pr(S_1 > K \cap S_2 > K) = \overline{C}(Q_1(S_1 > K), Q_2(S_2 > K)) \tag{3.50}$$

An increase in correlation increases the probability of exercise of the option and raises its value. A call option on the minimum is long correlation.

Consider now an option written on the maximum of the two underlying assets. The payoff may be decomposed (see Stulz, 1987) as

$$\max(\min((S_1, S_2) - K, 0) = \max(S_1 - K, 0) + \max(S_2 - K, \ 0)$$
$$- \max(\min((S_1, S_2) - K, 0) \tag{3.51}$$

The probability of exercise is then

$$\Pr(\max(S_1, \ S_2) > K) = \Pr(S_1 > K) + \Pr(S_2 > K) - \Pr(S_1 > K \cap S_2 > K)$$
$$= Q_1(S_1 > K) + Q_2(S_2 > K) - \overline{C}(Q_1(S_1 > K), \ Q_2(S_2 > K)) \tag{3.52}$$

An increase in correlation now causes a decrease of the probability of exercise of the option and its value. A call option on the maximum is short correlation.

An interesting question for the reader: Is the sign in the correlation position now due to the use of max(.) or min(.) functions in the payoffs? The answer is a resounding no. As a counterexample, the reader may verify that a put option on the maximum is long correlation, while a put on the minimum is short. What is instead relevant, and this result will be used repeatedly throughout the book, is the presence of AND rather than OR operators in the payoff functions.

3.8 CONDITIONAL PROBABILITIES

As copula functions represent joint distributions, it is very easy to use them to express conditional probabilities. In fact, using Bayes' theorem it is immediate to prove, for example

$$\Pr(H_Y \leq z | H_X \leq u) = \frac{C(u, z)}{u} \tag{3.53}$$

that is, the probability of observing an event in the lower tail for the first variable, given that we also observe a lower tail event for the second variable. The corresponding conditional probability in the upper tail can be accordingly derived using the survival copula defined above

$$\Pr(H_Y > z | H_X > u) = \frac{1 - u - z + C(u, \ z)}{1 - u} \tag{3.54}$$

It is also easy to prove that

$$\Pr(H_Y \le z \mid H_X = u) = \frac{\partial C(u, z)}{\partial u} \tag{3.55}$$

Conditional distributions like these are extensively used in pricing. Particularly useful will be the conditional Gaussian copula

$$\Pr(H_Y \le z \mid H_X = u) = \Phi\left(\frac{\Phi^{-1}(z) - \sqrt{\rho}\,\Phi^{-1}(u)}{\sqrt{1-\rho}}\right) \tag{3.56}$$

and the conditional *Student t* one

$$\Pr(H_Y \le z \mid H_X = u) = t_{v+1}\left(\sqrt{\frac{v+1}{t + t_v^{-1}(u)^2}}\,\frac{t_v^{-1}(z) - \sqrt{\rho}\,t_v^{-1}(u)}{\sqrt{1-\rho}}\right) \tag{3.57}$$

3.9 NON-PARAMETRIC MEASURES

Copula functions naturally lead to non-parametric measures of dependence or association. The first straightforward idea is to compute correlation among the probability integral transforms above. From the uniform distributions and copula results above we get

$$\rho_S = \frac{\int_0^1 \int_0^1 [C(u, z) - uz]\,du\,dz}{\sqrt{\int_0^1 u^2\,du - \left(\int_0^1 u\,du\right)^2}\sqrt{\int_0^1 z^2\,dz - \left(\int_0^1 z\,dz\right)^2}} = \frac{\int_0^1 \int_0^1 C(u, z)\,du\,dz - \left(\frac{1}{2}\right)^2}{\sqrt{\frac{1}{12}}\sqrt{\frac{1}{12}}}$$

$$= 12 \int_0^1 \int_0^1 C(u, z)\,du\,dz - 3 \tag{3.58}$$

where ρ_S is known as the rank correlation or Spearman's rho. It may be verified that $C(u, z) = \min(u, z)$ yields $\rho_S = 1$ and $C(u, z) = \max(u + z - 1, 0)$ leads to $\rho_S = -1$. The same results is true for other non-parametric measures such as Kendall's τ. The latter is linked to copula from the relationship

$$\tau = 4 \int_0^1 \int_0^1 C(u, z)\,dC(u, z) - 1 \tag{3.59}$$

Copula can then be specified in such as way as to fit a particular non-parametric figure. The Fréchet family is the simplest example. Take the Spearman ρ_S figure and recover

$$\rho_S = \alpha - \beta \tag{3.60}$$

while for the Kendall's *tau* figure the relationship is just a little more involved

$$\tau = (\alpha - \beta)(2 + \alpha + \beta)/3 \tag{3.61}$$

For the Gaussian copula we have instead

$$\rho_S = (6/\pi)\arcsin(\rho/2) \qquad \tau = (2/\pi)\arcsin\rho \tag{3.62}$$

where ρ is the correlation parameter.

3.10   TAIL DEPENDENCE

Copula functions enable us to model non-normality in a multidimensional setting, by separately addressing the aspects of non-normality. The first has to do with skewness and "fat tails" in the marginal distributions. Market return distributions can be modelled by fitting smile effects with the standard techniques, or by specifying appropriate time series models. The second aspect has to do with the structure of dependence across the distribution, and for extreme events. In particular, it is relevant whether extreme negative or positive movements in one market are associated to extreme movements in the others. A measure of this co-movement structure is the so-called *tail dependence index*. The tail dependence index is a conditional distribution and it is directly linked to the copula function. Using Bayes' theorem, the probability that a market experienced an event with probability z, conditional on a second market experiencing an event with the same probability, is

$$\Pr\left(H_X(x) \leq z \,|\, H_Y(y) \leq z\right) = \frac{C(z,z)}{z} \tag{3.63}$$

The lower tail dependence index is the limit of this conditional distribution for very extreme events, that is for z approaching 0 from above. The lower tail dependence index is then:

$$\lambda_L = \lim_{v \to 0^+} \frac{C(z,z)}{z} \tag{3.64}$$

By the same token, the upper tail dependence index is linked to the survival copula, with z approaching 1 from below:

$$\lambda_U = \lim_{v \to 1^-} \frac{1 - 2z + C(z,z)}{1-z} \tag{3.65}$$

As an exercise it is easy to check that, for the product copula, both the upper and lower tail dependence indexes are 0, and for the maximum copula they are both equal to 1. This is obvious: if two risks are orthogonal they remain so in the tails, and if two risks are perfectly dependent, such perfect dependence is preserved in the tails.

In cases of imperfect dependence it is not obvious whether such dependence fades away in the tails or not. As the simplest case, take the Fréchet family of copula above and check, simply using the linearity property of limits, that

$$\lambda_L = \lambda_U = \alpha \tag{3.66}$$

In other cases checking the tail index may not be so straightforward. However, it may be easily proved that for the Gaussian copula we have $\lambda_L = \lambda_U = 0$, provided that the correlation parameter ρ is different from 1, and extreme events are independent. A positive tail index indicates departure from the Gaussian behaviour. For the Student t copula, the tail dependence parameter λ (the same for upper and lower tails, due to symmetry of the Student t distribution) is instead

$$\lambda = 2t_{v+1}\left(\frac{\sqrt{v+1}\sqrt{1-\rho}}{\sqrt{1+\rho}}\right) \qquad (3.67)$$

with t_{v+1} the tail of a univariate Student t distribution. So, Student t copula provides tail dependence, except in the case $\rho = -1$.

3.11   CORRELATION ASYMMETRY

Dependence structure may also deviate from normality because of asymmetry. Technically, we may denote symmetry, or radial symmetry, as the case in which a copula function is equal to the corresponding survival copula, that is $C(u, z) = \overline{C}(u, z)$. Elliptical distributions display this symmetry relationship.

3.11.1   Correlation asymmetry: finance

Correlation asymmetry leads to the so-called phenomena of correlation smile or skew in finance. The price of bivariate put and call options is consistent with correlation figures that change across claims with different probabilities of exercise (that is different moneyness).

Example 3.4   *Bivariate digital options.* Consider the bivariate digital options in Example 3.1 above. Assume that value of the univariate digital put option is 20% for each of the underlying assets S_1 and S_2. For the sake of simplicity, we assume the risk-free discount factor to be equal to 1 ($v(t, T) = 1$). Consider a dependence structure represented by a Gaussian copula with a correlation parameter equal to 30%. The value of a bivariate digital call option is equal to

$$DP(S_1, S_2, t; K_1, K_2, T) = \Phi(\Phi^{-1}(0.2), \Phi^{-1}(0.2); 0.3) = 0.06614$$

Consider now the value of a bivariate digital call option with the same strikes. By arbitrage, the bivariate digital call is worth

$$DC(S_1, S_2, t; K_1, K_2, T) = v(t, T) - DP(S_1, t; K_1, T)$$
$$- DP(S_2, t; K_2, T) + DP(S_1, S_2, t; K_1, K_2, T)$$
$$= 1 - 0.2 - 0.2 + 0.06614 = 0.66614$$

Of course, by arbitrage the univariate call options have to be equal to 80% for both assets. One may now verify that

$$DC(S_1, S_2, t; K_1, K_2, T) = \Phi(\Phi^{-1}(0.8), \Phi^{-1}(0.8); 0.3) = 0.66614$$

and the price is consistent with the same copula function with same correlation parameter 30%.

Assume now that the dependence structure is Clayton, with parameter 0.2792. It may be verified that

$$DP(S_1, S_2, t; K_1, K_2, T) = \text{Clayton}(0.2, 0.2; 0.2792) = 0.06614$$

but now

$$DC(S_1, S_2, t; K_1, K_2, T) = \text{Clayton}(0.8, 0.8; 0.2792) = 0.6484 < 0.66614$$

Of course, the correct price is again 0.66614. If it were not so, in fact, one could exploit arbitrage gains. But what's wrong? It is the fact that both the bivariate put and call options are represented by the *same* copula function. This is possible with the Gaussian copula, because it is symmetric, but it is not possible with the Clayton one. In the latter case, we must pay attention to whether we specify the copula or the survival one – that is, whether we calibrate bivariate put or call options.

An important corollary of the asymmetry problem is that copula functions that are not symmetric provide asymmetric evaluations of call and put claims, given the same marginal probabilities. Alternatively, one could say that call and put options price different implied correlations.

Example 3.5 *Bivariate digital options (continued).* Take the same bivariate put option as in the previous example:

$$DP(S_1, S_2, t; K_1, K_2, T) = \Phi(\Phi^{-1}(0.2), \Phi^{-1}(0.2); 0.3) = 0.06614$$

Now compute the bivariate call options with the same marginals. Symmetry of the copula function implies that

$$DC(S_1, S_2, t; K_1, K_2, T) = \Phi(\Phi^{-1}(0.2), \Phi^{-1}(0.2); 0.3) = 0.06614$$

and that call and put options with the same marginals have the same value.
    Now take the Clayton copula case with parameter

$$DP(S_1, S_2, t; K_1, K_2, T) = \text{Clayton}(0.2, 0.2; 0.2792) = 0.06614$$

But now we have

$$DC(S_1, S_2, t; K_1, K_2, T) = 1 - 0.8 - 0.8 + \text{Clayton}(0.8, 0.8; 0.2792) = 0.0484$$

and the bivariate call option is worth less than the corresponding put. As the price of both the bivariate call and put is increasing in correlation, this means that put options, represented using the Clayton copula, imply more correlation for downward movements than for upward movements.

3.11.2 Correlation asymmetry: econometrics

The question is now whether a correlation asymmetry phenomenon is borne out by the data. While there is no wide evidence on implied information, apart for some markets, there is a developed stream of literature pointing to a robust evidence of asymmetric correlation in the equity market. In particular, correlation is found to be higher in periods of worse performance of the stock market.

The evidence provided (see Longin and Solnik, 2001 and Ang and Chen, 2002, among the first contributions) use the technique of the so-called *exceedance correlation*. Correlation is computed for subsamples including observations at least θ standard deviations above the mean value and compared with that measured with observations at least θ standard deviations below the mean. For symmetric distributions the correlation measures obtained should be equal. The typical finding is that the correlation in the below average sample is higher than that in the corresponding above average sample. Correlation is also checked for non-Gaussianity in the subsamples, showing in some cases (Ang and Chen, 2002) that departures from normality are due to correlation in lower percentiles. The test is a quadratic distance between the empirical exceedance figures and those of the normal distribution (which are different from the correlation figure on the overall sample because of the conditioning bias).

A possible extension of analysis to non-parametric association measures, namely rank correlation, is given by Dobric and Schmid (2005). They propose a measure, called conditional rank correlation, that is in the same spirit as the exceedance correlation idea. They observe that the Spearman rank correlation statistic can be written as

$$\rho_S = \frac{\int_0^1 \int_0^1 C(u, z)\, du\, dz - \int_0^1 \int_0^1 uz\, du\, dz}{\int_0^1 \int_0^1 \min(u, z)\, du\, dz - \int_0^1 \int_0^1 uz\, du\, dz} \tag{3.68}$$

From this representation one can easily devise a conditional rank correlation statistic

$$\rho_S(p; C(u, z)) = \frac{\int_0^p \int_0^p C(u, z)\, du\, dz - \int_0^p \int_0^p uz\, du\, dz}{\int_0^p \int_0^p \min(u, z)\, du\, dz - \int_0^p \int_0^p uz\, du\, dz} \tag{3.69}$$

and for radial symmetric copulas

$$\rho_S(p; C(u, z)) = \rho_S(p; \overline{C}(u, z)) \tag{3.70}$$

which is exactly in the same spirit as exceedance correlation.

3.12 NON-EXCHANGEABLE COPULAS

A problem with the use of many copula functions is that they are *exchangeable*. The term was first introduced in probability theory by De Finetti in the 1930s. A bivariate distribution is deemed exchangeable if $H(x, y) = H(y, x)$. It may easily be verified that all the copula functions presented above are endowed with this "exchangeability" property.

Is this a flaw or an advantage of copula functions? And, how can we extend the class of copula functions to include some "non-exchangeable" ones? In order to answer the first question, we have to investigate the economic meaning of exchangeability.

Consider two markets or currencies X and Y, with joint probability distribution $H(X, Y) = C(u, z)$. Non-exchangeability means that, for example

$$C(u, z) > C(z, u) \tag{3.71}$$

which implies that

$$\Pr\left(H_Y \leq z \,|\, H_X \leq u\right) = \frac{C(u, z)}{u} > \frac{C(z, u)}{u} = \Pr\left(H_X \leq z \,|\, H_Y \leq u\right) \tag{3.72}$$

In plain terms, if we take $u = 0.5$ and $z = 0.25$, this says that the joint probability that market Y falls below its lower quartile value, given that market X falls below its median value, is higher than the probability that market X falls below its lower quartile, given that Y falls below its median value.

In a sense, quoting a metaphorical statement that is sometimes used by analysts, one would say: "when market X catches a cold, market Y takes pneumonia". Non-exchangeability refers then to a *dominant* role of a market or risk factor with respect to others. A somewhat close concept is that of *contagion*: something that happens to a market propagates to the others more than the other way around.

Example 3.6 *German dominance.* Before the euro, the German dominance phenomenon was that whenever the German Deutschemark was weak against the dollar, peripheral currencies, such as the Italian lira, were weak against the Deutschemark and then even weaker against the dollar. On the contrary, when peripheral currencies were weak against the dollar, the stance of the Deutschemark was almost unaffected.

Example 3.7 *Credit risk contagion.* In contagion credit risk models default propagates from one firm to the others because of commercial links from one to the other. Consider a firm with many relationships with firms providing intermediate goods and services to it. Assume the latter firms are not diversified and only provide goods to the leader company. If the leader company defaults, all these firms will probably follow. If, instead, only one of them is caught into a default, the impact on the leader firm may not be relevant.

We see that accounting for non-exchangeability enables us to catch empirical regularities of markets and risk factors co-movements that are economically meaningful. Two questions remain. How do we measure non-exchangeability? And how do we generate non-exchangeable copulas?

In answer to the first question, a recent paper by Nelsen (2006) finds that the maximum level of non-exchangeability is

$$0 \leq \sup |C(u, z) - C(z, u)| \leq 1/3 \tag{3.73}$$

therefore, a natural measure of non-exchangeability is: $3 \sup |C(u, z) - C(z, u)|$.

Techniques to generate non-exchangeable copulas have not been studied in detail. One, due to Khoudraji (1995), is particularly useful. Given two exchangeable copula functions $C^*(u, z)$ and $C(u, z)$, the copula function

$$C^*(u^\kappa, z^\lambda)C(z^{1-\kappa}, u^{1-\lambda}) \qquad (3.74)$$

is non-exchangeable.

3.13 ESTIMATION ISSUES

The dependence structure can be calibrated or estimated using time series data or a cross-section of multivariate derivative prices, if available. Hybrid approaches combining implied and historical information are also possible: one could in fact estimate the model by a "historical simulation" approach by reconstructing a time series of implied probabilities and estimating the dependence structure among them.

Whatever the data, two main approaches may be followed. We just touch upon them, referring the reader to Cherubini *et al.* (2004) for details. The first approach is calibration. Non-parametric dependence statistics (such as Spearman's ρ or Kendall's τ quoted above) are estimated on the data and the copula function is calibrated in such a way as to yield the same parameter. The other approach is estimation and uses the maximum likelihood methodology. In order to write the log-likelihood we define the copula density as the joint density $f(x, y)$ that can be written as

$$c(u, z) = \frac{\partial^2 C(u, z)}{\partial u \, \partial z} \qquad (3.75)$$

The joint density $f(x, y)$ can be written as

$$f(x, y) = c(u, z) f_X(x) f_Y(y) \qquad (3.76)$$

where $f_i(.), i = X, Y$, are the marginal density functions. Based on this result, the log-likelihood from a sample of data X_j and $Y_j, j = 1, \ldots, N$, can be written as

$$L = \sum_{j=1}^{N} c(u, z) + \sum_{j=1}^{N} f_X(X_j) + \sum_{j=1}^{N} f_Y(Y_j) \qquad (3.77)$$

Notice that the log-likelihood can be divided in two parts, the first involving the dependence structure and the second involving the marginal densities. This feature makes available other estimation procedures beyond standard MLE. In particular one can use:

(i)   direct maximum likelihood estimation (MLE) of all the parameters of the model;
(ii) inference for the margin (IFM): the parameters of the marginal densities are estimated in a first stage, and used to compute the marginal distributions and to estimate the parameters of the copula density in the second stage;
(iii) canonical maximum likelihood (CML): ranks are used to estimate the copula function parameters directly.

3.14 LÉVY PROCESSES

In a paper dating back to 1973, Clark proposed the following model. Assume that you sample the log-returns on an asset over intervals of length τ. The returns you measure are actually

$$\ln\left[\frac{S\left(t_j+\tau\right)}{S\left(t_j\right)}\right]=\sum_{i=1}^{N_j}r_i \tag{3.78}$$

where N_j is the number of trades in the period $[t_j, t_j+\tau]$, and it is a random variable, while r_i are the log-returns of each transaction in the period, and are assumed i.i.d. Technically, the τ-period returns measured in this way are a subordinated stochastic process: more precisely, the variable N_j is the subordinator. Clark showed that this structure actually destroys the normality property of the returns (even though it is postulated at the transaction level), inducing excess kurtosis in the distribution. The subordinator moves volatility and volumes at the same time, so that in hectic phases of the market they both increase while they decrease when the number of transactions is lower.

While the target of Clark's approach was to jointly explain prices and volumes (see also Epps and Epps, 1976), the main idea behind the approach has been rediscovered by the most recent research on asset prices dynamics. The basic idea is that at some microscopic level, so to speak, the price process is not continuous, but it is subject to *jumps*. Actually, the genuine idea in Clark's approach is that the price process evolves only by jumps (*pure jump process*). This has led the recent research to propose a new dynamics for the prices of financial assets of the kind

$$S\left(t\right)=S\left(0\right)\exp\left[\mu t+\sigma Z\left(t\right)+\sum_{i=1}^{N(t)}X_i\right] \tag{3.79}$$

where $N(t)$ is the number of jumps, represented by a Poisson process with intensity θ. The variables X_i represent jumps and are i.i.d. random variable with density $f(.)$. For generality, a diffusion part is also included in the process. The product of the intensity and the density of the jumps (θf) is defined as the *Lévy density*, and the dynamics of the log price defined in this way is called a *Lévy process*. Actually, the rigorous definition of the Lévy process is more involved, calling for the concept of *infinitely divisible distribution* and the *Lévy–Kintchine* theorem (see Kyprianou *et al.*, 2005, and Cont and Tankov, 2003 for a detailed treatment). However, for all we need in this treatment, it is enough to say that a Lévy process is a general process made up by diffusion and a jump part. Apart from the pioneering model with jumps due to Merton (1976), the most well-known models among those that use jumps are due to Madan and Seneta (1987) (the so-called *variance gamma*, VG, model) and to Carr *et al.* (2002, 2003) (the so-called CGMY model). Finally, the most recent research in this field has addressed an issue that remains open: how to address dependence among variables driven by Lévy processes? An interesting result would be to identify the copula function that links together the marginal Lévy processes in a joint distribution. This extension of Sklar's theorem to jump processes was addressed by Kallsen and Tankov (2006), who suggest the adoption of *Lévy copulas*. Even though empirical applications are still on the way, this extension appears to be an interesting direction to follow.

REFERENCES AND FURTHER READING

Alexander, C.O. (1997) Volatility and correlation estimation: measurement, models and applications, in Alexander, C.O. (ed.) *Risk Management and Analysis*, vol. I (pp. 125–168). John Wiley & Sons, Chichester.

Alexander, C.O. (2001) Orthogonal GARCH, in Alexander, C.O. (ed.) *Mastering Risk* (pp. 21–38). Prentice Hall.

Andersen, T.G., Bollerslev, T., Diebold, F.X. & Labys, P. (2001) The distribution of realized exchange rate volatility, *Journal of the American Statistical Association*, **96**, 42–55.

Andersen, T.G., Bollerslev, T., Diebold, F.X. & Labys, P. (2003) Modelling and forecasting realized volatility, *Econometrica*, **71**, 579–625.

Ang, A. & Chen, J. (2002) Asymmetric correlations of equity portfolios, *Journal of Financial Economics*, **63** (3), 443–494.

Baba, Y., Engle, R.F., Kraft, D.F. & Kroner, K.F. (1991) *Multivariate Simultaneous Generalized ARCH* (mimeo).

Bollerslev, T. (1986) Generalised autoregressive conditional heteroskedasticity, *Journal of Econometrics*, **31**, 307–327.

Bollerslev, T. (1987) A conditionally heteroskedastic time series model for security prices and rates of return data, *Review of Economics and Statistics*, **59**, 542–547.

Bollerslev, T. (1990) Modelling the coherence in short run nominal exchange rates: A multivariate generalised ARCH model, *Review of Business Economics and Statistics*, **72**, 498–505.

Bollerslev, T. & Mikkelsen, H.O. (1996) Modelling and pricing long memory in stock market volatility, *Journal of Econometrics*, **73**, 151–184.

Bollerslev, T., Chou, R.Y. & Kroner, K.F. (1992) ARCH modeling in finance, *Journal of Econometrics*, **52**, 5–59.

Boudoukh, J., Richardson, M. & Whitelaw, R.F. (1997) Investigation of a class of volatility estimators, *Journal of Derivatives*, **4** (3), 63–72.

Breeden, D.T. & Litzenmberger, R.H. (1978) Prices of state contingent claims implicit in option prices, *Journal of Business*, **51**, 621–651.

Brigo, D. & Mercurio, F. (2001) Displaced and mixture diffusions for analytically tractable smile models, in H. Geman, D. Madan, S.R. Pliska & T. Vorst (eds) Mathematical Finance – Bachelier Congress 2000. Springer, Berlin, Heidelberg, New York.

Carr, P., Geman, H., Madan, D.B. & Yor, M. (2002) The fine structure of asset returns: An empirical investigation, *Journal of Business*, **75**, 305–332.

Carr, P., Geman, H., Madan, D.B. & Yor, M. (2003) Stochastic volatility for Levy processes, *Mathematical Finance*, **13**, 345–382.

Cherubini, U., Luciano, E. & Vecchiato, W. (2004) *Copula Methods in Finance*. John Wiley, & Sons, Chichester.

Clark, P. (1973) A subordinate stochastic process model with finite variance for speculative prices, *Econometrica*, **41**, 135–155.

Cont, R. & Tankov, P. (2003) *Financial Modelling with Jump Processes*. Chapman & Hall, CRC.

Cox, J.C. (1975) *Notes on option pricing I: Constant elasticity of variance diffusions*. Working Paper, Stanford University.

Derman, E. & Kani, I. (1994) Riding on a smile, *Risk*, **7**, 32–39.

Dobric, J. & Schmid, F. (2005) Non parametric estimation of lower tail dependence λL in bivariate copulas, *Journal of Applied Statistics*, **32** (4), 387–407.

Driessen, J., Maenhout, P. & Vilkov, G. (2005) *Option-implied correlations and the price of correlation risk*. Working Paper.

Duan, J.C. (1995) The GARCH option pricing model, *Mathematical Finance*, **5**, 13–32.

Dupire, B. (1993) Model art, *Risk*, **6** (10), 118–121.

Dupire, B. (1994) Pricing with a smile, *Risk*, **7** (1), 18–20.

Embrechts, P., McNeil, A. & Straumann, D. (1999) *Correlation and dependence in risk management: Properties and pitfalls.* ETHZ Working Paper.

Engle, R.F. (1982) Autoregressive conditional heteroskedasticity with estimates of the variance of U.K. inflation, *Econometrica*, **50**, 987–1008.

Engle, R.F. (1995) *ARCH: Selected Readings.* Advanced Texts in Econometrics, Oxford University Press.

Engle, R.F. (2002) Dynamic conditional correlation: A simple class of multivariate generalized conditional heteroschedasticity model, *Journal of Business Economics and Statistics*, **20**, 339–350.

Engle, R.F. & Bollerslev, T. (1986) Modelling the persistence of conditional variances, *Econometric Reviews*, **5**, 1–50.

Engle, R.F. & Gonzales-Rivera, G. (1991) Semiparametric ARCH models, *Journal of Business Economics and Statistics*, **9** (4), 345–359.

Engle, R.F. & Kroner, K.F. (1995) Multivariate simultaneous generalized ARCH, *Econometric Theory*, **11**, 122–150.

Engle, R.F. & Mezrich, J. (1996) GARCH for Groups, *Risk*, **9**, 8.

Engle, R.F., Lilien, D.M. & Robins, R.P. (1987) Estimating time varying risk premia in the term structure: The ARCH-M model, *Econometrica*, **55** (2), 391–407.

Engle, R.F., Ng, V.K. & Rotschild, M. (1990) Asset pricing with a factor ARCH covariance structure: Empirical estimates for Treasury bills, *Journal of Econometrics*, **45**, 213–238.

Epps, T.W. & Epps, M.L. (1976) The stochastic dependence of security price changes and transaction volumes: Implications for the mixture of distributions hypothesis, *Econometrica*, **44**, 305–321.

Frees, E.W. & Valdez, E. (1998) Understanding relationships using copulas, *North American Actuarial Journal*, **2**, 1–25.

Garman, M.B. & Klass, M.J. (1980) On the estimation of security prices volatilities from historical data, *Journal of Business*, **53** (1), 61–65.

Geman, H. (2002) Pure jump Levy processes for asset price modelling, *Journal of Banking and Finance*, **26**, 1297–1316.

Gibbons, J.D. & Chakraborti, S. (1992) *Non Parametric Statistical Inference.* Marcel Dekker, New York.

Glosten, L.R., Jagannathan, R. & Runkle, R. (1993) Relationship between the expected value and volatility of the nominal excess returns on stocks, *Journal of Finance*, **48**, 1179–1801.

Hamilton, J.D. (1994) *Time Series Analysis.* Princeton University Press, Princeton, NJ.

Heston, S.L. (1993) A closed form solution for options with stochastic volatility with applications to bonds and currency options, *Review of Financial Studies*, **6**, 327–343.

Hull, J. & White, A. (1987) The pricing of options on assets with stochastic volatility, *Journal of Finance*, **42**, 281–300.

Jarrow, R.A. & Rudd, A. (1982) Approximate option evaluation for arbitrary stochastic processes, *Journal of Financial Economics*, **10**, 347–369.

Joe, H. (1997) *Multivariate Models and Dependence Concepts.* Chapman & Hall, London.

Kallsen, J. & Tankov, P. (2006) Characterization of dependence of multidimensional Lévy processes using Lévy copulas, *Journal of Multivariate Analysis*, **97**, 1151–1172.

Koudraji, A. (1995) *Contributions a l'étude des copules et à la modelization des valeurs extremes bivariées.* PhD Thesis, Université Laval, Québec, Canada.

Kyprianou, A., Shoutens, W. & Wilmott, P. (2005) *Exotic Options and Advanced Lévy Processes.* John Wiley & Sons, Chichester.

Longin, S. & Solnik, B. (2001) Extreme correlation of international equity markets, *Journal of Finance*, **56**, 649–676.

Madan, D.B. & Seneta, E. (1987) The VG for share market returns, *Journal of Business*, **63**, 511–524.

Marris, D. (1999) *Financial option pricing and skewed volatility.* Working Paper.

Merton, R. (1976) Option pricing when underlying stock returns are discontinuous, *Journal of Financial Economics*, **3**, 125–144.

Nelson, D.B. (1991) Conditional heteroskedasticity in asset returns: A new approach, *Econometrica*, **59** (2), 347–370.

Nelsen, R.B. (1999) *An Introduction to Copulas*. Springer-Verlag, New York.

Nelsen, R.B. (2006) *Extremes of Exchangeability*. Working Paper.

Parkinson, M. (1980) The extreme value method for estimating the variance of the rate of return, *Journal of Business*, **53** (1), 61–65.

Rebonato, R. (2000) *Volatility and Correlation*. John Wiley & Sons, Chichester, UK.

Rogers, L.C.G. & Satchell, S.E. (1991) Estimating variance from high, low and closing prices, *Annals of Applied Probability*, **1**, 504–512.

Rogers, L.C.G., Satchell, S.E. & Yoon, Y. (1994) Estimating the volatility of stock prices: A comparison of methods that use high and low prices, *Applied Financial Economics*, **4**, 241–247.

Rubinstein, M. (1994) Implied binomial trees, *Journal of Finance*, **49**, 771–818.

Shimko, D. (1994) Bounds of probability, *Risk*, **6**, 33–37.

Sklar, A. (1959) Fonctions de ripartitions à n dimensions et leur marges, *Publications de l'Institut Statistique University of Paris*, **8**, 229–231.

Taylor, S.J. (2005) *Asset Price Dynamics, Volatility and Predictions*. Princeton University Press, Princeton, NJ.

Yang, D. & Zhang, Q. (2000) Drift independent volatility estimation based on high, low, open and close prices, *Journal of Business*, **73** (3), 477–491.

4

Cash Flow Design

4.1 INTRODUCTION

The purpose of this chapter is to recall some elementary notions on structured bonds introducing, at the same time, some new notions concerning object-oriented programming. In particular we will introduce a synthetic introduction to patterns and two new UML diagrams: Activity diagrams and Sequence diagrams. Furthermore we will look in depth into the way Java handles dates and time periods and will build a complete Java application for the generation of a bond schedule. At the end of the chapter we will explain how to design a cash flow generator for a coupon bond with indexed coupons.

Bond portfolio managers and other investors are faced with challenges when they consider pricing and purchasing structured bonds: for example, the future cash flows generated by structured bonds can be linked to unknown future interest rates or equity market level. Moreover, structured bonds may include embedded options that allow the issuers to call them in before maturity. What is a fair price for a structured bond? How can the risks of a portfolio of structured bonds be managed? As we have already stated, these are the key questions that should be addressed in this book. In order to find (or to suggest) an answer to these questions we have, first of all, to address some more practical issues. Among these, of special relevance for all practical purposes, are those related to the building of cash flows and discounting factors. This, in turn, is related to the ability to manage calendar dates and schedules, and this will be addressed immediately in the next section (and the bad news is that this is not as simple as one would imagine) in which we also discuss some issue about software design.

We will then take into consideration questions linked to the calculation of coupon cash flows and nominal amounts. For educational purpose we can split both the coupon and the repayment calculation into two main classes:

- known amounts (deterministic)
- unknown amounts (not deterministic).

As far as the coupon computation is concerned, this separation is equivalent to distinguish fixed interest payment at known dates (deterministic cash flow) from floating coupon (including in the latter options like caps and floors). Furthermore, many structured bonds provide the issuers with the option to call in the bonds before maturity, at a set of prespecified times; these times often correspond to the coupon dates of the bonds. Since options are contingent claims, this kind of proviso transforms the principal amount into a stochastic variable making it unpredictable. More precisely we will speak of *callability* when the issuer, as above, has the right to repay the bond before the maturity date on the call dates. These bonds are referred to as callable bonds. Most callable bonds allow the issuer to repay the bond at par. In exchange for this, the issuer has to pay a premium, the so-called call premium. We will speak of *putability* when the bond holder has the right to force the issuer to repay the bond before the maturity date on the put dates. From the point of view of exercise dates, we can distinguish among three main categories:

- A Bermudan callable has several call dates, usually coinciding with coupon dates.
- A European callable has only one call date. This is a special case of a Bermudan callable.
- An American callable can be called at any time up to the maturity date.

The issuer's decision whether or not to call in a given bond at a given time depends critically upon the value of interest rates at that time. It is worth noting that, although it is apparent that early exercise becomes more attractive to the issuer as interest rates decline, computing the precise point at which early exercise is optimal requires, in general, intensive numerical calculations. Other products contain different kinds of option (e.g. convertible bonds) which give the owner the right to exchange the nominal repayment with a position in equities according to a predefined conversion plan. Just to summarize some definitions, we report a short list of the principal types of bond we will encounter throughout this book.

4.2   TYPES OF BONDS

4.2.1   Floaters and reverse floaters

Floaters and *reverse floaters* have a coupon that is not known at the time the bonds are issued. Instead, the coupons depend on the movement of future interest rates. For both floater and reverse floater bonds, coupons are determined by the prevailing LIBOR rate at the time the previous coupon was paid. If interest rates go up, floater coupons go up and reverse floater coupons go down. The coupon is reset periodically.

4.2.2   Convertible bonds

A convertible bond is the type of bond that can be converted into shares of stock in the issuing company, usually at some pre-announced ratio. A convertible bond will typically have a lower coupon rate for which the holder is compensated by the value of the holder's ability to convert the bond into shares of stock. In addition, the bond is usually convertible into common stock at a substantial premium to its market value.

Other convertible securities include: exchangeable bonds – where the stock underlying the bond is different from that of the issuer; convertible preferred stock (similar valuation-wise to a bond, but lower in seniority in the capital structure); and mandatory convertible securities (short duration securities, generally with high yields, that are obligatorily convertible upon maturity into a variable number of common shares based on the stock price at maturity).

4.2.3   Equity-linked notes

An equity-linked note combines the characteristics of a zero or low coupon bond or note with a return component based on the performance of a single equity security, a basket of equity securities, or an equity index. In the latter case, the security would typically be called an equity index-linked note. Equity-linked notes come in a variety of styles.

Example 4.1 World Bank USD S&P 500® Equity Linked Bonds. In 10 November 2004, The World Bank launched USD denominated bonds linked to the performance of the S&P 500® Index. The bonds were placed with US investors, who would like to participate in the upside of the performance of the equity index and want principal protection and a minimum return. The bonds have an annual coupon of 1.15% and, at maturity, investors receive 100% of the principal and a supplemental payment linked to the average annual return of the S&P 500® Index as described in the terms of the notes. Deutsche Bank was the sole underwriter for the bonds.

BOND CHARACTERISTICS

Amount: USD 10 405 000
Settlement date: 26 November 2004
Maturity date: 26 November 2011
Coupon: 1.15%
Minimum redemption amount: 100%
Redemption amount: 100% plus a supplemental payment calculated based on the average performance of the S&P 500® Index on annual fixing dates as described in the terms of the notes
Denomination: USD 1000
Clearing system: DTC
ISIN Code: US459056HJ94

(*Source*: www.worldbank.org/debtsecurities).

4.2.4 Inflation-linked bonds

Inflation-linked bonds, in which either the principal amount or the coupon is indexed to inflation. The interest rate is lower than for fixed rate bonds with comparable maturity. However, as the principal amount grows, the payments increase with inflation. The government of the United Kingdom was the first to issue inflation-linked Gilts in the 1980s. Treasury Inflation-Protected Securities (TIPS) and I-bonds are examples of inflation-linked bonds issued by the US government.

4.2.5 Asset-backed securities

Asset-backed securities are bonds whose interest and principal payments are backed by underlying cash flows from other assets. Examples of asset-backed securities are mortgage-backed securities (MBS), collateralized mortgage obligations (CMOs) and collateralized debt obligations (CDOs). A cash flow collateralized debt obligation, or cash flow CDO, is a structured finance product that typically securitizes a diversified pool of debt assets. These assets, corporate loans for instance, are transfered into different classes of bonds (known as tranches) that pay investors from the cash flows they generate. Cash flow CDOs offer investors access to a diversified and actively managed portfolio of credit risks in a single investment that provides enhanced returns corresponding to each investor's appetite for risk. Investors in CDO senior and mezzanine bonds can earn high returns relative to similarly rated asset-backed securities. CDO equity investors can earn leveraged returns. Cash flow CDOs offer the asset managers and issuing institutions a range of benefits, depending on the structure and motivation of each transaction. Asset managers can increase assets under management achieving some protection from market value volatility. Issuing institutions can sell off portfolio credit risk, reduce regulatory capital requirements and lower funding costs. Cash flow CDOs should be distinguished from market value CDOs, which are not discussed in this chapter. Whereas market value CDOs are managed to payoff liabilities through the trading and sale of collateral, cash flow CDOs are managed to payoff liabilities from the interest and principal payments of collateral. This means that unlike market value CDOs, cash flow CDOs focus primarily on managing the credit quality of the underlying portfolio rather than the volatility of its market value.

4.3 TIME AND SCHEDULER ISSUES

When specifying payment dates and interest rates on swaps and bonds, it is very important that both sides of the transaction agree on dates on which payments will occur and on how the amounts payable will be calculated. In this context calendar and date manipulation issues are of very special importance independently on the particular structured product you want to trade. Handling the financial calendar is actually very complicated, so in this section we briefly review only some of the more important aspects.

From a general point of view there are many different ways in which financial securities require the generation of a time schedule from parametric data (first date, last date, time interval between two consecutive dates, etc.) and the calculation of the number of days between two dates. For example day count is used to compute the number of days in accrued interest and the number of days in a coupon period. As we will see, the method of counting days has an important influence on some derivatives securities. We have then two major issues to be addressed in order to build a schedule:

- How to build schedule dates.
- How to calculate time interval between consecutive dates.

The first point should be very simple (if it were not for) holiday dates or, more generally, non-business days. In this case we need to "adjust" the date, choosing an appropriate business day as near as possible to the original date. How to do this is discussed below.

4.3.1 Payment date conventions

We refer to a "Business Day Convention" as a convention of adjusting dates specified or determined in respect of a transaction, e.g. a payment or fixing date. As we said, the adjustment is necessary because the date in question may fall on a day that is not a "business day".

Under the 2000 ISDA Definitions, a business day in relation to a particular place (e.g. Tokyo) is a day on which commercial banks and foreign exchange markets settle payments and are open for general business in that place (i.e. Tokyo). If place is not specified, the business day will be determined by reference to the currency payable on the particular payment date by reference to the financial centres indicated for such currency set out in the 2000 ISDA Definitions or the Annex. For example, if euro is the currency of payment, the TARGET settlement day will be deemed to the business day in the absence of any other agreement. If more than one currency is involved, the business day would be determined in respect of each such currency.

The relevant business day conventions are:

- *Following business day convention*, where the date will be the first following day that is a Business Day.
- *Modified following business day convention*, where the date will be the first following day that is a business day (i.e. same as following business day convention) unless the first following business day is in the next calendar month, in which case that date will be the first preceding day that is a business day. So if the date specified is "28 February" and the first following business day is 1 March, the date will instead be 27 February (if it is a business day).
- *Preceding business day convention*, where the date is the first preceding date that is a business day.
- *Modified preceding business day convention*. The rationale of this convention is similar to the modified following business day described above. In this case the date will be the first preceding day that is a business day unless this day is in the previous month, in which case that date will be the first following business day.
- *End of month*. Using the end of month convention would involve picking the last good business day in the month.
- *IMM*. International Money Market or IMM days are the third Wednesday in March, June, September and December.

Let us now discuss the other relevant aspect: how to count days between two dates.

4.3.2 Day count conventions and accrual factors

An accrual method or day count convention is used to calculate an accrual factor, which represents the fraction of a year that relates to a given period. There are two components that make up an accrual factor. The first component uses a day count convention to determine how many days fall in the accrual period, which will be the numerator in the calculation of the accrual factor. The second component is a day count convention to determine the number of days that make up a full period, which will be the denominator in the calculation of the accrual factor.

In Table 4.1 we report the description of some convention currently used. Please note that this table is not complete, and for all operational purpose we strongly advise the reader to consult ISDA papers for precise and up to date definitions.

Table 4.1   Some conventions currently in use

Accrual method	Description
365/360	The number of accrued days is calculated on the basis of a year of 365 days. The accrual factor is the number of accrued days divided by 360.
Actual/365	The number of accrued days is equal to the actual number of days between the effective date and the terminating date. The accrual factor is the number of accrued days divided by 365.
Actual/360	The number of accrued days is equal to the actual number of days between the effective date and the terminating date. The accrual factor is the number of accrued days divided by 360.
Actual/Actual	The number of accrued days is equal to the actual number of days between the effective date and the terminating date. Calculation of the accrual factor assumes the year basis to be 365 days for non-leap years and 366 for leap years.

Table 4.1   (Continued)

Accrual method	Description
	If a short stub period (<1 year) contains a leap day, the number of days is divided by 366, otherwise the number of days is divided by 365.
30/360 (ISDA)	The number of accrued days is calculated on the basis of a year of 360 days with 12 30-day months with two exceptions. First, if the last date of the accrual period falls on the 31st of a month, and the first date of the period falls on a day other than the 30th or 31st of a month, then the month that includes the last day will be considered to have 31 days. Second, if the last date of the accrual period falls on the last day of February, the month of February will not be extended to a 30-day month. The accrual factor is calculated as the number of accrued days divided by 360.
30E/360	The number of accrued days is calculated on the basis of a year of 360 days with 12 30-day months. If either the first date or last date of the accrual period falls on the 31st of a month, that month will be shortened to a 30-day month. If the last day of the accrual period falls on the last day of February, the month of February will not be extended to a 30-day month. The accrual factor is calculated as the number of accrued days divided by 360.

4.4   JSCHEDULER

In this section we describe a simple Java application designed to build a generic schedule from initial data in parametric form. Our approach will be to follow as closely as possible a correct object-oriented approach, so we will list all the classes we need to do our job. Since we would like to provide the reader with concrete software tools we will describe, step by step, the implementation of the code starting from the beginning: how Java handles calendar and date.

4.4.1   Date handling in Java

The core language offers several classes for dealing with dates and times:

* `java.util.GregorianCalendar` (a subclass of the abstract `Calendar` class.)
* `java.util.Date`
* `java.text.DateFormat` and its subclass `java.text.SimpleDateFormat`

The `GregorianCalendar` can be used to represent a specific date according to the Gregorian calendar (and the Julian calendar before that). Methods are provided to compare calendar objects such as whether one date came before or after another. The `java.util.Calendar` cbase class, which is abstract, holds static methods that give information such as the current date and time. For example if you type

```
Calendar this_moment = Calendar.getInstance ( );
System.out.println(this_moment);
```

you will get a string like this

```
java.util.GregorianCalendar[time=1147876622875,areFieldsSet=
true,areAllFieldsSet=true, lenient=true,zone=sun.util.
calendar.ZoneInfo[id="Europe/Berlin",offset=3600000,
dstSavings=3600000,useDaylight=true,transitions=143,lastRule
=java.util.SimpleTimeZone[id=Europe/Berlin,offset=3600000,
dstSavings=3600000,useDaylight=true,startYear=0,startMode=2,
startMonth=2,startDay=-1,startDayOfWeek=1,startTime=3600000,
startTimeMode=2,endMode=2,endMonth=9,endDay=-1,endDayOfWeek
=1,endTime=3600000,endTimeMode=2]],firstDayOfWeek=2,
minimalDaysInFirstWeek=4,ERA=1,YEAR=2006,MONTH=4,
WEEK_OF_YEAR=20,WEEK_OF_MONTH=3,DAY_OF_MONTH=17,DAY_OF_YEAR
=137,DAY_OF_WEEK=4,DAY_OF_WEEK_IN_MONTH=3,AM_PM=1,HOUR=4,
HOUR_OF_DAY=16,MINUTE=37,SECOND=2,MILLISECOND=875,
ZONE_OFFSET=3600000,DST_OFFSET=3600000]
```

in which you can find (in a patient manner) everything you want to know about the present time. To keep track of time, Java counts the number of milliseconds from the start of 1 January 1970. This means, for example, that 2 January 1970, began 86 400 000 milliseconds later. Similarly, 31 December 1969, began 86 400 000 milliseconds before 1 January 1970. The Java Date class keeps track of those milliseconds as a long value. Because long is a signed number, dates can be expressed before and after the start of 1 January 1970. The largest positive and negative values expressible by the long primitive can generate dates forward and backward about 290 000 000 years, which suits most people's schedules. The Date class, found in the java.util package, encapsulates a long value representing a specific moment in time. One useful constructor is Date(), which creates a Date object representing the time the object was created. The getTime() method returns the long value of a Date object.

The class DateFormat can generate several date and time strings. One purpose of the DateFormat class is to create strings in ways that humans can easily deal with them. However, because of language differences, not all people want to see a date in exactly the same way. Someone in England may prefer to see "25 December 2000", while someone in the United States may be more accustomed to seeing "December 25, 2000". So when an instance of a DateFormat class is created, the object contains information concerning the particular format in which the date is to be displayed. To use the default format of the user's computer, you can apply the getDateInstance method to create the appropriate DateFormat object:

```
DateFormat df = DateFormat.getDateInstance();
```

The DateFormat class is found in the java.text package.

You can convert a Date object to a string with the format method. This is shown in the following demonstration program:

```
import java.util.*;
import java.text.*;

public class NowString {
  public static void main(String[] args) {
```

```
        Date now = new Date();
        DateFormat df = DateFormat.getDateInstance();
        String s = df.format(now);
        System.out.println("Today is " + s);
    }
}
```

The getDateInstance method shown in the code above, with no arguments, creates
an object in the default format or style. Java also provides some alternative styles for
dates, which you can obtain through the overloaded getDateInstance(int style).
DateFormat also provides some ready-made constants that you can use as arguments
in the getDateInstance method. Some examples are SHORT, MEDIUM, LONG and
FULL, which are demonstrated in the program below:

```
import java.util.*;
import java.text.*;

public class StyleDemo {
    public static void main(String[] args) {
        Date now = new Date();

        DateFormat df  = DateFormat.getDateInstance();
        DateFormat df1 = DateFormat.getDateInstance
                            (DateFormat.SHORT);
        DateFormat df2 = DateFormat.getDateInstance
                            (DateFormat.MEDIUM);
        DateFormat df3 = DateFormat.getDateInstance
                            (DateFormat.LONG);
        DateFormat df4 = DateFormat.getDateInstance
                            (DateFormat.FULL);
        String s  = df.format(now);
        String s1 = df1.format(now);
        String s2 = df2.format(now);
        String s3 = df3.format(now);
        String s4 = df4.format(now);

        System.out.println("(Default) Today is " + s);
        System.out.println("(SHORT)   Today is " + s1);
        System.out.println("(MEDIUM)  Today is " + s2);
        System.out.println("(LONG)    Today is " + s3);
        System.out.println("(FULL)    Today is " + s4);
    }
}
```

That program outputs the following:

```
(Default) Today is Nov 8, 2000
(SHORT)   Today is 11/8/00
(MEDIUM)  Today is Nov 8, 2000
```

| (LONG) | Today is November 8, 2000 |
| (FULL) | Today is Wednesday, November 8, 2000 |

You can also use the DateFormat class to create Date objects from a String, via the parse() method. This particular method can throw a ParseException error, so you must use proper error-handling techniques. A sample program that turns a String into a Date is shown below:

```java
import java.util.*;
import java.text.*;

public class ParseExample {
   public static void main(String[] args) {
      String ds = "November 1, 2000";
      DateFormat df = DateFormat.getDateInstance();
      try {
         Date d = df.parse(ds);
      }
      catch(ParseException e) {
         System.out.println("Unable to parse " + ds);
      }
   }
}
```

The parse() method is a useful tool for creating arbitrary dates.

Another way to create an object representing an arbitrary date is to use the following constructor of the GregorianCalendar class, found in the java.util package:

```java
GregorianCalendar(int year, int month, int date)
```

Note that for the month, January is 0, February is 1, and so on, up to December, which is 11. Since those are not the numbers most of us associate with the months of the year, programs will probably be more readable if they use the constants of the parent Calendar class: JANUARY, FEBRUARY and so on. For example, for

```java
GregorianCalendar firstFlight = new GregorianCalendar(2006,
CalendarMAY, 17);
```

a shorter form is available

```java
GregorianCalendar firstFlight = new GregorianCalendar
(2006, 05, 17);
```

Previously we explained how to turn Date objects into Strings. You will do the same again; but first, you need to convert a GregorianCalendar object to a Date. To do so, you will use the getTime() method, which GregorianCalendar inherits from its parent Calendar class. The getTime() method returns a Date corresponding to a GregorianCalendar object. You can put the whole process of creating a

GregorianCalendar object, converting it to a Date, and getting and outputting the corresponding String in the following program:

```
import java.util.*;
import java.text.*;

public class Flight {

    public static void main(String[] args) {
        GregorianCalendar firstFlight=new GregorianCalendar(1903,
                                    Calendar.DECEMBER, 17);
        Date d = firstFlight.getTime();
        DateFormat df = DateFormat.getDateInstance();
        String s = df.format(d);
        System.out.println("First flight was " + s);
    }
}
```

Sometimes it is useful to create an instance of the GregorianCalendar class representing the day the instance was created. To do so, simply use the GregorianCalendar constructor taking no arguments, such as:

```
GregorianCalendar thisday = new GregorianCalendar();
```

Note the similarities between the Date() constructor and the GregorianCalendar() constructor: both create an object, which in simple terms, represents today.

The GregorianCalendar class offers methods for manipulating dates. One useful method is add(). With the add() method, you can add such time units as years, months and days to a date. To use the add() method, you must supply the field being increased, and the integer amount by which it will increase. Some useful constants for the fields are DATE, MONTH, YEAR and WEEK_OF_YEAR. One important side effect of the add() method is that it changes the original date. Sometimes it is important to have both the original date and the modified date. Unfortunately, you cannot simply create a new GregorianCalendar object set equal to the original. The reason is that the two variables have a reference to one date. If the date is changed, both variables now refer to the changed date. Instead, a new object should be created. The following example will demonstrate this:

```
import java.util.*;
import java.text.*;

public class ThreeDates {
    public static void main(String[] args) {
        GregorianCalendar gc1 = new GregorianCalendar(2000,
                                    Calendar.JANUARY, 1);
        GregorianCalendar gc2 = gc1;
        GregorianCalendar gc3 = new GregorianCalendar(2000,
                                    Calendar.JANUARY, 1);
        //Three dates all equal to January 1, 2000
```

```
    gc1.add(Calendar.YEAR, 1);
    //gc1 and gc2 are changed
    DateFormat df = DateFormat.getDateInstance();

    Date d1 = gc1.getTime();
    Date d2 - gc2.getTime();
    Date d3 = gc3.getTime();

    String s1 = df.format(d1);
    String s2 = df.format(d2);
    String s3 = df.format(d3);

    System.out.println("gc1 is " + s1);
    System.out.println("gc2 is " + s2);
    System.out.println("gc3 is " + s3);
  }
}
```

After the program is run, gc1 and gc2 are changed to the year 2001 (because both objects are pointing to the same underlying date representation, which has been changed). The object gc3 is pointing to a separate underlying date representation, which has not been changed.

4.4.2 Data models

JScheduler will be a very simple application that will produce a generic schedule composed by a vector of dates. The input data should be as simple as possible, in particular we want to produce the schedule starting from a reduced set of parameters which are:

- First date
- First regular date
- Last date
- Last regular date
- Interval
- Day count
- Market
- Day convention.

The appearance of the control panel is shown in Figure 4.1.

The reason you must distinguish between the first date and first regular date (and the same for last) is due to the possibility of handling one or two stub periods. By default, values of the first date and the first regular date will be the same (and the same is true for the last date). The first regular date and the last regular date identify the period with regular frequency (in which the interval between two consecutive dates is the same). If there is a stub period at the beginning of our schedule, one has to put the value of the first date different from that of the first regular date, the interval between these two dates is the initial stub period. The same can be done if one wants to put a final stub period, in this case values of the last date and the last regular date should be different from each other. The parameter Interval refers

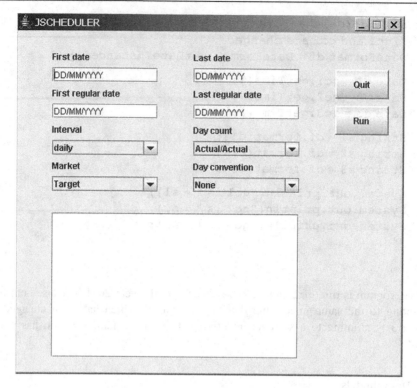

Figure 4.1   The JScheduler panel control

to the periodicity of the regular section of the scheduler; it is a parameter with a predefined set of possible values which are identified by the following constant:

```
public static final int daily      = 0;
public static final int weekly     = 1;
public static final int biweekly   = 2;
public static final int monthly    = 3;
public static final int quarterly  = 4;
public static final int fourmonthly = 5;
public static final int semiannual = 6;
public static final int annual     = 7;
public static final int expiry     = 9;
```

These must be defined in a particular class, as we will soon see. The parameter "Day count" refers to the convention followed for day counting as described in Section 4.3.2. Possible values for this parameter are:

```
public static final int _actact = 0;
public static final int _365act = 1;
public static final int _act365 = 2;
```

```
public static final int _act360 = 3;
public static final int _a30360 = 4;
public static final int _e30360 = 5;
public static final int _365360 = 6;
public static final int _365365 = 7;
```

Market parameter is related to the market calendar of bank holidays, but for the moment we can neglect this constant since we will not use it. Finally, the field "Day convention" will permit the user to define the particular convention followed by the calculation engine for those days that are not business days. Possible values for this parameter are:

```
public static final int unadjusted   = 0;
public static final int preceding    = 1;
public static final int following    = 2;
public static final int modpreceding = 3;
public static final int modfollowing = 4;
```

The calculation engine should be able to produce schedules for any combination of values of these parameters, but what if we want to write a code which, in addition, could be easily modified if one or more of the possible values for the previous parameters undergo a change? Let us suppose, for example, that we are delivering the engine when we suddenly discover that our customers wish to handle a new bond that is characterized by a two-month periodicity (this always happens the day before delivery!). In this case we should modify the range of possible values for the parameter Interval and, in addition, we should modify the calculation engine in order to take into account this new possible value. From a general point of view this could be a complicated matter! The essence of good coding is reusability; this means that when we design our code we should always keep in mind the possibility that in future our code might need to be extended. If we have designed it well, then we will simply have to add features; on the other hand, if we have designed it badly, then we will have to rewrite the existing code. So the problem is: How should we design our procedures in order to maximize reusability or, in other words, to minimize the rewriting of existing code?

A very powerful answer to this problem consists in the use of abstract classes which, in Java, are called "interface". The advantage in using interfaces is that we can write multiple classes that implement the same interface and use them without rewriting all the interface routines. This is, beyond any doubt, one of the most important advantages of object-oriented design.

Let us see how to implement this in practice. We will define a class CPeriod which contains all the methods we need to generate a schedule. First, let us look at the properties and the constructor of the class:

```
public class CPeriod {

    /* properties *
    private GregorianCalendar    firstDate;
    private GregorianCalendar    lastDate;
    private GregorianCalendar    firstRegularDate;
    private GregorianCalendar    lastRegularDate;
```

```
private int   codDayCount   = -1;
private int   codAdjustment = -1;
private int   codFrequency  = -1;

private ArrayList  unadjustedDates;
private ArrayList  adjustedDates;
private double     intervalBetweenDates[];

public CPeriod(String firstDate,
               String  lastDate,
               String  firstRegularDate,
               String  lastRegularDate,
               int     codDayCount,
               int     codAdjustment,
               int     codFrequency)
{
   DateFormat df = DateFormat.getDateInstance(DateFormat.SHORT);
   try
   {
      System.out.println("");

      Date _firstDate = df.parse(firstDate);
      Date _lastDate = df.parse(lastDate);
      Date _firstRegularDate = df.parse(firstRegularDate);
      Date _lastRegularDate = df.parse(lastRegularDate);

      this.firstDate = new GregorianCalendar();
      this.lastDate = new GregorianCalendar();
      this.firstRegularDate = new GregorianCalendar();
      this.lastRegularDate = new GregorianCalendar();

      unadjustedDates = new ArrayList();
      adjustedDates = new ArrayList();

      this.firstDate.setTime(_firstDate);
      this.lastDate.setTime(_lastDate);
      this.firstRegularDate.setTime(_firstRegularDate);
      this.lastRegularDate.setTime(_lastRegularDate);

      this.codFrequency = codFrequency;
      this.codDayCount = codDayCount;
      this.codAdjustment = codAdjustment;
   }
   catch(ParseException e)
   {
      System.out.println("Unable to parse String Date");
   }
}
   ...
}
```

CPeriod has 10 properties

```
private GregorianCalendar   firstDate;
private GregorianCalendar   lastDate;
private GregorianCalendar   firstRegularDate;
private GregorianCalendar   lastRegularDate;

private int                 codDayCount = -1;
private int                 codAdjustment = -1;
private int                 codFrequency = -1;

private ArrayList           unadjustedDates;
private ArrayList           adjustedDates;
private double              intervalBetweenDates[];
```

We have already described the first four parameters (we note only the use of the GregorianCalendar type). codDayCount, codAdjustment and codFrequency are three integer values which contain the information about the particular conventions followed in the building of schedule; finally we have two ArrayList which contain the set of dates (unadjusted and adjusted) produced by the calculation engine and a double array whose elements are time intervals between consecutive dates (the time unit is the year).

The createSchedule method is the most important procedure of our class. In this implementation we use the interface concept in order to write a method that can build a schedule without knowing the periodicity of the schedule itself. This can be done using an interface – a class in which all methods are defined as abstract.

```
public interface IInterval
{
   public abstract int      period();
   public abstract int      periodMultiplier();
   public abstract String   periodCode();

}
```

This interface has three methods, the first, period(), should return an integer that specifies the time unit of the interval (defined in the class GregorianCalendar in the java.util package), periodMultiplier() specifies the number of time units of the interval and, finally, periodCode() returns a string code. Note that none of the previous methods returns a specific value since they are all abstract. The concrete implementation is demanded to other classes which are specialization of IInterval. For example a semi-annual periodicity is implemented with the following class:

```
public class CInterval_Semiannual implements IInterval
{
   public int period() {
      // TODO Auto-generated method stub
      return GregorianCalendar.MONTH;
   }
```

```
    public int periodMultiplier() {
      // TODO Auto-generated method stub
      return 6;
    }
    public String periodCode() {
      return "6M";
    }
}
```

Note that, in this case, in place of the keyword extends we will find implements. We can build a set of classes each implementing a particular time interval, and the complete hierarchy is shown in Figure 4.2.

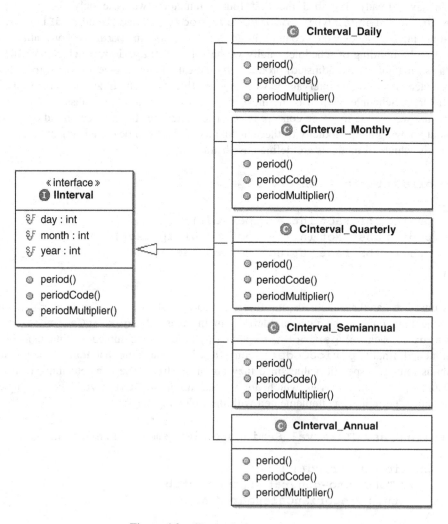

Figure 4.2   CInterval class strucuture

Let's go a step forward and define a class that can be used to build a generic object of type Interval, we refer to this class as a "factory". This is the implementation of the class `CInterval_Factory`:

```
public class CInterval_Factory {
     public static final int daily     = 0;
     public static final int monthly   = 1;
     public static final int quarterly = 2;
     public static final int semiannual= 3;
     public static final int annual    = 4;

     public IInterval createInstance(int code)
     {
     switch(code)
     {
     case daily:
        return new CInterval_Daily();
     case monthly:
        return new CInterval_Monthly();
     case quarterly:
        return new CInterval_Quarterly();
     case semiannual:
        return new CInterval_Semiannual();
     case annual:
        return new CInterval_Annual();
     }
     return null;
   }
}
```

The reason for this apparent complication should soon be clear; for the moment we ask the reader to note that this class is actually very simple. We define a set of constant for the most important kind of periodicity and we then insert a single method: `createInstance()`. This method simply takes an integer value as input which codifies the particular time interval and returns the corresponding class. Please note that the signature of this method

```
public IInterval createInstance(int code)
```

declares that the type of the object returned is `IInterval` (the interface class previously described). If you remember our discussion about abstraction in Chapter 2, you should not be surprised to find that the method itself actually returns objects of different types. In fact all these objects are derived from the interface `IInterval` and one of the most important consequences of inheritance is the complete compatibility among a class and its subclasses.

The Factory class is used by the `createSchedule()` method in which we create an object of type `CInterval_Factory`

```
CInterval_Factory   factoryInterval   = new CInterval_Factory();
```

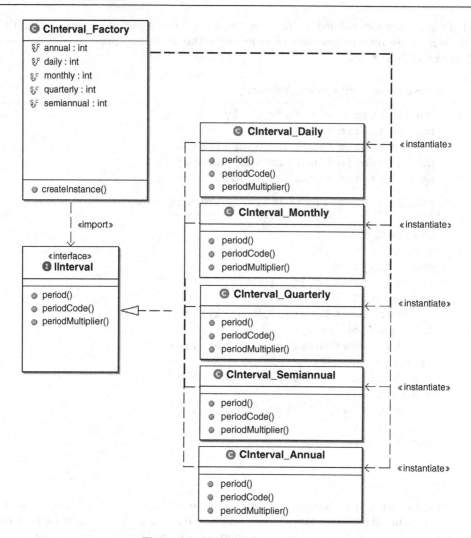

Figure 4.3   CInterval Factory pattern

this object is then used to create an instance of the appropriate class for periodicity handling

```
IInterval freq  = factoryInterval.createInstance(codFrequency);
```

Note that the "freq" object is defined to be of type `IInterval`, and `codFrequency` is the parameter that specifies what is the particular object we need. The complete code of the `createSchedule()` method is then

```
public ArrayList createSchedule()
{
   GregorianCalendar currentDate = (GregorianCalendar)
   firstRegularDate.clone();
```

```
/* create an object of type Interval */
CInterval_Factory   factoryInterval
= new CInterval_Factory();
IInterval freq = factoryInterval.createInstance
(codFrequency);
```

```
if(firstDate.before(firstRegularDate))
   unadjustedDates.add(firstDate);
```

```
while(currentDate.before(lastRegularDate))
{
   unadjustedDates.add(currentDate.clone());
   currentDate.add(freq.period(),freq.period
   Multiplier());
}
unadjustedDates.add(currentDate.clone());
```

```
if(lastDate.after(lastRegularDate))
   unadjustedDates.add(lastDate);
```

```
return unadjustedDates;
}
```

The method produces a schedule by means of the method `add()` of the class
`GregorianCalendar`, note that in this method `period` and `periodMultiplier` are
return values of the object `freq`. What is the advantage of this apparently cumbersome
design? Let's suppose that we need to extend our program in order to consider a two-month
periodicity. In this case we have simply to perform two operations:

1. Add a new class:

```
public class CInterval_Bimonthly implements IInterval {

   public int period() {
      // TODO Auto-generated method stub
      return GregorianCalendar.MONTH;
   }

   public int periodMultiplier() {
      // TODO Auto-generated method stub
      return 2;
   }

   public String periodCode() {
      // TODO Auto-generated method stub
      return "2M";
   }
}
```

which implements the same interface of the other classes.

2. Update the Factory class, including a new branch for the switch statement and a new constant for the identification of the chosen periodicity:

```
public class CInterval_Factory {
    public static final int daily       = 0;
    public static final int monthly     = 1;
    public static final int quarterly   = 2;
    public static final int semiannual  = 3;
    public static final int annual      = 4;
    public static final int bimonthly   = 5;

    public IInterval createInstance(int code)
    {
      switch(code)
      {
      case daily:
        return new CInterval_Daily();
      case monthly:
        return new CInterval_Monthly();
      case quarterly:
        return new CInterval_Quarterly();
      case semiannual:
        return new CInterval_Semiannual();
      case annual:
        return new CInterval_Annual();
      case bimonthly:
        return new CInterval_Bimonthly();
      }
      return null;
    }
}
```

We do not need to modify any other part of the code, in particular we do not touch class CPeriod or other classes not connected with the periodicity. The new structure of interval classes is shown in Figure 4.4.

The same pattern can be followed implementing the adjustSchedule() method which, as the name itself suggests, perform all the calculations needed to adjust a holiday date into a working day according to a specified convention. The source code of the method is reported below:

```
public ArrayList adjustSchedule()
{
    GregorianCalendar  date      = null;
    CDateUtility      dateUtility = new CDateUtility();

    Iterator i = unadjustedDates.iterator();

    if(codAdjustment > 0)
    {
```

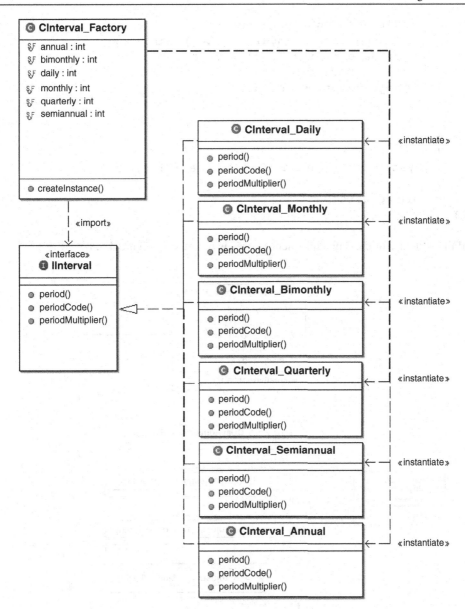

Figure 4.4 The new strucuture of Interval classes

```
/* create an object of type Day Adjustment */
CDayAdjustment_FactoryfactoryDayAdj =
new CDayAdjustment_Factory();
IDayAdjustment adj =
factoryDayAdj.createInstance(codAdjustment);

while(i.hasNext())
{
```

```
          date = (GregorianCalendar)
          ((GregorianCalendar)i.next()).clone();
          if(dateUtility.IsHoliday(date))
             adj.modify(date);
          adjustedDates.add(date);
      }
   }
   else
   {
       System.out.println("Code not valid!");
   }
   return adjustedDates;
}
```

and the structure of the day adjustment classes is reported in Figure 4.5.

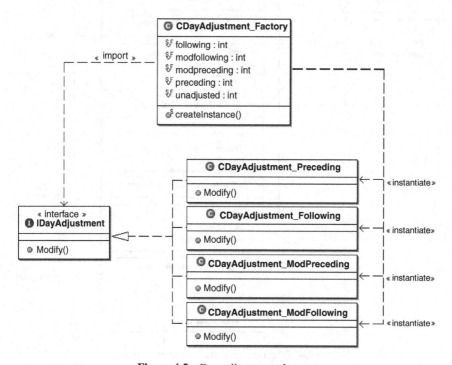

Figure 4.5   Day adjustment classes

The interface is very simple

```
public interface IDayAdjustment
{
   public abstract void modify(GregorianCalendar
   unadjustedDate);
```

```
    public CDateUtility dateUtility = new CDateUtility();
}
```

The method "modify" takes as input an object of type `GregorianCalendar` which represents the unadjusted date. The class `CDayAdjustment_Factory` contains the methods `createInstance()` that builds the correct object according to the input parameter code:

```
public class CDayAdjustment_Factory {

    public static final int unadjusted = 0;
    public static final int preceding = 1;
    public static final int following = 2;
    public static final int modpreceding = 3;
    public static final int modfollowing = 4;

        /**
        */
        public static IDayAdjustment createInstance
        (int code)
        {
            switch(code)
            {
            case preceding:
                return new CDayAdjustment_Preceding();
            case following:
                return new CDayAdjustment_Following();
            case modpreceding:
                return new CDayAdjustment_ModPreceding();
            case modfollowing:
                return new CDayAdjustment_ModFollowing();
            default:
                return null;
            }
        }
}
```

Finally, the last method of `CPeriod` class is `createIntervals()` which calculates intervals between consecutive dates according to a specified day count convention. The source code is reported below, in this case the pattern previously discussed involves the `CDayCount` class, the interface `IDayCount` and its subclasses.

```
public double[] createIntervals()
{
    GregorianCalendar    begin = null;
    GregorianCalendar    end   = null;
    /* create an object of type CDayCount_Factory */
    CDayCount_Factory dayCountFactory = new CDayCount_Factory();
    /* create an instance of the appropriate Day Count object */
```

```
IDayCount dayCount = dayCountFactory.createInstance
(codDayCount);

intervalBetweenDates = new double[adjustedDates.size()];
for(int i = 0;i < adjustedDates.size() - 1;i++)
{
   begin = (GregorianCalendar)((GregorianCalendar)
   adjustedDates.get(i)).clone();
   end = (GregorianCalendar)((GregorianCalendar)
   adjustedDates.get(i+1)).clone();

   double delta = dayCount.Calculate(begin,end);
      intervalBetweenDates[i] = delta;
   }
   return intervalBetweenDates;
}
```

4.4.3 Design patterns

This example is a particular case of a more general way of programming design which is called "Design Patterns". Design patterns are recurring solutions to software design problems you find again and again in real-world application development. Patterns are about design and interaction of objects, as well as providing a communication platform concerning elegant, reusable solutions to commonly encountered programming challenges. More precisely, a design pattern is a general repeatable solution to a usually occurring problem in software design; a design pattern isn't a finished design that can be transformed directly into code, but is a description or template for how to solve a problem that can be used in many different situations. Design patterns typically show relationships and interactions between classes or objects, without specifying the final application classes or objects that are involved. Design patterns gained popularity in computer science after the book *Design Patterns: Elements of Reusable Object-Oriented Software* was published in 1994 (Gamma *et al.*). That same year, the first Pattern Languages of Programs conference was held, and the following year the Portland Pattern Repository was set up for the documentation of design patterns.

Design patterns can be classified on the basis of multiple criteria, the most common of which is the basic underlying problem they solve. According to this criterion, design patterns can be placed into various classes, some of which are:

- Fundamental patterns
- Creational patterns
- Structural patterns
- Behavioural patterns
- Concurrency patterns
- Architectural patterns.

For the moment we will take into consideration creational patterns. These are design patterns that deal with object creation mechanisms, trying to create objects in a manner suitable to the situation. The basic form of object creation could result in design problems or add complexity to the design. Creational design patterns solve this problem by somehow controlling this object creation. One of this pattern is the so-called Factory Method pattern which we have previously used for the schedule generation.

4.4.4   The Factory Method pattern

The Factory Method pattern, like other creational patterns, deals with the problem of creating objects (products) without specifying the exact class of object that will be created.

The main classes in the Factory Method pattern are the **creator** and the **product**. The creator needs to create instances of products, but the concrete type of product should not be hard coded in the creator – subclasses of the creator should be able to specify the subclasses of product to use. To achieve this an abstract method (the Factory Method) is defined on the creator. This method is defined to return a product. Subclasses of creator can override this method to return instances of appropriate subclasses of product.

In our previous program we have implemented a parametric version of the Factory Method, the creator was the class Factory (i.e. `CInterval_Factory`), the product is one of the Concrete classes which are subclasses of the Interface class (i.e. `CInterval_Annual` which implements `IInterval`).

4.5   CASH FLOW GENERATOR DESIGN

From the point of view of the coupon design, the most important features of a bond are:

- *Nominal, principal or face amount*: The amount over which the issuer pays interest, and which has to be repaid.
- *Issue price*: The price at which investors buy the bonds when they are first issued. The net proceeds that the issuer receives are calculated as the issue price, less the fees for the underwriters, times the nominal amount.
- *Maturity date*: The date by which the issuer has to repay the nominal amount. As long as all payments have been made, the issuer has no more obligations to the bond holders after the maturity date. The length of time until the maturity date is often referred to as the term or simply maturity of a bond. The maturity can be any length of time, although debt securities with a term of less than one year are generally designated money market instruments rather than bonds. Most bonds have a term of up to 30 years. Some bonds have been issued with maturities of up to 100 years, and some even do not mature at all. These are called perpetuities. In early 2005, a market developed in euro for bonds with a maturity of 50 years. For example, in the market for US Treasury securities, there are three groups of bond maturities:

  - short term (Bills): maturities up to one year
  - medium term (Notes): maturities between one and 10 years
  - long term (Bonds): maturities greater than 10 years.

- *Coupon*: The interest rate that the issuer pays to the bond holders. Usually this rate is fixed throughout the life of the bond. It can also vary with a money market index, such as LIBOR, or it can be more exotic. The name "coupon" originates from the fact that in the past, physical bonds were issued which had coupons attached to them. On coupon dates the bond holder would give the coupon to a bank in exchange for the interest payment.

- *Coupon dates*: The dates on which the issuer pays the coupon to the bond holders. In the USA, most bonds are semi-annual, which means that they pay a coupon every six months.

In the following sections we will sketch an object-oriented analysis for a cash flow generator in the case of a generic interest rate product but first of all let us introduce a new UML tools: the activity diagram.

4.5.1 UML's activity diagram

In many ways UML activity diagrams are the object-oriented equivalent of flow charts and data-flow diagrams (DFDs). They are used to explore the logic of:

- a complex operation
- a complex business rule
- a single use case
- several use cases
- a business process
- software processes.

In UML there are, as usual, more things to say. For practical purpose we will use these types of diagram as a sort of flow chart, ignoring many of the most advanced aspects; nevertheless, we will give a glance at the general characteristics of these diagram.

An activity diagram consists of the following behavioural elements:

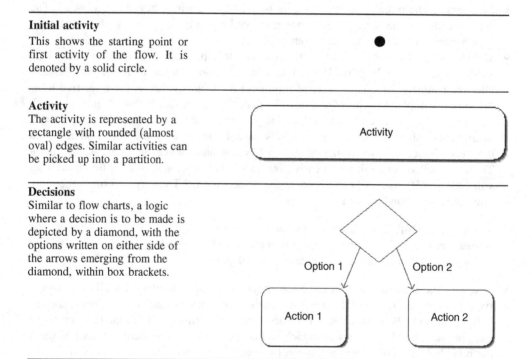

Initial activity
This shows the starting point or first activity of the flow. It is denoted by a solid circle.

Activity
The activity is represented by a rectangle with rounded (almost oval) edges. Similar activities can be picked up into a partition.

Decisions
Similar to flow charts, a logic where a decision is to be made is depicted by a diamond, with the options written on either side of the arrows emerging from the diamond, within box brackets.

Signal
When an activity sends or receives a
message, that activity is called a
signal. Signals are of two types:
input signal (message receiving
activity) shown by a concave
polygon and output signal (message
sending activity) shown by a convex
polygon.

Input Signal

Output Signal

Concurrent activities
Some activities occur
simultaneously or in parallel.
Such activities are called
concurrent activities. For
example, listening to the lecturer
and looking at the blackboard is a
parallel activity. This is
represented by a horizontal split
(thick dark line) and the two
concurrent activities next to each
other, and the horizontal line
again to show the end of the
parallel activity.

Activity 1   Activity 2

Final activity
The end of the activity diagram is
shown by a bull's eye symbol,
also known as a final activity.

In Figure 4.6 we show the diagram that describes the generation of a generic cash flow. This diagram represents little more than a draft, but nevertheless it is useful to give a global vision of the various activities that contribute to the building of the cash flow. Various activities are in general self-explanatory although it is worth while to describe each of them briefly, since this will help us in the next step: the definition of the data model. Let us start from the Date Computation block, which contains four activities:

- *Calculation Date Generation*: Its presence is optional and contains a schedule composed by useful dates for the calculation of the coupon besides fixing or payment dates. This is used, for example, in some structured product in which coupons are calculated by a sum of the values reached by an index in a certain time interval.
- *Payment Date Generation*: This is simply the schedule of payment.
- *Fixing Date Generation*: The schedule containing dates in which the index is fixed.
- *Repayment Date Generation*: For an amortizing bond it contains the dates at which we have the notional repayment, while, for a bullet bond, it contains only the expiration date.

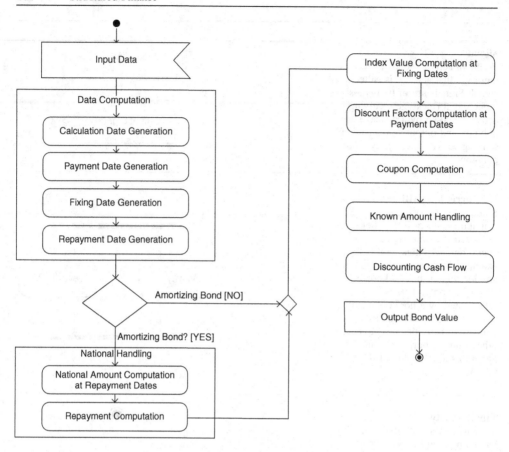

Figure 4.6 Generation of a generic cash flow

All these schedules do not necessarily have to be calculated inside the same computational procedure. This is only a conceptual scheme; the implementation in a software program can be different – for example, our cash flow generator could read these schedules from an external file or they could be passed by another routine, etc. After this block we find a decision, we have to decide if the bond is a bullet bond or not. If we have an amortizing bond we have to calculate the notional amount for each payment date and eventually the repayment. This last calculation is not necessary in all those cases in which the notional is used only for coupon calculation and is not exchanged during the life of the structured product, as in a plain vanilla swap.

The other activities are self-explanatory except, perhaps, the "Known Amount Handling". With this name we want to refer to the computation of known coupon or, in general, some other known contribution to the current coupon.

With this diagram in mind we can face the next step of the project phase: the data model.

4.5.2 An important guideline to the data model for derivatives: FpML

An approach to be avoided in the planning of a software project is to reinvent the wheel. In the definition of a data model for an interest rate product we have an important guideline, which is the FpML standard (see Appendix B for a short introduction). Since the best way to introduce a new argument is to proceed with a practical example, let us see how FpML can model some trades based on a simple swap. This example is based on documentation that is freely available on the website http://www.fpml.org/.

Example 4.2 On 12 December 2005 Bank 1 and Bank 2 enter into an ISDA swap agreement with each other. The terms of the contract are:

- Effective date: 14 December 2005
- Termination date: 14 December 2010
- Notional amount: EUR 50 000 000
- Bank 1 pays the floating rate every six months, based on six-month LIBOR, on an ACT/360 basis
- Bank 2 pays the 6% fixed rate every year on a 30E/360 basis
- The swap is non-compounding, non-amortizing and there are no stub periods. There is no averaging of rates. The business day convention for adjusting the calculation dates is the same as that used for payment date adjustments.

The complete XML file is reported in Appendix B for reference. In this paragraph we will analyse it component by component. To the higher level, according to the FpML standard, a trade concerning a swap can be represented in this way:

```
<?xml version="1.0" ?>
- <!--
        == Copyright (c) 2002-2003. All rights reserved.
        == Financial Products Markup Language is subject to the FpML
           public license.
        == A copy of this license is available at http://www.fpml.
           org/documents/license
  -->
- <FpML version="4-0" xsi: type="DataDocument"
     xmlns:xsi="http://www.w3.org/2001/XMLSchemainstance"
     xsi:schemaLocation="http://www.fpml.org/2003/FpML-4-0 ../
     fpml-main-4-0.xsd"
     xmlns="http://www.fpml.org/2003/FpML-4-0">
  +<trade>
  +<party id="BANK 1">
  +<party id="BANK 2">
  </FpML>
```

As we can see, the document is formed by three blocks: trade and two parties. The trade block is in turn composed by a tradeHeader and a swap. The tradeHeader contains general information about the trade itself, such as Bank Id, Effective date of trade, and so on. For our purposes the most interesting part of the document is the swap component. Let us look at this part.

```
-<swap>
  <!-- Bank 1 pays the floating rate every 6 months, based on 6M
  LIBOR, on an ACT/360 basis -->
 -<swapStream>
     <payerPartyReference href="BANK 1" />
     <receiverPartyReference href="BANK 2" />
   + <calculationPeriodDates id="floatingCalcPeriodDates">
   + <paymentDates>
   + <resetDates id="resetDates">
   + <calculationPeriodAmount>
   </swapStream>
   <!--Bank 2 pays the 6%fixed rate every year on a 30E/360
     basis-->
 -<swapStream>
     <payerPartyReference href="BANK 1" />
     <receiverPartyReference href="BANK 2" />
   + <calculationPeriodDates id="fixedCalcPeriodDates">
   + <paymentDates>
   + <calculationPeriodAmount>
   </swapStream>
 </swap>
```

The swap is clearly composed of two legs which are modelled by the entity swapStream (which in turn is a particular case of the entity InterestRateStream). Each swapStream is composed of the following entities:

- **calculationPeriodDates**: This is a global complex type defining the parameters used to generate the calculation period dates schedule, including the specification of any initial or final stub calculation periods. A calculation period schedule consists of an optional initial stub calculation period, one or more regular calculation periods and an optional final stub calculation period. In the absence of any initial or final stub calculation periods, the regular part of the calculation period schedule is assumed to be between the effective date and the termination date. No implicit stubs are allowed, i.e. stubs must be explicitly specified using an appropriate combination of firstPeriodStateDate, firstRegularPeriodStartDate and lastRegularPeriodEndDate. This complex type contains the following types:

  - *effectiveDate*: The first day of the term of the trade. This day may be subject to adjustment in accordance with a business day convention.
  - *terminationDate*: The last day of the term of the trade. This day may be subject to adjustment in accordance with a business day convention.
  - *calculationPeriodDatesAdjustments*: The business day convention to apply to each calculation period end date if it would otherwise fall on a day that is not a business day in the specified financial business centres.

- *firstPeriodStartDate*: The start date of the calculation period if the date falls before the effective date. It must only be specified if it is not equal to the effective date. This date may be subject to adjustment in accordance with a business day convention.
- *firstRegularPeriodStartDate*: The start date of the regular part of the calculation period schedule. It must only be specified if there is an initial stub calculation period.
- *lastRegularPeriodEndDate*: The end date of the regular part of the calculation period schedule. It must only be specified if there is a final stub calculation period.
- *calculationPeriodFrequency*: The frequency at which calculation period end dates occur with the regular part of the calculation period schedule and their roll date convention.

Each type may, in turn, be a complex type, and as the complete description of the FpML structure is clearly out of the scope of this book, we refer the interested reader to the original documentation that is easily available at the website cited above. In our case the `calculationPeriodDates` fragment is the following:

```
<calculationPeriodDates
  id="floatingCalcPeriodDates">
   <effectiveDate>
     <unadjustedDate>2005-12-14</unadjustedDate>
     <dateAdjustments>
       <businessDayConvention>NONE</businessDayConvention>
     </dateAdjustments>
   </effectiveDate>
   <terminationDate>
     <unadjustedDate>2010-12-14</unadjustedDate>
 <dateAdjustments>
 <businessDayConvention>MODFOLLOWING</businessDayConvention>
   <businessCenters
     id="primaryBusinessCenters">
       <businessCenter>DEFR</businessCenter>
     </businessCenters>
   </dateAdjustments>
 </terminationDate>
 <calculationPeriodDatesAdjustments>
    <businessDayConvention>MODFOLLOWING
      </businessDayConvention>
   <businessCentersReference
     href="primaryBusinessCenters" />
 </calculationPeriodDatesAdjustments>
 <calculationPeriodFrequency>
    <periodMultiplier>6</periodMultiplier>
    <period>M</period>
    <rollConvention>14</rollConvention>
 </calculationPeriodFrequency>
</calculationPeriodDates>
```

- **paymentDates**: A type defining parameters used to generate the payment dates schedule, including the specification of early or delayed payments. It contains either a reference to the associated calculation period dates component defined elsewhere in the document or a list of parameters in the case the calculation dates are different from the payment dates. The list of parameters in the last case is the following:

- *paymentFrequency*: The frequency at which regular payment dates occur. If the payment frequency is equal to the frequency defined in the calculation period dates component, then one calculation period contributes to each payment amount. If the payment frequency is less frequent than the frequency defined in the calculation period dates component, then more than one calculation period will contribute to a payment amount. A payment frequency more frequent than the calculation period frequency, or one that is not a multiple of the calculation period frequency, is invalid.
- *firstPaymentDate*: This is the first unadjusted payment date. This element must only be included if there is an initial stub.
- *lastRegularPaymentDate*: This is the last regular unadjusted payment date. This element must only be included if there is a final stub. All calculation periods after this date contribute to the final payment.
- *payRelativeTo*: This specifies whether the payments occur relative to each adjusted calculation period start date, adjusted calculation period end date or each reset date.
- *paymentDaysOffset*: If early payment or delayed payment is required, this specifies the number of days offset when the payment occurs relative to what would otherwise be the unadjusted payment date.
- *paymentDatesAdjustments*: This is the business day convention to apply to each payment date if it would otherwise fall on a day that is not a business day in the specified financial business centres.

The following is the fragment of code for our case

```
<paymentDates>
  <calculationPeriodDatesReference
    href="floatingCalcPeriodDates" />
  <paymentFrequency>
    <periodMultiplier>6</periodMultiplier>
    <period>M</period>
  </paymentFrequency>
  <payRelativeTo>CalculationPeriodEndDate</payRelativeTo>
  <paymentDatesAdjustments>
    <businessDayConvention>MODFOLLOWING</businessDayConvention>
    <businessCentersReference
      href="primaryBusinessCenters" />
  </paymentDatesAdjustments>
</paymentDates>
```

- **resetDates**: A type defining the parameters used to generate the reset dates schedule and associated fixing dates. The reset dates are determined relative to the calculation periods schedules dates. For the complete description, see the FpML documentation.
- **calculationPeriodAmount**: A type defining the parameters used in the calculation of fixed or floating rate period amounts or for specifying a known calculation period amount or known amount schedule. The contents of this complex type are

either

- *calculation*: The parameters used in the calculation of fixed or floaring rate period amounts.

or

- *knownAmountSchedule*: The known calculation period amount or a known amount schedule expressed as explicit known amounts and dates.

The related fragment in our example is

```
<calculationPeriodAmount>
  <calculation>
    <notionalSchedule>
      <notionalStepSchedule>
        <initialValue>50000000.00</initialValue>
        <currencycurrencyScheme="http://www.fpml.org/ext/
         iso4217">EUR</currency>
      </notionalStepSchedule>
    </notionalSchedule>
    <floatingRateCalculation>
      <floatingRateIndex>LIBOR</floatingRateIndex>
      <indexTenor>
        <periodMultiplier>6</periodMultiplier>
        <period>M</period>
      </indexTenor>
    </floatingRateCalculation>
    <dayCountFraction>ACT/360</dayCountFraction>
  </calculation>
</calculationPeriodAmount>
```

Many other features, such as like amortizing, in arrears coupon, etc., can be handled by this powerful data model. To build a complete set of classes to reproduce the complexity of FpML is clearly beyond the objectives of this text. Instead we will take inspiration for a minimal set of classes which can help us to design the process roughly described in Figure 3.6. The first classes we draw are:

- **CCalculation**: This class contains all the information needed to perform coupon calculation; it contains reference to other classes, precisely:

  - *IDayCount*: This is the interface for day count calculation previously described;
  - *ICompoundingMethod*: This is an interface to handle the generic compounding method. Remember that by the use of interfaces we avoid the need to define each implementation in complete detail at design time;
  - *CDiscounting*: This is the class that contains methods to perform cash flow discount. From a correct object-oriented point of view, this class should also be used like an interface;
  - *CNotional*: This class should handle all the calculations concerning the notional. It refers to other classes (CNotionalStepRule and CAmountSchedule).

– *CFloatingRate*: This class contains all the information for the computation of the coupon stochastic component.

The UML class diagram is depicted in Figure 4.7. Note that the CFloatingRate class in the figure has a reference to the interface IIndex which contains information about the coupon index. The UML diagram for the interface IIndex, together with some additional classes, is shown in Figure 4.8.

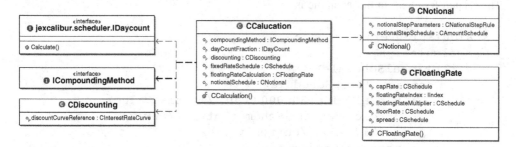

Figure 4.7   CCalculation class

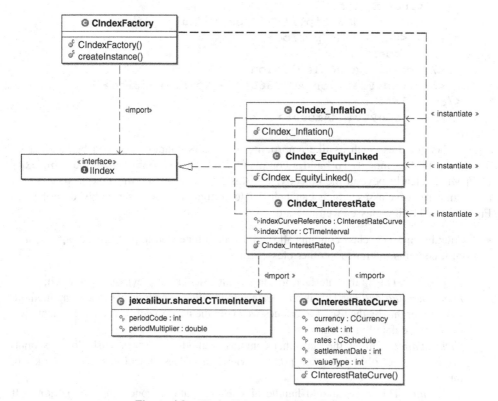

Figure 4.8   CIndexFactory and related classes

Finally, the Notional Amount and the Calculation information are collected into a single class, CCalculationPeriodAmount, which, in turn, is included in our main class CInterestRateStream. The UML diagram is show in Figure 4.9

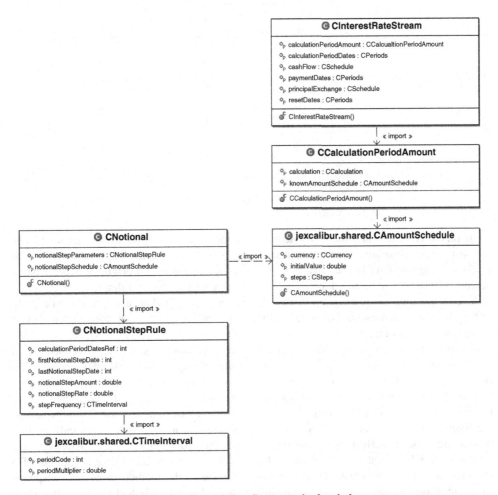

Figure 4.9   CInterestRateStream and related classes

Once you define the classes that describe your problem, you will find it very useful to describe the interaction of the objects with each other. In the UML context this can be easily done by using the so-called "sequence diagram".

4.5.3   UML's sequence diagram

UML sequence diagrams model the flow of logic within your system in a visual manner, enabling you to document and validate your logic, and are commonly used for analysis and design purposes. The invocation of methods in each object, and the order in which the invocation occurs, is captured in this kind of diagram. A sequence diagram is two-dimensional in nature. On the horizontal axis, it shows the life of the objects it represents,

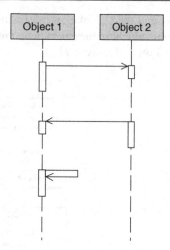

Figure 4.10   Sequence diagram

while on the vertical axis it shows the sequence of the creation or invocation of these objects. Because it uses class name and object name references, the sequence diagram is very useful in elaborating and detailing the dynamic design, the sequence and origin of invocation of objects. Hence, the sequence diagram is one of the most widely used diagrams in UML.

A sequence diagram is made up of objects and messages. Objects are represented exactly as they have been represented in all UML diagrams – as rectangles with the underlined class name within the rectangle itself.

The reason why they are called sequence diagrams should be obvious: the sequential nature of the logic is shown via the ordering of the messages (the horizontal arrows). The first message starts in the top left corner, the next message appears just below that one, and so on. The dashed lines hanging from the boxes are called object lifelines, representing the life span of the object during the scenario being modelled. The long, thin boxes on the lifelines are activation boxes, also called method-invocation boxes, which indicate that processing is being performed by the target object/class to fulfil a message. Messages are indicated on UML sequence diagrams as labelled arrows; when the source and target of a message is an object or class, the label is the signature of the method invoked in response to the message. Return values are optionally indicated using a dashed arrow with a label indicating the return value. A strongly related argument is that of a Collaboration diagram for which we suggest the interested reader should consult the link reported in the reference section.

4.6   THE CLEG CLASS

We can now design the last class: CLeg. As the name suggests, this class refers to a generic interest rate leg. It contains a reference to an instance of the CInterestRateStream, which contains all we need to compute schedule, floating rate and so on, and a reference to an interface for a generic coupon payoff. The UML diagram is shown in Figure 4.11. For the sake of simplicity we have designed only two payoffs: a plain vanilla cap-floor coupon and a floater coupon.

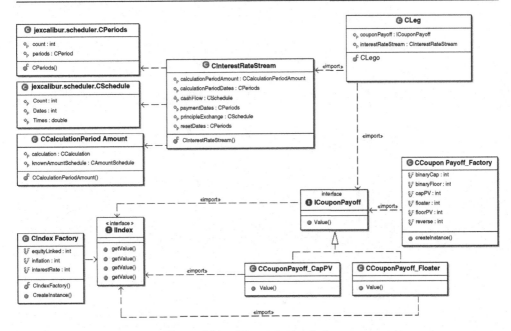

Figure 4.11   CLeg and related classes

REFERENCES AND FURTHER READING

Java date handling is well described in:

http://java.sun.com/j2se/1.4.2/docs/api/java/util/GregorianCalendar.html.

and reference therein. For a complete introduction to the Design Patterns we strongly suggest the reader to start with:

Gamma, E., Helm, R., Johnson, R.B. & Vlissides, J. (1995) *Design Patterns: Elements of Reusable Object Oriented Software*. Addison-Wesley.

5
Convertible Bonds

5.1 INTRODUCTION

We begin our study of structured products by examining equity-linked securities. These products are conceived to make an investment contingent on the performance of a stock or a market index.

In this, as in the following chapters, we will organize our discussion along three main lines, corresponding to the three basic questions one has to address to understand and evaluate a structured product.

- The first question is whether the derivative product in the structure is used to modify the coupon plan or the repayment plan: in other terms, we ask whether only the interest flow is at risk or is repayment of the principal also stochastic. In this chapter, the focus will be on cases in which the derivative contract is exclusively used to modify the repayment schedule of the principal.
- The second question is about the sensitivity to equity risk: its shape, sign and magnitude. As for the shape, we must first recognize whether exposure to equity risk is linear or not. In the typical case of nonlinear option-like exposures, further questions arise about the sign of the exposure to equity directional movements (*delta* effect), the impact of convexity (*gamma* effect) and the effects of changes in volatility (*vega* effect). In jargon, we must understand whether we are long/short the underlying and long/short volatility.
- The third question is which derivative products represent the "main course" of the structure and what are instead ancillary features. In a different metaphor, we must understand the type of car we are driving before focusing on its "optional" features. Of course, optional features are part of the cost, but they generally make little difference whether you are driving an Aston Martin or a Ferrari.

5.2 OBJECT-ORIENTED STRUCTURING PROCESS

We will strive to follow and describe structuring process and IT implementation jointly. After all, building a structured product actually amounts to conceiving an *aggregation* of financial objects, such as:

- a standard debt contract, with fixed or floating payments, called the "*host* contract" under the International Accounting Standard – in the setting above, this is the bond;
- one or more nonlinear derivative contracts, determining the main mission of the contract: being long or short on some equity risk factor and/or the corresponding volatility;
- one or more derivative contracts that are "ancillary" to the products and are used to modify and modulate the overall risk and value of the structure.

As usual we may take as our reference point the data model according to FpML. We choose to model an option as an entity, which is composed by:

- a set of underlying financial assets;
- a payoff function;
- an exercise period;
- a discount function.

Furthermore, it can contain a reference to a generic interface defining a pricing algorithm.

The objects above will be specified in classes that will be discussed in detail when it is required by the structuring process. The first requirement is, of course, the determination of "financial asset".

5.2.1 Financial asset class

This class is simply an abstract class which defines a generic financial asset. For the time being it is sufficient to model this class with two attributes: a double number, `level`, which specifies the value of the asset in a generic measure unit, and another double, `volatility`, which specifies the standard deviation of the log-return of `level`. For our purpose it is not important how volatility is calculated, it can be historical or implied. Since this class is an abstract, one needs to have one or more subclasses. For the time being we define two subclasses: `CEquity` and `COption`. `COption`, in turn, has as an attribute a reference to `CFinancialAsset` in order to store information about its underlying asset. Using the `CLeg` class defined in Chapter 4, we can form more complex types of products.

5.3 CONTINGENT REPAYMENT PLANS

Consider $P(t, T : c)$ the value of the bond with coupon payment c and repayment in a single sum at maturity T: we make the latter assumption because it is very commonly used in the market. A more general notation, which would not change the discussion below, would be $P(t, T : c, k)$ with k a deterministic repayment plan.

Assume we want to make the repayment plan stochastic in this structure. In a very general setting, designing a contingent repayment plan implies the definition of a set of objects:

- A set of securities, S_i, objects of the `CFinancialAsset` class, that will be eligible for delivery to repay the loan.
- A physical amount of each security n_i that will be eligible for delivery for each asset in the set.
- A set of dates $t_j \leq T$ in which the loan could be repaid.
- A function $f(P(t_j, T : c), n_i S_i(t_j))$ designing the possible repayment options.

The function chosen will typically identify the party that will benefit from the optionality – that is, the party that has the right to exercise the option. On the one hand, if we set

$$\max \left[P\left(t_j, T : c\right), n_i S_i\left(t_j\right) \right] \tag{5.1}$$

it is clear that the option will be at the disposal of the party who lends the money, that is investor, or the holder of the bond: it is in fact in his interest to be repaid with the most valuable asset. On the other hand, setting

$$\min\left[P\left(t_j, T:\mathbf{c}\right), n_i S_i\left(t_j\right)\right] \tag{5.2}$$

gives the repayment option to the borrower: it is in the interest of the issuer to repay the obligation by the least valuable asset.

The choice of asset to be exchanged denotes the kind of product. Notice that, in principle, the asset can be cash, say a unit $(n = 1 + r_g)$, in which case we would have

$$\max\left[P\left(t_j, T:\mathbf{c}\right), 1 + r_g\right] \tag{5.3}$$

and the bond contains an option at the disposal of the investor. The investor then holds the right to redeem the bond at par plus a premium of r_g (that is, to sell it for the face value of $1 + r_g$) at time t_j. The bond is *putable*. In fact, the payoff function can be rewritten as

$$\max\left[P\left(t_j, T:\mathbf{c}\right), 1 + r_g\right] = P\left(t_j, T:\mathbf{c}\right) + \max\left(\left(1 + r_g\right) - P\left(t_j, T:\mathbf{c}\right), 0\right) \tag{5.4}$$

that is, as a position in the bond plus a put option. On the contrary, the function

$$\min\left[P\left(t_j, T:\mathbf{c}\right), 1 + r_g\right] \tag{5.5}$$

identifies the prepayment option in favour of the issuer. The bond is *callable*, and can be written as

$$\max\left[P\left(t_j, T:\mathbf{c}\right), 1 + r_g\right] = P\left(t_j, T:\mathbf{c}\right) - \max\left(P\left(t_j, T:\mathbf{c}\right) - \left(1 + r_g\right), 0\right) \tag{5.6}$$

So, in this very introductory treatment, the contingent repayment clause amounts to a position in an option written on the bond itself. The callability/putability property can be jointly represented in the form

$$P\left(t_j, T:\mathbf{c}\right) - \omega \max\left(\omega\left(P\left(t_j, T:\mathbf{c}\right) - \left(1 + r_g\right)\right), 0\right) \tag{5.7}$$

with $\omega = 1$ denoting callability and $\omega = -1$ representing putability.

In more general applications, the terms of the repayment can be changed, allowing us to switch either to a different repayment schedule or to a different security, representing a totally different risk factor. In particular, debt repayment can be substituted by the delivery of equity stocks. It is the case of convertible and reverse convertible bonds that we address here. In terms of our object-oriented approach this calls for the definition of a `CPayoff` class. The definition of this class will accompany most of our work from now on. We start by the simplest one.

5.3.1   Payoff class

The `CPayoff` class contains all we need to compute the payoff of our option. In principle we can think of it as an abstract container in which we find information about

- contractual features (the strike price, in our simple example);
- the algorithm which defines the payoff for every market scenario.

The CPayoff class is an abstract class, a sort of interface to decouple the computational section of the program from the specific payoff with which we are dealing. Each specific payoff must be implemented as a concrete class. In the example given in the UML diagram in Figure 5.2, we have designed only two different payoffs for the most common type of options: a call and a put plain vanilla without path dependency. In these cases the methods value() are simply defined as:

```
public double value(double[] s)
{
    double payoff  = 0.0;
    if(s[s.length - 1] > strike)
      payoff = s[s.length - 1] - strike;

    return payoff;
}
```

for the plain vanilla call and

```
public double value(double[] s)
{
    double payoff = 0.0;
    if(s[s.length - 1] < strike)
      payoff = strike - s[s.length - 1];
    return payoff;
}
```

for the put. It is worth noting that in both cases we consider the payoff as a function of a vector of values: in fact, the value of the underlying asset at the exercise date is represented as s[s.length - 1] where s.length is the dimension of the vector. It simply means that it takes the last element of the array. This structure, however, makes the class fully flexible to accommodate more sophisticated path dependent payoffs, as we will see below.

In order to specify the option, the underlying asset s has to be defined. In the callability/putability setting above the underlying asset s is simply the forward price of the bond $P(t, T: c)$. In the more general setting below, denoting convertible bonds, it can be either a stock or an equity index.

5.4 CONVERTIBLE BONDS

Assume a convertible bond with coupon plan c. Assume that at time τ the investor has the option to convert, that is to exchange, the product against n units of the asset S. Analytically, this means that at time τ the value of the convertible bond (PC) will be

$$PC\,(\tau,\,T;\,\mathbf{c}) = \max\,(PC\,(\tau,\,T;\,\mathbf{c})\,,\,nS\,(\tau)) \tag{5.8}$$

where $P(\tau,\,T:\mathbf{c})$ is the value of the bond in case it is not converted, and $S(\tau)$ is the unit price of the asset. The function max(.) makes it clear that the option is in favour of the investor, and the value of the product at time τ can be written as

$$PC(\tau,\,T;\,\mathbf{c}) = \max(PC(\tau,\,T;\,\mathbf{c}),\,nS(\tau)) = P(\tau,\,T;\,\mathbf{c}) + n\max\left[S(\tau) - \frac{P(\tau,\,T;\,\mathbf{c})}{n},\,0\right] \tag{5.9}$$

and the product includes n call options with a strike equal to $P(\tau,\,T:\mathbf{c})/n$. No arbitrage requires the value of the product to be equal to its replicating portfolio:

$$PC\,(t,\,T;\,\mathbf{c}) = P\,(t,\,T;\,\mathbf{c}) + n\,\text{CALL}\left(S,\,t;\,\frac{P\,(\tau,\,T;\,\mathbf{c})}{n},\,\tau\right) \tag{5.10}$$

Of course, if the bond can be converted only at maturity, then $P(T,\,T:\mathbf{c})/n = 1/n$. If the conversion option can, instead, be exercised before maturity at time $\tau < T$, the options embedded in the product are "exchange options" between the stock and the bond. Standard martingale pricing arguments suggest that these n options should be priced as call options struck at the forward price of the bond. If one has reason to think of the stock as being significantly correlated with the term structure, the risk-adjusted drift of the stock should be adjusted for such correlation, and the evaluation should be carried out under the *forward martingale measure*.

Example 5.1 *LYONs.* In 1985 Merrill Lynch launched the so-called *Liquid Yield Option Notes* (LYONs) for two clients. LYONs are zero-coupon-bonds that are callable, putable or convertible at a set of dates.

5.4.1 Exercise class

In many instances convertible bonds allow the conversion choice to be made at several points in time over the life of the contract. This choice, while granting more flexibility to the investor, makes life more difficult for quantitative analysts. The "convertibility" option is in fact represented by a set of n *Bermudan* or *American* call options with time-varying strikes. In fact, the contract will include a set of conversion dates $t_j \leq T$. At each conversion date t_j, the value of the product will be

$$PC\,(t_j,\,T;\,\mathbf{c}) = P\,(t_j,\,T;\,\mathbf{c}) + n\max\left[S\,(t_j) - \frac{P\,(t_j,\,T;\,\mathbf{c})}{n},\,0\right] \tag{5.11}$$

conditional on the fact that conversion has not been done up to time t_{j-1}. The early exercise feature of course increases the value of the product. This is an example of the ancillary options described in the introduction.

The exercise period is described through a hierarchy of classes which has, at the higher level, an abstract class named `CExercise`.

`CExercise` is the abstract base class defining the way in which options may be exercised. It has the following attributes:

- `expirationDate`: An object of type `GregorianCalendar`. The last day within an exercise period for an American style option. For a European style option it is the only day within the exercise period.
- `expirationTime`: The latest time (in years from valuation date) for exercise on expirationDate.
- `expirationTimeUnit`: This is an integer number which specifies the time unit of the field `expirationTime`. Possible values are `GregorianCalendar.DAY_OF_MONTH`, `GregorianCalendar.MONTH` and `GregorianCalendar.YEAR`.

Among its methods, one is of utmost importance: `earlyExerciseValue( )`. This method is used to calculate the option value in the case of early exercise and is used by some of the pricing algorithms we will discuss subsequently. We overload this method with three different signatures:

```
public abstract double earlyExerciseValue(double
    intrinsicValue, double continuationValue);
public abstract double earlyExerciseValue(double
    intrinsicValue, double continuationValue,
    double exerciseTime);
public abstract double earlyExerciseValue(double intrinsicValue,
    double continuationValue,
    GregorianCalendar
    exerciseDate);
```

The method takes the `intrinsicValue` of an option and the `continuationValue` as input, and returns the appropriate value according to exercise type. The implementation of this method varies, of course, for the different kinds of exercise.

- `CEuropeanExercise`

  - Superclass: `CExercise`

    o This class has no proper methods or parameters. Despite this, it must be defined in order to have a concrete class for European exercise. In this case the `earlyExerciseValue( )` method simply ignores the `intrinsicValue` and return always the `continuationValue`.

- `CAmericanExercise`

  - Superclass: `CExercise`

    o `commencementDate`: The first day of the exercise period for an American style option.

o For this class, the `earlyExerciseValue()` method returns the maximum value between `intrinsicValue` and `continuationValue`:

```
public double earlyExerciseValue(double intrinsicValue,
   double continuationValue)
{
   return Math.max(intrinsicValue, continuationValue);
}
```

- **CBermudaExercise**

  - Superclass: `CExercise`

    o `exerciseDates:` The dates define the Bermudan option exercise times and the expiration date. The last specified date is assumed to be the expiration date.
    o `exerciseTimes:` The same information as above expressed in years.

When dealing with Bermuda exercise we need first of all to understand if we are inside an exercise period or not. For this reason, the method takes the evaluation time as input (both in the form of date or of time measured in years). For the sake of simplicity we suppose that the exercise dates are a discrete set. The best way to store this information in a Java structure is to use a Hashtable. For a complete definition of the characteristic and use of Hashtable in Java the reader is invited to consult the Sun website `http://java.sun.com/j2se` – in particular the page `http://java.sun.com/j2se/1.3/docs/api/java/util/Hashtable.html` (valid, of course, at the time of writing this book). In extreme synthesis a Hashtable is a structure which maps keys to values as a dictionary. The advantage of using this structure, instead of a simple vector for example, is that this class has a certain number of efficient methods to search for a particular value. In this case we will use a Hashtable to store the exercise data for Bermuda exercise. In the main application we define the exercise dates using the exercise times as keys in the following way[1]

```
Hashtable exerciseTimes = new Hashtable(50,0.75f);

exerciseTimes.put(new Double(1.0),"15/06/2006");
exerciseTimes.put(new Double(2.0),"15/06/2007");
exerciseTimes.put(new Double(3.0),"15/06/2008");
exerciseTimes.put(new Double(4.0),"15/06/2009");
exerciseTimes.put(new Double(5.0),"15/06/2010");
```

We have set five exercise dates (including expiration) equally spaced in time. The `earlyExerciseValue()` method for this option type returns the

---

[1] The parameters in the constructor of a Java Hashtable are the *capacity* and the *load factor*. We do not get into details about the value of these parameters, we limit ourselves to remind that the capacity of the table has to be somewhat larger than the number of elements you plan to look up. The more spare capacity you give, the faster the lookup. There are of course diminishing returns. Typically, you specify about 25% more capacity than you have elements and a load factor of 0.75 which controls automatic growth of the lookup table when it gets too full. More details on that in the references about Java language.

continuationValue except in those cases in which calendar time coincides with an exercise date. The Java implementation can be something like this:

```
public double earlyExerciseValue(double intrinsicValue,
                    double continuationValue,
                    double exerciseTime)
{
  if(exercisePeriod.containsKey(new Double(exerciseTime)))
    return Math.max(intrinsicValue,continuationValue);
  else
    return continuationValue;
}
```

Having used a Hashtable as container we can easily check if the exerciseTime is valid by simply recalling the containsKey method of Hashtable class.

The complete UML diagram for the Exercise classes is reported in Figure 5.1.

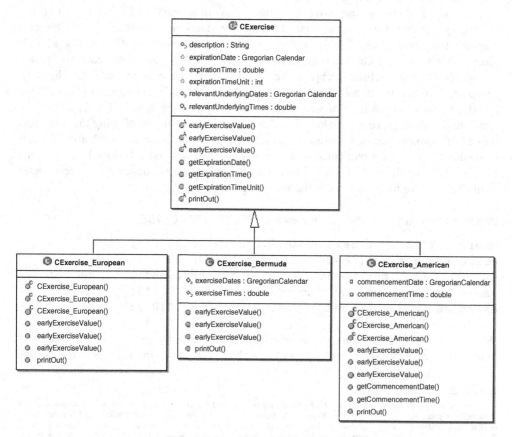

Figure 5.1 Exercise period classes

5.5   REVERSE CONVERTIBLE BONDS

Assume a product in which the choice to repay the debt in terms of equity instead of cash is left to the borrower. Of course, one would settle for the cheapest repayment method. The payoff will be

$$PC(\tau, T; \mathbf{c}) = \min(PC(\tau, T; \mathbf{c}), nS(\tau)) \tag{5.12}$$

The product embeds a put option at the disposal of the issuer:

$$PC(\tau, T; \mathbf{c}) = P(\tau, T; \mathbf{c}) - n\max\left[\frac{P(\tau, T; \mathbf{c})}{n} - S(\tau), 0\right] \tag{5.13}$$

By arbitrage, then, the value of the product consists of two parts:

$$PC(t, T; \mathbf{c}) = P(t, T; \mathbf{c}) - n\,\mathrm{PUT}\left[S, t; \frac{P(\tau, T; \mathbf{c})}{n}, \tau\right] \tag{5.14}$$

i.e. a long position in a zero-coupon bond and a short position in n put options.

These products, known as reverse convertible bonds, are particularly risky. Of course, being short an option is a particularly risky business. First, it enables us to earn little money if nothing happens and to lose a lot if the market moves against the short end of the contract. Second, selling an option implies a negative gamma and vega position: if one hedges against the event of a drop in the market, he remains exposed to losses from movements of the market in both directions as well as to increases in volatility. It is for these reasons that typically these products include a more stringent condition for the exercise of the option, conditioning the exercise of the option to a second event. The usual choice is to include a barrier in the option.

5.6   BARRIERS

Barriers represent a very common provision in convertible bonds. We show below examples of applications to both convertibles and reverse. Barrier options are derivative products whose exercise is conditional on the price of the underlying asset reaching a barrier level h in a given time period (typically the lifetime of the option itself). Barrier options may be classified as: (i) *down* and *up* depending on whether the barrier is lower or higher than the price of the underlying asset; or (ii) *in* and *out* depending on whether the option is activated or made void when the barrier is reached.

5.6.1   Contingent convertibles: Co.Cos

Take a normal convertible bond and assume that an investor can choose to be repaid in terms of stocks as opposed to cash if the following events take place:

1. The value of the stock is above a strike price.
2. The company's stock has reached an upper level set above the strike price itself before the option has to be exercised.

The second event is what gives the name "contingent" to the convertible bond (technically, *upside contingency*), and actually amounts to the inclusion of a barrier in the product. The conversion option is then an *up-and-in* call option. The value of the security would be

$$PC(t, T; \mathbf{c}) = P(t, T; \mathbf{c}) + n \, UIC \left[S, t; \frac{P(\tau, T; \mathbf{c})}{n}, \tau, h \right] \tag{5.15}$$

where UIC denotes the value of the *up-and-in* call.

An obvious symmetry relationship between barrier options enables us to identify the value added to the product by the barrier. In fact, it is intuitive that buying an *in* and an *out* option amounts to buying a plain vanilla option. In our example

$$UIC \left[S, t; \frac{P(\tau, T; \mathbf{c})}{n}, \tau, h \right] + UOC \left[S, t; \frac{P[\tau, T; \mathbf{c})}{n}, \tau, h \right] = CALL \left[S, t; \frac{P[\tau, T; \mathbf{c})}{n}, \tau \right]$$

$$\tag{5.16}$$

where UOC denotes an *up-and-out* option. We may than compute

$$PC(t, T; \mathbf{c}) = P(t, T; \mathbf{c}) + n \, CALL \left[S, t; \frac{P(\tau, T; \mathbf{c})}{n}, \tau \right] - UOC \left[S, t; \frac{P(\tau, T; \mathbf{c})}{n}, \tau, h \right]$$

$$\tag{5.17}$$

and the value of the *up-and-out* call represents the value of the *upside contingency* included in the product.

5.6.2 Contingent reverse convertibles

Assume a contract under which the issuer may repay its debt in terms of equity stock if the following events take place:

1. The value of the stock is below some strike level k at time τ.
2. The value of the stock has decreased below some barrier h by time τ.

In this case the product could be broken down into a plain bond and a short position in a *barrier option*. The derivative product embedded in the reverse convertible is a *down-and-in* put option (DIP). The value of the product will then be

$$PC(t, T; \mathbf{c}) = P(t, T; \mathbf{c}) - n \, DIP \left(S, t; \frac{P(\tau, T; \mathbf{c})}{n}, \tau, h \right) \tag{5.18}$$

As in the previous case, the value of the barrier can be singled out. So, the value of the product can be divided into three parts:

$$PC(t, T; \mathbf{c}) = P(t, T; \mathbf{c}) - n \, PUT \left[S, t; \frac{P(\tau, T; \mathbf{c})}{n}, \tau \right] + DOP \left[S, t; \frac{P(\tau, T; \mathbf{c})}{n}, \tau, h \right]$$

$$\tag{5.19}$$

where DOP denotes the *down-and-out* put option, representing the value of the barrier added to the product.

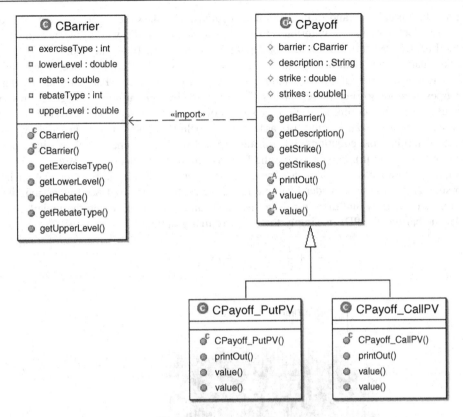

Figure 5.2   The payoff model

5.6.3   Introducing barriers in the Payoff class

In Figure 5.2 we introduce the barrier in the class CPayoff and in the following we will see how to introduce a more interesting payoff, and in doing that we would test the validity of our class structure.

5.6.4   Parisian option: a short description

A problem with standard barrier options is that they can be easily manipulated, particularly if the underlying asset is illiquid. A financial engineering solution to this problem is offered by the so-called Parisian option. Parisian options are essentially a crossover between barrier options and Asian options. They have predominant barrier option features in that they can be knocked in or out depending on hitting a barrier from below or above; and they differ from standard barrier options in that extreme outlier asset movements will not trigger the Parisian – to activate or extinguish the trigger, the asset must lie outside or inside the barrier for a predetermined time period t. For example, an up-and-out Parisian call option becomes extinguished if the underlying asset remains above a predetermined barrier level for a prescribed length of time. Compared to standard barrier options, it can be more beneficial for the holder of a Parisian option on a volatile asset.

Because of its highly path-dependent nature, Parisian options cannot be solved via a closed form method and common methods involve the consideration of the PDE, the use of a Laplace transform, and finite difference methods. The classic paper on pricing Parisian options under continuous monitoring is that of Chesney *et al.* (1997) who show the evaluation of the Laplace transform followed by a rapid inversion via the Euler method.

Like many other path-dependent exotics, solving the PDE on a lattice using finite differences is generally the most reliable method, and in the case of Parisians and barriers, this is even more so. For these options, there are 16 differential equations governing the various cases. Considering all the combinations of down, up, in-and-out Parisian calls and puts, and then assessing whether the asset price is below or above the strike price, we are able to determine the equations. By considering a three-dimensional problem (time, price and duration of out/in), one can solve the PDE via finite differences on a lattice. Referring to Figure 5.3, we can see that, in general, the barrier divides the integration region into two subregions. Let us consider a simple model using the Black and Scholes assumptions of constant volatility and take, for example, an up-and-out option. When the underlying is under the barrier, the PDE is simply that of an ordinary option:

$$\frac{\partial f}{\partial t} + \frac{1}{2}\sigma^2 S^2 \frac{\partial^2 f}{\partial S^2} + rS\frac{\partial f}{\partial S} - rf = 0$$

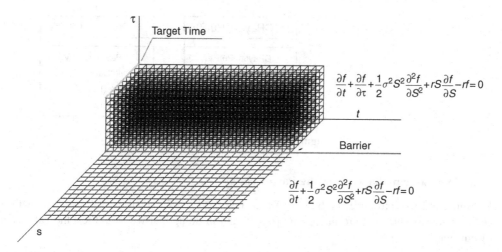

Figure 5.3   Integration region for Parisian option pricing

When the underlying is above the barrier, the option value is a function not only of S (underlying level) and t (expiration time) but also of a new variable, τ, which is the time the underlying lies outside the barrier itself. The PDE becomes

$$\frac{\partial f}{\partial t} + \frac{\partial f}{\partial \tau} + \frac{1}{2}\sigma^2 S^2 \frac{\partial^2 f}{\partial S^2} + rS\frac{\partial f}{\partial S} - rf = 0$$

Example 5.2   Consider the following LYONs contract. It was issued by General Mills, and is a debt issue convertible into 13.0259 shares of common stock for any $1000 of principal amount. Conversion is conditional on the event that the closing price of General Mills is greater than a barrier level for 20 days out of a set of 30 consecutive days in a quarter. As we see, exercise of conversion is in this case conditional on a Parisian-like feature.

5.7 PRICING ISSUES

We now turn to the pricing issues involved in a structured product. The replicating portfolio approach immediately delivers the price as the sum of the financial assets involved. Once the "host contract" has been defined and the derivative contracts have been described, the price of the structured product clearly has to be equal to the algebraic sum of the two. Arguments of disagreement about the price can then emerge mainly about the pricing algorithms of the single components of the replicating portfolio.

The price of the "host contract" is obtained by applying the appropriate discount factor curve to the cash flows. In this case most of the argument about the price may be due to the discount factor that one prefers to use. Is it more reasonable to use the zero coupon curve "bootstrapped" from the swap rates, or some other curve? Should we take into account the default probability of the issuer? Some of these issues are standard and are left to the "knowledge of the market" of the structurer, some others will be covered in later chapters.

Here we focus on the pricing complexity coming from the derivative part of the product. This may actually raise most of the arguments about the "fair price" of a contract and may occur for two reasons:

(a) the statistical model used for the underlying assets
(b) the complexity of the structure of derivative contracts.

If we have plain vanilla European options we could first use the celebrated standard Black and Scholes formulas, and then try to refine the model by accounting for volatility smiles and term structures. Many choices can be made. One could use, among the others, (i) stochastic volatility models; (ii) local volatility models; (iii) implied trees. Other models that are on the research frontier today, or have not yet been written, may well become the market standard tomorrow.

The problem is compounded in cases in which the derivative involved is exotic. Different exotic products would call for numerical procedures, rather than closed form approximations. And again, it may be the case that new methods, or new refinements of old methods, would gather momentum in the market practice. For all of these reasons we would not like to redesign our software at any change of fashion in the market. So what we need, as usual, is a way to implement things in order to maximize code reusability and maintenance. As we will see, we need the *Strategy Pattern* to accomplish that.

5.7.1 Valuation methods for barrier options: a primer

Evaluating a barrier option amounts to solving a bivariate problem involving two events: (i) the contract ends in the money; (ii) the barrier is hit or is not hit. Notice that the second event is path-dependent, and for this reason, barrier options are also called *quasi-path-dependent*. This suggests a standard classification of barrier options models.

- The first strategy exploits the dynamic structure of the underlying asset. A solution is obtained either by an explicit solution to the corresponding PDE equation or by application of the reflection principle.
- The second strategy exploits static replication techniques using plain vanilla options. Plain vanilla options are set at a discrete sequence of dates in such a way as to replicate the value of the payoff as time elapses.

The second strategy is best understood if one considers that in real-world applications barriers are monitored at discrete times. This implies, for example, that the value of a *down-and-out* call (put) option could be computed as the joint probability that the option is above the barrier at all monitoring dates and above (below) the strike at the final date.

5.7.2   The Strategy Pattern

The Strategy Pattern (Figure 5.4) basically consists of decoupling an algorithm from its host, and encapsulating the algorithm into a separate class. More simply put, an object and its behaviour are separated and put into two different classes. This allows us to switch the algorithm we are using at any time.

This has several advantages. First, if you have several different behaviours that you want an object to perform, it is much simpler to keep track of them if each behaviour is a separate class, and not buried in the body of some method. Should you ever want to add, remove, or change any of the behaviours, it is a much simpler task, since each one is its own class. Each such behaviour or algorithm encapsulated into its own class is called a *Strategy*.

When you have several objects that are basically the same, and differ only in their behaviour, it can be beneficial to make use of the Strategy Pattern. Using Strategies, you can reduce these several objects to one class that uses several Strategies. The use of Strategies also provides a nice alternative to subclassing an object to achieve different behaviours. When you subclass an object to change its behaviour, the behaviour it executes is static. If you wished to change what it does, you would need to create a new instance of a different subclass and replace that object with your new creation. With Strategies, however, all you need to do is switch the object's strategy, and it will immediately alter its behaviour. Using Strategies also eliminates the need for many conditional statements. When you have several behaviours together in one class, it is difficult to choose among them without resorting to conditional statements. If you use Strategies, you do not need to check for anything, since the current strategy just executes without asking questions.

In this chapter we shall use three different approaches to price an option (Figure 5.5):

- analytical, based on the Black and Scholes formula or some modification;
- binomial tree;
- Monte Carlo simulation.

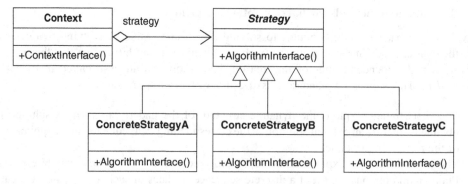

Figure 5.4   The Strategy pattern UML diagram

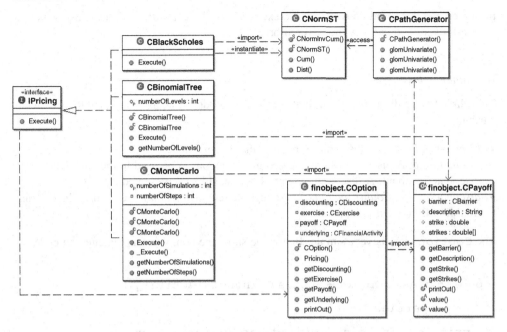

Figure 5.5 Our pricing algorithm UML diagram

Each algorithm has a method called `Execute()` which takes the object to price as input. We will see soon how this is going to perform.

5.7.3 The Option class

We have finally reached at the end of our process, and in Figure 5.6 we can find the UML diagram of the `COption` class. All of the subclasses constituting this class have been

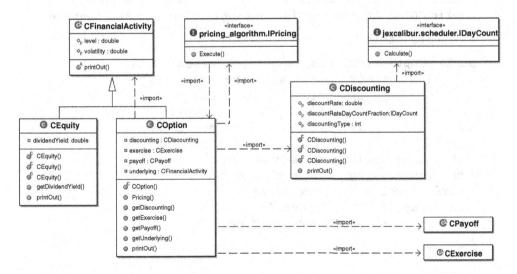

Figure 5.6 `COption` class

presented and discussed above, with the exception of the class CDiscounting, which is straightforward and can now be covered briefly.

Discounting class

This class defines discounting information. We can model this class, including the following attributes:

- *discountingType*: The discounting method that is applicable.
- *discountRate*: A discount rate, expressed as a decimal, to be used in the calculation of a discounted amount. A discount amount of 5% would be represented as 0.05.
- *discountRateDayCountFraction*: A discount day count fraction to be used in the calculation of a discounted amount.

The COption class is very simple. Below we show the complete implementation code:

```
public class COption extends CFinancialActivity {

    /* properties */

    private CFinancialActivity underlying    = null;
    private CExercise          exercise      = null;
    private CPayoff            payoff        = null;
    private CDiscounting       discounting   = null;
    private IPricing           pricingModel  = null;

    /* inspectors */

    public CFinancialActivity getUnderlying(){return underlying;}
    public CExercise getExercise()              {return exercise;}
    public CPayoff getPayoff()                  {return payoff;}
    public CDiscounting getDiscounting()   {return discounting;}

    /* constructors */

    public COption(CDiscounting       discounting,
                   CFinancialActivity underlying,
                   CExercise          exercise,
                   CPayoff            payoff,
                   IPricing           pricingModel)
    {
      this.discounting   = discounting;
      this.underlying    = underlying;
      this.exercise      = exercise;
      this.payoff        = payoff;
      this.pricingModel  = pricingModel;
    }

    /* methods */
```

```
public double Pricing()
{
  return pricingModel.Execute(this);
}

public void printOut()
{
  System.out.println("\n");
  payoff.printOut();
  exercise.printOut();
  underlying.printOut();
  discounting.printOut();
  System.out.println("");
}
}
```

5.7.4   Option pricing: a *Lego*-like approach

Let us suppose we want to price a simple plain vanilla European call option. First, we have to build the fundamental blocks, i.e. payoff, exercise, underlying activity and pricing method. In this case, in a professional setting, it is of utmost importance to use the factory pattern described in the previous chapter, but for the sake of simplicity we will not use that approach in this chapter. As we have already discussed, our "Lego bricks" are implemented by the following classes:

- CPayoff;
- CExercise;
- CDiscounting;
- IPricing.

We can instantiate the corresponding objects using the following instructions:

```
double      S          = 32000.0; // level of underlying asset
double      sigma      = 0.15000; // standard deviation of log ret
double      K          = 31500.0; // exercise price
double      T          = 0.25000; // expiry (years)
double      r          = 0.02500; // interest rate
CPayoff     payoff     = new CPayoff_CallPV(K);
CExercise   exercise   = new CExercise_European(T,
                           GregorianCalendar.YEAR);
CDiscounting           discounting = new CDiscounting(r);
CFinancialActivity     equity      = new CEquity(S, sigma);
IPricing               priceModel  = new CBlackScholes();
```

We have chosen to valuate the option using a simple Black–Scholes procedure. Now we can instantiate an object called anEuropeanOption using one of the constructors of the COption class:

```
COption anEuropeanOption = new COption(discounting,
                                       equity,
                                       exercise,
                                       payoff,
                                       priceModel);
```

Finally we can calculate the option price by invoking the `Pricing()` method which, in turn, simply returns the result of the `Execute()` method of the price model passed in input.

```
double price = anEuropeanOption.Pricing();
```

If you run the program in the CD, this is the result you should obtain in the Eclipse console:

```
Running Black & Scholes Algorithm

Payoff type              : Call Plain Vanilla
Exercise price           = 31500.0
Exercise type            : European
Expiration               = 0.25 years
Underlying value         = 32000.0
Underlying volatility    = 0.15(15.0%)
Discounting rate         = 0.025(2.5%)

Fair Value = 1335.3716477670241
```

To price the put option on the same underlying we simply change the payoff, writing

```
payoff = new CPayoff_PutPV(K);
```

and the output of the program will be

```
Running Black & Scholes Algorithm

Payoff type              : Put Plain Vanilla
Exercise price           = 31500.0
Exercise type            : European
Expiration               = 0.25 years
Underlying value         = 32000.0
Underlying volatility    = 0.15(15.0%)
Discounting rate         = 0.025(2.5%)
Fair Value = 639.1106024039582
```

In the same simple way we can price different kinds of option with different algorithms. For example, let us assume that we wish to price the same put as above, but with an early exercise. We only have to build an appropriate algorithm, for example a binomial tree, with 1000 steps:

```
priceModel = new    CBinomialTree(1000);
```

and define a new exercise type

```
exercise = new   CExercise_American(0,T, GregorianCalendar.
                 YEAR);
```

Now create a new object

```
COption anAmericanOption = new COption(discounting,
                                       equity,
                                       exercise,
                                       payoff,
                                       priceModel);
```

and a call to the `Pricing()` method will produce the following output:

```
Running Binomial Tree...
Number of levels = 1000

Payoff type              : Put Plain Vanilla
Exercise price           = 31500.0
Exercise type            : American
First Exercise Time      = 0.0 years
Last Exercise Time       = 0.25 years
Underlying value         = 32000.0
Underlying volatility = 0.15(15.0%)
Discounting rate         = 0.025(2.5%)

Fair Value = 649.6099105839411
```

We can easily extend the Black–Scholes pricing class in order to include the computation of a simple plain vanilla barrier option. Let us define

H	:	barrier level
R_{out}	:	"out" option Rebate
R_{in}	:	"in" option Rebate
$1\,H > K$	=	1 if $H > K$, 0 otherwise
τ	=	$T - t$
υ	=	$r - d - \sigma 2/2$
ω	=	1 for call option and -1 for put option
θ	=	1 for "down" option and -1 for "in" option

and

$$\max(\omega) = \omega \max(\omega H, \omega K)$$

$$B\&S(y, K, \tau, r, d, \sigma, \omega) = \omega y \exp[-d(T - t)]N(\omega d_1) - \omega \exp[-r(T - t)]KN(\omega d_2)$$

The formalism is that of Zhang (1998) to which the interested reader is referred for the theoretical background and further details.

Down-and-in call / Up-and-in put

Consider the following function:

$$
\text{DCUP} = \left(\frac{H}{y}\right)^{2v/\sigma^2} \left\{ \text{B\&S}\left[\left(\frac{H^2}{y}\right), \max(\omega), \omega\right] + \theta\left[\max(\omega) - K\right]\exp(-r\tau) N \right.
$$

$$
\left\{ \omega d_2\left[\left(\frac{H^2}{y}\right), \max(\omega)\right]\right\} + 1_{\theta H > \theta K}\left\{\text{B\&S}(y, K, -\theta) - \text{B\&S}(y, H, -\theta)\right.
$$

$$
+ \theta(H - K)\exp(-r(T - t)) N\left[-\theta d_2(y, H)\right]\}
\tag{5.20}
$$

then

$$
\text{Down-and-in call} = \text{DCUP}(\omega = 1, \theta = 1)
$$

$$
\text{Up-and-in put} = \text{DCUP}(\omega = -1, \theta = -1)
$$

Down-and-in put / Up-and-in call

$$
\text{UCDP} = \left(\frac{H}{y}\right)^{2v/\sigma^2} \left\{ \text{B\&S}\left(\frac{H^2}{y}, K, \theta\right) - \text{B\&S}\left(\frac{H^2}{y}, H, \theta\right) \right.
$$

$$
\left. + \omega(H - K)\exp(-r\tau) N\left[\theta d_2(H, y)\right]\right\} 1_{H > K} + \left\{\text{B\&S}[y, \max(\omega), -\theta]\right.
$$

$$
+ \left[\max(\omega) - K\right]\exp(-r\tau) N\left[\omega d_2(y, \max(\omega))\right]\}
\tag{5.21}
$$

$$
\text{Down-and-in put} = \text{UCDP}(\omega = -1, \theta = 1)
$$

$$
\text{Up-and-in call} = \text{UCDP}(\omega = 1, \theta = -1)
$$

Down-and-out call / Up-and-out put

$$
\text{DCUPOT} = \text{B\&S}[y, \max(\omega), \theta] - \left(\frac{H}{y}\right)^{2v/\sigma^2} \text{B\&S}\left[\frac{H^2}{y}, \max(\omega), \theta\right]
$$

$$
+ \theta\left[\max(\omega) - K\right]\exp(-r\tau)\left[N(\theta d_2(y, \max(\omega))) - \left(\frac{H}{y}\right)^{2v/\sigma^2}\right.
$$

$$
N\left(\theta d_2\left(\frac{H^2}{y}, \max(\omega)\right)\right)\right]
\tag{5.22}
$$

$$
\text{Down-and-out call} = \text{DCUPOT}(\omega = 1, \theta = 1, \max(1))
$$

$$
\text{Up-and-out put} = \text{DCUPOT}(\omega = -1, \theta = -1, \max(-1))
$$

Up-and-out call / Down-and-out put

$$
\text{UCDPOT} = 1_{H>K} \left\{
\begin{array}{l}
[\text{B\&S}\,(y, K, \omega) - \text{B\&S}\,(y, H, \omega) + \theta\,(H - K)\exp\,(-r\tau) \\[2mm]
N\,(\omega d_2\,(y, H))] - \left(\dfrac{H^2}{y}\right)^{2v/\sigma^2} \left[\text{B\&S}\left(\dfrac{H^2}{y}, K, \omega\right)\right. \\[4mm]
\left. - \text{B\&S}\left(\dfrac{H^2}{y}, H, \omega\right)\right. \\[4mm]
\left. + \theta\,(H - K)\exp\,(-r\tau)\,N\,(\omega d_2\,(H, y))\right]
\end{array}
\right\}
\tag{5.23}
$$

$$
\text{Up-and-out call} = \text{UCDPOT}(\omega = 1, \theta = -1)
$$
$$
\text{Down-and-out put} = \text{UCDPOT}(\omega = -1, \theta = 1)
$$

Rebate

For a barrier option of the type "in", a rebate is paid at option expiry if the option itself ends without activation. If the amount of rebate is R_{in}, its value is computed as

$$
\text{RBIN} = \exp\,(-r\tau)\,R_{\text{in}}\left\{ N\,[\theta d_2\,(y, H)] - \left(\dfrac{H}{y}\right)^{2v/\sigma^2} N\,[\theta d_2\,(H, y)] \right\}
\tag{5.24}
$$

For a barrier option of the type "out", two possible situations are usually considered:

(i) the value R_{out} is paid at expiry;
(ii) R_{out} is paid when the barrier is reached.

In the first case the actual value of rebate is given by

$$
\text{ROUT} = \exp\,(-r\tau)\,R_{\text{out}}\left\{ N\,[-\theta d_2\,(y, H)] + \left(\dfrac{H}{y}\right)^{2v/\sigma^2} N\,[\theta d_2\,(H, y)] \right\}
\tag{5.25}
$$

In the second case we have

$$
\text{ROUT} = R_{\text{out}}\left\{ \left(\dfrac{H}{y}\right)^{q_1(r-\eta)} N\,[\theta Q_1\,(r - \eta)] + \left(\dfrac{H}{y}\right)^{q_{-1}(r-\eta)} N\,[\theta Q_{-1}\,(r - \eta)] \right\}
\tag{5.26}
$$

where

$$
\psi\,(s) = \sqrt{v^2 + 2s\sigma^2}
$$
$$
Q_i = \dfrac{\ln(H/y) + i\tau\psi\,(s)}{\sigma\sqrt{\tau}}, \quad i = 1, -1
$$
$$
q_i = \dfrac{v + i\psi\,(s)}{\sigma^2}, \quad i = -1, 1
$$

We add this formula to the `CBlackScholes` class. For the sake of code reusability it is necessary for the interface of this class to remain unchanged. For this reason we keep the `Execute()` method as the main method of the class, and the only change occurs inside this method, but this is not directly connected to other classes that will continue to use the `CBlackScholes` class in the same way. Let us have a look to the new implementation of the `Execute()` method:

```
public double Execute(COption option)
{
   if(option.getPayoff().getBarrier() == null){
     return BS_PlainVanilla(option);
   }
   else{
     return BS_Barrier(option);
   }
}
```

Note that a necessary condition for this method to work is that we have correctly initialized to `null` the attribute `barrier` in the constructor of the `CPayoff` class. Below we show the source code of the constructor:

```
public abstract class CPayoff
{
   /* attributes */

   protected String description = "";
   protected double strike = 0;
   protected double[]   strikes   = null;
   protected CBarrier   barrier   = null;

   /* inspectors */

   public double   getStrike()    {return strike;}
   public double[] getStrikes()  {return strikes;}
   public String   getDescription(){return description;}
   public CBarrier getBarrier()  {return barrier;}

   /* methods */

   public abstract double value(double s);
   public abstract double value(double[] s);
   public abstract void printOut();
}
```

We can price a barrier option by simply putting together all the "Lego" bricks in this way

```
CBarrier  barrier = new CBarrier(30000,30000);
exercise  =   new CExercise_European(T, GregorianCalendar.YEAR);
payoff    =   new CPayoff_CallDownOut(K, barrier);
```

```
priceModel  =   new CBlackScholes();

COption aBarrierOption = new COption(discounting,
                                     equity,
                                     exercise,
                                     payoff,
                                     priceModel);

price = aBarrierOption.Pricing();
```

REFERENCES AND FURTHER READING

Asquith, P. (1995) Convertible bonds are not called late, *Journal of Finance*, **50** (4), 1275–1289.

Barone-Adesi, G., Bermudez, A. & Hatgioannides, J. (2003) Two-factors convertible bonds evaluation using the method of characteristics/finite elements, *Journal of Economic Dynamics and Control*, **27** (10), 1801–1831.

Boyle, P.P. & Lau, S.H. (1994) Bumping up against the barrier with binomial method, *Journal of Derivatives*, 6–14.

Bowie, J. & Carr, P. (1994) Static simplicity, *RISK*, **7** (8), 44–50.

Brennan, M.J. & Schwartz, E.S. (1977) Convertible bonds: Valuation and optimal strategies of call and conversion, *Journal of Finance*, **32** (5), 1699–1715.

Brennan, M.J. & Schwartz, E.S. (1980) Analyzing convertible bonds, *Journal of Financial and Quantitative Analysis*, **15** (4), 907–929.

Brennan, M.J. & Schwartz, E.S. (1997) The evaluation of the American put option, *Journal of Finance*, **32**, 449–462.

Broadie, M., Glasserman, P. & Kou, S. (1997) A continuity correction for discrete barrier options, *Mathematical Finance*, **7**, 325–349.

Carr, P. & Chou, A. (1997) Breaking barriers, *RISK*, **10** (9), 139–145.

Carr, P., Ellis, K & Gupta, V. (1998) Static hedging of exotic options, *Journal of Finance*, **53**, 1165–1190.

Chesney, M., Jeanblanc-Picque, M. & Yor, M. (1997) Brownian excursions and Parisian barrier options, *Advances in Applied Probability*, **29** (1), 165–184.

Cheung, W. & Nelken, I. (1994) Costing the converts, *RISK*, **7**, 47–49.

Derman, E., Engener, D. & Kani, I. (1994) *Static option replication*. Working Paper, Goldman Sachs.

Geman, H. & Yor, M. (1996) Pricing and hedging double-barrier options, *Mathematical Finance*, **6**, 365–378.

Harding, J., Hegde, S.P. & Mateti, R.S. (2005) *Extending the LYONs Pricing Model* (Mimeo).

Heynen, R.C. & Kat, H.M. (1994) Partial barrier options, *Journal of Financial Engineering*, **2**, 253–274.

Hirsa, A., Cortadon, G. & Madan, D.B. (2003) The effect of model risk on the valuation of barrier options, *The Journal of Risk Finance*, Winter.

Ho, T.S.Y. & Pfeffer, D.M. (1996) Convertible bonds: model, value, attribution and analytics, *Financial Analysts Journal*, **52** (5), 35–44.

Hung, M.Y. & Wang, J.Y. (2002) Pricing convertible bonds subject to credit risk, *Journal of Derrivatives*, **10**, 75–87.

Ingersoll, J. Jr. (1977) A contingent claim valuation of convertible securities, *Journal of Financial Economics*, **4**, 289–322.

Kunitomo, N. & Ikeda, M. (1992) Pricing options with curved boundaries, *Mathematical Finance*, **2**, 275–298.

Lau, K.W. & Kwok, Y.K. (2004) Anatomy of options features in convertible bonds, *Journal of Futures Markets*, **24** (6), 513–532.

Mayers, D. (1998) Why firms issue convertible bonds: The matching of financial and real options, *Journal of Financial Economics*, **47** (1), 83–102.

McConnell, J.J. & Schwartz, E.S. (1986) LYON taming, *Journal of Finance*, **41**, 561–576.

Merton, R.C. (1973) Theory of rational option pricing, *Bell Journal of Economics and Management Science*, **4**, 141–183.

Myneny, R. (1992) The pricing of the American option, *Annals of Applied Probability*, **2**, 1–23.

Nyborg, K.G. (1996) The use and pricing of convertible bonds, *Applied Mathematical Finance*, 167–190.

Reiner, E. & Rubinstein, M. (1991) Breaking down the barriers, *RISK*, **4** (8), 28–35.

Rich, D. (1994) The mathematical foundation of barrier option pricing theory, *Advances in Futures and Options Research*, 267–311.

Ritchken, P. (1995) On pricing barrier options, *Journal of Derivatives*, 19–28.

Roberts, G.O. & Shortland, C. (1997) Pricing barrier options with time dependent coefficient, *Mathematical Finance*, **7** (1), 83–93.

Rogers, L.C.G. & Stapleton, E.J. (1997) Fast accurate binomial pricing, *Finance and Stochastics*, **2**, 3–17.

Rogers, L.C.G. & Zane, O. (1997) Valuing moving barrier options, *Journal of Computational Finance*, **1** (1), 5–11.

Stein, J.C. (1992) *Convertible bonds as "back door" financing*. NBER Working Paper.

Takahashi, A., Kobayashi, T. & Nakagawa, N. (2001) Pricing convertible bonds with default risk, *Journal of Fixed Income*, **11**, 20–29.

Tsiveriotis, K. & Fernandez, C. (1998) Valuing convertible bonds with credit risk, *Journal of Fixed Income*, **8**, 95–102.

Wilckens, S. & Röder, K. (2003) Reverse convertibles and discount certificates in the case of constant and stochastic volatilities, *Financial Markets and Portfolio Management*, **17** (1), 76–102.

Zhang, P.G. (1998) *Exotic options, 2nd edition*, World Scientific.

6

Equity-Linked Notes

6.1 INTRODUCTION

Structured products in which the derivative is included in the repayment plan may be very risky, particularly if they entail a short position in the option. In fact, the investor remains exposed to the risk that the exercise of the option could erode most, if not all, of the principal invested. It is for this reason that derivatives are included in the coupon plan of many structured products.

In this chapter we will present a review of the main choices available to structure a coupon plan. We will touch upon the main techniques used to structure single coupon products. Again, one would have to differentiate the main risk involved in the products – that is, the stock or the index to which the coupon is linked – from optionalities included to adjust the price and the riskiness of the product. We will see that these targets would quite naturally lead us to use exotic options, such as barrier, Asian and multivariate (basket and rainbow) options.

6.2 SINGLE COUPON PRODUCTS

The simplest example of a structured coupon plan is provided by equity-linked notes (ELNs) with a single coupon payment. In their simplest form, they promise full repayment of principal, and interest payment at maturity, based on the performance of a stock or an equity index. The coupon is typically written as

$$\text{Coupon} = \max\left[\frac{S(T) - S(0)}{S(0)}, \ r_g\right] \tag{6.1}$$

where T is the maturity date of the bond, 0 is the issuance date, and r_g is the guaranteed return. As $S(0)$ is known and fixed from the origin all through the lifetime of the contract, it may be considered as a constant, and we may rescale the value of the underlying asset by this value. The coupon payoff is then

$$\text{Coupon} = \max\left(s(T) - 1, \ r_g\right) = r_g + \max\left(s(T) - (1 + r_g), \ 0\right) \tag{6.2}$$

with $s(T) \equiv S(T)/S(0)$. The coupon is then made up by a deterministic component r_g and a call option. The value of the product at any time t is then

$$\text{ELN}(t) = v(t, T)(1 + r_g) + \text{Call}\left[s(t), t; 1 + r_g, T\right] \tag{6.3}$$

The leverage feature, and the value of the derivative component of the contract, are tuned by the strike price of the option, and thus by the guaranteed return r_g. In order to understand the nature of the contract, recall that the call option corresponds to a long position in the underlying asset funded with debt. Moreover, the amount of debt embedded in the call option is equal to the product of the strike times the risk-neutral probability that the option ends in the money: that is, $(1 + r_g)Q(s(T) > 1 + r_g)$. Then, the equity-linked product corresponds to the replicating portfolio

$$\text{ELN}(t) = v(t, T)(1 + r_g)(1 - Q(s(T) > 1 + r_g)) + \Delta_c s(t) \tag{6.4}$$

From this point of view, the product supplies a dynamic capital-protected trading strategy. The main task of this product is then to provide exposure to equity risk. Of course, the product itself is less flexible than a freely managed dynamic trading strategy. In order to improve the product, a structurer would ask what could go wrong as the market moves in one direction or the other, and what ancillary options could be introduced to ease these problems.

In particular, the options are easy to see:

- As the underlying asset moves down, the equity content of the investment vanishes. Following a huge decrease in the market, the investor may remain locked into a zero-coupon bond for a very long maturity.
- As the underlying asset moves up, the interest cost suffered by the issuer increases, owing to the increase of both leverage and equity returns. In principle, following a sharp increase in the market the prospects of interest costs can become exhorbitant and foreshadow liquidity problems for the borrower.

Enhancing the flexibility of the product would then call for contractual provisions directed to

- reset the strike in case of a massive decrease in the equity market;
- reduce the participation of the interest payments to equity return;
- condition the indexation scheme on an upper barrier;
- allow either the issuer or the investor to put an end to the contract before maturity.

6.2.1   Crash protection

As pointed out previously, a problem with the standard equity-linked note is that following a huge decrease in the market the investor participation in the equity market may vanish. If the investor cannot get out of the contract or sell the note on the secondary market, he may remain locked into an unwanted zero-coupon bond investment. A natural way to solve this problem is to include a clause stating that if the market falls down to a barrier h, with respect to the initial value, the strike is automatically reset down to that value. This clause is called "*crash protection*".

From the point of view of the replicating portfolio, an equity-linked note ELN featuring a crash protection clause can be represented as a position in two barrier options. Formally, the replicating portfolio is

$$\text{ELN}(t) = v(t, T)(1 + r_g) + \text{DOC}\left[s(t), t; 1 + r_g, T, h\right] + \text{DIC}\left[s(t), t, h, T, h\right] \tag{6.5}$$

and includes a down-and-out call with the original strike and barrier h, and a down-and-in call with the same barrier and strike h. In plain words, if the barrier h is reached, the initial call option embedded in the product vanishes and is substituted by another one with strike h. Recalling again the symmetry between "out" and "in" options we get

$$\text{ELN}(t) = v(t, T)(1 + r_g) + \text{Call}\left[s(t), t; 1 + r_g, T\right] + \text{DIC}\left[s(t), t, h, T, h\right]$$
$$- \text{DIC}\left[s(t), t, 1 + r_g, T, h\right] \tag{6.6}$$

It is then possible to disentangle the value of the crash protection clause in the product as

$$\text{Crash protection} = \text{DIC}\left[s(t), t, h, T, h\right] - \text{DIC}\left[s(t), t, 1 + r_g, T, h\right] \tag{6.7}$$

Notice that as the value of call options is decreasing in the strike price, the value of the crash protection is positive, and increases the value of the product. This comes as no surprise, of course, as the option to reset the strike downward is in favour of the investor.

Structuring the crash protection clause: setting the strike

Consider an equity-linked note indexed at the Italian stock market. The structurer may be willing to grant a "crash protection" to increase the value of the product. Which choice variables can he adjust to set up the product and tune up the value of the crash protection itself? One such variable is of course the level of the barrier. The value of the crash protection clause is not a monotone function of the barrier. Of course, it is very close to zero if the barrier is very high and close to $1 + r_g$, but it also tends to zero as the barrier tends to zero. In fact, decreasing the barrier has a negative impact on the value of the second down-and-in option, i.e. the one with strike $1 + r_g$. On the other hand, this downward effect on the first down-and-in call is mitigated by the upward impact associated to a reduction of the strike down to the barrier level.

Structuring the crash protection clause: outside barrier options

An alternative choice is to link the downward revision of the strike to a decrease in another market. In our case, the equity-linked note is indexed to the Italian stock market, while the crash protection is triggered by a decline of a global market index (the MSCI global index, for example). This structure is reasonable because it stresses the role of the "crash protection" as a tool by which to address the impact of systematic risk on the value of the structure: an investor is interested in a long position exposure to the Italian equity risk factor, but wants to be protected from global equity risk.

In the above framework, the crash protection clause would entail an "outside" barrier option. An outside barrier option is an option in which the underlying asset and the barrier trigger are different variables. Of course, the value of the barrier option, and consequently of the crash protection clause, would increase with the dependence structure of the two assets: the underlying and the trigger. Outside barrier options have not been exaustively studied.

The closed form solution in the standard Black–Scholes setting was provided by Heynen and Kat (1994) and Carr (1995). A recent paper by Cherubini and Romagnoli (2006), that we briefly review here, proposes a link between the dependence structure of the two variables and that of the events connected to them. Assume that there is a specific dependence structure between the two markets; in our case, the Italian stock index and the MSCI global index, represented by the copula function $C(Q_1, Q_2)$. The question is: What is the consistent (compatible, would be the correct term in statistics) dependence structure of the Italian stock index and the running minimum of the MSCI global index? Cherubini and Romagnoli found that

$$\overline{C}\left(\overline{Q}_1, \overline{Q}_{M2}\right) = \overline{C}\left(\overline{Q}_1, \overline{Q}_{M2}, \overline{Q}_2\right) = \overline{C}\left(\overline{Q}_1, \min\left(\overline{Q}_{M2}, \overline{Q}_2\right)\right) \tag{6.8}$$

where $\overline{C}\left(\overline{Q}_1, \overline{Q}_2\right)$ denotes the survival copula of the two markets, $\overline{Q}_i$ the survival marginals and $\overline{Q}_{M2}$ the survival marginal of the running maximum of the second variable (the MSCI index in our case). In plain words, we have recovered the dependence structure of the joint event that the option on the Italian index ends in the money and the MSCI remains above the barrier until expiration of the contract. Using this pricing kernel, the price of the outside barrier option can be easily computed by numerical integration.

Exploiting the dependence structure between the underlying asset and the barrier variable enables the structurer to adjust the value of the crash protection clause in a very flexible way. Figure 6.1 shows the difference in value of the cash protection clause under different copula functions.

Note that the value is higher with the Clayton copula than with the Gaussian one. The reason for that rests on the impact of tail dependence on the value of outside barrier options. As it is intuitive, higher tail dependence decreases the value of *knock-out* options in favour of *knock-in* options because it increases the probability that an extreme event in the underlying asset may be associated with an extreme event in the trigger variable.

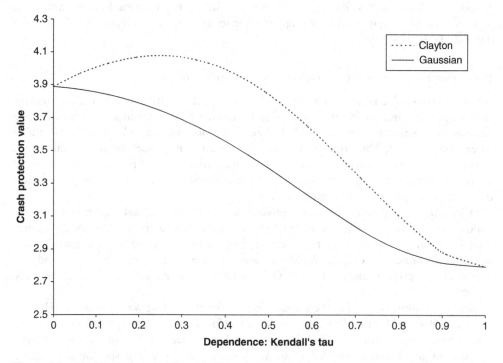

Figure 6.1   Outside crash protection with different dependence structures: Gaussian vs Clayton copula

6.2.2   Reducing funding cost

From the point of view of the issuer, a problem with this kind of product is that it may raise the cost of funding to extremely high levels if the equity market booms. In such a case, the increase in debt service costs may endanger the soundness of the borrower. We briefly review here three straightforward solutions to this problem that are usually implemented in the market.

Participation rate

A very easy way to curb this possibility is to index the interest payment to a percentage of the performance of the equity market. The percentage is called participation rate. In this case the coupon is

$$\text{Coupon} = \max \left[\alpha \frac{S(T) - S(0)}{S(0)}, r_g \right] \tag{6.9}$$

where α is the participation rate. The value of the product will then be

$$\text{ELN}(t) = v(t, T)(1 + r_g) + \alpha \, \text{Call} \left[s(t), t; \ 1 + r_g, T \right] \tag{6.10}$$

Call spreads

A more radical approach to reduce the cost of funding to a fixed amount, if the market performs above a given level, is to use either a call spread or a barrier option. In the first case the payoff will be

$$\text{Coupon} = \min \left\{ \max \left[\frac{S(T) - S(0)}{S(0)}, r_g \right], r_{cap} \right\} \tag{6.11}$$

where obviously $r_{cap} > r_g$. Considering that $\min(a, b) = a - \max(a - b, 0)$ we obtain that

$$\text{Coupon} = \max \left[\frac{S(T) - S(0)}{S(0)}, r_g \right] - \max \left\{ \max \left[\frac{S(T) - S(0)}{S(0)}, r_g \right] - r_{cap}, 0 \right\} \tag{6.12}$$

from which

$$\text{Coupon} = \max \left(\frac{S(T) - S(0)}{S(0)}, r_g \right) - \max \left(\frac{S(T) - S(0)}{S(0)} - r_{cap}, 0 \right) \tag{6.13}$$

Up-and-out option

An alternative way to reduce the cost of funding is to make the indexed payment conditional on the underlying variable growing beyond a given threshold over the life of the contract. Of course, this amounts to the inclusion of a barrier in the call option. The type of barrier is clearly up-and-out.

6.2.3 Callability/putability: compound options

A more radical way of addressing the problem in which the value of the embedded option could move in either direction during the life of the contract, is to terminate the contract before its natural maturity.

Consider the problem in which the underlying asset may decrease, leaving the investor locked into a financial product that yields much less than expected. This problem could be addressed by granting the investor the opportunity to get out of the contract as soon as its value falls below a given threshold. Consider a structured product with payoff

$$ELN(T) = 1 + r_g + \max\left(S(T) - (1 + r_g), 0\right) \tag{6.14}$$

and assume that the investor may terminate the contract at time τ, and retrieve his principal. Then, the value of the product at the time of exercise of the option would be

$$ELN(\tau) = \max\left[1, v(\tau, T)(1 + r_g) + \text{CALL}(s, \tau; 1 + r_g, T), 0\right]$$
$$= v(\tau, T)(1 + r_g) + \text{CALL}(s, \tau; 1 + r_g, T) + \max[1 - v(\tau, T)(1 + r_g)$$
$$- \text{CALL}(s, \tau; 1 + r_g, T), 0] \tag{6.15}$$

The value of the early termination of the contract is then a put option held by the investor against the issuer. The strike price of the option is

$$1 - v(t, T)(1 + r_g) \tag{6.16}$$

and the underlying asset is represented by the call option $\text{CALL}(s\tau, \tau, 1 + r_g, T)$. An option taking another option as its underlying asset is called a *compound option*. Allowing for putability introduces a compound option into the contract.

If one allows for stochastic interest rates, the pricing problem becomes even more involved. In fact, notice that the strike can be written as

$$1 - v(\tau, T)(1 + r_g) = v(\tau, T)(r(\tau, T) + r_g) \tag{6.17}$$

where $r(\tau, T)$ is the interest rate return on the risk-free asset for an investment stating at time τ and maturing at time T. From this point of view, putability can be viewed as a spread option. Its payoff would be in fact

$$\max\left[(v(\tau, T)r_g + v(\tau, T)r(\tau, T) - \text{CALL}(s, \tau; 1 + r_g, T), 0\right] \tag{6.18}$$

It is evident that a change of numeraire (namely, using the discount factor $v(t, T)$ as numeraire) may simplify the pricing formula. Under the $Q(T)$ forward martingale measure we have in fact

$$v(t, T)E_{Q(t)} \max\left[r_g + r(\tau, T) - \frac{\text{CALL}\left(s, \tau; 1 + r_g, T\right)}{v(\tau, T)}, 0\right] \tag{6.19}$$

By the same token, consider the case in which the underlying asset may increase by a substantial rise in the cost of funds. The problem can be addressed by granting the issuer the right to get out of the contract as soon as its cost rises above a given threshold. The value of the product at the time of exercise of the option would then be

$$ELN(\tau) = \min\left[1, v(\tau, T)(1 + r_g) + CALL\left(s, \tau; 1 + r_g, T\right), 0\right]$$
$$= v(\tau, T)(1 + r_g) + CALL\left(s, \tau; 1 + r_g, T\right) - \max\left[CALL\left(s, \tau; 1 + r_g, T\right)\right.$$
$$\left. -(1 - v(\tau, T)(1 + r_g)), 0\right] \tag{6.20}$$

and it is easy to see that this is a call type of option. Callability – which is a very standard feature in fixed income products – becomes quite complex even in very simply structured product such this example. In fact, exactly as in the putability example above, callability becomes a *compound spread option* with payoff

$$\max\left\lfloor CALL\left(s, \tau; 1 + r_g, T\right) - v(\tau, T)r(\tau, T) - v(\tau, T)r_g \right\rfloor \tag{6.21}$$

In general, putability and callability can be represented in the same formula by writing

$$ELN(\tau) = v(\tau, T)(1 + r_g) + CALL\left(s, \tau; 1 + r_g, T\right)$$
$$- \rho \max\left[\omega\, CALL\left(s, \tau; 1 + r_g, T\right) - \rho\left(1 - v(\tau, T)(1 + r_g)\right), 0\right] \tag{6.22}$$

with $\rho = 1$ for callable notes and $\rho = -1$ for putable bonds.

Compound option: pricing issues

Considering a Black–Scholes environment, the payoff for a European compound option is given by:

$$\max\left\{0, \phi PV_t\left[\max\left(0, \eta S^* - \eta X_u | T\right] - \phi X\right\}\right. \tag{6.23}$$

where S^* is the value of the stock underlying the underlying option, X_u is the underlying strike price and X is the compound strike. τ is the expiry date of the compound and T is the expiry date of the underlying option. The parameters ϕ and η are binary variables that take values of v or 1. The value -1 is given as 1 when the underlying option is a call, and -1 when the underlying option is a put. Parameter ϕ is v of m 1 when the compound is a call and -1 when the compound is a put.

This application of compound options was first considered by Geske (1977), followed similarly by Geske (1979), Selby & Hodges (1987). The variables considered when valuing a compound option are:

- price of the underlying asset of the underlying option (S);
- exercise prices of underlying option and the compound option (X_1 and X_2);
- dividend payments (if any) on the underlying asset (q);
- risk-free rate (r);
- expiry dates for the underlying option (T_1) and the compound option (T_2).

The four formulas for pricing the options are:

(1) call on call:

$$\text{CALL}_{\text{Call}} = S\,e^{-qT_2}M\,(a_1, b_1, \rho) - X_2 e^{-rT_2}M\,(a_2, b_2, \rho) - e^{-rT_1}X_1 N(a_2) \qquad (6.24)$$

(2) call on put:

$$\text{CALL}_{\text{put}} = -S\,e^{-qT_2}M\,(-a_1, -b_1, \rho) + X_2\,e^{-rT_2}M\,(-a_2, -b_2, \rho) - e^{-rT_1}X_1 N(-a_2)$$
$$(6.25)$$

(3) put on call:

$$\text{Put}_{\text{call}} = X_2\,e^{-rT_2}M\,(-a_2, b_2, -\rho) - S\,e^{-qT_2}M\,(-a_1, b_1, -\rho) + e^{-rT_1}X_1 N(-a_2) \quad (6.26)$$

(4) put on put:

$$\text{Put}_{\text{Put}} = -X_2\,e^{-rT_2}M\,(a_2, -b_2, -\rho) + S\,e^{-qT_2}M\,(a_1, -b_1, -\rho) + e^{-rT_1}X_1 N(a_2) \quad (6.27)$$

where the variables are defined as:

$$a_1 = \frac{\ln\,(S/S^*) + \left(r - D + 0.5 \cdot \sigma^2\right)\tau}{\sigma\sqrt{T\tau_1}} \qquad (6.28)$$

$$a_2 = a_1 - \sigma\sqrt{T\tau_1} \qquad (6.29)$$

$$b_1 = \frac{\ln\,(S/X_2) + \left(r - D + 0.5 \cdot \sigma^2\right)\tau}{\sigma\sqrt{T\tau_2}} \qquad (6.30)$$

$$b_2 = b_1 - \sigma\sqrt{T\tau_2} \qquad (6.31)$$

and S^* is the critical stock price for which the following criteria holds:

$$\text{CALL}\,(S^*,\ X_1,\ D,\ r,\ \sigma,\ T_2 - T_1) = X_2 \qquad (6.32)$$

This can be solved iteratively using the Newton–Rhapson method.

For overlapping Brownian increments, we can denote the correlation of the compound and underlying options as $\rho = \sqrt{\tau/T}$. Also note that, in the equations, $M(a, b, \rho)$ is the bivariate cumulative distribution function.

Pricing of a compound option using the Option class

The pricing of a compound option in our Java framework is very simple. First we have to define a new pricing model implementing the previously discussed formulas. It is very natural to build a new class which is a subclass of the `CBlackScholes` class (see Figure 6.2)

We shall also define the `CNormBivariate` class which contains methods for the computation of the cumulative binormal distribution. The algorithm used is described in the classic work *Options, Futures and Other Derivatives* (Hull, 2003).

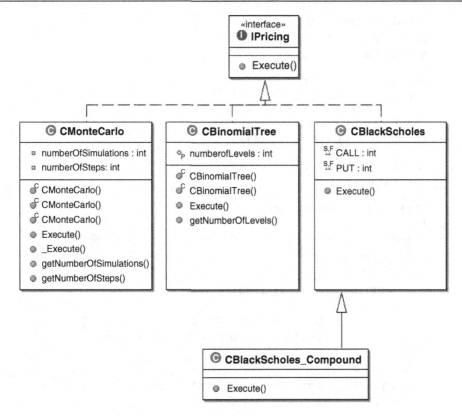

Figure 6.2   The CBlackScholes_Compound class

```
package pricing_algorithm;

public class CNormBivariate {
  /**
   *-----------------------------------------------------------
   */
  public double Cum( double a,
                     double b,
                     double rho)
  {
    CNormST    N       = new CNormST();
    double AA[] = {0.325303, 0.4211071, 0.1334425,
                   0.006374323};
    double BB[] = {0.1337764, 0.6243247, 1.3425378,
                   2.2626645};

    double d     =  0;
    double somma =  0;
    double rho1  =  0;
    double rho2  =  0;
```

```
double delta =  0;
double NA    =  0;
double NB    =  0;

int  i      =  0;
int  j      =  0;

if(rho == 1) rho = 0.999999999;
if(rho == -1) rho = -0.999999999;

NA = N.Cum(a);
NB = N.Cum(b);

if(a <= 0 && b <= 0 && rho <= 0)
{
   somma = 0;
   for(i = 1; i <= 4; i++)
   {
      for(j = 1; j <= 4; j++)
         {
             somma = somma + AA[i - 1] * AA[j - 1] *
             f(BB[i - 1], BB[j - 1], a, b, rho);
         }
   }
   return Math.sqrt(1 - rho * rho) * somma /
   Math.PI;
}
else
{
   if(a * b * rho <= 0)
   {
      if(a <= 0)
      {
      return NA - Cum(a, -b, -rho);
      }
      else if(b <= 0)
      {
      return NB - Cum(-a, b, -rho);
      }
      else if(rho <= 0)
      {
      return NA + NB - 1 + Cum(-a, -b, rho);
      }
   }
   else
   {
       d = Math.sqrt(a * a - 2 * rho * a * b + b * b);
       rho1 = (rho * a - b) * Math.signum(a) / d;
```

```
            rho2 = (rho * b - a) * Math.signum(b) / d;
            delta = 0.25 * (1 - Math.signum(a) * Math.signum(b));
            return Cum(a, 0, rho1) + Cum(b, 0, rho2) - delta;
        }
      }
      return 0;
}
/**
*-----------------------------------------------------------
*/
private double f( double x,
                  double y,
                  double a,
                  double b,
                  double rho,)
                  {
   double a_prime = 0;
   double b_prime = 0;
   double f = 0;
   double d = 0;

   d = Math.sqrt(2 * (1 - rho * rho));
   a_prime = a / d;
   b_prime = b / d;

   f = a_prime * (2 * x - a_prime) + b_prime *
       (2 * y - b_prime) +
       2 * rho * (x - a_prime) * (y - b_prime);
   return Math.exp(f);
}
```

This is the code for the `CBlackScholes_Compound` class:

```
package pricing_algorithm;

import finobject.COption;

public class CBlackScholes_Compound extends CBlackScholes {

   /**
   * note: this method overwrite the Execute method of the super
     class
   * CBlackScholes
   */

   public double Execute(COption option){
      return BS_Compound(option);
   }
```

```
/**
*-----------------------------------------------------------------
* Function Name
* @author Giovanni Della Lunga
* @param option the option to be evaluated
* @return option fair value
*/
private double BS_Compound(COption option)
{
   System.out.println("Running Black & Scholes Algorithm for
   Compound Option");
   option.printOut();

   CNormST           N   = new CNormST();
   CNormBivariate    M   = new CNormBivariate();

   double price = 0;

   /* gathering information about the compound and underlying
      option */
   double    T1    = option.getExercise().getExpirationTime();
   double    K1    = option.getPayoff().getStrike();
   double    r     = (option.getDiscounting()).
                        getDiscountRate();
   double    q     = 0;
   int       theta1 = 0;

   if((option.getPayoff()).value(K1 + 1) > 0 )
      theta1 = 1;
   else
      theta1 = -1;

   COption underOption = new COption();
   underOption          = (COption)option.getUnderlying();

   double    T2          = underOption.getExercise().
                              getExpirationTime();
   double    K2          = underOption.getPayoff().getStrike();
   double    S0          = underOption.getUnderlying().getLevel();
   double    sigma       = underOption.getUnderlying()
                              .getVolatility();
   int       theta2     = 0;

   if((underOption.getPayoff()).value(K2 + 1) > 0 )
      theta2 = 1;
   else
      theta2 = -1;

   /* first of all we search for the asset price at time T1
```

for which the underlying option value at time T1 equals K1 where T1 is the exercise time of the compound option and K1 its strike value. The computation of this value is performed with a simple Newton–Rapson algorithm. For a more robust procedure we strongly suggest to replace with the secant method.

```java
*/

double zero         = 0;
double optionPrice  = 0;
double delta        = 0;
double correction   = 0;
double S            = S0;
double ERROR        = 1e-6;

do{
  optionPrice = BS_Formula(theta2,S, K2, T1, r,q,sigma);
  zero        = K1 - optionPrice;
  delta       = BS_Delta(theta2,S, K2, T1, r,q,sigma);
  correction  = zero/delta;
  S           = S + correction;
}while(Math.abs(correction) > ERROR);

double a1 = (Math.log(S0/S) + (r - q +0.5*sigma*sigma)*T1)/
          (sigma*Math.sqrt(T1));
double a2 = a1 - sigma*Math.sqrt(T1);

double b1 = (Math.log(S0/K2) + (r - q +0.5*sigma*sigma)*T2)/
          (sigma*Math.sqrt(T2));
double b2 = b1 - sigma*Math.sqrt(T2);

double ert1 = Math.exp(-r*T1);
double ert2 = Math.exp(-r*T2);
double eqt2 = Math.exp(-q*T1);
double rtt  = Math.sqrt(T1/T2);

if(theta1 == CALL && theta2 == CALL){
   price = S0 * eqt2 * M.Cum( a1, b1, rtt) - K2*ert2 *
   M.Cum( a2, b2, rtt)- ert1 * K1 * N.Cum( a2);
}
else if(theta1 == CALL && theta2 == PUT){
   price = K2 * ert2 * M.Cum(-a2,-b2, rtt) - S0 * eqt2 *
   M.Cum(-a1,-b1, rtt)- ert1 * K1 * N.Cum(-a2);
}
else if(theta1 == PUT && theta2 == CALL){
   price = K2 * ert2 * M.Cum(-a2, b2,-rtt) - S0 * eqt2 *
   M.Cum(-a1, b1,-rtt)+ ert1 * K1 * N.Cum(-a2);
}
else if(theta1 == PUT && theta2 == PUT){
   price = S0 * eqt2 * M.Cum( a1,-b1,-rtt) - K2 * ert2 *
```

```
     M.Cum( a2,-b2,-rtt)+ ert1 * K1 * N.Cum( a2);
   }
   return price;
 }
}
```

Now we can simply generalize the previously discussed code in order to price a Compound Option. It is worth noting that we only have to define a simple Option as an underlying of the compound option. The code is:

```
//-----------------------------------------------------------------
// Compound Option

exercise = new CExercise_European(T, GregorianCalendar.YEAR);
payoff   =  new CPayoff_PutPV(K);

COption simpleOption = new COption(discounting,
                                  equity,
                                  exercise,
                                  payoff,
                                  null);

exercise    = new CExercise_European(0.5 * T,
              GregorianCalendar.YEAR);
payoff      = new CPayoff_CallPV(900.0);
priceModel  = new CBlackScholes_Compound();

COption compoundOption = new COption(discounting,
                                     simpleOption,
                                     exercise,
                                     payoff,
                                     priceModel);

price = compoundOption.Pricing();
```

6.3 SMOOTHING THE PAYOFF: ASIAN OPTIONS

A possible problem with the kind of product we have just described is that the payoff is linked to a realization of the performance of the index in the very distant future. A typical maturity for these products is five years. So, in order to evaluate the product, one has to figure out the risk-neutral distribution of the underlying asset five year from now. This raises two problems. The first, which we will not discuss here, is that five-year options are not traded on the market, and we do not have a unique and precise market price for the derivative contract at hand. The second – even assuming that a market for five-year options existed – is that their price would probably be very high. Intuitively, this is due to the obvious fact that the degree of uncertainty about the performance of the underlying asset is growing with the length of its horizon. Who can know what the stock market values will be in five years?

There are two obvious ways to solve this problem. The first is to index the coupon to some average value sampled over a period rather than at a point in time. The second is to abandon the single coupon structure and switch to the design of an indexed coupon stream. Here we discuss the first solution, i.e. that of smoothing the payoff.

In terms of payoff notation, we have

$$\text{Coupon} = \max \left[\frac{\sum_{i=1}^{n} S(t_i)/n - S(0)}{S(0)}, r_g \right] \tag{6.33}$$

where $\{t_1, t_2, \ldots, t_n\}$ is a set of dates.

The coupon is then decomposed as

$$\text{Coupon} = \max \left[\sum_{i=1}^{n} s(t_i)/n - 1, r_g \right] = r_g + \max \left[\sum_{i=1}^{n} s(t_i)/n - (1 + r_g), 0 \right] \tag{6.34}$$

and the option involved is an Asian option. More exactly, it is an "arithmetic average Asian option".

6.3.1 Price approximation by "moment matching"

The arithmetic average option is one of the few pricing problems that do not have a closed form solution under the Black–Scholes model. The reason is that linear combinations of log-normal variables are not log-normally distributed, and their distribution is unknown. The most effective pricing solution is to resort to simulation, as we will discuss below. For the time being, we illustrate here an approximation technique, based on "moment matching". The typical algorithm used is that proposed by Turnbull and Wakeman (1991). The basic assumption is that under the risk-neutral probability measure Q the underlying asset follows the geometric Brownian motion, as in the standard Black–Scholes framework

$$dS(t) = (r - q)S(t)\,dt + \sigma S(t)\,dZ(t) \tag{6.35}$$

where q is the instantaneous dividend yield.

The idea is to compute the first two moments of the distribution of the average price, denoted $A(t_n)$, and imagine an "auxiliary" geometric Brownian motion yielding the same moments. The price is obtained by applying the Black–Scholes formula on this "auxiliary" process. Assume that the sample of dates is $\{t_1, t_2, \ldots, t_n\}$. Then the algorithm consists of the following steps:

- Compute the *forward* price at each reference date t_i: $F_i = \exp[(r - q)(t_i - t)S(t)]$
- Compute the first moment of forward prices: $S(t)[F_1 + F_2 + \ldots F_i + \ldots F_n]/n \equiv S(t)M_1$. This represents the first moment of the risk-neutral distribution: $E_Q(A(t_n)) = S(t)M_1$.

- Compute the second moment of forward prices. To this purpose, define a matrix **M** of dimension n such that the diagonal elements are

$$m_{ii} = S^2(t)\exp\left[(2(r-q)+\sigma^2)(t_i - t)\right] \tag{6.36}$$

and the off-diagonal elements are

$$m_{ij} = S^2(t)m_{ii}\exp\left[(r-q)(t_j - t)\right] \tag{6.37}$$

with $t_j > t_i$. Then, define $\mathbf{e}'\mathbf{M}\mathbf{e} = S^2(t)M_2$, with $\mathbf{e}$ the unit vector. Then, under the risk-neutral measure the second moment from the origin of the average price is $E_Q(A^2(t_n)) = S^2(t)M_2$.
- Assume an "auxiliary" process $A^*(t)$ with dynamics

$$dA(t) = (r-q_A)A^*(t)\,dt + \sigma_A A^*(t)\,dz(t) \tag{6.38}$$

and a starting value $A^*(t) = S(t)$. Obviously the distribution of the $A^*(t_n)$ would be log-normal with moments

$$E_Q(A^*(t_n)) = S(t)\exp[(r-q_A)(t_n - t)]$$
$$E_Q(A^{*2}(t_n)) = S^2(t)\exp[(2(r-q_A)+\sigma_A^2)(t_n - t)] \tag{6.39}$$

- we calibrate q_A and σ_A, computing by "moment matching"

$$M_1 = \exp[(r-q_A)(t_n - t)]$$
$$M_2 = \exp[(2(r-q_A)+\sigma_A^2)(t_n - t)] \tag{6.40}$$

- Compute the value of the Asian option using the Black–Scholes formula with parameters q_A and σ_A.

6.3.2 Variable frequency sampling and seasoning process

In typical Asian option applications to equity-linked notes, the sampling frequency is often scheduled to change over the life to the contract. In a typical contract, say on a five-year maturity, the final reference value for the computation of the coupon would be a combination of

- monthly frequency samples for the first and second years
- quarterly frequency samples for the third and four years
- half-year frequency samples for the fifth year.

Of course, this structure is conceived to modulate the smoothing effect over the life span of the product. In particular, such a smoothing effect would decrease as time elapses.

Another effect linked to the passage of time is due to the fact that the option undergoes a "seasoning process". At a given point in time τ, the value of the option would in fact depend on the accrued average process $A(\tau)$. However, the value of a seasoned Asian option can be easily transformed into that of an unseasoned one, provided we have a rescaling factor and a suitable change of the strike. Given the original strike k and a number p of observations already collected over the life of the option (out of the total number of n), the strike is reset to the value

$$k^* = [p/(n-p)](k - A_p) + k$$

where A_p is the average value of the p observations collected. The value of the seasoned Asian option is then

$$\text{SAsian} = [(n-p)/p](\text{Asian}(s(\tau), \tau; k^*, t_n))$$

6.4 DIGITAL AND CLIQUET NOTES

We pointed out above that the long maturity of a single equity-linked coupon may be a problem, but smoothing the payoff function may help to address it. A more radical solution, however, would be to move beyond the single coupon structure. One would design a stream of coupons whose values are totally or partially determined by the performance of some stock or market index. Here we review some basic choices that the structurer may consider.

6.4.1 Digital notes

The first choice is that of a fixed payment if the market index is above some given strike level at some reference date. For the sake of simplicity assume the reference dates $\{t_1, t_2, \ldots, t_n\}$. The description of the coupon is in this case digital

$$\text{Coupon}(t_i) = \begin{cases} c & S(t_i) > \beta S(t_0) \\ 0 & S(t_i) \le \beta S(t_0) \end{cases} \tag{6.41}$$

where β is a barrier parameter that sets the strike of the option. This structure is particularly used in a multivariate setting, and will be discussed below. It is also known as an "altiplano" note. The coupon plan is represented by a stream of digital options.

The price of a digital option (DC) is particularly easy to recover. From Breeden and Litzenberger (1978) we have that the price of a digital call, with strike K and exercise T, is given by

$$\text{DC}(S, t; K, T) = -\frac{\partial \text{Call}(S, t; K, T)}{\partial K} \tag{6.42}$$

This representation is valid for all pricing models, and only rests on the assumption of absence of arbitrage. It may easily be verified that in the Black–Scholes setting we have

$$\text{DC}(S, t; K, T) = v(t, T)\Phi\left[\frac{\ln(F(S, T)/K) - \sigma^2(T-t)}{\sigma\sqrt{T-t}}\right] \tag{6.43}$$

where $F(S, T) \equiv S(t)/v(t, T)$ is the *forward price* of S for delivery at time T.

6.4.2 Cliquet notes

Consider the following coupon plan. Coupons are paid at dates $\{t_1, t_2, \ldots, t_n\}$. In each period the coupon, or part of it, is determined on the basis of the performance of the reference stock or equity index in the same period. That is, the coupon paid at time t_i is given by

$$\text{Coupon}(t_i) = \max\left[\frac{S(t_i) - S(t_{i-1})}{S(t_{i-1})}, 0\right] \tag{6.44}$$

The coupons are given by a sequence of at-the-money options struck at the beginning of the coupon period and paid at the end of it. Products like these are called *forward start options*. A sequence of forward start options are called *cliquet options* (or *ratchet options*). For these reasons such structured products are called *cliquet notes*.

It is easy to see how to modify the payoff in order to set bounds to interest payments. For example, to set a cap r_{cap} to the coupon, it is easy to resort to a call spread:

$$\text{Coupon}(t_i) = \max\left[\frac{S(t_i) - S(t_{i-1})}{S(t_{i-1})}, 0\right] - \max\left[\frac{S(t_i) - (1 + r_{\text{cap}})S(t_{i-1})}{S(t_{i-1})}, 0\right] \tag{6.45}$$

and the interest payment is capped. This option is sold by the investor to the issuer, thus reducing the value of both the coupon stream and the product.

6.4.3 Forward start options

In most models the price of forward start options is obtained by the property of linear homogeneity of the price in the underlying asset and the strike. Explicitly, we have

$$\text{CALL}\,(cS(t)\,;\,cK, T) = v(t, T)\, E_Q[\max\,(cS(T) - cK, 0)] =$$
$$= v(t, T)\, c E_Q[\max\,(S(T) - K, 0)] = c\,\text{CALL}\,(S(t)\,;\,K, T) \tag{6.46}$$

Assume one wants to price, at time t, an option starting at time τ with strike $\alpha S(\tau)$. At time τ the value of the option will be $\text{Call}(S(\tau), \tau; \alpha S(\tau); T)$. Using linear homogeneity we have

$$\text{CALL}\,(S(\tau)\,;\,\alpha S(\tau),\ T - \tau) = c\,\text{CALL}\left[\frac{S(\tau)}{c};\ \frac{\alpha S(\tau)}{c},\ T - \tau\right] \tag{6.47}$$

If we define: $c \equiv S(\tau)/S(t)$ we can compute

$$\text{CALL}\,(S(\tau)\,;\,\alpha S(\tau),\,T - \tau) = S(\tau)\,\frac{\text{CALL}\,(S(t)\,;\,\alpha S(t),\,T - \tau)}{S(t)} \tag{6.48}$$

This defines a static replicating portfolio for the option. Actually, the value of the forward start option at time t with τ amounts to N stocks, with N given by

$$N = \frac{\text{CALL}\,(S(t)\,;\,\alpha S(t),\,T - \tau)}{S(t)} \tag{6.49}$$

Computing the expected value under the risk-neutral measure Q and discounting back to time t we get

$$v(t, \tau) E_Q(S(\tau)) N = N \frac{v(t, \tau) q(t, \tau) S(t)}{v(t, \tau)} = Nq(t, \tau) S(t) \qquad (6.50)$$

where $q(t, \tau)$ is the cumulated flow of dividends from time t to τ. Using the definition of N we get

$$\text{FSCALL}(S(t), t; \tau, \alpha S(\tau), T) = q(t, \tau) \text{CALL}(S(t), t; , \alpha S(t), T - \tau) \qquad (6.51)$$

The analysis may be carried over to time varying volatility by simply substituting the forward volatility in the equation above. Accounting for stochastic volatility makes life more difficult as the pricing formula requires a change in measure (see Musiela and Rutkowski, 2005, quoted in Chapter 1.)

6.4.4 Reverse cliquet notes

Consider a product like the following. Coupon is paid as a lump sum at maturity of the note, time t_n. The coupon is determined according to the function

$$\text{Coupon} = \max \left[D - \sum_{i=1}^{n} \min \left[\frac{S(t_i) - S(t_{i-1})}{S(t_{i-1})}, 0 \right], 0 \right] \qquad (6.52)$$

where D is a percentage sum and the set of reference dates is $\{t_0, t_1, \ldots, t_{n-1}, t_n\}$. The rationale of the product is very simple. The investor is initially endowed with a large coupon D (typically around 50%). In each period the performance of the stock or market index S is recorded. Positive performances leave the coupon unaffected, while negative performances are progressively subtracted from the coupon.

Intuitively, the product is long the underlying asset. In fact, interest income is progressively lowered by decreases of the stock. If the market goes up, then it is good news. It is less intuitive to understand what happens with changes in volatility. Some glance on the sign on this sensitivity can be obtained if we understand the kind of derivative product embedded in the structure. The answer is evident if we rewrite the payoff in a slightly different way

$$\text{Coupon} = \max \left[D - \sum_{i=1}^{n} \max \left[1 - \frac{S(t_i)}{S(t_{i-1})}, 0 \right], 0 \right] \qquad (6.53)$$

The coupon is then a put option with strike D. The underlying asset is a sum of forward start put options, that is a *cliquet put* option. The investor is then selling a *cliquet put option* to the issuer. An increase in volatility would then increase the value of the option, and the value of the product for the investor would decrease. By the same token, an increase in the underlying asset would decrease the value of the option, raising the value of the product for the investor. The product is then long in the underlying asset and short in volatility, just like in the *reverse* convertible case in the previous chapter. The underlying asset is a *cliquet* option. It is then not surprising that these products are known as *reverse cliquet* notes.

Remark 6.1 Why not use the cumulative decrease of the stock rather than a sum of decreases over the subperiods? That would have been an alternative. In this case the product would be

$$\text{Coupon} = \max \left[D - \max \left(1 - \frac{S(t_n)}{S(t_0)}, \ 0 \right), \ 0 \right] \tag{6.54}$$

The difference between the two products of course hinges on the difference between a cliquet option and the corresponding European option. We leave the reader to analyse the structure.

6.5 MULTIVARIATE NOTES

We saw above that smoothing was a tool to modulate the risk of a product by a reduction of volatility. Another tool to achieve the same task is *diversification*. Selling a product whose coupon is linked to a basket of underlying assets instead of a single asset enables us to change the risk structure of the product. This also brings another dimension into the picture, that of correlation. The analysis of these products should then account for this new feature and should be conducted on two levels. First, one should ask how the dependence structure is actually changing the risk/return nature of the product: in other words, the question is whether the product is providing diversification or concentration of risks. Second, as correlation is bound to change, one should ask how correlation changes may impact on the value of the product: the question is whether a position is long or short in correlation.

In a very general way, multivariate notes can be written as

$$\text{Coupon}(t_j) = f\left(S_i(t_j); \ i = 1, \ 2, \ \ldots, \ p; \ i = 1, \ 2, \ \ldots, \ n\right) \tag{6.55}$$

As for univariate notes, one may both conceive either a single coupon at maturity or a stream of coupons paid at dates $\{t_1, t_2, \ldots, t_n\}$. The difference is that now the payoffs are functions of the $\{S_1, S_2, \ldots, S_p\}$ stocks according to a multivariate function $f(.)$. The shape of the function determines whether the product is long or short in correlation. From the shape of the function itself it is not easy to give a straight answer to this question. We provide, however, a rule of thumb that may be very helpful to get an answer.

6.5.1 The AND/OR rule

Consider a product with some payoff function $f(S_1, S_2, \ldots, S_p)$. The following is a simple rule of thumb to determine the sign of the position with respect to correlation. If the function involves logical AND operators ($\cap$), the product is long in correlation. If the function involves OR operators ($\cup$), then the product is short in correlation.

In other words, one should look through the contract and search statements of the kind: "The coupon is paid if both event A AND B take place", and in such case the value of the contract will increase with dependence between A and B. Alternatively, if one runs into statements like: "The coupon is paid if event A OR B takes place" the value of the contract will decrease with correlation.

Going back to the chapter on correlation, we know that AND operators are linked to joint distributions and copula functions. So, the probability attached to the statement "... both events A AND B take place" would be

$$Q(A \cap B) = C(Q_A, Q_B) \tag{6.56}$$

where $C(u, z)$ is a copula function and Q_A and Q_B are the marginal distributions. Copula functions increase with dependence. The probability that both events would take place also increases and so does the price of the payoff attached to it under the contract.

Notice that if the coupon were linked to the complement sets, it would also increase with correlation. Consider in fact the statement "... if NEITHER A OR B takes place". Despite how it may looks at first sight, this is an AND statement, involving the complement sets ("A does not take place AND B does not take place"). The probability attached to it is

$$Q(\overline{A} \cap \overline{B}) = \overline{C}(\overline{Q}_A, \overline{Q}_B) = \overline{Q}_A + \overline{Q}_B - 1 + C\left(1 - \overline{Q}_A,\ 1 - \overline{Q}_B\right) \qquad (6.57)$$

where $\overline{Q}_A = 1 - Q_A, \overline{Q}_B = 1 - Q_B$ and $\overline{C}(u, z)$ is the survival copula. Notice that the survival copula also increases with dependence.

Contrary to that, it is easy to see that the probability attached to the statement "... if event A OR B take place takes place" would be represented by

$$Q(A \cup B) = 1 - Q(\overline{A} \ AND \ \overline{B})$$
$$= 1 - \overline{C}(\overline{Q}_A,\ \overline{Q}_B) = 1 - \overline{Q}_A - \overline{Q}_B + 1 - C\left(1 - \overline{Q}_A,\ 1 - \overline{Q}_B\right)$$
$$= Q_A + Q_B - C(Q_A,\ Q_B) \qquad (6.58)$$

Notice that the probability now decreases with the value of the copula function, and also with the dependence between events A and B.

6.5.2 Altiplanos

Consider a digital product indexed to a set of events. Typically each event in the set is defined by

$$A_i(t_j) \equiv S_i(t_j) \le BS_i(t_0) \qquad (6.59)$$

where B is a barrier value. The event takes place if the value of a stock S_i at time t_j is below some strike level $BS_i(t_0)$. We can observe such events for a basket of $i = 1, 2, ..., p$ stocks.

Actually one could define the event in a more sophisticated way in, for example, the following structure which is very common in many contracts. Consider a set of dates $t_{j1} < t_{j2} < ..., < t_{jk}$, where $t_{j-1} < t_{j1}$ and $t_{jk} = t_j$. Define the event

$$A_i(t_j) \equiv \bigcup_{q=1}^{k} S_i(t_{jq}) \le BS_i(t_0) \qquad (6.60)$$

More explicitly, the period of time ranging from t_{j-1} to t_j is partitioned in subintervals. The event is defined as the case in which the value of a stock falls below the strike level $BS_i(t_0)$ at the end of at least one of the subintervals. In plain words, the event is defined as the case in which the stock breaches the barrier in the period from t_{j-1} to t_j.

An *Altiplano* is a structured product paying a fixed coupon at time t_j if none of the events described above has taken place. Formally, consider the following characteristic function

$$\chi_j = \begin{cases} 0 & \bigcup_{i=1}^{p} A_i(t_j) \\ 1 & \bigcap_{i=1}^{p} \overline{A}_i(t_j) \end{cases} \qquad (6.61)$$

where $\overline{A}_i(t_j)$ is the complement of $A_i(t_j)$. The payoff of an Altiplano is given by

$$\text{Coupon}(t_j) \equiv c\,\chi_j$$

where c is a fixed coupon. In other words, an Altiplano pays a fixed coupon at time t_j if no asset has breached the barrier in the period, or, analogously, if all the stocks have remained above the barrier. It is easy to check that this product is long in correlation. In fact, the value of the coupon is

$$cv(t,\ t_j)Q(\chi_j) = cv(t,t_j)Q\left[\bigcap_{i=1}^{p}\overline{A}_i(t_j)\right] = cv(t,t_j)\overline{C}_j\left[\overline{Q}_1(t_j),\ \overline{Q}_2(t_j),\ldots,\overline{Q}_p(t_j)\right] \quad (6.62)$$

where $\overline{Q}_i(t_j)$ is the marginal probability attached to the event $\overline{A}_i(t_j)$, and $\overline{C}_j(.)$ is the corresponding survival copula.

In some of these products the relationship between dependence and value can be more complex than this. Some products in fact include the so-called "*memory*" feature. When the event takes place in an *Altiplano with memory*, the coupon is paid for the corresponding maturity and for all of the previous maturities for which the event has not occurred. Formally, the coupon is defined as

$$\text{Coupon}(t_j) = c\,\chi_j + c\sum_{m=1}^{j-1}(1-\chi_m) \quad (6.63)$$

The price may be written as

$$cv(t,t_j)Q\left[\bigcap_{i=1}^{p}\overline{A}_i(t_j)\right] + cv(t,t_j)\sum_{m=1}^{j-1}Q\left[\bigcup_{i=1}^{p}A_i(t_m)\right] \quad (6.64)$$

It is clear that the memory part is decreasing with correlation. In fact, for each time t_m we have

$$Q\left[\bigcup_{i=1}^{p}A_i(t_m)\right] = 1 - \overline{C}_m\left[\overline{Q}_1(t_m),\overline{Q}_2(t_m),\ldots,\overline{Q}_p(t_m)\right] \quad (6.65)$$

So, whether the product is long or short in correlation is an empirical question related to the relative weight of the two parts in the payoff: the Altiplano part and memory. Obviously, the longer the time to maturity of the note, the more the memory part is likely to be relevant, and the product could well be short in correlation.

6.5.3 Everest

An alternative to a digital payoff is to index the amount of payment – and not only if the payment would take place – to the performance of a set of stocks or markets. So, for example, assume a single coupon paid at maturity T, generally defined as

$$\text{Coupon}(T) = \max\left[f\left(\frac{S_1(T)}{S_1(0)}, \frac{S_2(T)}{S_2(0)}, \ldots, \frac{S_n(T)}{S_n(0)}\right) - (1+r_g), 0\right] \quad (6.66)$$

A usual choice is

$$\text{Coupon}(T) = \max\left[\min\left(\frac{S_1(T)}{S_1(0)}, \frac{S_2(T)}{S_2(0)}, \ldots, \frac{S_n(T)}{S_n(0)}\right) - (1+r_g), 0\right] \qquad (6.67)$$

This choice defines the so-called Everest note. In this product, the coupon is given by a rainbow option, namely a call option on the minimum out of a set of assets.

The intuitive AND/OR rule suggests that the product is long in correlation. Actually, the option would be exercised if the worst performance in the basket is greater than the strike. But this implies that all performances should be above the strike. This is a clear AND statement, and the Everest note is long in correlation. The statement may be proved formally. While referring the reader to Chapter 8 in Cherubini *et al.* (2004) for a more extensive treatment, we provide here the basic steps of the proof. The idea is that, according to Breeden and Litzenberger (1978), we may write

$$-\frac{\partial\,\text{CallMin}\,(s_1, s_2, \ldots, s_n, t; \eta, T)}{\partial\eta} = v(t, T)Q\,(s_1(T) > \eta, s_2(T) > \eta, \ldots, s_n(T) > \eta)$$
$$(6.68)$$

for every strike η (remember the definition $s_i(T) \equiv S_i(T)/S_i(0)$). Integrating both sides from $(1+r_g)$ to infinity we get

$$\text{CallMin}\,(s_1, s_2, \ldots, s_n, t; 1+r_g, T) = v(t, T)\int_{1+r_g}^{\infty} Q(s_1(T) > \eta, s_2(T) > \eta, \ldots, s_n(T) > \eta)\,\mathrm{d}\eta$$
$$(6.69)$$

Using copula functions we get

$$\text{CallMin}\,(s_1, s_2, \ldots, s_n, t; 1+r_g, T) = v(t, T)\int_{1+r_g}^{\infty} \overline{C}_T\left[\overline{Q}_1(\eta), \overline{Q}_2(\eta) \ldots \overline{Q}_n(\eta)\right]\,\mathrm{d}\eta \quad (6.70)$$

where $\overline{Q}_n(\eta) \equiv Q(s_n(T) > \eta)$. The value of the product is then an increasing function of copulas and is therefore increasing with dependence, as we wanted to prove.

Remark 6.2 Consider a coupon indexed to the maximum performance in the set. Formally,

$$\text{Coupon}(T) = \max\left[\max\left(\frac{S_1(T)}{S_1(0)}, \frac{S_2(T)}{S_2(0)}, \ldots, \frac{S_n(T)}{S_n(0)}\right) - (1+r_g), 0\right] \qquad (6.71)$$

The AND/OR rule in this case predicts that the product is short in correlation. In fact, the coupon pays more than the guaranteed return if at least one of the stocks in the basket records a better performance. This is a clear OR statement that points to a inverse relationship between dependence and the value of the product. Again, intuition may be rigorously verified. Without loss of generality, let us take the bivariate case. It is immediate to verify (see also Stultz, 1982), that

$$\max\left[\max\left(\frac{S_1(T)}{S_1(0)},\frac{S_2(T)}{S_2(0)}\right)-(1+r_g),0\right]=\max\left[\frac{S_1(T)}{S_1(0)}-(1+r_g),0\right]$$

$$+\max\left[\frac{S_2(T)}{S_2(0)}-(1+r_g),0\right]$$

$$-\max\left[\min\left(\frac{S_1(T)}{S_1(0)},\frac{S_2(T)}{S_2(0)}\right)-(1+r_g),0\right] \tag{6.72}$$

By arbitrage, the product is equivalent to a long position in two univariate call options and a short position in an Everest – that is, a call on the minimum of the two assets. Since, as we proved above, the call on the minimum is long in correlation, the call on the maximum is short.

6.5.4 Basket notes

Let us finally come to the most standard among the multivariate structured products, the so called basket note. In these notes the function used to define the underlying asset is an average, typically an arithmetic average. So the coupon is defined as

$$\text{Coupon}(T)=\max\left[\frac{1}{n}\sum_{i=1}^{n}\frac{S_i(T)}{S_i(0)}-(1+r_g),0\right] \tag{6.73}$$

To be more precise, this kind of structure is typically used when the underlying assets are stock indexes rather than individual stocks. In case of individual stocks, it is more usual to find a structure like

$$\text{Coupon}(T)=\max\left[\frac{\sum_{i=1}^{n}n_iS_i(T)}{\sum_{i=1}^{n}n_iS_i(0)}-(1+r_g),0\right] \tag{6.74}$$

where n_i denotes the physical units of the ith stock in the basket. In both cases, there is no need to resort to the AND/OR rule to determine the sign of the position with respect to correlation (even though it is quite straightforward). The products are clearly long in correlation.

A basket option is obviously more expensive than an Everest. In fact, whenever the Everest pays a coupon, the basket option pays more. Furthermore, the basket option may pay in cases in which the Everest does not. We leave the reader to prove that the basket coupon has to be cheaper than a coupon paying the maximum performance.

If we want to be more precise about the price, however, this simple product raises complex problems. The reason is that linear combinations of log-normal variables are not log-normally distributed. The problem is actually the same as the one we encountered to evaluate arithmetic average Asian options. Exactly as in that problem one could approximate the price by a moment-matching algorithm. The natural alternative is simulation, which is usually preferred because the curse of pricers is that it is very common to run into both problems in the same contract. A typical payoff in fact is that of a basket Asian note, written as

$$\text{Coupon}(T)=\max\left[\frac{1}{p}\sum_{j=1}^{p}\sum_{i=1}^{n}\frac{S_i(t_j)}{S_i(0)}-(1+r_g),\ 0\right] \tag{6.75}$$

where t_j are dates at which the reference portfolio is evaluated. In cases like this, there is not much one can do to produce an accurate price, and Monte Carlo simulation emerges like the mandatory solution.

6.6   MONTE CARLO METHOD

Numerical methods that are known as Monte Carlo methods can be loosely described as statistical simulation systems, where statistical simulation is defined in quite general terms to be any method that utilizes sequences of random numbers to perform the simulation. Monte Carlo methods have been used for centuries, but only in the past several decades has the technique gained the status of a full-fledged numerical method capable of addressing the most complex applications. The name "Monte Carlo" was coined by Metropolis (inspired by Ulam's interest in poker) during the Manhattan Project of Second World War, because of the similarity of statistical simulation to games of chance, and because the capital of Monaco was a centre for gambling and similar pursuits. Statistical simulation methods may be contrasted to conventional numerical discretization methods, which typically are applied to ordinary or partial differential equations that describe some underlying physical or mathematical system. In many applications of Monte Carlo, the underlying dynamic process is simulated directly, and there is no need to even write down the differential equations that describe the behaviour of the system. The only requirement is that the system can be described by probability distribution functions (p.d.f.'s). Once the p.d.f.'s are known, the Monte Carlo simulation can proceed by random sampling from the p.d.f.'s. Many simulations are then performed (multiple "trials" or "histories") and the desired result is taken as an average over the number of observations (which may be perhaps millions of observations). In many practical applications, one can predict the statistical error (the "variance") in this average result, and hence an estimate of the number of Monte Carlo trials that are needed to achieve a given error.

Although it is natural to think that Monte Carlo methods are used to simulate random, or stochastic, processes, since these can be described by p.d.f.'s, this coupling is actually too restrictive because many Monte Carlo applications have no apparent stochastic content, such as the evaluation of a definite integral or the inversion of a system of linear equations. However, in these cases and others, one can pose the desired solution in terms of p.d.f.'s, and while this transformation may seem artificial, this step allows the system to be *treated* as a stochastic process for the purpose of simulation and hence Monte Carlo methods can be applied to simulate the system.

6.6.1   Major components of a Monte Carlo algorithm

Let us now describe briefly the major components of a Monte Carlo method. The primary components of a Monte Carlo simulation method include the following:

- *Probability distribution functions (p.d.f.'s)*: The mathematical system must be described by a set of p.d.f.'s.
- *Random number generator*: A source of random numbers uniformly distributed on the unit interval must be available.
- *Sampling rule*: A prescription for sampling from the specified p.d.f.'s, assuming the availability of random numbers on the unit interval, must be given.

- *Scoring (or tallying)*: The outcomes must be accumulated into overall tallies or scores for the quantities of interest.
- *Error estimation*: An estimate of the statistical error (variance) as a function of the number of trials and other quantities must be determined.
- *Variance reduction techniques*: Methods for reducing the variance in the estimated solution to reduce the computational time for Monte Carlo simulation.

6.6.2 Monte Carlo integration

We would like to evaluate the following definite integral:

$$I = \int_a^b g(x)\,dx \tag{6.76}$$

where we assume that $g(x)$ is real valued (r.v.) on $(-\infty, +\infty)$. The idea is to manipulate the definite integral into a form that can be solved by the Monte Carlo method. To do this, we define the following function on $[a, b]$,

$$f(x) = \begin{cases} 1/(b-a), & a \le x \le b \\ 0, & \text{otherwise} \end{cases} \tag{6.77}$$

and insert (6.76) into (6.77) to obtain the following expression for the integral I:

$$I = \frac{1}{b-a} \int_{-\infty}^{+\infty} g(x)f(x)\,dx \tag{6.78}$$

Note that $f(x)$ can be viewed as a uniform p.d.f. on the interval $[a, b]$. Given that $f(x)$ is a p.d.f., we observe that the integral on the right-hand side of (6.78) is simply the expectation value for $g(x)$:

$$I = \frac{1}{b-a} \int_{-\infty}^{+\infty} g(x)f(x)\,dx = \frac{1}{b-a}\langle g \rangle \tag{6.79}$$

We now draw samples $\{x_n\}$ from the p.d.f. $f(x)$, and for each $\{x_n\}$ we will evaluate $g(x_n)$ and form the average G,

$$G = \frac{1}{N}\sum_{n=1}^{N} g(x_n) \tag{6.80}$$

But (6.80) states that the expectation value for the average of N samples is the expectation value for $g(x)$, $G = \langle g \rangle$, hence

$$I \approx \hat{I} = \frac{1}{b-a}\left[\frac{1}{N}\sum_{i=1}^{N} g(x_n)\right] \tag{6.81}$$

Thus we can *estimate* the true value of the integral I on $[a, b]$ by taking the average of N observations of the integrand, with the r.v. x sampled uniformly over the interval $[a, b]$.

Recall that (6.80) related the true variance in the average G to the true variance in g,

$$\text{var}(G) = \frac{1}{N}\text{var}(g) \tag{6.82}$$

Although we do not know var(G), since it is a property of the p.d.f. $f(x)$ and the real function $g(x)$, it is a constant. Furthermore, if we associate the error in our estimate of the integral I with the standard deviation, then we might expect the error in the estimate of I to decrease by the factor $N^{-1/2}$.

We call (6.81) the crude Monte Carlo estimator. Formula (6.82) for its standard error is important for two reasons. First, it tells us that the standard error of a Monte Carlo analysis decreases with the square root of the sample size. If we quadruple the number of realizations used, we will half the standard error. Second, standard error does not depend upon the dimensionality of the integral (6.76). Most techniques of numerical integration – such as the trapezoidal rule or Simpson's method – suffer from the curse of dimensionality. When generalized to multiple dimensions, the number of computations required to apply them increases exponentially with the dimensionality of the integral. For this reason, such methods cannot be applied to integrals of more than a few dimensions. The Monte Carlo method does not suffer from the curse of dimensionality. It is as applicable to a 1000-dimensional integral as it is to a one-dimensional integral.

While increasing the sample size is one technique for reducing the standard error of a Monte Carlo analysis, doing so can be computationally expensive. A better solution is to employ some technique of variance reduction. These techniques incorporate additional information about the analysis directly into the estimator. This allows them to make the Monte Carlo estimator more deterministic, and hence have a lower standard error.

6.6.3 Sampling from probability distribution functions

Transformation of p.d.f.'s

In order to give a complete discussion of sampling, we need to explain transformation rules. Given a p.d.f. $f(x)$, one defines a new variable $y = y(x)$, and the goal is to find the p.d.f. $g(y)$ that describes the probability that the r.v. y occurs. First of all, we need to restrict the transformation $y = y(x)$ to be unique, because there must be 1-to-1 relationship between x and y in order to be able to state that a given value of x unambiguously corresponds to a value of y. Given that $y(x)$ is 1-to-1, then it must either be monotone increasing or monotone decreasing, since any other behaviour would result in a multiple-valued function $y(x)$.

Let us first assume that the transformation $y(x)$ is monotone increasing, which results in $dy/dx > 0$ for all x. The transformation must conserve probability, i.e. the probability of the r.v. x' occurring in dx about x must be the same as the probability of the r.v. y' occurring in dy about y, since if x occurs, the 1-to-1 relationship between x and y requires, that y takes place. But by definition of the p.d.f.'s $f(x)$ and $g(y)$,

$$f(x)\,dx = \text{prob}(x \le x' \le x+dx)$$
$$g(y)\,dy = \text{prob}(y \le y' \le y+dy)$$

(6.83)

The transformation implies that these probabilities must be equal. Equality of these differential probabilities yields

$$f(x)\,dx = g(y)\,dy$$

(6.84)

and one can then solve for $g(y)$:

$$g(y) = f(x)/[dy/dx]$$

(6.85)

This holds for the monotone increasing function $y(x)$. It is easy to show that for a monotone decreasing function $y(x)$, where $dy/dx < 0$ for all x, the fact that $g(y)$ must be positive (by definition of probability) leads to the following expression for $g(y)$:

$$g(y) = f(x)/[-dy/dx]$$

(6.86)

Combining the two cases leads to the following simple rule for transforming p.d.f.'s:

$$g(y) = f(x)/|dy/dx|$$

(6.87)

For multidimensional p.d.f.'s, the derivative $|dy/dx|$ is replaced by the Jacobian of the transformation, which will be described later when we discuss sampling from the Gaussian p.d.f.

Sampling via inversion of the c.d.f.

Since the r.v. x and the c.d.f. $F(x)$ are 1-to-1, one can sample x by first sampling $y = F(x)$ and then solving for x by inverting $F(x)$, or $x = F^{-1}(y)$. The c.d.f. is uniformly distributed on $[0, 1]$, which is denoted $U[0, 1]$. Therefore, we simply use a random number generator (RNG) that generates $U[0, 1]$ numbers, to generate a sample ξ from the c.d.f. $F(x)$. Then the value of x is determined by inversion, $x = F^{-1}(\xi)$. The inversion is not always possible, but in many important cases the inverse is readily obtained.

We summarize below the steps for sampling by inversion of the c.d.f.:

- *Step 1*: Sample a random number ξ from $U[0, 1]$
- *Step 2*: Equate ξ with the c.d.f.: $F(x) = \xi$
- *Step 3*: Invert the c.d.f. and solve for x: $x = F^{-1}(\xi)$

6.6.4 Error estimates

For finite but at least moderately large n, we can supplement the estimate of our integral $\hat{I}$ with a confidence interval. For this purpose, let

$$\sigma = \sqrt{\frac{1}{N-1}\sum_{i=1}^{N}\left(I_i - \hat{I}\right)^2}$$

(6.88)

denote the sample standard deviation of our estimation and let α_δ denote the $1 - \delta$ quantile of the standard normal distribution, then

$$\hat{I} \pm \alpha_{\delta/2} \frac{\sigma}{\sqrt{N}}$$

is an asymptotically valid $1 - \delta$ confidence interval for $\hat{I}$.

6.6.5   Variance reduction techniques

Many practitioners have some intuitive familiarity with the Monte Carlo method from their work. At an elementary level, it is a surprisingly simple concept, but it can be computationally expensive to use. It is easy to code Monte Carlo analyses that take hours or even days to run. To speed up analyses – to make them run in minutes as opposed to days – users need to employ techniques such as variance reduction. These techniques are easy to learn, but they are NOT intuitive. To use them, users need a sophisticated understanding of how and why the Monte Carlo method works.

Standard techniques of variance reduction include:

- common random numbers
- antithetic variates
- control variates
- importance sampling, and
- stratified sampling.

For a general description of these methods we refer the interested readers to Jäckel (2002) and Glasserman (2003). In this section we shall briefly describe common random numbers (in connection with the problem of sensitivities estimates), antithetic variates and control variates.

Common random numbers

In practice, the evaluation of price sensitivities is often as important as the evaluation of prices. For hedging purposes, when managing a lot of derivatives, it is also important to know the risk exposure. Whereas prices for some derivatives can be observed in the market, their sensitivities to parameter changes typically cannot, and must therefore be computed. Sensitivity measures of derivatives for which closed-form formulas do not exist have to be computed numerically. However, highly precise estimates with the brute force method can take a long time to be achieved. *Variance reduction techniques* reduce the mean standard error and can be used to speed up simulations by achieving a specified level of precision with a smaller number of trials. In this section we will discuss a very simple approach to estimating price sensitivities, especially delta with finite difference approximation. The reader is referred to Glasserman (2003) for a complete discussion on this important subject.

Consider the problem of computing the delta of the Black–Scholes price of a European call:

$$\Delta = \frac{\partial C}{\partial S_0} \tag{6.89}$$

where C is the option price and S_0 is the current stock price. A crude estimate of delta could be obtained by generating a terminal stock price

$$S(T) = S(0) \exp\left[\left(r - \frac{1}{2}\sigma^2\right) T + \sigma\sqrt{T} Z\right]$$
(6.90)

from the current stock price $S(0)$, and a second, independent terminal stock price

$$S_\varepsilon(T) = (S(0) + \varepsilon) \exp\left[\left(r - \frac{1}{2}\sigma^2\right) T + \sigma\sqrt{T} Z'\right]$$
(6.91)

from the perturbed initial price $(S(0) + \varepsilon)$ with Z and Z' independent. For each terminal price, a discounted payoff can be computed

$$C(S_0) = e^{-rT} \max[0, \ S(T) - K]$$
(6.92)

$$C(S_0 + \varepsilon) = e^{-rT} \max[0, \ S_\varepsilon(T) - K]$$
(6.93)

A crude estimation of delta is then provided by the finite difference approximation

$$\tilde{\Delta} = \frac{C(S_0 + \varepsilon) - C(S_0)}{\varepsilon}$$
(6.94)

By generating n independent replications of $S(T)$ and $S_\varepsilon(T)$ we can calculate the sample mean of n independent copies of $\tilde{\Delta}$. As $n \to \infty$ this sample mean converges to the true finite difference ratio. At this point one could think that to get an accurate estimate of Δ we should make ε as small as possible. However, since we generate $S(T)$ and $S_\varepsilon(T)$ independently of each other, we have

$$\mathrm{Var}(\tilde{\Delta}) = \varepsilon^{-2}\{\mathrm{Var}[C(S_0 + \varepsilon)] + \mathrm{Var}[C(S_0)]\} = O(\varepsilon^{-2})$$
(6.95)

so the variance of $\tilde{\Delta}$ becomes very large if we make ε small! To get an estimator that converges to Δ we must let ε decrease slowly as n increases, resulting in slow overall convergence. Better estimators can generally be improved using the method of *common random numbers* which, in this context, simply uses the same random number Z in the estimation of both $S(T)$ and $S_\varepsilon(T)$. If we denote by Δ^* the finite difference approximation thus obtained, we have that, for fixed ε, the sample mean of independent replications of Δ^* also converges to the true value of Δ. However, the variance of this estimator is now given by

$$\mathrm{Var}(\hat{\Delta}) = \varepsilon^{-2}\{\mathrm{Var}[C(S_0)] + \mathrm{Var}[C(S_0 + \varepsilon)] - 2\,\mathrm{Cov}[C(S_0), \ C(S_0 + \varepsilon)]\}$$
(6.96)

because $C(S_0)$ and $C(S_0 + \varepsilon)$ are no longer independent. In particular, if they are positively correlated, then Δ^* has smaller variance than $\tilde{\Delta}$. It is possible to demonstrate that this is indeed the fact due to monotonicity of the function mapping Z to C. Thus the use of common random numbers reduces the variance of the estimate of delta.

Antithetic variates

The antithetic variate method is one of the most widely used variance reduction techniques. Let

$$Y = g(x_1, x_2, \cdots, x_n) \tag{6.97}$$

be generated from a random sample

$$(x_1, x_2, \cdots, x_n) \tag{6.98}$$

of independent standard normal numbers. Now generate a second variable

$$Y^* = g(-x_1, -x_2, \cdots, -x_n) \tag{6.99}$$

from the random sample

$$(-x_1, -x_2, \cdots, -x_n) \tag{6.100}$$

which is also a standard normal distribution. Then

$$E\left[\frac{Y + Y^*}{2}\right] = \frac{E[Y] + E[Y^*]}{2} = E[Y] \tag{6.101}$$

is also an unbiased estimator with

$$\mathrm{Var}\left[\frac{Y + Y^*}{2}\right] = \frac{\mathrm{Var}[Y]}{2} + \frac{\mathrm{Cov}[Y, \ Y^*]}{2} \tag{6.102}$$

If $\mathrm{Cov}[Y, \ Y^*] < \mathrm{Var}[Y]$ then $\mathrm{Var}\left[\frac{Y + Y^*}{2}\right] < \mathrm{Var}[Y]$.

As $E\left[\frac{Y + Y^*}{2}\right]$ uses twice as many replications as $E[Y]$, we must account for differences in computational requirements. Thus, for antithetics to increase efficiency, we require

$$2 \cdot \mathrm{Var}\left[\frac{Y + Y^*}{2}\right] < \mathrm{Var}[Y] \tag{6.103}$$

which means

$$\mathbf{Cov[Y, Y^*] < 0} \tag{6.104}$$

As in the previous discussion about common random numbers, it is possible to prove that this is the case if the relationship between the random number set and the pricing function is monotonic. This argument can be adapted to show that the method of antithetic variates increases efficiency in pricing a European put and other options that monotonically depend on inputs. Caution must be used in other cases where this assumption is questionable (e.g. some kind of barrier options).

Control variates

Consider a crude Monte Carlo estimator:

$$\frac{1}{N}\sum_{k=1}^{N} f(U^{[k]}) \tag{6.105}$$

Let ξ be a real-valued function for which the mean

$$\mu_\xi = E[\xi(U)] \tag{6.106}$$

is known. We shall refer to the random variable $\xi(U)$ as a **control variate**. Consider the random variable $f^*(U)$ based on this control variate:

$$f^*(U) = f(U) - c\left(\xi(U) - \mu_\xi\right) \tag{6.107}$$

for some constant c. By construction, $\psi = E[f^*(U)]$, so we can estimate ψ with the Monte Carlo estimator

$$\frac{1}{N}\sum_{k=1}^{N} f^*(U^{[k]}) = \frac{1}{N}\sum_{k=1}^{N}(f^*(U^{[k]}) - c[\xi(U^{[k]}) - \mu_\xi]) \tag{6.108}$$

This will have a lower standard error than the crude estimator (6.105) if the standard deviation σ^* of $f^*(U)$ is smaller than the standard deviation σ of $f(U)$. This will happen if $\xi(U)$ has a high correlation ρ with the random variable $f(U)$, in which case random variables $c\xi(U)$ and $f(U)$ will tend to offset each other in (6.107). We formalize this observation by calculating

$$\sigma^* = \text{stdev}(f(U) - c[\xi(U) - \mu_\xi]) = \text{stdev}\left(f(U) - c\xi(U)\right)$$

$$= \sqrt{\sigma^2 + c^2\sigma_\xi^2 - 2c\sigma\sigma_\xi\rho} \tag{6.109}$$

where σ_ξ is the standard deviation of $\xi(U)$. Obviously, σ^* will be smaller than σ if

$$\rho > \frac{c\sigma_\xi}{2\sigma} \tag{6.110}$$

It can be shown that σ^* is minimized by setting

$$c = \frac{\sigma\rho}{\sigma_\xi} \tag{6.111}$$

in which case

$$\sigma^* = \sigma\sqrt{1-\rho^2} \tag{6.112}$$

Often, ρ and σ_ξ are unknown, which makes determining the optimal value for c problematic. We can estimate ρ and σ_ξ with a separate Monte Carlo analysis. Alternatively, if ξ closely approximates f, c might simply be set equal to 1. As the above description indicates, the key to the method of control variates is finding a function ξ that closely approximates f, and for which $E[\xi(U)]$ is easy to calculate. A well-known case of this type of relationship is that of an arithmetic average Asian option and the corresponding geometric average option.

6.6.6   Pricing an Asian option with JMC program

As we have discussed in the previous section, the method of control variates replaces the evaluation of an unknown expected value with the evaluation of the difference between the unknown quantity and a related quantity whose expected value is known. Here, the unknown quantity of interest is the value C_A of an average-price Asian call option whose payout at expiration is $\max(A - K, 0)$, where A is the arithmetic average of the underlying asset prices during the holding period. The related quantity with known expectation is the value C_G of an Asian option whose payout is $\max(G - K, 0)$, where C_G is the geometric average. Because of the log-normality of the stock price model, an analytic expression is available for C_G but not for C_A. In particular, if

$$G = \left(\prod_{j=1}^{m} S_{t_j} \right)^{1/m} \tag{6.113}$$

then

$$C_G = \exp(-rT) \left[\exp\left(\mu_G + \frac{1}{2}\sigma_G^2 \right) N(d_1) - KN(d_2) \right] \tag{6.114}$$

where

$$\mu_G = \ln(S_0) + \left(r - q - \frac{1}{2}\sigma^2 \right) \frac{T+h}{2} \qquad h = T/m$$

$$\sigma_G^2 = \sigma^2 h \frac{(2m+1)(m+1)}{6m}$$

$$d_1 = \frac{\mu_G - \ln(K) + \sigma_G^2}{\sigma_G}$$

$$d_2 = d_1 - \sigma_G$$

and m is the number of point used to estimate the average. We have included these formulas in a new class derived from the `CBlackScholes` class that we named `CBlackScholes_GeometricAsian` (see Figure 6.3).

The code of the `Execute()` method is shown below.

```
package pricing_algorithm;

import finobject.COption;

public class CBlackScholes_GeometricAsian extends
   CBlackScholes {
   /**
   * note: this method overwrite the Execute method
     of the super class
   * CBlackScholes
   */
   public double Execute(COption option){
```

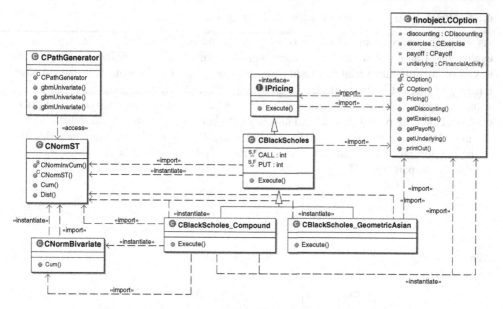

Figure 6.3   The complete CBlackScholes class and its subclasses

```
    return BS_GeometricAsian(option);
}
private double BS_GeometricAsian(COption option)
{
    System.out.println("Running Black & Scholes Algorithm for
    Geometric Asian Option");
    option.printOut();

    CNormST N   =   new CNormST();

    double price = 0;

    double S = (option.getUnderlying()).getLevel();
    double sigma = (option.getUnderlying()).
                getVolatility();
    double K = (option.getPayoff()).getStrike();
    double  r = (option.getDiscounting()).
            getDiscountRate();
    double T  = (option.getExercise()).
            getExpirationTime();

    int m_ave  =(option.getPayoff()).getNrFixing();

    double  h = T / (double)m_ave;
    double mg = Math.log(S) + (r - sigma * sigma / 2) *
                (T + h) / 2.0;
```

```
    double  sg = Math.sqrt((sigma * sigma) * h * (2 * m_ave + 1)
                * (m_ave + 1) / (6 * m_ave));
    double d1  = (mg - Math.log(K) + sg * sg) / sg;
    double d2 = d1 - sg;

    price = Math.exp(-r * T) * (Math.exp(mg + sg * sg / 2) *
            N.Cum(d1) - K * N.Cum(d2));
    return price;
    }
}
```

To price an Asian option with a crude Monte Carlo we have extended the pricing classes, adding a new class named `CMonteCarlo` which, as usual, implements the `IPricing` interface.

```
public class CMonteCarlo implements IPricing {

    /* parameters */
    private int numberOfSimulations;
    private int numberOfSteps;

    /* inspectors */

    public int getNumberOfSimulations()
    {return numberOfSimulations;}
    public int getNumberOfSteps() {return numberOfSteps;}

    /* constructors */

    public CMonteCarlo(){}

    public CMonteCarlo(int numberOfSimulations,
    int numberOfSteps)
    {
        this.numberOfSimulations = numberOfSimulations;
        this.numberOfSteps = numberOfSteps;
    }

        public CMonteCarlo(int numberOfSimulations)
    {
        this.numberOfSimulations = numberOfSimulations;
        this.numberOfSteps = 1;
    }

    /* methods */

    public double Execute(COption option)
    {
        System.out.println("Running Monte Carlo Simulation...");
        System.out.println("Number of Simulations = " +
                        numberOfSimulations);
```

```
        option.printOut();

        numberOfSteps++;
        int i              = 0;
        double price       = 0;
        double T           = (option.getExercise()).
                                getExpirationTime();
        double r           = (option.getDiscounting()).
                                getDiscountRate();
        double stdev       = (option.getUnderlying()).
                                getVolatility();
        double S           = (option.getUnderlying()).getLevel();

        double riskNeutralDrift = r - 0.5*stdev*stdev;
        double sqrtDeltaT       = Math.sqrt(T/(numberOfSteps-1));
        double discount         = Math.exp(-r*T);

        double[] y                   = new double[numberOfSteps];

        CPathGenerator generator = new CPathGenerator(numberOf
                                    Steps, numberOfSimulations);
        price = 0;
        for(i = 0; i < numberOfSimulations; i++)
        {
           generator.gbmUnivariate(S,
             stdev,
             sqrtDeltaT,
             riskNeutralDrift,
             y);

             price += (option.getPayoff()).value(y);
        }
        price *= discount/numberOfSimulations;

        return price;
     }
  }
```

The CMonteCarlo class uses the CPathGenerator class to generate the log-normal path for the underlying. This class could be easily generalized to include a more complicated stochastic process.

```
  public class CPathGenerator
  {
     private int nStep = 0;
     private int nPath = 0;

     public CPathGenerator(int nStep, int nPath)
     {
```

```
        this.nStep = nStep;
        this.nPath = nPath;
    }

    public boolean gbmUnivariate(double iniValue,
                                 double stdev,
                                 double sqrDt,
                                 double drift,
                                 double[][] path)
    {
        double z = 0;

        Random gen = new Random();

        for (int i     = 0; i < nPath; i++){
            path[i][0]= iniValue;
            for (int j = 1; j < nStep; j++){
                        z = CNormST.CNormInvCum(gen.nextDouble());
                path[i][j] = path[i][j-1] * Math.exp((drift
                        * sqrDt + stdev*z)*sqrDt);
            }
        }
        return true;
    }

    public boolean gbmUnivariate(double iniValue,
                                 double stdev,
                                 double sqrDt,
                                 double drift,
                                 double[] path)
    {
        double z = 0;

        Random gen = new Random();

        path[0]    = iniValue;
        for (int j = 1; j < nStep; j++){
            z = CNormST.CNormInvCum(gen.nextDouble());
            path[j]= path[j-1] * Math.exp((drift * sqrDt +
                    stdev*z)*sqrDt);
        }
        return true;
        }
    }
```

Using a crude Monte Carlo simulation to estimate the arithmetic average Asian option is equivalent to considering the estimator $C_A = E\left[C_A^i\right]$, where C_A^i is the simulated value for the ith path. In this case, the control variates technique is equivalent to using the estimator.

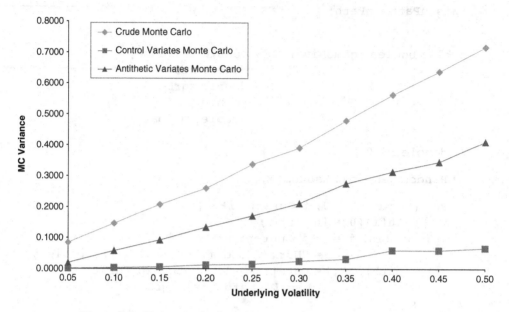

Figure 6.4   Variance reduction with respect to the underiying volatility

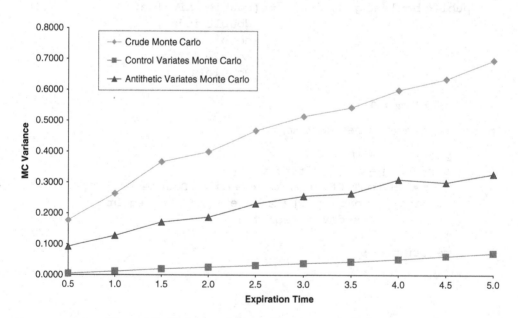

Figure 6.5   Variance reduction with respect to expiration time

$$C_A = E[C_A^i + C_G - C_G^i] = E[C_A^i] + C_G - E[C_G^i] = E[C_A^i]$$

Using C_G as a control variate reduces the variance because it "steers" the estimate towards the correct value. Running the program in the CD you can find that the decrease in variance is impressive. In Figures 6.4 and 6.5 we report the Monte Carlo variance for different times to expiration and different values for the underlying volatility. As we can see, the effect of reduction is much more pronounced than that obtained with more standard techniques as antithetic variates.

REFERENCES AND FURTHER READING

Boyle, P.P. (1977) Options: a Monte Carlo approach, *Journal of Financial Economics*, **4**, 323–338.

Boyle, P.P. & Tse, Y.K. (1990) An algorithm for computing values of options on the maximum or minimum of several assets, *Journal of Financial and Quantitative Analysis*, **25**, 215–227.

Boyle, P.P., Broadie, M. & Glasserman, P. (1997) Monte Carlo methods for security pricing, *Journal of Economic Dynamics and Control*, **21**, 1267–1321.

Boyle, P.P., Evnine, J. & Gibbs, S. (1989) Numerical evaluation of multivariate contingent claims, *Review of Financial Studies*, **2**, 241–250.

Carr, P. (1995) Two extensions to barrier options evaluations, *Applied Mathematical Finance*, **2**, 173–209.

Cherubini, U. & Romagnoli, S. (2006) *Outside barrier options*. Working Paper, University of Bologna.

Cherubini, U. & Romagnoli, S. (2007) *The dependence structure of running maxima and minima: Results and option pricing applications*. Working Paper, University of Bologna.

Cherubini, U., Luciano, E. & Vecchiato, W. (2004) *Copula Methods in Finance*. John Wiley & Sons, Chichester.

Dupire, B. (ed.) (1998) *Monte Carlo Methodologies and Applications for Pricing and Risk Management*. Risk Books, London.

Fishman, G.S. (1996) *Monte Carlo Concepts, Algorithms and Applications*. Springer-Verlag, New York.

Geman, H. & Eydeland, A. (1995) Domino effect, *RISK*, **8** (4), 65–67.

Geman, H. & Yor, M. (1993) Bessel processes, Asian options and perpetuities, *Mathematical Finance*, **3**, 349–375.

Geman, H., El Karoui, N. & Rochet, J.C. (1995) Changes of numeraire, changes of probability measures and pricing of options, *Journal of Applied Probability*, **32**, 443–458.

Geske, R. (1977) The valuation of corporate liabilities as compound options, *Journal of Financial and Quantitative Analysis*, **12** (4), 541–552.

Geske, R. (1979) The valuation of compound options, *Journal of Financial Economics*, **7**, 63–82.

Glasserman, P. (2003) *Monte Carlo Methods in Financial Engineering*. Springer, Berlin, Heidelberg, New York.

Heynen, R. & Kat, H. (1994) Crossing barriers, *RISK*, **7** (6), 46–51.

Hull, J. (2003) *Options, Futures and Other Derivatives*. Prentice Hall, New Jersey.

Jäckel, P. (2002) *Monte Carlo Methods in Finance*. John Wiley & Sons, Chichester.

Kat, H. (2002) *Structured Equity Products*. John Wiley & Sons Finance Series, Chichester.

Kemna, A.G.Z. & Vorst, T. (1990) A pricing method for options based on average asset values, *Journal of Banking and Finance*, **14**, 113–129.

Selby, M. & Hodges, S. (1987) On the evaluation of compound options, *Management Science*, **33**, 347–355.

Stulz, R.M. (1982) Options on the minimum and the maximum of two risky assets: Analysis and applications, *Journal of Financial Economics*, **10**, 161–185.

Turnbull, S.M. & Wakeman, L.M. (1991) A quick algorithm for pricing European average options, *Journal of Financial and Quantitative Analysis*, **26**, 377–389.

7
Credit-Linked Notes

7.1 INTRODUCTION

Defaultable bonds are debt instruments issued by entities that are subject to default risk – that is, the risk that they may be unable to fully repay interest and principal. Typical issuers subject to the risk of default are corporate entities (think of Enron, WorldCom, Parmalat, Cirio), municipal entities (think of Orange county) or countries (think of Mexico, Russia, or Argentina).

Strictly speaking, standard defaultable bonds may not be considered proper structured products. However, it is clear that they carry at least two sources of risk. The first has to do with the structure of the product and how its value may change with term structure. The second has to do with the characteristics of the issuer and how the value of the products can change while its credit standing changes. Nowadays it is possible to separate these sources of risk by using new instruments, called *credit derivatives*. For this reason, it is natural to include these securities among the structured products. They may in fact be thought to be made up of a plain product and some credit derivative contracts. Actually, financial engineering can be used to modify the mix of market risk and credit risk in a product, and one could also synthetically build a corporate bond independently from the fact that the issuer has actually issued debt.

7.2 DEFAULTABLE BONDS AS STRUCTURED PRODUCTS

To see why defaultable bonds may be considered structured products, assume that the credit risk can be sold to some other party. Formally, define $DP(t, T:c)$ the value at time t of the bond with coupon payment c and repayment in a single sum at maturity T. Denote instead $P(t, T:c)$ the value of the contract if it were issued by a default-free issuer (the US Treasury, for example). We have

$$DP(t, T:c) = P(t, T:c) - \text{default risk premium} + \varepsilon \qquad (7.1)$$

The value of the defaultable contract will be lower than the corresponding default-free contract, apart from the friction factors accounted for by ε. The friction factors could be due to differences in liquidity or fiscal treatment, institutional and contractual features, etc. Assume that one could purchase insurance on the value of the bond at maturity $\tau \leq T$. We know that a standard could be to buy a put with a given strike price k, with payoff

$$\max(k - DP(\tau, T:c), 0) \qquad (7.2)$$

In this case one ensures the value of the investment with respect to a stop loss value equal to k. Actually, this insurance covers two main sources of risk: (i) the risk of a term structure increase and a decrease of $P(t, T : \mathbf{c})$; (ii) the risk of an increase in the default risk premium. Of course, frictions may also play a role.

7.2.1 Expected loss

If one buys insurance for repayment of the principal in full by time T, he would buy the payoff

$$1 - DP(T, T : \mathbf{c}) \tag{7.3}$$

This product provides protection against default. It is called *default put* option. In fact, two things can happen with bond $DP(T, T : \mathbf{c})$ at maturity. The firm has not defaulted by time T, and the bond is worth the principal ($DP(T, T : \mathbf{c}) = 1$). Alternatively, the firm may have defaulted and the bond is worth less than the principal, the so-called recovery rate ($DP(T, T : \mathbf{c}) = RR$), Defining $1_{\tau \leq T}$ the indicator function spotting the default event, the value of the defaultable bond would be

$$DP(T, T : \mathbf{c}) = (1 - 1_{\tau \leq T}) + 1_{\tau \leq T}RR = 1 - 1_{\tau \leq T}(1 - RR) = 1 - 1_{\tau \leq T}LGD \tag{7.4}$$

where $LGD \equiv 1 - RR$ is called *loss given default*. The payoff of the option providing insurance against default is then

$$1 - DP(T, T : \mathbf{c}) = 1_{\tau \leq T}LGD \tag{7.5}$$

The value of the default put option at time t would then be

$$DefPut(t, T) = v(t, T)E_Q[\max(1 - DP(T, T : \mathbf{c}), 0)] = v(t, T)E_Q[1_{\tau \leq T}LGD] = v(t, T)EL \tag{7.6}$$

where EL is the *expected loss*.

A defaultable bond is then a structured product consisting of a default-free bond and a default put option.

$$DP(t, T : \mathbf{c}) = P(t, T : \mathbf{c}) - DefPut(t, T) \tag{7.7}$$

In fact, at time T it will be exactly: $DP(T, T : \mathbf{c}) = 1 - 1_{\tau \leq T}LGD$.

Ways to provide insurance against default, technically called "selling protection", are offered by credit derivatives. Credit derivatives are just institutional ways to buy and sell the options described above.

7.2.2 Credit spreads

Defaultable bonds issued by a particular entity may just be considered as another fixed income asset class. As for all other fixed income classes, the bonds in this class can be represented by a discount factor curve. The discount factor $v^*(t, \tau)$ gives the value at time t of 1 unit of currency paid at time τ by a defaultable entity. The corresponding discount factor of the default-free entity is denoted by $v(t, \tau)$. The value of the defaultable bond can then be expressed as

$$DP(t, T; \mathbf{c}) = \sum_{i=1}^{n} cv^*(t, t_i) + v^*(t, t_n) \tag{7.8}$$

The discount factor curve can be expressed in terms of a yield curve. Depending on the compounding regime, we may denote the term structure $i^*(t, T)$ defined from

$$i^*(t, T) = \left(\frac{1}{v^*(t, T)}\right)^{1/(\tau - T)} - 1 \tag{7.9}$$

By the same token we compute $i(t, T)$ from

$$i(t, T) = \left(\frac{1}{v(t, T)}\right)^{1/(T - t)} - 1 \tag{7.10}$$

Alternatively, we could use continuous compounding

$$r^*(t, T) = -\frac{\ln(v^*(t, T))}{T - t} \qquad r(t, T) = -\frac{\ln(v(t, T))}{T - t} \tag{7.11}$$

The difference in value can then be expressed in terms of yield spreads. This is the so-called credit spread term structure

$$cs(t, T) = r^*(t, T) - r(t, T) \tag{7.12}$$

The credit spread (cs) term structure refers to the difference between the defaultable and the default-free zero-coupon curves. The value of a defaultable zero-coupon bond is

$$DP(t, T : 0) = v^*(t, T) = v(t, T)[1 - E_Q(1_{\tau \leq T} LGD)] \tag{7.13}$$

From this, the credit spread term structure can be written as

$$cs(t, T) = -\frac{\ln[v^*(t, T)/v(t, T)]}{T - t} = -\frac{\ln[1 - E_Q(1_{\tau \leq T} LGD)]}{T - t} \tag{7.14}$$

and credit spreads convey the same information content as prices.

7.3   CREDIT DERIVATIVES

Credit derivatives were introduced at the beginning of the 1990s to enable financial institutions to transfer credit risk, just like IRS were traditionally used to transfer interest rate risk. For this reason the main technical tool used is that of the swap contract, even though spread options have recently gathered momentum.

Before illustrating the technical features of the main contracts used in the market, we review the basic choices that have to be made in the financial engineering of "credit protection". The first feature is the design of the payoff, that may be:

- linked to a specific reference obligation or to a set of obligations;
- determined by a credit event or a price;
- referred to the expected loss or the credit spreads.

The second feature is the design of the payment that may be

- fixed payment (up-front premium);
- periodic fixed payments (running basis premium);
- periodic floating payments plus spread (running basis spread).

7.3.1   Asset swap spread

The *asset swap* (ASW) is a product which, properly speaking, is not a credit derivative but is extensively used in the evaluation of credit risk. An asset swap can be seen as a package of two products: a bond, which in principle may be defaultable or not, and a plain vanilla interest rate swap. Under an asset swap two parties exchange the flows of a bond, plus up-front payment if the bond price is below par against floating payments, plus a spread and up-front payment if the bond quotes above par.

Without loss of generality, assume that the bond $DP(\tau, T : \mathbf{c})$ quotes below par. Two parties engage in an asset swap on this product. Payments are scheduled at times $\{t, t_1, t_2, \ldots, t_n = T\}$. Date t is the evaluation period. The party paying the fixed leg would pay $1 - DP(t, T : \mathbf{c})$ at time t and will pay the coupon c on all the following dates. The present value of the fixed leg would then be

$$1 - DP(t, T; \mathbf{c}) + c \sum_{j=1}^{n} v(t, t_j) \tag{7.15}$$

The party paying the floating leg would pay coupons indexed to the default-free curve plus a spread s. Apart from convexity and timing adjustments that we rule out for simplicity, the present value of the floating leg would be, as in standard *IRS* deals,

$$1 - v(t, T) + s \sum_{j=1}^{n} v(t, t_j) \tag{7.16}$$

An important point to notice is that the payments of the fixed and the floating legs have been discounted using the default-free term structure. This means that we rule out the event of default of either of the two parties in the swap contract. Of course, this may not be the case (actually, it is not) in the real world. Namely, three sources of credit risk are involved in this transaction: default of the issuer of the underlying security, default of the party providing protection, and default of the party purchasing protection. Our analysis here is limited to the first credit risk source. The other sources, known under the name of "counterparty risk", will be discussed in a later chapter.

As is well known, swap contracts are structured in such a way that the floating and fixed legs have the same value at the origin of the contract. So, the asset swap spread s is determined from the equality

$$1 - DP(t, T; \mathbf{c}) + c \sum_{j=1}^{n} v(t, t_j) = 1 - v(t, T) + s \sum_{j=1}^{n} v(t, t_j) \tag{7.17}$$

Recalling the definition of swap rate 'sr'

$$sr = \frac{1 - v(t, T)}{\sum_{j=1}^{n} v(t, t_j)} \tag{7.18}$$

we can compute

$$s = c - \text{sr} + \frac{1 - \text{DP}(t, T; \mathbf{c})}{\sum\limits_{j=1}^{n} v(t, t_j)} \tag{7.19}$$

So, the spread is made up of two components. The first is the difference between the coupon and the swap rate. The second is the up-front payment divided by the sum of the discount factors. It is particularly on the latter component that the spread carries information. To see this, consider what would happen to the asset swap on the corresponding default-free bond $P(t, T; \mathbf{c})$. Remember that the present value of this bond is

$$P(t, T; \mathbf{c}) = \sum\limits_{j=1}^{n} cv(t, t_j) + v(t, T) \tag{7.20}$$

Substituting in the asset swap spread formula we get

$$s = c - \text{sr} + \frac{1 - P(t, T; \mathbf{c})}{\sum\limits_{j=1}^{n} v(t, t_j)}$$

$$= c - \text{sr} + \frac{1 - \sum\limits_{j=1}^{n} cv(t, t_j) - v(t, T)}{\sum\limits_{j=1}^{n} v(t, t_j)} = c - \text{sr} - c + \frac{1 - v(t, T)}{\sum\limits_{j=1}^{n} v(t, t_j)} = 0 \tag{7.21}$$

from the definition of swap rate. So, any positive spread is a measure of the underlying bond being below par by more than it should be if it had been evaluated using the discount factor curve $v(t, \tau)$. Of course, credit risk could be just one of the possible explanations for this underpricing. Others could be liquidity, tax effects, and the like.

7.3.2 Total rate of return swap

A total return swap (TRS), or a total rate of return swap (TRORS), is simply a swap of the "total return" on a security against a sequence of payments. The total return is defined as the sum of coupon payments and capital gains or losses over the period.

Securities may be equities (*equity swaps*), corporate bonds, tranches, commodities and so on. To stick to our problem, consider our defaultable bond $\text{DP}(t, T; \mathbf{c})$. For the sake of simplicity, assume that the product is a zero-coupon bond ($c = 0$), and that we have a total return swap providing protection of the investment up to time t_j. Payments are assumed to be scheduled on the dates $\{t_1, t_2, \ldots, t_j \leq T\}$ The party providing insurance pays

$$\frac{\text{DP}(t_i, T; 0) - \text{DP}(t_{i-1}, T; 0)}{\text{DP}(t_{i-1}, T; 0)} \tag{7.22}$$

and the party purchasing insurance pays a spread s over LIBOR.

$$\frac{1}{v(t_{i-1}, t_i)} - 1 + s = i(t_{i-1}, t_i) + s \tag{7.23}$$

Notice that

$$\frac{DP(t_i, T; 0) - DP(t_{i-1}, T; 0)}{DP(t_{i-1}, T; 0)} = \frac{1}{v^*(t_{i-1}, t_i)} - 1 = i^*(t_{i-1}, t_i) \tag{7.24}$$

As typically the value at origin is assumed to be zero, we have

$$\sum_{i=1}^{n} v(t, t_i) E_{Q(t_i)}(i^*(t_{i-1}, t_i)) = \sum_{i=1}^{n} v(t, t_i) E_{Q(t_i)}(i(t_{i-1}, t_i)) + \sum_{i=1}^{j} v(t, t_i) s \tag{7.25}$$

where $Q(t_i)$ denotes the *forward martingale measure* for payments to be made at time t_i.
    The spread of the total return swap is then

$$s = \frac{\sum_{i=1}^{n} v(t, t_i) E_{Q(t_i)}(i^*(t_{i-1}, t_i) - i(t_{i-1}, t_i))}{\sum_{i=1}^{n} v(t, t_i)} \tag{7.26}$$

As for the ASW contract above, it is immediate to check that if the underlying asset of the total return swap is default-free, we have $s = 0$.
    We may now discuss the basic properties of a total return swap, in view of the payoff features pointed out in the previous section. We may make some remarks.

- The payoff is linked to a specific security. Actually, the set of securities allowed is much larger than the defaultable securities. Any investment may be the underlying of a total return swap.
- Payments are not contingent to a specific event, but are only determined by realizations of the underlying asset. These can be determined either by changes of the credit quality or by other factors.
- The underlying is typically a rate of return on a security.

From these arguments it emerges that total return swaps may not be properly defined as "credit derivatives". Actually, the value of the premium is linked to the credit standing of the issuer, and may be severely affected by deterioration of its credit quality. However, many other events and risk factors may impact on it. On one hand, institutional and liquidity features specific to a given security may be priced in the premium. On the other hand, the premium may respond to changes in the shape of the term structure, irrespective of what happens to the credit spread.

7.3.3   Credit default swap

A credit default swap (CDS) is a proper credit derivative product. Its structure closely resembles an insurance product and the events against which it is meant to provide insurance are defaults or similar "credit events".
    The typical CDS structure is that of a swap. One party buys protection against some default event ("*protection buyer*") and pays a premium, typically on a running basis. The stream of payments due by the protection buyer is called the "*premium leg*" of the swap. The other party, the protection seller, faces the obligation, until maturity of the swap, to pay the losses incurred by the protection buyer as a result of a certified "*credit event*". The

losses are referred to a principal amount determined in the contract. This insurance service is called the *"protection leg"*.

Unlike the total return swap, the CDS is a standardized product. The underlying asset is not a specific issue, but rather a "name", denoting an issuer. When a credit event occurs, the protection seller makes up for losses on general exposures to the "name" under the contract. Depending on the type of contract, it can be settled in cash: in some "digital" contracts the obligation is a fixed sum, in other cases the loss-given default to be refunded is determined by experts. The most usual settlement agreement remains, however, a *physical delivery*. The protection buyer is then allowed to deliver whatever debt obligation was issued by the "name", receiving the nominal value. Of course, the natural choice would be to deliver those instruments that are worth less. In other words, the protection buyer holds a *"quality option"* or *"delivery option"*, like that typical of the futures markets. It is this feature that provides the CDS market with the same product standardization and liquidity as that of the futures markets themselves. So, everybody holding an exposure with respect to a given "name" will be interested in trading a CDS on that name; also, everybody interested in structuring products linked to the credit quality of a name would use a CDS as a way to provide "synthetic" credit risk.

The credit event is also standardized under the ISDA agreement. Eligible credit events are:

- Bankruptcy
- Obligation acceleration
- Obligation default
- Failure to pay
- Moratorium/Repudiation
- Restructuring.

Different credit events may have impact on the value of the contract. This certainly applies to contracts selecting the "restructuring" credit event. In this case in fact, there may be a clear "moral hazard" problem with the party purchasing protection. The party holding insurance against default on some exposure may have a strong incentive to force debt restructuring with the issuer to collect the payment from the protection seller. It is for this reason that protection premia for a CDS with this "restructuring" clause are typically higher.

In order to describe the payments expected for the two legs we make the simplifying assumption that payments occur at the end of the coupon period. The payment from the protection seller at the end of any coupon period (time t_i) can be represented as

$$\mathbf{1}_{t_{i-1} < \tau \leq t_i} \text{LGD} \tag{7.27}$$

where $\mathbf{1}_{t_{i-1} < \tau \leq t_i}$ is the indicator function taking value 1 if default occurs between time t_{i-1} and time t_i. At time t_i the protection buyer will pay instead

$$\mathbf{1}_{t_{i-1} < \tau} s \tag{7.28}$$

where now the indicator function $\mathbf{1}_{t_{i-1} < \tau}$ spots that the issuer has survived up to time t_{i-1}. The term s is the fixed premium paid on a running basis. It is in fact assumed that if the "name" defaults in a period, the contract ends in that period.

We will now address the problem of evaluating the payments of the two legs. Denote by $\overline{Q}(t) = \Pr(\mathbf{1}_{t<\tau})$ the survival probability of the issuer up time t under the risk-neutral measure. The present value of each payment of the protection leg is then

$$v(t, t_i)[\overline{Q}(t_{i-1}) - \overline{Q}(t_i)] \, \text{LGD} \tag{7.29}$$

that is the discounted value of the probability of observing default between time t_{i-1} and time $t_i[\overline{Q}(t_{i-1}) - \overline{Q}(t_i)]$, times the payment to be done (LGD). By the same token, the present value of each payment in the premium leg is given by

$$v(t, t_i)\overline{Q}(t_{i-1})s \tag{7.30}$$

that is, the discounted value of the premium times the probability that the "name" had survived up to the period. As in the previous case of total return swaps, notice that the payments are discounted by the default-free discount factor, meaning that we do not take into account the default risk of the two parties involved in the swap.

Credit default swaps, together with all other swap contracts, share the feature that no capital is exchanged at the origin of the contract. So, the value of a CDS at inception is zero. Assuming that the swap consists of n payments, we have at the origin

$$\sum_{i=1}^{n} v(t, t_i)\overline{Q}(t_{i-1})s_n = \sum_{i=1}^{n} v(t, t)\left[\overline{Q}(t_{i-1}) - \overline{Q}(t_i)\right] \text{LGD} \tag{7.31}$$

where s_n is the premium charged for an n period protection.

So, to comment on the general differences between CDS and other credit derivatives, we can use the bullet points of the section above:

- The payoff is not linked to a specific security, but to all of the obligations issued by the "name" .
- Payments are contingent to a specific event, defined and specified under a standard ISDA template.
- The underlying is a "name", an abstract term to denote the credit standing of an issuer.

These features have made the CDS market the most liquid tool to hedge credit risk, very much in the same way as the IRS market has been the ideal tool to transfer interest rate risk without unbundling fixed income portfolios.

7.3.4 The FpML representation of a CDS

The XML schema for a CDS, developed by the International Swaps and Derivatives Association (ISDA), contains nearly 400 required or optional information components, whose composition is dependent on numerous contingencies. As usual we present a general overview of the relevant data structure, the interested reader is referred to the original documentation (FpML 4.0 – Credit Derivative Component DefinitionsRecommendation 2 April 2004). The XML schema contains a complex type called `CreditDefaultSwap` which is composed of the following elements:

- *generalTerms*: This element contains all the data that appears in the section entitled "1. General Terms" in the 2003 ISDA Credit Derivatives Confirmation.

- *feeLeg*: This element contains all the terms relevant to defining the fixed amounts/payments per the applicable ISDA definitions.
- *protectionTerms*: This element contains all the terms relevant to defining the applicable floating rate payer calculation amount, credit events and associated conditions to settlement, and reference obligations.
- Either

  - *cashSettlementTerms*: This element contains all the ISDA terms relevant to cash settlement for when cash settlement is applicable. ISDA 2003 Term: Cash Settlement.

  Or

  - *physicalSettlementTerms*: This element contains all the ISDA terms relevant to physical settlement for when physical settlement is applicable. ISDA 2003 Term: Physical Settlement.

Each of these elements is in turn defined appropriately by a particular complex type. From the FpML internet site you can also download a very interesting set of ISDA confirmation documents which refer to CDS transactions. For each transaction you can find the corresponding FpML file.

The following is the schema fragment for CDS extracted from file `fpml-cd-4-0.xsd`:

```
<xsd:complexType name = "CreditDefaultSwap">
  <xsd:complexContent>
    <xsd:extension base = "Product">
      <xsd:sequence>
        <xsd:element name = "generalTerms" type
         = "GeneralTerms">
          <xsd:annotation>
            <xsd:documentation xml:lang
            = "en">This element contains
            all the data that appears in the
            section entitled "1.
            General Terms" in the 2003 ISDA
            Credit Derivatives Confirmation.
            </xsd:documentation>
          </xsd:annotation>
        </xsd:element>
        <xsd:element name = "feeLeg" type = "FeeLeg">
          <xsd:annotation>
            <xsd:documentation xml:lang = "en">
            This element contains all the
            terms relevant to defining
            the fixed amounts/payments per the
            applicable ISDA definitions.
            </xsd:documentation>
          </xsd:annotation>
        </xsd:element>
```

```
       <xsd:element name = "protectionTerms" type
       = "ProtectionTerms">
         <xsd:annotation>
           <xsd:documentation xml:lang = "en">
           This element contains all the
           terms relevant to defining
           the applicable floating
           rate payer calculation amount,
           credit events and associated
           conditions to settlement,
           and reference obligations.
           </xsd: documentation>
         </xsd:annotation>
       </xsd:element>
       <xsd:choice minOccurs = "0">
         <xsd:element name = "cashSettlementTerms"
         type ="CashSettlementTerms">
           <xsd:annotation>
             <xsd: documentation xml:lang = "en">
             This element contains all the
             ISDA terms relevant to
             cash settlement for when
             cash settlement is applicable.
             ISDA 2003 Term: Cash
             Settlement.
             </xsd:documentation>
           </xsd:annotation>
         </xsd:element>
         <xsd:element name =
         "physicalSettlementTerms" type =
         "PhysicalSettlementTerms">
           <xsd:annotation>
             <xsd:documentation xml:lang
             = "en">This element contains
             all the ISDA terms relevant to
             physical settlement for when
             physical settlement is
             applicable. ISDA 2003 Term:
             Physical Settlement.
             </xsd:documentation>
           </xsd:annotation>
         </xsd:element>
       </xsd:choice>
     </xsd:sequence>
   </xsd:extension>
 </xsd:complexContent>
</xsd:complexType>
```

This structure could be used as a guide to design an object-oriented description of this type of derivative. From a general point of view, as the reader should have understood, there is no unique solution to the problem of building a hierarchy of classes. For example, we should use classes from Chapter 4 (particularly `CInterestRateStream` and related classes) to build a generic `Swap` class from which we could inherit a `CreditDefaultSwap` adding specific attributes of this type of derivative. These attributes can be designed, keeping in mind the previously discussed FpML scheme. Of course this crucially depends on the kind of application we are thinking of. For example, if pricing is our main concern, then, to information of the `Swap` class, we should add a list of default probability for each payment date. Nevertheless, strictly speaking, default probabilities are not attributes of a CDS so it should be a better approach to build a class that includes the pricing model used. This model should calculate default probabilities from the general information contained in the `CreditDefaultSwap` class. According to this last approach we should define a generic class which we should call (following FpML schema) `ProtectionTerm`, designed to collect all information about the underlying financial asset of our CDS.

7.3.5   Credit spread options

We have seen that the market refers to the swap technique to transfer credit risk in very much the same way as it does for interest risk. It seems that these markets are destined to develop in a similar way. The natural development is that of introducing products that enable us to enter these swap transactions, just as the Swaptions market allows us to do for IRS. Actually, this development is on the way, and markets have been developed for:

- *Asset swap spread options*: They allow us to enter an asset swap spread at a future date for a given spread. Actually, these are nothing but spread options on the difference between the yield to maturity of the asset and the swap rate for the corresponding maturity.
- *Credit default swap options*: They allow us to enter a credit default swap at a future date for a given premium. In concept, they are very similar to Swaptions (in fact they are also called CDSwaptions), and the pricing techniques are very similar to those used for the default-free corresponding product (see Hull and White, 2003; Jamshidian, 2004; Brigo and Morini, 2005).

7.4   CREDIT-LINKED NOTES

Credit derivatives, and credit default swaps in particular, represent important tools with which to set up structured products. Credit-linked notes are the most straightforward example. The idea is to synthetically provide investors with exposure to the default risk of a "name", in exchange for a higher return.

Let us describe the deal. A trust engages in the following operations:

- It raises funds for an amount $LP(t, T: \mathbf{c})$ by issuing a note with maturity T.
- It buys L nominal of the default-free asset $P(t, T: \mathbf{c})$.
- It enters a CDS contract with a dealer, selling protection on "name" X for a nominal amount equal to L.
- In exchange for the protection service, the trust earns a premium equal to s_n paid on a running basis.

- If the "name" of the CDS contract survives to the end of the investment horizon T, the trust would pay $c + s_n$ interest on a running basis.
- If the "name" of the CDS defaults at time $\tau \leq T$, the trust uses the collateral amount $LP(\tau, T : c)$ to face its protection obligation, paying $L \times LGD$ to the CDS counterparty and reducing the principal of the note issued by the same amount.

In analytical terms, the structure of the credit-linked note (CLN) can be summarized as follows:

$$CLN = P(t, T : c) - CDS(t, T : s) \qquad (7.32)$$

A credit-linked noted is then the sum of a long position in a default-free security and a short position in a CDS (selling protection). The deal is summarized in the scheme below.

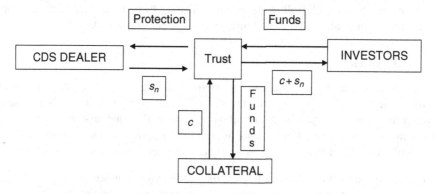

Figure 7.1   A credit-linked note

7.5   CREDIT PROTECTION

Under a general perspective, credit risk is not only, or directly, connected with the event of default of an entity. Credit risk is also the change in value of an obligation due to the modified perception in the market that default could occur at some time in the future. Many events can bring about this change of perception, but the most relevant are decisions from the rating agencies. Changes in rating or in the outlook from S&P, Moody's or Fitch have relevant impact on the market evaluation of bonds.

In some cases, one may find clauses aimed at protecting the value of the investments from these events. These clauses are sometimes referred to as "credit protection". Consider a product with coupons paid at dates $\{t_0, t_1, t_2, \ldots, t_n\}$. The typical definition of a coupon with credit protection is

$$c(t_{j-1}, t_j) \equiv c + \sum_{i=1}^{m} s_i \mathbf{1}_i(t_{j-1}) \qquad (7.33)$$

where i denotes the credit rating scale (for example AAA $= 1$, AA $= 2$, $\ldots$, C $= m$). $\mathbf{1}_i(t)$ denotes the indicator function taking value 1 if the credit rating class of the issuer is i at time t. The spread s_i represents the value to be added to the coupon corresponding to the rating class.

The value of the product would then be

$$DP(t, t_n; \mathbf{c}) = \sum_{i=1}^{n} v^*(t, t_i)c + v^*(t, t_n) + \sum_{j=1}^{n} \sum_{i=1}^{m} v^*(t, t_j)s_i Q(1_i(t_{j-1})) \qquad (7.34)$$

The price of the product then involves the evaluation of a stream of digital options in which the underlying asset is the rating class of the issuer. The idea is that if the issuer is downgraded, the negative impact on the present value of the cash flows is mitigated by an increase in the nominal value of the coupon. The ideal tool used to price the credit protection clause is of course the credit *transition matrix*, giving the probability that the obligor could move from rating class i to rating class j in the unit of time. Transition matrices are supplied by the rating agencies, even though it must be remembered that, in pricing applications like this, they should be converted under the risk-neutral measure (see Jarrow *et al.*, 1997). Assume that you have a risk-neutral credit transition matrix

$$\mathbf{Q} \equiv \begin{bmatrix} q_{11} & q_{21} & \cdots & q_{1k} \\ q_{21} & q_{22} & \cdots & \vdots \\ \vdots & \vdots & & \vdots \\ q_{k1} & q_{k2} & \cdots & q_{kk} \end{bmatrix} \qquad (7.35)$$

with q_{ij} is the joint probability that the issuer is in the rating class i at time t and in rating class j at time $t+1$. Assuming that the transition matrix is constant, the probability of moving from rating class i at time t and in rating class j at time $t+n$ is given by the elements of the matrix $\mathbf{Q}^n$. Denote $\mathbf{q}_i^n$ the ith row of this matrix. If we assume that, at the evaluation time t, the issuer belonged to class i, the price of the defaultable bond with credit protection can then be expressed in compact form as

$$DP(t, t_n; \mathbf{c}) = \sum_{j=1}^{n} v^*(t, t_i)c + v^*(t, t_n) + s_i v^*(t, t_1) + \sum_{j=1}^{n} v^*(t, t_j) \mathbf{q}_i^{j-1} \mathbf{s} \qquad (7.36)$$

where $\mathbf{s}$ is an m-dimension vector with elements s_i.

Example 7.1 A bond issued by Telecom Italy on 30 July 1999 for maturity in 10 years was paying a fixed 6.125% coupon plus credit protection, as described in Table 7.1.

Table 7.1 Credit protection example

Moody's	Standard and Poor's	Spread
Baa1	BBB +	15 bp
Baa2	BBB	45 bp
Baa3	BBB −	95 bp
Ba1 or lower	BB + or lower	195 bp

In case of disagreement between the rating agencies, the worst rating would be selected.

7.6   CALLABLE AND PUTABLE BONDS

The problem of pricing callability and putability features is obviously much more involved in the case of defaultable bonds, because the exercise of the corresponding option depends on two sources of risk: interest rate and credit risk.

To highlight the greater complexity, consider a problem that would not actually make sense for default-free bonds: a callable/putable floating rate note. Denote by $\mathrm{DFRN}(t, T)$ a floating rate note issued by a defaultable entity. Coupons are reset and paid at dates $\{t_0, t_1, t_2, \ldots, t_n = T\}$. For the sake of simplicity, let us assume a "natural lag" scheme of indexation. Coupon is reset at time t_{j-1} and paid at time t_j. The coupon is indexed to the default-free term structure and is formally defined as

$$c\left(t_{j-1}, t_j\right) = \frac{1}{v(t_{j-1}, t_j)} - 1 \tag{7.37}$$

The value of the coupon at the reset date is then

$$v^*(t_{j-1}, t_j)c(t_{j-1}, t_j) = v^*(t_{j-1}, t_j)\left[\frac{1}{v(t_{j-1}, t_j)} - 1\right] = \frac{v^*(t_{j-1}, t_j)}{v(t_{j-1}, t_j)} - v^*(t_{j-1}, t_j) \tag{7.38}$$

Adding and subtracting 1, we get

$$v^*(t_{j-1}, t_j)c(t_{j-1}, t_j) = \frac{v^*(t_{j-1}, t_j)}{v(t_{j-1}, t_j)} - 1 + (1 - v^*(t_{j-1}, t_j)) \tag{7.39}$$

So, the coupon of a defaultable floater can be broken down into two parts. The first part depends on the ratio $v^*(t_{j-1}, t_j)/v(t_{j-1}, t_j)$, and so on the credit spread. The second part, $1 - v^*(t_{j-1}, t_j)$, is a typical floating rate coupon, with the peculiarity that it is indexed to the defaultable interest rate. As in all the standard floating rate notes, if one adds the discounted value of the coupons and the principal, one gets the value of a short-term note. In particular, the note will quote at par at any coupon reset date. At any reset time t_i we have then

$$\mathrm{DFRN}(t_i, t_n) = \sum_{j=i+1}^{n} E_Q[v^*(t_i, t_{j-1})v^*(t_{j-1}, t_j)c(t_{j-1}, t_j)]$$

$$= \sum_{j=i+1}^{n} E_Q\left[v^*(t_i, t_{j-1})\left(\frac{v^*(t_{j-1}, t_j)}{v(t_{j-1}, t_j)} - 1\right)\right] + 1 \tag{7.40}$$

Computing the value requires determining the dynamics of the credit spread and its dependence with the term structure of the defaultable issuer. Notice that the term that keeps the value of the floating rate note away from par is very similar to the discounted present value of a protection leg in a CDS contract, the counterparty of this contract being the issuer of the bond. To see this, recall that

$$\frac{v^*(t_{j-1}, t_j)}{v(t_{j-1}, t_j)} - 1 = 1_{t_{j-1} \leq \tau < t_j}\mathrm{LGD} \tag{7.41}$$

which is actually the promised payment of a protection seller on a CDS swap. The only problem here is that the issuer is providing insurance against himself. So, counterparty risk cannot be reasonably ignored.

Assume now that the product is callable at time t_i for a value equal to $1 + k$. We have

$$\min(\text{DFRN}(t_i, t_n), 1 + k) = \text{DFRN}(t_i, t_n) - \max(\text{DFRN}(t_i, t_n) - (1 + k), 0)$$

$$= \text{DFRN}(t_i, t_n) - \max\left[E_Q\left[\sum_{j=i+1}^{n} v^*(t_i, t_{j-1}) \right.\right.$$

$$\left.\left. \times \left(\frac{v^*(t_{j-1}, t_j)}{v(t_{j-1}, t_j)} - 1 \right) \right] - k, 0 \right] \qquad (7.42)$$

Notice that the value of the call option depends on the credit spreads. The underlying asset of the call option is a stream of payments. The pricing problem is very similar to that of an option on a credit default swap.

7.7 CREDIT RISK VALUATION

We now give a brief account of valuation issues of credit risk. Our review will be necessarily synthetic and selective. The readers interested in a more detailed treatment are referred to many excellent books available: among others, we quote Cossin and Pirrotte (2000), Bielecki and Rutkowski (2001), Duffie and Singleton (2003), Lando (2004). What is common to all the pricing models is the goal to provide a satisfactory representation of the two main figures involved in credit risk evaluation: the probability of default (or the complement, the survival probability) and the recovery rate (or the complement, the loss-given default figure). Given a model for these two figures, we can compute their product, the *expected loss*, which is the main ingredient to recover a price for all the products surveyed above. The main difference in the approach to this problem is in the pricing tool used. The general and well-known taxonomy of credit risk models denote as *structural models* those using option-pricing theory to evaluate credit risk, and as *reduced form* models those using term structure theory to explain credit spread behaviour. Apart from borderline cases, this taxonomy is quite satisfactory and we follow it here.

7.7.1 Structural models

In structural models, corporate liabilities are evaluated by decomposing their payoffs in linear and nonlinear products, and using standard option-pricing theory to price them. The seminal paper in this literature is due to Merton (1974), even though the world famous Black and Scholes (1973) was already targeted at the pricing of corporate liabilities. The basic idea is the following. Assume that a bond is issued to fund an entrepreneurial project that will give its payoff at time T. The payoff is denoted $V(T)$. Assume that this project is funded using a zero-coupon bond whose face value is B and has a maturity matching the end of the project T. At maturity, the value of debt will be

$$D(T, T; 0) = \min[B, V(T)] \qquad (7.43)$$

In order to isolate the nonlinearity due to default risk, notice that we have

$$D(T, T; 0) = B - \max[B - V(T), 0] \qquad (7.44)$$

Default risk is measured as a short position in a put option written on the value of assets for a strike price equal to the face value of debt. By the same token, using the decomposition

$$D(T, T; 0) = V(T) - \max[V(T) - B, 0] \tag{7.45}$$

it is easy to see that what is left after repayment of debt, that is equity, is a call option with the same underlying, strike price and exercise dates.

Assuming that the value of the project follows a geometric Brownian motion, one may use the Black–Scholes formula to price both equity and debt. In particular, debt is valued as

$$D(t, T; 0) = V(t)\Phi(-d_1) + v(t, T)B\Phi(d_2)$$
$$d_1 = \frac{\ln[V(t)/(Bv(t, T))] + \sigma_V^2(T - t)}{\sigma_V\sqrt{T - t}} \tag{7.46}$$
$$d_2 = d_1 - \sigma_V\sqrt{T - t}$$

where σ_V is the volatility of the value of the firm. Adding and subtracting $v(t, T)B$ we get

$$D(t, T; 0) = v(t, T)B + V(t)\Phi(-d_1) - v(t, T)B\Phi(-d_2)$$
$$= v(t, T)B - [-V(t)\Phi(-d_1) + v(t, T)B\Phi(-d_2)] \tag{7.47}$$

and the part in square brackets represent the short position in the put option measuring credit risk. Notice that we could further write

$$D(t, T; 0) = v(t, T)B\left[1 - \Phi(-d_2) + \frac{V(t)}{v(t, T)B}\Phi(-d_1)\right]$$
$$= v(t, T)B\left[1 - \Phi(-d_2)\left(1 - \frac{V(t)}{v(t, T)B}\frac{\Phi(-d_1)}{\Phi(-d_2)}\right)\right] \tag{7.48}$$

By standard option-pricing theory we know that the probability exercise of a put option under the Black–Scholes model is $\Phi(-d_2)$. In this model, exercise of the put option means default of the bond, so we can write $\mathrm{DP} = \Phi(-d_2)$. We can then recognize

$$D(t, T; 0) = v(t, T)B[1 - \mathrm{DP}(1 - \mathrm{RR})] \tag{7.49}$$

where the formula for the *recovery rate* (RR) can be easily extracted by comparison. This way of representing the formula is particularly suggestive of the basic principle and idea behind structural models. Both the default probability and the loss-given default figures are determined by a single state variable, which is the value of the firm. This idea is responsible for both the elegance and the lack of flexibility of such models.

This lack of flexibility does not have to do with the stylized structure of the model. In fact, while in the seminal Merton's paper the structure of the bond is kept very simple, assuming a zero-coupon bond and the possibility of default only at maturity, successive extensions have been proposed to account for coupon bonds (Geske, 1977), covenants and seniority structures (Black and Cox, 1976), warrants and convertible debt (Bensoussan *et al.*, 1995a, 1995b).

While representing an elegant and informative approach to the evaluation of corporate securities, structural models do not generally provide a good fit to the real market data. This poor fit shows up in three empirical regularities:

- Typically, reasonable values for leverage of the firm and volatility of assets produce credit spreads which are too low with respect to those observed in the market.
- Undervaluation is particularly relevant for short-term maturities: a typical credit spread term structure in the Merton model shows a hump and zero intercept.
- Undervaluation is particularly relevant for high credit standing obligors.

Several answers have been proposed as possible solutions to these problems. Anderson and Sundaresan (1996) suggest that the owner of the firm may engage in a strategic rescheduling process to exploit the bankruptcy costs at the expense of bondholders. Along the same lines, Leland (1994) and Leland and Toft (1996) allow the owner of the firm to terminate the process in such a way as to optimize the value of equity, again at the expense of debt. An alternative explanation for the failure of structural models to fit the data stems from the fact that the value of the firm is not directly observed and this lack of transparency may affect the prices in the market. In this spirit Cherubini and Della Lunga (2001) propose a conservative assessment of the probability of default by using a default probability interval, in line with the MaxMin–Expected–Utility framework in Gilboa and Schmeidler (1989). However, this approach is not able to account for the strong undervaluation of credit spreads for short maturities. This is due to the main assumption on which the model was built – that is, the representation of the value of the firm as an adapted diffusion process. The need to account for higher credit spreads for shorter maturities can be achieved either by allowing for a jump process in the value of the firm (Zhou, 2001), so dropping the diffusion process assumption, or by relaxing the adapted process hypothesis. The latter route was first followed by Duffie and Lando (2001), who propose a model with endogenous bankruptcy in which the market is assumed to observe a noisy signal of the value of the firm at discrete times. Recently, several extensions of this model have been provided. Baglioni and Cherubini (2006) model a bias in the signal showing that such bias could be responsible for the undervaluation of high credit standing obligors. Herkommer (2006) introduces correlation between the value of the firm and noise, and finds evidence of negative correlation. Other approaches based on imperfect information, concerning both the value of the firm and the default thresholds, have been proposed (Giesecke, 2001; CreditGrades™, 2001).

7.7.2 Reduced form models

The reason for the elegance of structural models, that the dynamics of the value of the firm determines both the default probability and the loss-given default, is also their main reason for flaw. The value of the firm is not a sufficient statistic for the event of default, and in some cases, like sovereign risk, may also not even be defined. Moreover, even if it were a sufficient statistic for the default event, it could definitely not be so for the recovery rate. What one can recover on debt, in fact, is often the outcome of a complex and time-consuming process. If the default case is brought before the court, the time to recovery may be very lengthy and difficult to predict, particular under some jurisdictions (e.g. the Italian one). If, as happens most often, the case is handled by rescheduling renegotiations among the parties, the outcome itself is unpredictable, as it comes from a complex game under which many optimal strategies bring to *absolute priority violations*. This phenomenon points to the fact that, in the end, the natural priority in the repayment of funds in case of crisis (such as pay all the debt before paying equity) may be violated. The Anderson and Sundaresan strategic debt service model is the first and simplest example. Many more cases of absolute priority violations do occur in the real world, particularly in cases (most of them) in which many lender are involved, with different exposures. These situations provide the natural recipe for blackmail behaviour that is very difficult to model and predict. All of these arguments have convinced some of the scholars in credit risk to give up the economics of the problem in favour of a more statistically oriented approach. The basic idea is to come up with reasonable statistical models for the two quantities involved: default and recovery rate.

Default risk

Concerning the modelling of default probability, the first idea that may come to mind is to model the default event as a Poisson process. The parameter describing the process is called intensity and defines the instantaneous probability of observing an event. In this application, of course, we are interested in the default event. The probability of observing n default events in a time span from t to T is

$$\exp(-\lambda(T-t))\frac{(\lambda(T-t))^n}{n!} \tag{7.50}$$

The probability of observing 0 events is the survival probability beyond time T, and is as simple as

$$\exp(-\lambda(T-t)) \tag{7.51}$$

Assume, for the sake of simplicity and for a conservative assessment, a zero recovery rate. The price of a defaultable zero-coupon bond maturing at T is then

$$D(t, T; 0) = v(t, T)Q(\tau > T) = v(t, T)\exp(-\lambda(T-t)) \tag{7.52}$$

The credit spread is

$$-\ln\left[\frac{D(t, T; 0)}{v(t, T)}\right]/(T-t) = -\ln[\exp(-\lambda(T-t))]/(T-t) = \lambda \tag{7.53}$$

The credit spread structure is then flat at the same level as the default intensity. If one may not consider a flat term structure realistic, the model can be extended by making the instantaneous intensity process stochastic. In this case the survival probability would be

$$Q(\tau > T) = E_Q\left[\exp\left(-\int_t^T \lambda(u)\,du\right)\right] \tag{7.54}$$

A natural choice would be to resort to mean-reversion diffusive process

$$d\lambda(t) = k(\bar{\lambda} - \lambda(t))\,dt + \sigma\lambda^\alpha(t)\,dz^*(t) \tag{7.55}$$

The instantaneous probability converges towards a long run mean value $\bar{\lambda}$. Notice that for $\alpha = 0$ and $\alpha = 0.5$ the stationary distribution is known: it is normal and gamma, respectively.

The survival probability has closed form solutions, and are given in classical factor models of the term structure models, namely Vasicek (1977) and CIR (Cox et al., 1985).

$$Q(\tau > T) = \left[\exp\left(-\int_{t}^{T} \lambda(u)\, du \right) \right] = \exp[A(T-t) - B(T-t)\lambda(t)]$$

The value of the defaultable zero coupon under the assumption of zero recovery rate is then

$$D(t, T; 0) = E_Q[v(t, T)Q(\tau > T)] = v(t, T)Q_T(\tau > T) \tag{7.56}$$

where Q_T is the T-time forward martingale measure: $Q_T(\tau > T) = E_{Q(T)}[Q(\tau > T)]$.

Recovery risk

Models taking into account recovery risk are more recent. In most models, in which recovery is assumed constant, the extension of the analysis above is immediate. Actually, a defaultable zero-coupon bond can be considered as a portfolio of two bonds: the default-free bond and a fictitious bond with same default probability and recovery rate equal to zero. In other terms, it is easy to see that

$$D(t, T: 0) = v(t, T)[\text{RR} - (1 - \text{RR})Q_T(\tau \leq T)] \tag{7.57}$$

The recovery rate can be either defined on the "Treasury equivalent value" of the bond (Jarrow and Turnbull, 1995) or on the "market value" of the bond (Duffie and Singleton, 1999). If one assumes the recovery rate to be stochastic, but orthogonal to the other risk factors (that is, interest rate risk and default probability), the extension of this formula is immediate by substitution of the expected value of the recovery rate for the value RR above. Distributions with finite support, such as the Beta, are typically used to estimate the expected recovery rate. In some cases, both the default intensity and the recovery rate are not distinguished in the credit spread figure. In the Duffie and Singleton model, in fact, we have

$$D(t, T: 0) = E_Q\left[\exp\left(-\int_{t}^{T} [r(u) + \lambda(u)(1 - \text{RR})\, du] \right) \right] \tag{7.58}$$

where $r(u)$ is the instantaneous default-free rate and RR is the "recovery of market value".

If one is interested in disentangling the recovery rate and the default event, it may be relevant to investigate whether they may be correlated. Actually, in structural models recovery rates and default probabilities can be shown to be negatively correlated. Evidence of such negative correlation has been confirmed in many empirical applications (Frye, 2000 and Altman et al., 2004). On economic grounds, this evidence is explained with the co-movement of these variables across the business cycle. When the trend of the economy is strong, default is less likely, the value of firms is higher, and the amount that can be recovered in case of default is correspondingly higher. When the economy is in a recession, many defaults are likely to occur and for each of them one expects to recover a lower value. Consistent with this evidence, one would like to separately model these two sources of risk, breaking down credit risk into default risk and recovery risk: furthermore, recovery should be modelled under the risk-neutral measure. The literature on this issue is not yet very extensive. Madan and Unal (1998) propose a model to back out recovery risk from junior and senior debt. Jarrow (2000) proposes a model to accomplish the same task using equity and debt. Finally Guo *et al.* (2005) model the recovery process in a structural-like approach distinguishing between a default intensity and a bankruptcy intensity: in some sense, models like these try to bridge the gap from reduced form models to structural models in a way similar to that of "strategic debt service" models.

7.8   MARKET INFORMATION ON CREDIT RISK

From the above bird's-eye review of the main credit risk models, it emerges that there are many sources of information from which to recover a consistent estimate of default risk. If one were to make a classification, one could first distinguish between historical and implied credit risk measures. Historical measures are mainly supplied by the rating agencies, as well as private databases of banks and other financial intermediaries. Implied information is instead extracted from market quotes of securities issued from or on some obligor. Among these sources providing implied information we may further distinguish between security-specific or issuer-specific information. Typical example of security-specific source of information is the asset swap spread. Typical examples of issuer-specific information are stock prices and CDS quotes. At the time of writing, it would seem that most of the debate, both among practitioners and in the academic literature, is about the relative information content of equity and CDS.

7.8.1   Security-specific information: asset swap spreads

We saw that asset swap spreads convey information about the undervaluation of an asset. So, if one is interested in measuring the specific risk of a single bond, a look at the ASW spread could give a global view of how the market prices the issue.

The best way to illustrate the procedure and the problems is by an example. Consider that one has to evaluate the risk of a bond issued by Nippon Telecom. The bond pays a fixed coupon equal to 6% of the nominal value, and promises repayment of principal at maturity, on 25 March 2008. On 20 February 2001 the market was quoting an asset swap spread of 38.3 basis points. The market typically uses this information as an estimate of the default intensity of the issue. Of course, on rigorous grounds the only information that is possible to recover from this figure is the degree of undervaluation of the bond. Credit risk can be just one of many other possible explanations: liquidity issues, fiscal features, left alone outright mis-pricing.

If the issue has been assigned a rating, one can check how much specific information is embedded in the asset swap rate by simply comparing the spread with those quoted for similar issues of the same rating class. At that time, the NTT issue above was rated A − from Standard and Poor's. Figure 7.2 shows the comparison between the asset swap spread and the credit spread of the closest rating classes (A and BBB). The picture shows that around the seven-year maturity, corresponding to the maturity of the bond, the asset swap spread is actually included in the range between the BBB and A spreads. More precisely, the BBB spread was 43 bp against 26 bp for the A spread.

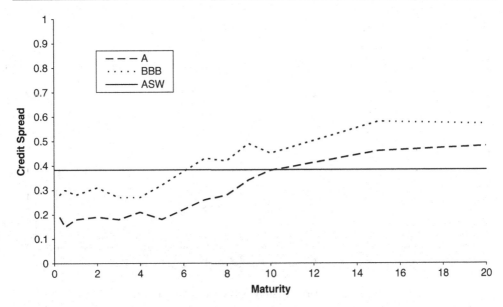

Figure 7.2   Asset swap and rating spread curve information. NTT, 6%, 25/3/2008, evaluations, 20/02/2001

7.8.2   Obligor-specific information: equity and CDS

In the analysis above, we saw that one can actually resort to extreme choices between information specific to a given security and specific to a rating class. In the first choice, the significance of the results can be affected by the specific features of the security under analysis, while in the second it can be noisy for the many different obligors and securities represented in the rating class. A good compromise between a security-specific and rating-specific default probability information is offered by the equity market and/or by the CDS market. Thanks to their liquidity, these markets represent the most preferred source of information about the credit standing of obligors.

As an example of these sources of information, Figure 7.3 reports the time series of stock prices and CDS quotes for Parmalat in the year preceding the default event that took place in December 2003. It can be seen that, particularly in periods of crisis, the stock and CDS quotes behave as in a mirror image. In February 2003, for example, Parmalat proposed a new large bond issue to the market. Since Parmalat was also reporting a large liquidity, this issue came as a surprise to the market. As Figure 7.3 shows, when the issue was withdrawn the stock price tumbled suddenly, and at the same time the CDS quotes spiked up.

Equity information

Structural models suggest equity as a natural choice of obligor-specific information. As a matter of fact, if equity is a call option on the asset value of the firm, the probability that this option will expire worthless at the end of the business project, or that it would reach zero before the end of it, corresponds to the probability of default of the obligor. Notice that using equity also solves the problem of distinguishing default probability and loss-given default in the expected loss figure. In fact, apart from absolute priority violations or strategic

Figure 7.3   Parmalat story: CDS and common stock

debt service behaviour, the residual claim nature of equity ensures that its value has to be zero under the default scenario.

Moody's KMV approach: Building upon this idea the Moody's KMV model extracts from equity data expected default frequencies. The target is to use such information to extract two unknown key variables: the value of the firm, V, and its volatility, σ_V. These values are recovered by solving a nonlinear system of two equations. The first is the Black–Scholes formula yielding the value of the stock $S(t)$

$$S(t) = V(t)\Phi(d_1) - v(t, T)B\Phi(d_2) \tag{7.59}$$

The second equation enables us to fit the volatility of the stock. From Ito's lemma we have

$$\sigma_s S(t) = \sigma_V V(t)\Phi(d_1) \tag{7.60}$$

The system is solved by an iterative procedure and from the estimates of V and σ_V one computes the so called *distance to default* (DD) figure

$$DD(t) = \frac{\ln(V(t)/B)) + (\mu - 0.5\sigma_V^2)}{\sigma_V} \tag{7.61}$$

where μ is the estimated rate of growth of assets (meaning that we are under the objective probability measure). This figure is finally used to recover the empirical frequency of default from a database.

Maximum likelihood approach: An alternative to the above algorithm is to resort to maximum likelihood estimation of the parameters. The idea stems from the distribution

$$\ln\left(\frac{V(t)}{V(t-\delta)}\right) \sim \Phi\left((\mu - 1/2\sigma_V^2)\delta, \sigma_V\sqrt{\delta}\right) \tag{7.62}$$

Assuming one could observe $V(t)$, a possible way to estimate the parameters would be by maximizing the log-likelihood

$$L(V(t_i), i = 1, 2, \ldots, n, \mu, \sigma_V) = -\frac{n-1}{2} \ln(2\pi) - \ln \sigma_V^2 - \sum_{i=2}^{n} \ln V(t_i)$$

$$-\frac{1}{2} \sum_{i=2}^{n} \left[\ln \left(\frac{V(t_i)}{V(t_{i-1})} \right) - \mu(t_i - t_{i-1}) \right] \quad (7.63)$$

Duan (1994, 2000) shows how to modify the likelihood in order to account for the fact that the value of assets $V(t)$ cannot be directly observed. Assuming that one observes a derivative $g(V(t))$ instead of $V(t)$, with a delta equal to Δ_g, one can write a *log-likelihood on transformed data*

$$L(g(V(t_i)), i = 1, 2, \ldots, n, \mu, \sigma_V) = -\frac{n-1}{2} \ln(2\pi) - \ln \sigma_V^2 - \sum_{i=2}^{n} \ln V^*(t_i, \sigma_V)$$

$$-\sum_{i=2}^{n} \ln |\Delta_g(t_i, \sigma_V)| - \frac{1}{2} \sum_{i=2}^{n} \left[\ln \left(\frac{V^*(t_i, \sigma_V)}{V^*(t_{i-1}, \sigma_V)} \right) \right.$$

$$\left. - \mu(t_i - t_{i-1}) \right] \quad (7.64)$$

At any iteration, the values of $V^*(t)$ and the corresponding deltas are computed on the basis of the volatility value σ_V. Further elaborations on this subject were provided by Ericsson and Reneby (2003), Brockman and Turtle (2003), Duan *et al.* (2004), and Bruche (2004).

CDS information

A CDS market competes with equity for obligor-specific information. Credit default swap is in fact a very liquid market, at least for the most important "names", and the underlying of the contract is not a single bond, but the whole set of debt obligations of the "name". Looking at CDS also helps us to investigate the term structure of the default probability, and this is made possible for obligors for which CDS contracts are quoted for several maturities. In this case, it is possible to "*bootstrap*" the term structure of the default probability in a very similar manner to that by which we usually back out the zero-coupon factor curve from swap rates.

More specifically, let us assume that a CDS spread s_1 is quoted for protection over a one-year horizon. For the sake of simplicity, assume that the spread is paid in one instance at the end of the year, and is paid even if the name has defaulted. By the definition of a CDS spread we have

$$v(t, t_1)s_1 = v(t, t_1) \left[1 - \overline{Q}(t_1) \right] \text{LGD} \quad (7.65)$$

from which it is immediate to recover

$$1 - \frac{s_1}{\text{LGD}} = \overline{Q}(t_1) \quad (7.66)$$

This can be substituted in the two-year CDS

$$\sum_{i=1}^{2} v(t, t_i)\overline{Q}(t_{i-1})s_2 = \sum_{i=1}^{2} v(t, t_1)\left[\overline{Q}(t_{i-1}) - \overline{Q}(t_i)\right]LGD \qquad (7.67)$$

to recover $\overline{Q}(t_2)$, and so on.

Example 7.2   In Table 7.2 we report the market bid–ask quotes for protection on FIAT on December 2002.

Using the above bootstrap procedure, we compute the default probability depicted in Figure 7.4.

Table 7.2   CDS on Fiat – 25 December 2002

Maturity	Bid	Ask
1 year	145	155
3 years	170	175
5 years	180	183
10 years	195	215

Data is given in basis points.

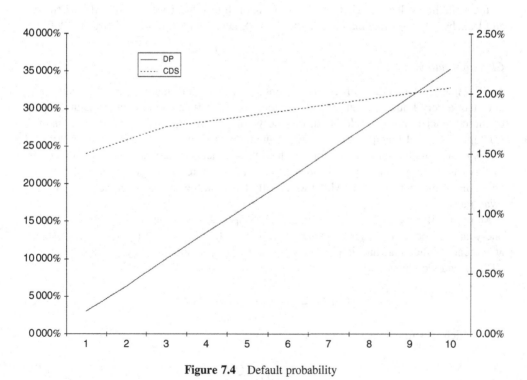

Figure 7.4   Default probability

Integrating rating and market information: Moody's Market Implied Ratings (MIR)

Moody's has recently proposed a model to bridge together qualitative information – that is, information contained in the rating assigned to an issuer – with quantitative information – that is, information implicit in credit products and equity. This technology has been given the name of *Market Implied Ratings* (MIR). The idea is to monitor the distance between the median spread of the rating to which the issuer belongs and its own rating, estimated from market data. The idea is to spot cases in which the spread departs from the levels typical of the corresponding rating class, as early warnings of future credit events. It is the latest development of the attention the rating agencies have devoted to the signals emerging from the markets.

REFERENCES AND FURTHER READING

Altman, E., Resti, A. & Sironi, A. (2001) "The link between default and recovery rates: Theory, empirical evidence and implications", *The Journal of Business*, **78**, 2203–2228.

Anderson, R. & Sundaresan, S. (1996) Design and valuation of debt contracts, *Review of Financial Studies*, **9** (1), 37–68.

Bensoussan, A., Crouhy, M. & Galai, D. (1995a) Stochastic equity volatility related to the leverage Effect I: Equity volatility behaviour, *Applied Mathematical Finance*, **1**, 63–65.

Bensoussan, A., Crouhy, M. & Galai, D. (1995b) Stochastic equity volatility related to the leverage effect I: Valuation of European equity options and warrants, *Applied Mathematical Finance*, **2**, 43–59.

Bielecki, T. & Rutkowski, M. (2001) *Credit Risk: Modelling, Valuation and Hedging*. Springer Finance, Berlin.

Black, F. & Cox, J. (1976) Valuing corporate securities: Some effect of bond indenture provisions, *Journal of Finance*, **31** (2), 351–367.

Black, F. & Scholes, M. (1973) The pricing of options and corporate liabilities, *Journal of Political Economy*, **81**, 637–654.

Brigo, D. & Morini, M. (2005) *CDS Market Formulas and Models*. Working paper.

Brockman, P. & Turtle, H. (2003) A barrier option framework for corporate security valuation, *Journal of Financial Economics*, **67**, 511–529.

Bruche, M. (2004) *Estimating Structural Bond Pricing Models via Simulated Maximum Likelihood*. Working Paper.

Cherubini, U. & Della Lunga, G. (2001) Liquidity and credit risk, *Applied Mathematical Finance*, **8**, 79–95.

Cox, J.C., Ingersoll, J.E. & Ross, S.A. (1985) A theory of the term structure of interest rates, *Econometrica*, **53**, 385–407.

CreditGrades™ (2001) *Technical Document*. RiskMetrics Group.

Cossin, D. & Pirrotte, F. (2001) *Advanced Credit Risk Models*, John Wiley & Sons, Chichester, UK.

Duan, J.C. (1994) Maximum likelihood estimation using price data of the derivative contract, *Mathematical Finance*, **4** (2), 155–167.

Duan, J.C. (2000) Correction: maximum likelihood estimation using price data of the derivative contract, *Mathematical Finance*, **10**, 461–462.

Duan, J.C., Gauthier, G. & Simonato, J. (2004) *On the Equivalence of the KMV and the Maximum Likelihood Methods for Structural Credit Risk Models*. Working Paper.

Duffie, D. & Lando, D. (2001) Term structure of credit spreads with incomplete accounting information, *Econometrica*, **69**, 633–664.

Duffie, D. & Singleton, K. (1999) Modelling term structure of defaultable bonds, *Review of Financial Studies*, **12**, 687–720.

Duffie, D. & Singleton, K. (2003) *Credit Risk: Pricing, Measurement and Management.* Princeton University Press.

Frye, J. (2000) Collateral damage, *RISK*, April, 91–94.

Giesecke, K. (2001) *Default and Information.* Working Paper, Cornell University.

Gilboa, I. & Schmeidler, D. (1989) Maximin expected utility with non-unique prior, *Journal of Mathematical Economics*, **18**, 141–153.

Hull, J. & White, A. (2003) *The Valuation of Credit Default Swap Options.* Rothman School of Management. Working Paper.

Jamshidian, F. (2004) Valuations of credit default swaps and swaptions, *Finance and Stochastics*, **8**, 343–371.

Jarrow, R. (2001) Default parameter estimation using market prices, *Financial Analysts Journal*, **57** (5), 75–92.

Jarrow, R. & Turnbull, S. (1995) Pricing derivatives on financial securities subject to credit risk, *Journal of Finance*, **50**, 53–86.

Jarrow, R. & Turnbull, S. (2000) The intersection of market and credit risk, *Journal of Banking and Finance*, **24**, 271–299.

Lando, D. (2004) *Credit Risk Modeling: Theory and Applications.* Princeton University Press.

Leland, H. (1994) Corporate debt value, bond covenants and optimal capital structure, *Journal of Finance*, **51**, 347–364.

Leland, H. & Toft, K. (1996) Optimal capital structure, endogenous bankruptcy, and the term structure of credit spreads, *Journal of Finance*, **29**, 449–470.

Madan, D. & Unal, H. (1998) Pricing the risks of default, *Review of Derivatives Research*, **2**, 121–160.

Merton, R. (1974) On the pricing of corporate debt: The risk structure of interest rates, *Journal of Finance*, **29**, 449–470.

Unal, H., Madan, D. & Guntay, L. (2003) Pricing the risk of recovery in default with absolute priority violations, *Journal of Banking and Finance*, **27** (6), 1001–1025.

Zhou, C. (2001) The term structure of credit risk with jump risk, *Journal of Banking and Finance*, **25**, 2015–2040.

Basket Credit Derivatives and CDOs

8.1 INTRODUCTION

In this chapter we extend the review of credit-linked notes, introducing the kinds of products that have made up most of the structured finance market since the 1990s. Since then, structured finance has been mostly synonymous with basket (or multi-name) credit products that mainly originated from the securitization business. The term *securitization* means changing into "security" – that is, a tradable asset, something that would have not been tradable otherwise. On the "buy" side, the counterparties interested in this business are actually investors that would like to acquire exposure to a wider variety of risk factors, which could not be achieved otherwise under the regulation. On the "sell" side, the market is made up by financial intermediaries that are interested in getting rid of exposures to some risk factors. Of course, setting up a securitization factor requires the selection of: (i) the kind of risk factor to be transferred; (ii) the distribution of this risk; and (iii) the allocation of risk to different categories of investors. On point (i), examples of kinds of risk transferred are greatly differentiated (credit, real estate, commodities, and others) even though most of the examples are related to credit risk exposures. On point (ii), choosing a "basket" of risk exposures, rather than a single one, enables one to model the distribution of the price of the security that is created. As for the third point, determining a particular "priority" structure enables a change in both the quantity and the quality of the exposures for each of the classes of securities issued. The new kind of securities issued constitutes a new kind of product, denoted as a "tranche". For the valuation of these products, a central role is played by the choice of the risk factors in the basket, and particularly how they interact and fit together as a single risk factor. For this reason, the dependence structure among the risk factors is the key feature of the products in this market. Tranches are in fact also called "correlation products". As a result of these developments, financial innovation has created new techniques and new markets to hedge and transfer the risk involved in these products. As single-name credit derivatives has paved the way to turn defaultable bonds into a set of structured finance products, and to synthetically create credit risk exposures, multi-name (or "basket") credit derivatives have spurred the development of the transfer of credit risk portfolios and to synthetically create exposures to correlation.

8.2 BASKET CREDIT DERIVATIVES

Consider a default swap defined in much the same way as that described in Chapter 7, except for a feature. It is going to provide protection against a subset of default events in a basket, say the first or the nth default, or the first n defaults of the names in the basket. As for standard CDS contracts, the protection seller may face either the obligation to deliver a fixed sum for any of the defaults or can accept physical delivery of debt contracts of the "name" under default.

Of course, the value of products like these are largely affected by the dependence structure of the credit quality of "names" of the basket. Assume one buys protection on the event of the first default in a "basket". For the sake of simplicity, let us assume that the LGD of the names are roughly the same. Let us also assume that the protection extends over to time T, and, in case of default, is paid at that time. On the other hand, the premium payment from the protection buyer is assumed to be done *up-front* at the origin of the contract – that is, at time t. The value of the *first-to-default* will then be

$$\text{FTD} = v(t, T)\text{LGD}(1 - Q(\tau_1 > T, \tau_2 > T, \dots, \tau_n > T)) \tag{8.1}$$

where τ_i are the default times of the $i = 1, 2, \dots, n$ names in the basket. If one recalls the AND/OR rule, it is evident that the product is short in correlation. In fact, the product yields a positive payoff if at least one of the names in the basket defaults by time T. If the default times are orthogonal, we have in fact

$$\text{FTD} = v(t, T)\text{LGD}(1 - Q(\tau_1 > T)Q(\tau_2 > T) \dots Q(\tau_n > T)) \tag{8.2}$$

while, in the case of perfect dependence, we have

$$\text{FTD} = v(t, T)\text{LGD}(1 - \min(Q(\tau_1 > T), Q(\tau_2 > T), \dots Q(\tau_n > T)) \tag{8.3}$$

and the value is lower.

8.3   PRICING ISSUES: MODELS

We saw before that most of the value of multivariate products is due to the dependence structure. For this reason these products are called "correlation products". The AND/OR rule used above for first-to-default swaps or valuations performed under the extreme assumptions of independence and perfect dependence can be used to gauge the sign of the exposure to correlation.

8.3.1   Independent defaults

In the case of independence of the default times we may, for example, use the binomial distribution to estimate, as q, the probability that a firm in the basket could default by time T. Accordingly, the probability that x firms would default by time T is given by

$$Q(x) = \binom{n}{x} q^x (1 - q)^{n-x} \tag{8.4}$$

The value of protection on the first x names is then given by

$$\text{FTD}(x) = \text{LGD} \sum_{k=1}^{x} k \binom{n}{k} q^k (1 - q)^{n-k} + x\text{LGD} \sum_{k=x+1}^{n} \binom{n}{k} q^k (1 - q)^{n-k} \tag{8.5}$$

Sticking to the case of orthogonal defaults, another natural choice is to extend the reduced form model. So, for example, the joint survival probability of the n names is

$$Q(\tau_1 > T, \tau_2 > T, \dots; \tau_n > T) = \exp(-(\lambda_1 + \lambda_2 + \dots \lambda_n)(T - t)) \tag{8.6}$$

Actually, the instantaneous probability of experiencing one default is determined by a global intensity given by the sum of the individual intensities

$$\Lambda = \lambda_1 + \lambda_2 + \ldots + \lambda_n \tag{8.7}$$

Likewise, the formula can be extended to the first x defaults. We have

$$\text{FTD}(x) = \text{LGD} \sum_{k=1}^{x} k \frac{\exp(-\Lambda(T-t))(\Lambda(T-t))^k}{k!} + x\,\text{LGD} \sum_{k=x+1}^{n} \frac{\exp(-\Lambda(T-t))(\Lambda(T-t))^k}{k!} \tag{8.8}$$

8.3.2   Dependent defaults: the Marshall–Olkin model

The most straightforward extension of the reduced form model to allow for dependent defaults is provided by Marshall and Olkin (1967) multivariate extension of the Poisson process. These models were introduced in credit risk modelling by Duffie and Singleton (1998) and also discussed in Li (2000). Esposito (2001) showed that this approach leads to closed form solutions or approximations for many basket derivative products. Here we follow his exposition to illustrate the model. To keep things simple, consider a model with two names, and assume that there are two idiosyncratic shocks that may lead to the default of each name, and a common shock that may lead to the default of both names. Define by λ_i, $i = 1, 2$, the intensity of the idiosyncratic shocks and by λ_{12} that of the common shock. According to the Marshall–Olkin model, the joint probability that name i will survive beyond time T_i is

$$Q(\tau_1 > T_1, \tau_2 > T_2) = \exp(-\lambda_1(T_1 - t) - \lambda_2(T_2 - t) - \lambda_{12}(\max(T_1, T_2) - t)) \tag{8.9}$$

In pricing applications generally we will have $T_1 = T_2 = T$, so that

$$Q(\tau_1 > T, \tau_2 > T) = \exp(-(\lambda_1 + \lambda_2 + \lambda_{12})(T - t)) \tag{8.10}$$

and the model provides an extension of the analysis of the previous section in which the global intensity is

$$\Lambda = \lambda_1 + \lambda_2 + \lambda_{12} \tag{8.11}$$

The marginal survival probability is

$$Q(\tau_i > T) = \exp(-(\lambda_i + \lambda_{12})(T - t)) \tag{8.12}$$

The dependence between the default times is

$$\rho(\tau_1, \tau_2) = \frac{\lambda_{12}}{\lambda_1 + \lambda_2 + \lambda_{12}} \tag{8.13}$$

Based on the calibration of marginal survival probabilities and the correlation of default times one can then evaluate the total default intensity Λ and the joint survival probability as

$$Q(\tau_1 > T, \tau_2 > T) = \exp(-(\lambda_1 + \lambda_2 + \lambda_{12})(T - t)) \tag{8.14}$$

The main problem with this model is that the number of shocks, and so the corresponding number of intensity figures to be calibrated from the market, grows exponentially with the dimension of the problem. To see this, consider the case with $n = 3$. In this case the system would be exposed to seven shocks: three idiosyncratic shocks, three shocks common to each couple and one shock common to all of the three names. The total intensity would be

$$\Lambda = \lambda_1 + \lambda_2 + \lambda_3 + \lambda_{12} + \lambda_{13} + \lambda_{23} + \lambda_{123} \tag{8.15}$$

and the joint survival probability would be

$$Q(\tau_1 > T, \tau_2 > T) = \exp(-\Lambda(T - t)) \tag{8.16}$$

The bivariate marginal survival probability for the first two variables, would be for example

$$Q(\tau_1 > T, \tau_2 > T) = \exp(-(\lambda_1 + \lambda_2 + \lambda_{12} + \lambda_{13} + \lambda_{23} + \lambda_{123})(T - t)) \tag{8.17}$$

and the marginal survival probability of the first name would be

$$Q(\tau_1 > T) = \exp(-(\lambda_1 + \lambda_{12} + \lambda_{13} + \lambda_{123})(T - t)) \tag{8.18}$$

The default time correlation between the first two names would then become

$$\rho(\tau_1, \tau_2) = \frac{\lambda_{12} + \lambda_{123}}{\lambda_1 + \lambda_{13} + \lambda_2 + \lambda_{23} + \lambda_{12} + \lambda_{123}} \tag{8.19}$$

The problem becomes more and more complex as n gets larger. In general, the marginal survival probability of the first name would be

$$Q(\tau_1 > T) = \exp\left[-\left(\lambda_1 + \sum_{i=2}^{n} \lambda_{1i} + \sum_{i=3}^{n} \lambda_{2i} + \ldots \lambda_{12\ldots n}\right)(T - t)\right] \tag{8.20}$$

The model is then very flexible, and perhaps even too flexible. One could in principle design shocks affecting subsets of "names" across the whole power set of 2^n events (one of the events being of course that of no shock). Esposito (2001) suggests that the model should be restricted to n idiosyncratic shocks and a common shock affecting the whole system. The global intensity would then be

$$\Lambda = \sum_{i=1}^{n} \lambda_i + \lambda_{123\ldots n} \tag{8.21}$$

The pairwise correlation would be equal across all the names

$$\rho(\tau_i, \tau_j) = \frac{\lambda_{123\ldots n}}{\sum_{i=1}^{n} \lambda_i + \lambda_{123\ldots n}} \tag{8.22}$$

and the marginal survival probability would be

$$Q(\tau_i > T) = \exp(-(\lambda_i + \lambda_{123\ldots n})(T - t)) \tag{8.23}$$

as in the bivariate model. Under this restriction, the model is particularly easy to calibrate. Of course, a promising feature of the model remains that it can be enhanced to design shocks only affecting subsets of the names. This feature has attracted particular attention in recent literature on credit risk, in the models called the *contagion approach*.

8.3.3 Dependent defaults: copula functions

An approach that enables us to account for default dependence, and is largely used in basket credit derivatives pricing, is that of copula functions. The joint default probability is represented as

$$Q(\tau_1 \leq T, \ \tau_2 \leq T, \ \ldots \tau_n \leq T) = C(Q_1(\tau_1 \leq T), \ Q_2(\tau_2 \leq T), \ldots Q_n(\tau_n \leq T)) \qquad (8.24)$$

where $Q_i(\tau_i \leq T)$ is the marginal default probability of the *i*th name. Likewise, one can fit the joint survival probabilities

$$Q(\tau_1 > T, \ \tau_2 > T, \ldots \tau_n > T) = \overline{C}(Q_1(\tau_1 > T), \ Q_2(\tau_2 > T), \ldots Q_n(\tau_n > T)) \qquad (8.25)$$

The typical copula function used is the Gaussian one,

$$C(Q_1, \ Q_2, \ \ldots Q_n) = \Phi_n(\Phi^{-1}(Q_1), \Phi^{-1}(Q_2), \ \ldots, \ \Phi^{-1}(Q_n); \Sigma) \qquad (8.26)$$

where $\Phi_n(.; \Sigma)$ is the *n*-dimensional standard normal distribution with correlation matrix Σ. In order to allow for tail dependence, and correlation among extreme financial crises, one can resort to the so-called T-copula

$$C(Q_1, \ Q_2, \ \ldots Q_n) = T_n(T^{-1}(Q_1), \ T^{-1}(Q_2), \ldots, T^{-1}(Q_n); \ \Sigma, \ \gamma) \qquad (8.27)$$

where $T_n(.; \Sigma, \gamma)$ is the *n*-dimensional standardized Student-*t* distribution with correlation matrix Σ and γ degrees of freedom. As is well known, a lower value of degrees of freedom generates tail dependence, while, as the degrees of freedom grow larger and larger, the distribution approaches the multivariate normal. Actually, disentangling the effects of correlation and tail dependence on the market co-movement of credit spreads remains an open issue.

The flexibility of the copula function approach is that it allows us to separate the specification of the marginal distribution of default times, so that samples of correlated default times can be calibrated and simulated. Typically, the model is calibrated in two steps:

1. A historical sample of marginal default probabilities is estimated from CDS quotes.
2. The dependence structure is calibrated on such samples by a canonical maximum likelihood (CML) estimation.

The reader is referred to Cherubini *et al.* (2004) for a broader discussion of the subject.

8.3.4 Factor models: conditional independence

While standard copula models lead to the Monte Carlo simulation as the technique available for pricing, the imposition of a more restrictive structure to the model enables us to exploit an alternative pricing tool. These models represent what is called the *factor copula* approach. The approach is excellently surveyed in Burtshell *et al.* (2005), and we follow that review here.

Gaussian Copula

The idea in some sense bridges together a structural approach and the construction of the Marshall–Olkin model mentioned above. The data-generating process of the default of each obligor i is driven by a state variable V_i, that may be thought of as the value of the firm or the "distance to default" in a structural model. This variable is assumed to be a function of a common factor M and an idiosyncratic shock ε_i.

$$V_i = \rho_i M + \sqrt{1 - \rho_i^2}\, \varepsilon_i \qquad (8.28)$$

Without any loss of generality, both the common factor and the idiosyncratic factor may be rescaled in such a way as to have a variance equal to 1. This, of course, amounts to rescaling the state variable in the same way. The covariance between the state variables of two obligors is $\operatorname{cov}(V_i, V_j) = \rho_i \rho_j$. If we further assume that both the common and the idiosyncratic shocks are normally distributed, it is clear that the set of state variables are also normally distributed. This leads to a model for the default times that actually looks like the Gaussian copula approach that we saw before

$$C(Q_1,\ Q_2, \ldots Q_n) = \Phi_n(\Phi^{-1}(Q_1),\ \Phi^{-1}(Q_2), \ldots,\ \Phi^{-1}(Q_n); \Sigma) \qquad (8.29)$$

Yet, actually a factor model imposes a richer structure to the design of dependence. This structure shows up in the particular shape of the correlation matrix. It is assumed that it may be decomposed in a reduced rank matrix (the rank being 1 in the one-factor model), and a diagonal matrix (as the idiosyncratic factors are assumed to be uncorrelated). This structure allows for a relevant simplification of the pricing technique. As a matter of fact, under this structure the conditional default probability distribution of each name with respect to the common factor M is independent of default of the others. Furthermore, we know that such conditional distribution corresponds to the partial derivative of the copula function. So,

$$Q(V_i \le v_i | M = m) = \frac{\partial C(Q_i(v_i),\ Q_M(m))}{\partial Q_M(m)} \qquad (8.30)$$

In many cases, this formula is available in closed form. The most straightforward example is that of the Gaussian copula for which

$$\frac{\partial C(Q_i(v_i),\ Q_M(m))}{\partial Q_M(m)} = \Phi\left(\frac{\Phi^{-1}(Q_i) - \rho_i \Phi^{-1}(Q_M)}{\sqrt{1 - \rho_i^2}}\right) = \Phi\left(\frac{\Phi^{-1}(Q_i) - \rho_i m}{\sqrt{1 - \rho_i^2}}\right) \qquad (8.31)$$

The joint conditional default distribution of the n names can then be written as

$$Q(V_1 \le v_1,\ V_2 \le v_2 \ldots V_n \le v_n | M = m) = \prod_{i=1}^{n} \frac{\partial C(Q_i(v_i),\ Q_M(m))}{\partial Q_M(m)} \qquad (8.32)$$

The unconditional one is

$$Q(V_1 \le v_1, \ V_2 \le v_2 \ldots V_n \le v_n) = \int_{-\infty}^{\infty} \prod_{i=1}^{n} \frac{\partial C(Q_i(v_i), \ Q_M(m))}{\partial Q_M(m)} f(m) \, \mathrm{d}m \qquad (8.33)$$

where $f(m)$ is the probability density function of the common factor. In the Gaussian case we have

$$Q(V_1 \le v_1, \ V_2 \le v_2 \ldots V_n \le v_n) = \int_{-\infty}^{\infty} \prod_{i=1}^{n} \Phi\left(\frac{\Phi^{-1}(Q_i) - \rho_i m}{\sqrt{1 - \rho_i^2}}\right) \phi(m) \, \mathrm{d}m \qquad (8.34)$$

where $\phi(.)$ denotes the density of the univariate standard normal distribution.

Stochastic correlation

An extension of the Gaussian model is suggested by Andersen and Sidenius (2005) and is based on a switching regime structure for the correlation:

$$V_i = (\mathbf{1}_X \rho_{il} + (1 - \mathbf{1}_X)\rho_{ih})M + \sqrt{1 - (\mathbf{1}_X \rho_{il} + (1 - \mathbf{1}_X)\rho_{ih})^2} \ \varepsilon_i \qquad (8.35)$$

where ρ_{il} and ρ_{ih} are the values of correlation in the low and high state respectively and $\mathbf{1}_X$ is a Bernoulli variable taking value 1 in the low-correlation state and zero otherwise. This variable is assumed to be a function of a set of random variables X. The conditional distribution is, of course, a mixture of Gaussian distributions

$$\frac{\partial C(Q_i(v_i), \ Q_M(m))}{\partial Q_M(m)} = p\Phi\left(\frac{\Phi^{-1}(Q_i) - \rho_{il} m}{\sqrt{1 - \rho_{il}^2}}\right) + (1 - p)\Phi\left(\frac{\Phi^{-1}(Q_i) - \rho_{ih} m}{\sqrt{1 - \rho_{ih}^2}}\right) \qquad (8.36)$$

where p is the risk-neutral probability associated to $\mathbf{1}_X = 1$. Of course, the structure of the correlation could have been designed in a more complex way, including more than one regime. In the limit, correlation could have been modelled as a continuous random variable, in which case the conditional distribution would have been

$$\frac{\partial C(Q_i(v_i), \ Q_M(m))}{\partial Q_M(m)} = \int_0^1 \Phi\left(\frac{\Phi^{-1}(Q_i) - \rho_i m}{\sqrt{1 - \rho_i^2}}\right) \mathrm{d}P(\rho_i) \qquad (8.37)$$

where P is the probability distribution of the correlation figure ρ_i.

Student t and double t copulas

The model can be very easily extended beyond the Gaussian copula. For example, one could change the model in (8.28) to

$$\sqrt{X} \ V_i = \rho_i M + \sqrt{1 - \rho_i^2} \ \varepsilon_i \qquad (8.38)$$

where X is a random variable independent of the common and idiosyncratic shock, and such that v/X follows a χ_v^2 (a chi-squared distribution with v degrees of freedom). As a result, the transformed state variables $\sqrt{X}\,V_i$ would follow a Student t distribution. This model was applied to credit risk issues by Frey and McNeil (2003) and Mashal *et al.* (2003). The covariance between the ith and the jth state variables is equal to $\rho_i\rho_j v/(v-2)$ (provided of course $(v>2)$).

A further extension, known as the "double t" model, was provided by Hull and White (2004). The factor model is

$$V_i = \rho_i\sqrt{\frac{v}{v-2}}X\,M + \sqrt{1-\rho_i^2}\sqrt{\frac{v^*}{v^*-2}}Y\,\varepsilon_i \qquad (8.39)$$

In this model both the common and the idiosyncratic factors are modelled as Student t variables with different degrees of freedom v and v^*.

Archimedean copulas

Archimedean copulas can also be considered as generated by a factor model. In this case, the common factor M is assumed to be endowed with a density $f(m)$, endowed with Laplace transform

$$\psi(s) \equiv \int_0^\infty \exp(-sm)f(m)\,\mathrm{d}m \qquad (8.40)$$

Define latent variables

$$V_i = \psi\left(-\frac{\ln Q_i}{m}\right) \qquad (8.41)$$

where Q_i are uniformly distributed random variables, independent of m. The conditional distribution function is

$$\frac{\partial C(Q_i,\ Q_M(m))}{\partial Q_M(m)} = \exp(-m\psi^{-1}(Q_i)) \qquad (8.42)$$

This can be verified, computing

$$\int_0^\infty \frac{\partial C(Q_i,\ Q_M(m))}{\partial Q_M(m)}f(m)\,\mathrm{d}m = \int_0^\infty \exp(-m\psi^{-1}(Q_i))f(m)\,\mathrm{d}m = \psi(\psi^{-1}(Q_i)) = Q_i \qquad (8.43)$$

where we have used the definition of a Laplace transform above.

Now, as conditional distributions are independent we get

$$Q(V_1 \le v_1,\ V_2 \le v_2 \ldots V_n \le v_n | M = m) = \prod_{i=1}^{n}\frac{\partial C(Q_i(v_i),\ Q_M(m))}{\partial Q_M(m)} = \exp\left(-m\sum_{i=1}^{n}\psi^{-1}(Q_i)\right)$$
$$(8.44)$$

The unconditional distribution is obtained by integrating over the domain of the common factor M. Recalling again the definition of a Laplace transform, we may write,

$$Q(V_1 \leq v_1, \; V_2 \leq v_2 \ldots V_n \leq v_n) = \int_0^\infty \exp\left(-m \sum_{i=1}^n \psi^{-1}(Q_i)\right) f(m)\, \mathrm{d}m = \psi\left(\sum_{i=1}^n \psi^{-1}(Q_i)\right)$$

$$(8.45)$$

and the joint distribution is a copula function of the Archimedean class. For example, taking the common factor density $f(m)$ to be the gamma distribution with parameter $1/\alpha$, we have that $\psi(s) = (1+s)^{-1/\alpha}$. So, $\psi^{-1}(u) = u^{1/\alpha} - 1$. The joint distribution is

$$Q(V_1 \leq v_1, \; V_2 \leq v_2 \ldots V_n \leq v_n) = \psi\left(\sum_{i=1}^n \psi^{-1}(Q_i)\right) = \left(\sum_{i=1}^n Q_i^{1/\alpha} - n + 1\right)^{-1/\alpha} \qquad (8.46)$$

which is the Clayton copula. Notice that, by comparison with the treatment in Chapter 3, the generating function of the copula is actually the inverse of the Laplace transform.

8.4   PRICING ISSUES: ALGORITHMS

8.4.1   Monte Carlo simulation

The most straightforward approach to pricing basket credit derivatives and CDOs is by Monte Carlo simulation. Once the proper copula function has been estimated and tested, the model may be simulated to recover samples of correlated default times. To keep the approach at the most general level, we may describe the procedure in two steps.

1. Draw n uniform random variables from copula $C(u_1, u_2, \ldots u_n)$.
2. Recover n times to default by inverting probability $\tau_i = Q^{-1}(u_i)$.

In models endowed with more structure, other Monte Carlo solutions can be used. Consider the copula factor models above: in general one could generate the systematic and the idiosyncratic factors and simulate the state variables V_i. In linear factor models the construction is straightforward. In Archimedean models the solution is provided by the so-called "Marshall–Olkin method", which is based on the Laplace transform. Recalling the notation used above, we may in full generality describe the simulation procedure as follows

1. Draw a random variable m with probability density $f(m)$.
2. Draw n uniform independent random variables from $Q_1, Q_2, \ldots, Q_n$.
3. Calculate the state variables

$$V_i = \psi\left(-\frac{\ln Q_i}{m}\right)$$

Of course remember, in case, that as the LGD figures are stochastic, they must be simulated as well.

8.4.2 The generating function method

The method that is most widely used in basket credit pricing is based on conditional independence. Once the proper copula factor model has been estimated, one knows, for each and every name in the basket, the conditional probability $Q\,(V_i \le v_i\,|M=m)$. We know that, if the model is well specified, these probabilities are independent. The problem is then to estimate

$$Q(V_1 \le v_1,\; V_2 \le v_2 \ldots V_n \le v_n|M=m) = \prod_{i=1}^{n} \frac{\partial C(Q_i(v_i),\; Q_M(m))}{\partial Q_M(m)} \qquad (8.47)$$

and to integrate the result over the common factor scenarios m.

A possible solution is to resort to generating functions. A natural choice, explored by Gregory and Laurent (2003) is to resort to the generating function of the binomial distribution. Sticking to the simplest case of homogeneous losses, the generating function of the number of defaults is

$$g_n(s) = E(s^n\,|\,m) = \prod_{i=1}^{n}(q_i(m)s + 1 - q_i(m)) = s^n q(n|m) + s^{n-1}q(n-1\,|\,m) + \ldots q(0\,|\,m)$$
$$(8.48)$$

So, estimating the conditional probability distribution of a number j of defaults in a set of n names amounts to computing the $q(j|m)$ coefficient. Actually, Laurent and Gregory also show how to allow for different, although deterministic, *loss-given default* figures. Actually, the loss process is defined on a discrete grid $L(j)$, $j = 1, 2, \ldots, n$. Then, the appropriate moment generating function is

$$g_L(s) = E(s^L\,|\,m) = \prod_{i=1}^{n}(q_i(m)s^{L(i)} + 1 - q_i(m))$$
$$= s^{L(n)}q(n\,|\,m) + s^{L(n-1)}q(n-1\,|\,m) + \ldots q(0\,|\,m) \qquad (8.49)$$

The conditional probability of losing an amount $L(j)$ is again given by the $q(j|m)$ coefficient. The coefficients of the polynomial can be computed by recursive formulas. The unconditional distribution is then obtained by integrating over the common factor scenarios

$$Q(L \le L^{(k)}) = \int_{-\infty}^{\infty} q(k|m)f(m)\,\mathrm{d}m \qquad (8.50)$$

The above approach could also be easily modified to allow for stochastic *loss-given default* figures, provided that they are independent of the number of default events and endowed with a common generating function $g_{\mathrm{LGD}}(s)$. In fact, assume that the probability distribution of the number of defaults n is endowed with a probability distribution with generating function $g_n(s)$ above. We ask the probability distribution of the sum $L = \mathrm{LGD}_1 + \mathrm{LGD}_2 + \ldots + \mathrm{LGD}_n$. This can be proved to be $g_n(g_{\mathrm{LGD}}(s))$. So, we have

$$g_L(s) = \prod_{i=1}^{n}(q_i(m)g_{\mathrm{LGD}}(s) + 1 - q_i(m)) \qquad (8.51)$$

8.5   COLLATERALIZED DEBT OBLIGATIONS

In Chapter 7 we showed that a corporate bond could actually be considered as a structured product composed of a default-free bond and a credit derivative. Furthermore, we noticed that a corporate bond could actually be created synthetically by structuring an equity-linked note: an intermediary would issue notes against funds collected from investors, and would invest the proceeds in default-free collateral while selling protection in a CDS contract for the same notional amount. It does not come as a surprise, then that by the same token a claim on a portfolio of credit exposures could be considered as a structured product involving basket credit derivatives. And, as in the equity-linked note in the univariate case, such a claim could probably be constructed synthetically by an intermediary selling protection on a basket of "names". Not only do these products exist in reality, but they also represent the most developed market for structured products. It is the Collateralized Debt Obligation (CDO) market. Exactly as in the univariate case, they may be cash or synthetic. Here we give a general description of a CDO, before focusing on different instances of the product in the following section.

8.5.1   CDO: general structure of the deal

In principle, a CDO is structured in much the same way as the credit-linked note discussed in Chapter 7. To start, consider a standard, so-called "*cash*" CDO. The purpose of the deal is to sell a basket of assets, namely in our case a set of debt instruments, to the general public (mainly institutional investors), for reasons that may carry advantages for the seller and the buyer. Sometimes, the deal is also referred to as "securitization", because it is bound to change into marketable "securities" whatever kind of asset the "originator" is willing to get rid of. The formal structure of a CDO deal is reported below. On the selling side, the originator sells a set of assets to an intermediary, called a *special purpose vehicle* (SPV). The SPV collects funds to pay for the assets by issuing securities. These securities are differentiated in a set of so-called "*tranches*", defined by different degrees of *seniority* of debt. By seniority hierarchy we mean a ranking according to which, in case of default events or in general losses on the assets, the *senior tranches* are affected after *junior tranches*. So, the income accruing from the assets sold from the originator to the SPV are passed through from the SPV to the final investors. Losses incurred on the assets are also passed through but they affect, and eventually may fully erode, *junior tranches* before the *senior* ones even begin to be affected. The process by which losses on the asset side are transferred to the tranches is called the *waterfall*. The first tranche to be affected by losses is the so-called *equity tranche* (in standard corporate finance, in fact, equity is the *residual claim*). *Mezzanine* is the tranche affected as soon as the equity tranche has been swept away. On the opposite end of the spectrum, *senior* and *supersenior* tranches are made much safer (Figure 8.1), because only massive losses can erode the principal invested in these tranches.

As an alternative structure, one could avoid the actual sale of the assets and only use credit derivatives to provide protection against losses on the assets themselves. This kind of product is called a *synthetic CDO*, and the structure is depicted in Figure 8.2. Differently from the cash CDO, on the asset side the SPV is just selling protection, typically by means of CDS. As at origin CDS are worth zero, the funds raised in exchange for the issuance of bonds have to be invested in default-free collateral. The interest rate risk of this investment is typically hedged by an interest rate swap. The proceeds from interest payments and

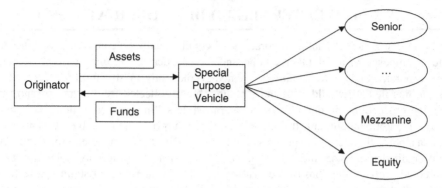

Figure 8.1   A "cash" CDO

CDS spreads are passed over to final investors. In case of defaults, the SPV pays for the losses by reducing the amount of collateral and the principal of the tranches accordingly. Of course, the reduction of the principal is structured according to the *tranching* and *waterfall* rules. Synthetic CDOs in which, on the liability side, the SPV raises funds are called *funded*. On the contrary, *unfunded* CDOs are structures in which both the asset and the liability sides of the SPV are represented by CDSs: in this case, typically the SPV is not even used in the deal.

Synthetic deals have become very popular in recent years, especially in Europe where over 90% of deals are synthetic. The rationale for such CDOs is to provide a flexible way to manage the credit portfolios without the need to sell assets and loans. From the point of view of the originators, CDOs have represented an opportunity to

- get rid of bad loans and reduce the amount of non-performing loans in the book;
- get rid of good loans providing very low spreads and absorbing, under the capital ratio regulation, a substantial amount of capital (*regulatory arbitrage*).

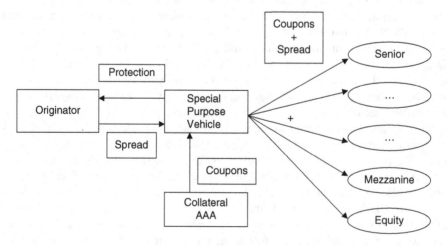

Figure 8.2   Synthetic CDO

From the point of view of investors, typically institutional investors, CDOs have represented an opportunity to

- invest in asset classes that otherwise would have not been permitted under the regulation;
- invest with the level of leverage and risk required;
- change the overall degree of diversification of the investor's portfolio.

As is clear from this broad introduction, the art of structuring CDOs amounts to choosing: (i) a tranching structure for the liability side and (ii) a degree of diversification for the asset side.

8.5.2   The art of tranching

In order to focus on the technique of tranching, let us assume for the time being that the asset side is made by a single exposure, whose value is V. To illustrate the setting, it is useful to refer to a structural model. The overall face value of debt is B, and is made up by a senior component whose face value is S and a junior component with face value J. Maturity of debt is at time T. From standard structural models the value of equity is

$$E_Q[v(t, T) \max(V(T) - B, 0)] \tag{8.52}$$

The overall market value of debt would be

$$v(t, T)B - E_Q[v(t, T) \max(B - V(T), 0)] \tag{8.53}$$

and that of senior debt

$$v(t, T)S - E_Q[v(t, T) \max(S - V(T), 0)] \tag{8.54}$$

The value of junior debt is obtained by subtracting senior debt from the overall debt

$$v(t, T)(B - S) - \{E_Q[v(t, T) \max(B - V(T), 0)] - E_Q[v(t, T) \max(S - V(T), 0)]\}$$
$$= v(t, T) J - \{E_Q[v(t, T) \max(B - V(T), 0)] - E_Q[v(t, T) \max(S - V(T), 0)]\} \tag{8.55}$$

So, the credit risk of the junior debt amounts to a position in a spread with two put options with strikes equal to the overall face value of debt and the face value of senior debt.

The jargon used in the CDO market is a little different from that used above, actually it is exactly the opposite, but is based on the same principle. Just rephrase the above setting defining losses instead of the value of assets as the state variable. So, for example, set $V(T) = 100 - L$ and define the face value of the global amount of debt to be $B = 100 - L_a$. Notice that in this case the value of equity is a put option, instead of a call:

$$E_Q[v(t, T) \max(V(T) - B, 0)] = E_Q[v(t, T) \max(L_a - L, 0)] \tag{8.56}$$

and the underlying asset of the option is the amount of losses instead of the value of assets. Given the probability distribution of losses, the general pricing formula for the equity tranche would then be

$$E_Q[v(t, T) \max(L_a - L, 0)] = v(t, T) \int_0^{L_a} Q(L \le u)\, du \tag{8.57}$$

As for the two tranches of debt, define $S = 100 - L_d$ as the face value of *senior* debt, so that the face value of *junior* debt is $J = B - S = L_d - L_a$.

Again, the value of senior debt will be

$$v(t, T)(100 - L_d) - E_Q[v(t, T) \max(L - L_d, 0)] \tag{8.58}$$

and credit risk is represented as a call instead of a put. Likewise, the credit risk in junior debt

$$v(t, T)(L_d - L_a) - \{E_Q[v(t, T) \max(L - L_a, 0)] - E_Q[v(t, T) \max(L - L_d, 0)]\} \tag{8.59}$$

is represented by a call spread.

We may now introduce some standard CDO jargon. We have introduced a new product, which is called a *tranche*, whose value at maturity depends on the amount of losses on a given asset. L_a is called the *attachment* point of the tranche, and denotes the level of losses at which the tranche begins to be eroded; L_d is called the *detachment* point and it is the level of losses at which the whole principal of the tranche is swept away. A tranche is called *equity tranche* if the attachment point is zero.

Just to practice with the model, assume that L is log-normally distributed, that is $L = \exp(x)$ where x is normally distributed with mean m and standard deviation s. In this case, obviously, the tranches could be priced in closed form, with formulas very similar to those in the Black and Scholes model. To illustrate very briefly, the overall expected loss (EL) would be

$$E_Q(L) = \exp(m + 0.5s^2) \tag{8.60}$$

The probability of observing an amount of losses less than L_a is

$$Q(L \le L_a) = \Phi\left(-\frac{\ln(E_Q(L)/L_a)}{s} + 0.5s\right) \tag{8.61}$$

The expected loss truncated to L_a is instead

$$E_Q(L|L \le L_a) = E_Q(L)\Phi\left(-\frac{\ln(E_Q(L)/L_a)}{s} - 0.5s\right) \tag{8.62}$$

The value of the equity tranche with detachment level L_a would then be

$$EL(0, L_a) = v(t, T)L_a\Phi\left(-\frac{\ln(E_Q(L)/L_a)}{s} + 0.5s\right)$$
$$-v(t, T)E_Q(L)\Phi\left(-\frac{\ln(E_Q(L)/L_a)}{s} - 0.5s\right) \tag{8.63}$$

Of course a straightforward arbitrage restriction requires

$$EL(L_a, L_d) = EL(0, L_d) - EL(0, L_a) \qquad (8.64)$$

So, any intermediate tranche has to be equal to the difference of two equity tranches taking the detachment and the attachment points of the intermediate tranche as strikes.

The very simple model sketched above already provides a tool for introducing in a simple way arguments that will be at the centre of our discussion in the following paragraphs.

- First, the value of tranches depends on the overall expected loss and its volatility. As for the sign of these effects, an increase in expected losses would decrease the value of all the tranches. In fact, equity tranches would be affected as long positions in put options, while senior tranches would be affected as short position in call options. Furthermore, as put options with higher strikes would be affected more, intermediate tranches would also decrease in value. The sign of a change in volatility would be instead opposite for equity tranches and senior tranches, simply because equity amounts to a long position in an option, while the senior tranche embeds a short position. The value of equity is positively affected by an increase in volatility, at the expense of the senior tranche. The impact on intermediate tranches, which are differences of two options, is not determined, and in general the relationship is not monotone.
- Second, if one could trade these tranches in a liquid market, he could extract from their prices information about the distribution of losses. Particularly, given the same value of overall expected losses, the values of the different tranches could convey information about losses in volatility. In this simple framework, this is the same concept as the implied volatility that we know in the options markets. Of course, it would be incorrect to extract implied volatility from the intermediate tranches, simply because they are call spreads and are not monotone (and therefore invertible) functions of volatility. So, the correct way to go would be to rely on implied volatility from the equity tranches and to compute the intermediate tranches by difference.
- Third, the prices of such products can be expressed in different ways. Tranches can be quoted in "up-front" terms, but more often they are quoted in terms of credit spreads. So, the expected figures for losses for the tranches are often translated into the spread in an asset swap transaction or a CDS fixed premium (for *unfunded* CDOs). Besides this, of course, these products, which are inherently nonlinear, could be quoted in terms of the "implied" parameter determining the distribution of losses: in this very simple treatment, this parameter is the "implied volatility", very much as in the options market. In the real market, in which the degree of diversification is considered as the main parameter in the distribution, the parameter quoted is the "implied correlation".

8.5.3 The art of diversification

Securitization products are intrinsically multivariate. So, the above analysis carries over once one has specified

$$L = L_1 + L_2 + \cdots + L_n \qquad (8.65)$$

Moving one step forward from the very simple model presented above, the underlying asset of the equity tranches involved in the product is now a sum of random variables, and the options embedded in the equity and senior tranches are *basket options*. Even without getting any deeper into the pricing issues, we can state that: (i) the value of the option on a basket cannot be higher than the value of a basket of options, so some diversification is provided to the tranches; (ii) the value of the basket option increases with correlation – think of the AND/OR rule.

Following these arguments, it is easy to see that the same lines of discussion above apply, once the term "correlation" is substituted for the term "volatility". So, the value of all the tranches is negatively affected by an increase in expected losses, while changes in volatility and correlation affect equity and senior tranches in different ways. As equity corresponds to a put option on the basket of losses, its value is increased by an increase in correlation. As, on the contrary, senior tranches involve a short position in a basket call option, it is clear that it is negatively affected by an increase in correlation. There is another way of looking at this argument, which highlights how tranching is enabled to reach different kinds of investors. The equity tranche is mainly affected by idiosyncratic shocks, which are progressively less relevant the more losses are generated by a systematic common factor. For the same reason, the equity tranche is also negatively affected by cross-section variance and heterogeneity of the exposures. For these reasons, the investors interested in equity tranches are funds that are specialized in the "fundamental" analysis and have no regulatory constraint to invest in non-rated assets. Most of them are *hedge funds* looking for "absolute return" deals. On the opposite side, the senior tranche is negatively affected by very pervasive and systematic phenomena, while it is almost immune to specific idiosyncratic default events: this kind of product is designed for large institutional investors seeking safe investments.

Of course, diversification is not always sought by investors. It may in fact be the case that some institutional investors are interested in more dependence, maybe even more than can be offered using the assets and the "names" available on the market. Structurers in this case may create correlation artificially using the so-called CDO^2 deals. A CDO^2 is a securitization structure in which the products on the asset side of the SPV are also tranches. The typical structure of a CDO^2 is depicted in Figure 8.3. There is an external "layer" with a set of "names", and an intermediate "layer" with a set of *tranches*, typically with the same *attachment* and *detachment* figures. Each basket in this intermediate layer constitutes what is also called a set of "*baby CDOs*". This set of CDO tranches represents the asset side of the SPV in the "*mother CDO*". Notice that each "name" may appear in more than one "baby CDO". This *overlapping* feature obviously increases the dependence structure among the "baby CDOs". Consider, for example, a large name whose default causes losses in the intermediate CDOs, and assume that it is represented in the basket of many of them: this, of course, gives rise to simultaneous losses in many intermediate CDOs, so artificially creating correlation among them. So, the higher the degree of overlapping among the "names", the higher the level of correlation generated on the asset side of the SPV. Of course, tuning the degree of overlapping enables the probability distribution of losses to be designed in a customized way. Formally, the loss of the jth "baby CDO" tranche is given by

$$LCDO_j = \min \left[\max \left(\sum_{i=1}^{n} \mathbf{1}_{ij} L_i - L_{aj}, \ 0 \right), \ L_{dj} \right] \tag{8.66}$$

where $\mathbf{1}_{ij}$ is an indicator function taking value 1 if the ith "name" is included in the jth intermediate tranche and zero otherwise, and L_{aj} and L_{dj} are its attachment and detachment points, respectively. The overall loss, which has to be shared by the tranches of the "mother CDO", is now

$$L = LCDO_1 + LCDO_2 + \cdots + LCDO_k \qquad (8.67)$$

where k is the number of "baby CDOs". Typically, losses are added, even though in principle a structurer could also think of different aggregation functions.

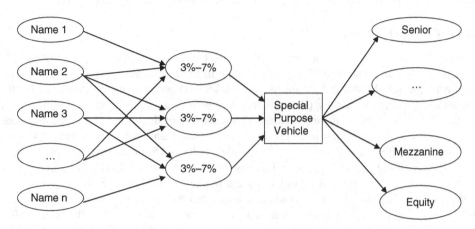

Figure 8.3   A CDO^2

Notice that the maximum amount of losses is given by the difference between detachment and attachment times the number of "baby CDOs". In the case shown in Figure 8.3, we have $4\% \times 3 = 12\%$ maximum loss. In the typical CDO^2 transaction the remaining amount of capital is invested in safe assets, represented by senior or supersenior tranches of *large* CDOs. A *large* CDO is a securitization deal in which the number n of assets or names is very large, so that it is not feasible to model the credit risk standing of each and every obligor: it is also said that the asset side is not *granular*. So, to complete the picture of the CDO^2 deal in the figure, the remaining 88% of principal could be invested in a senior tranche of a retail loan securitization, typically rated AAA.

To conclude, a feature that is often found in CDO^2 deals is the so-called *cross-subordination clause*. The rule gives an option to spread the losses across the entire set of "baby CDOs". So, if default of a name would overcome the attachment level of a "baby CDO", one would check whether the other "baby CDOs" have still room to absorb further losses. From the point of view of computation, this is equivalent to modifying the attachment and detachment levels of the "mother CDO". The details would be spelled out in the description of the pricing algorithm.

8.6   STANDARDIZED CDO CONTRACTS

Since 2003, some major global players introduced the idea of a market for standardized CDO contracts. Just like futures contracts for cash commodities or assets, such contracts would have been defined on a given notional description of the contract, representative of the major "names" in a market, with given maturities and tranches. Exactly as futures contracts, standardized CDOs were meant to provide a liquid tool to (i) hedge exposures in tranches in customized CDOs (*bespoke CDOs*) and (ii) take trading positions in the credit market, to exploit both the developments of the credit standing of the major "names" in the market and their co-movements (*correlation trading*). As finally happens with futures markets, the price transparency of the contract would enable implied information concerning credit risk correlation to be backed out. Nowadays, the standardized contracts traded in the market are the so-called *i-Traxx* indexes in Europe and the CDX indexes for the US market.

8.6.1   CDX and i-Traxx

CDX and *i-Traxx* are synthetic unfunded CDOs based on the most representative 125 "names" for different markets. *i-Traxx* specialize in the European market, but indexes are also available for the Australian and Asian markets. These indexes are produced by the International Indices Company (IIC). At the time of writing three benchmark indexes are produced: *i-Traxx Europe*, the main index, which consists of the main 125 European names; *i-Traxx Europe HiVol*, which includes the 30 European names with the highest five-year CDS spreads; and *i-Traxx Europe crossover*, which includes 45 sub-investment grade names. Furthermore, IIC offers several sector indexes. On the other hand, CDXs are administered by the CDS Index Company (CDSIndexCo) and marketed by Markit group.

We will focus on the two most standard indexes, that is the *i-Traxx Europe* and *CDX US*. Both indexes include 125 constituent names. The names are revised, and the index *rolled over* every six months. Maturities and tranches are also standardized. The standard maturities are 5, 7 and 10 years. The overall notional is 250 million. The tranches are reported in Table 8.1. We see that, apart from the equity tranches, the attachment and detachment points of the other tranches are different.

Table 8.1   i-Traxx and CDX quotes, five-year maturity, 27 September 2005

i-Traxx			CDX		
Tranche	Bid	Ask	Tranche	Bid	Ask
0–3%	23.5*	24.5*	0–3%	44.5*	45*
3–6%	71	73	3–7%	113	117
6–9%	19	22	7–10%	25	30
9–12%	8.5	10.5	10–15%	13	16
12–22%	4.5	5.5	15–30%	4.5	5.5

* Amount to be paid "up-front" plus 500 bp on a running basis.
Source: Lehman Brothers, *Correlation Monitor*, 28 September 2005.

The quote convention is that prices are expressed in basis points, and refer to CDS premia for selling and buying protection for the tranche. The important exception is the equity tranche, which is priced in terms of "up-front" plus 500 basis points on a running basis. The value of the tranches depends on: (i) the overall value of the relevant credit index; (ii) the expected loss of every name in the index; and (iii) the correlation among losses. In particular, as expected losses of the single names are priced in the market (and the availability of a transparent price is a requirement for inclusion in the index), the focus of the price is on correlation. Correlation is in fact an additional way of quoting standardized tranches.

8.6.2 Implied correlation

Implied correlation is that level of correlation (assuming correlation to be the same across all the names) which produces, using the standard pricing formula, the prices observed in the market. The concept is very much the same as implied volatility in the options market. In that case the standard pricing formula is that from the Black–Scholes model corresponding to Gaussian returns. Parallel to that, the standard pricing model for tranches is also based on the assumption of a Gaussian dependence structure, and it uses the *Gaussian copula* model.

What is strange, and breaks down the similarity between implied correlation and implied volatility, is that, at least in the beginning, the implied correlation was applied to all the tranches, including the intermediate ones. As we saw previously, this is incorrect. It would actually be like retrieving implied volatility from call spread prices in the option market. Call spread prices may well be non-monotone in volatility, just as intermediate tranches are generally non-monotone in correlation. The implied correlation concept can instead be correctly applied to equity tranches or senior tranches, which correspond to positions in options and are proved to be monotone in correlation. For this reason, after some years in which implied correlation had been applied to all the tranches, a new concept has been introduced, called *base correlation* to distinguish it from the past practice. *Base correlation* is the implied correlation that prices the equity tranches. So, for example, the base correlation for the CDX index refers to the correlation of the 0–3% equity tranche, the 0–7% equity tranche, and so on. The price of the mezzanine tranche is obtained by arbitrage, as specified above, by computing

$$EL(3\%, 7\%) = EL(0, 7\%) - EL(0, 3\%)$$

To distinguish this concept of base correlation, the old-fashioned way of extracting implied correlation from all the tranches has been called *compound correlation*, even though the use of this concept, particularly in credit analysis, has considerably decreased. So, typically in a report on the indexes we often find such information as that in Table 8.2. For example, a trader looking at that table could conjecture the possibility of a *cross-region* trade. Notice, in fact, that base correlation is markedly different between the US and the European market for equity and senior tranches, and in opposite directions. Furthermore, this contrasts with the other base correlations that are by and large similar in the two markets. An idea could then be, for example, to sell protection on the CDX equity tranche and buy protection on the corresponding i-Traxx equity tranche. One could actually have another idea, and assume that either of the two markets would converge towards a common shape of the base correlation curve. This could, for example, imply that the base correlation on the 0–3% equity tranche could increase while that on the 0–30% equity tranche could decrease. Buying exposure on the former and selling protection on the latter could be a promising business.

What we have introduced in the simple example above is a way of trading credit correlation, trying to gauge the future movements of the base correlation structure. That very closely recalls the activity of "*riding*" the yield curve in the fixed income market or betting on the smile curve in the options market. Actually, the smile (or skew) borrowed from the options market is nowadays largely used in the trading of standardized credit derivatives and is called the "*correlation smile*" or the "*correlation skew*". Just as in the options market, where we have been searching for years for new models to help to produce, and then predict, the volatility smile, the same is happening in the credit market. The quest is still open for models that enable us to understand

Table 8.2   i-Traxx and CDX correlation, five-year maturity, 27 September 2005

i-Traxx		CDX	
Tranche	Base correlation	Tranche	Base correlation
0–3%	12.3%	0–3%	6.6%
3–6%	23.5%	3–7%	22.6%
6–9%	31.8%	7–10%	31.1%
9–12%	38.8%	10–15%	41.0%
12–22%	55.5%	15–30%	66.3%

Source: Lehman Brothers, *Correlation Monitor*, 28 September 2005.

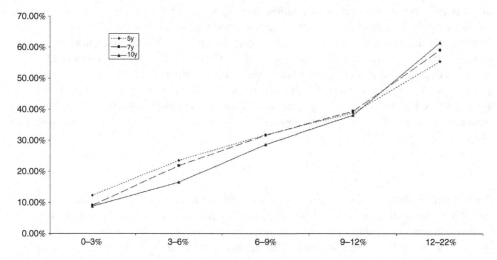

Figure 8.4   Base correlation of the i-Traxx tranches

and predict the correlation smile. Most of the models proposed have been surveyed in the first part of this chapter, but a full explanatory model has yet to be discovered.

In Figures 8.4 and 8.5 we report the base correlation skews for the same day as that in the illustration above for the CDX and i-Traxx markets, respectively.

8.6.3   "Delta hedged equity" blues

One of the most debated topics in the management of CDO investments is that of hedging. The issue has always been specially hot for lower tranches, and in particular for the equity tranche. Traditionally, the equity tranche was kept with the originator of the deal because it was too risky and unrated, and was used to send a signal to the market about the quality of the assets. However, it was too risky to leave the tranche unhedged. Ever since then, the problem of managing the risk of the equity tranche was a relevant issue. In these days, the practice of keeping the equity tranche with the originator is no longer available, particularly for regulatory reasons. Under the new regulatory framework, in fact, if the originator

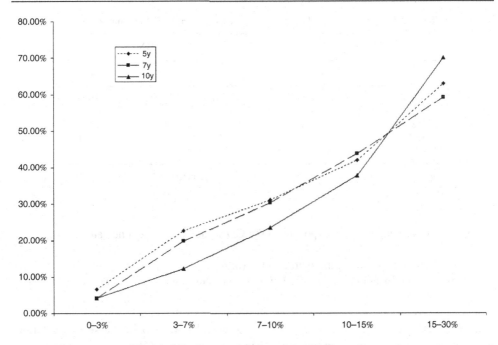

Figure 8.5 Base correlation of the CDX tranche

retains the equity tranche of a securitization deal, it is subject to capital requirement for the whole pool of securitized assets. Mainly for these reasons, in addition to the fact that it was a promising business opportunity, unregulated intermediaries, namely hedge funds, have taken over the job of handling the toxic waste of equity tranches generated by CDO deals. Of course, by the same token they have also taken over the practice and development of those techniques called "*delta hedged equity*". The financial crisis of May 2005, in which many hedge funds lost huge amounts of capital in these deals, shows however that the quest for good equity hedging strategies is by no means over. Here we provide a brief illustration of the problem, by keeping an eye on the May 2005 event.

Hedging a derivative contract can obviously be done with the underlying asset or other derivative contracts. Equity tranches make no difference and can be hedged

- buying protection on the whole index
- buying protection on other tranches.

As in standard derivatives, the quantity to be bought or sold to immunise a position is called *delta*. The delta reported for each tranche denotes the nominal amount for which one has to buy protection in order to hedge one unit of exposure to the tranche. To be explicit, in Table 8.3 we report, for the same day and markets as in the previous tables, the *deltas* of each tranche. So, for example, the *delta* of the equity tranche means that it is equivalent, in terms of sensitivity to index movement, to sell protection on the equity tranche for a nominal of 10m or on the whole index for a nominal amount of 190m.

Table 8.3   i-Traxx and CDX deltas, five-year maturity, 27 September 2005

i-Traxx		CDX	
Tranche	Delta	Tranche	Delta
0–3%	23.0	0–3%	19.0
3–6%	5.0	3–7%	5.5
6–9%	1.8	7–10%	1.8
9–12%	1.0	10–15%	1.0
12–22%	0.5	15–30%	0.5

Source: Lehman Brothers, *Correlation Monitor*, 28 September 2005.

So, in order to hedge a 10m exposure to the CDX equity tranche, one can

- buy protection on 190m of the whole index (*index hedged equity*)
- buy protection on about 34.5m (19.0/5.5) of the mezzanine trance (*mezzanine hedged equity*).

Until the crisis of May 2005, most hedge funds would have chosen the second solution, particularly because it was granting a much higher net margin (*carry*). Credit research of the period reports that the latter strategy was granting about 1.4m per annum as opposed to 0.9m offered by the index hedge solution. Of course, stability of the *deltas* is a major matter of concern. That was what actually happened in the weekend between Friday 6 May and Monday 9 May 2005. In front of a 3-bp increase of the index, the equity tranche increased substantially, with the up-front quote rising by 3.125%, but at the same time the mezzanine actually decreased by 16 bp. As at the time the leverage used for the mezzanine hedge was around 2.2, the decrease in the mezzanine spread contributed to a further 1.6% loss in the deal (Bank of America Securities, Credit Research, 9 May 2005).

8.7   SIMULATION-BASED PRICING OF CDOS

Owing to the high dimensionality of many of the structures, Monte Carlo methods are widely used to price credit derivatives and other credit structures such as CDOs. As we have already discussed in Chapter 6, Monte Carlo methods are generally fast and easy to implement and usually result in quite generic code implementation so that new structure can be introduced without great effort. The resulting pricing engine is easy to maintain and extend.

In this section we will discuss a very simple pricing model which is based on the simulation of default times for a series of names that represent the asset side of our CDO, the liability component being modelled with the set of securities issued by the CDO. We will show that the model can easily accommodate all the structures discussed here, including cash and synthetic CDOs as well as CDOs squared with or without *cross-subordination*.

Names and tranches are in turn implementation of the abstract `CFinancialActivity` class which we introduced in Chapter 5. The description of the two classes is shown in Figure 8.6.

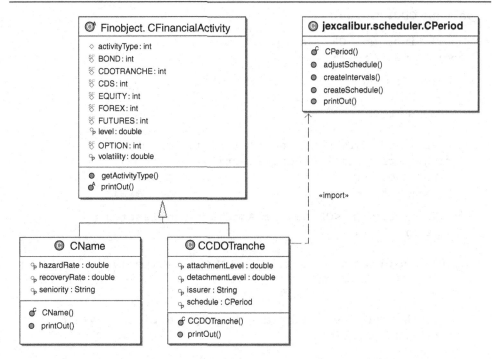

Figure 8.6 CName and CCDOTranche classes and their relationship with jExcalibur classes

8.7.1 The CABS (asset-backed security) class

In order to put together the CDO tranches with the names to which they refer, we will introduce a new class called **CABS**. In our simple model this class has only three attributes: a list of financial assets called **asset**; a second list of financial securities called **liability**; and a boolean parameter that specifies the type of subordination to be used in the computation of the tranche value. In the Java implementation we have used the ArrayList class for these attributes (see Figure 8.7 and the code below).

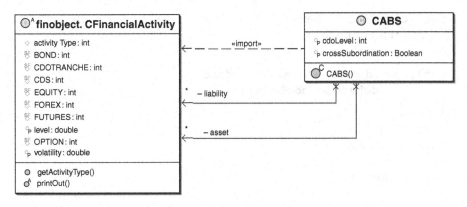

Figure 8.7 CABS class (note the association link between the two classes)

```java
package CDOPricing;

import finobject.CFinancialActivity;
import java.util.*;

public class CABS {
   /**
    * Attributes
    */
   private ArrayList<CFinancialActivity  asset;
   private ArrayList<CFinancialActivity  liability;
   private Boolean                        crossSubordination;
   private int                            cdoLevel;

   public ArrayList<CFinancialActivity> getAsset() {
      return asset;
   }
   public void setAsset(ArrayList<CFinancialActivity> asset) {
      this.asset = asset;
   }

   public ArrayList<CFinancialActivity> getLiability() {
      return liability;
   }

   public void setLiability(ArrayList<CFinancialActivity>
    liability) {
      this.liability = liability;
   }

   public Boolean getCrossSubordination() {
      return crossSubordination;
   }

   public void setCrossSubordination(Boolean crossSubordination) {
      this.crossSubordination = crossSubordination;
   }

   public int getCdoLevel() {
      return cdoLevel;
   }

   public void setCdoLevel(int cdoLevel) {
      this.cdoLevel = cdoLevel;
   }

   /**
    * Constructor
    */
   public CABS(){

   }
}
```

Both the asset list and the liability list can contain every financial asset, in particular the asset list can contain either names or tranches. The first case is the most straightforward and corresponds to the simple CDO in which we have a pool of credits (whose principal properties are described by the list of names) on the asset side and a set of tranches, which are issued with different seniorities, constituting the list of liabilities. If, in the asset list, we have CDO tranches, we obtain is a CDO Squared (CDO^2) deal as described above. In this case, which is obviously more difficult to handle than the previous one, we will have to specify how the losses from the elementary CDO tranches would propagate through the principal of the CDO^2 liabilities. As we will see in the following sections, the cross-subordination flag is meant to affect this propagation.

In short, the pricing process with Monte Carlo simulation can be decomposed in the following subprocesses:

- Generate a scenario of possible default times for each name. We generate n times (where n is the number of names) and for each value we check if this value is less than the expiration of CDO. If this is true then the status of the corresponding name is set to "defaulted".
- Calculate the potential losses due to defaulted names.
- Propagate the losses computed in the previous step in order to calculate the principal amount for each payment date of the tranche schedule (this was called the *waterfall mechanism*).
- The principal value for each payment date is accumulated during the scenario generation and a final average value is then calculated.
- Using the average nominal value and the coupon value of the tranche we can compute the average cash flow. The sum of the discounted value is the value of the tranche.

Let us now describe each step in deeper detail.

8.7.2   Default time generator

We suppose that individual names default according to a Poisson process with a constant default intensity λ for each name; the recovery rate is also assumed to a be a known constant value. The computation takes as input an exogenous correlation matrix, **R**, of dimension $n \times n$ (where n is the number of names) and the vector of n hazard rates. Using the covariance matrix we generate, for each Monte Carlo simulation, a vector of n correlated uniformly distributed random variables. The generation of these variates is done using the copula function technique. Finally, we compute default times by the inversion of exponential distribution

$$\tau_i = -\frac{\ln(u_i)}{\lambda_i}$$

where u_i is the generic uniformly distributed variable and λ_i is the ith name hazard rate.

The generation of random variates is done following the algorithms described in Cherubini *et al.* (2004). For the Gaussian copula we have

1. Find the Cholesky decomposition A of **R**.
2. Simulate n independent random variates $z = (z_1, \ldots, z_n)'$ from $N(0, 1)$

3. Set $x = Az$.
4. Set $u_i = \Phi(x_i)$ with $i = 1, 2, \ldots, n$ where Φ denotes the univariate standard normal distribution function.
5. $(y_1, \ldots, y_n)' = [F_1^{-1}(u_1), \ldots, F_n^{-1}(u_n)]$ where F_i denotes the ith marginal distribution.

Student t variates are generated according to

1. Find the Cholesky decomposition A of $\mathbf{R}$.
2. Simulate n independent random variates $z = (z_1, \ldots, z_n)'$ from $N(0, 1)$
2. Simulate a random variate s from χ_ν^2 independent of z.
3. Set $y = Az$.
4. Set $x = (\nu/s)^{1/2} y$.
5. Set $u_i = T_\nu(x_i)$ with $i = 1, 2, \ldots, n$, and where T_ν denotes the univariate Student t distribution function
6. $(y_1, \ldots, y_n)' = [F_1^{-1}(u_1), \ldots, F_n^{-1}(u_n)]$ where F_i denotes the ith marginal distribution.

As far as the Java implementation is concerned, we will again use the factory pattern. The generation of uniform distributions can be implemented using a generic interface named `IcopulaGenerator`; for each new copula-based generator we would like to design, we would have to add a standard class implementing this interface, as described in Figure 8.8.

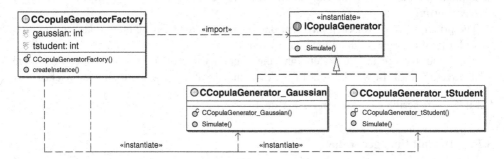

Figure 8.8   The CCopulaGenerator Factory Pattern

The uniform variates are used by the `Simulate` method of the `CDefaultTimes Generator` class. As we have previously pointed out, the output of the copula algorithm is compared with the expiration,of the CDO. If the value of the simulated default time is less than the CDO expiration, this means that we have a default event during the life of the product. In this case we set the status of the names to "defaulted", the status is memorized in an `ArrayList` called `NameStatus`.

8.7.3   The waterfall scheme

In order to compute the propagation of losses we have to distinguish two cases: simple CDO and squared CDO.

In the first case we compute the loss due to the generic defaulted name simply by multiplying the loss times the amount of the names in the pool of credits

$$\text{Loss} = (1 - \text{RecoveryRate}) * \text{Amount}$$

The loss is cumulated across all the names. In order to understand if the loss affects the nominal value of the tranche we compare the value with the attachment and detachment level of the tranche itself. The effective loss on the tranche is computed as

$$EL = \begin{cases} 0 & if \quad L < L_a \\ L - L_a & if \quad L_a < PL < L_d \\ L_d - L_a & if \quad L > L_d \end{cases}$$

where L is the loss simulated, EL is the effective loss on the tranches, L_a the attachment level and L_d is the detachment level. Since we have information about the default time, we can map each loss to the CDO schedule. At the end of this process we have a list of values for the residual nominal at each payment date.

For a squared CDO the computation is just a little more complicated. Remember that in this case the asset of CDO is formed by tranches too. If there is no cross-subordination, the computation is simply a reiteration of the previous one. We compute the effective loss for each tranche ("baby CDO") in the asset, cumulate all these losses and then propagate them to the "mother CDO" using the attachment and detachment levels of the latter.

If there is cross-subordination, potential losses in the asset tranches are simply summed up without tranching. The attachment and detachment levels of the squared CDO are also modified. We sum all the attachment levels of the asset tranches and this value is added to the attachment and the detachment levels of the CDO[2]. After this adjustment we can compute effective losses with the usual tranching mechanism applied to the cumulated losses of the asset tranches. The complete process is described in Figure 8.9.

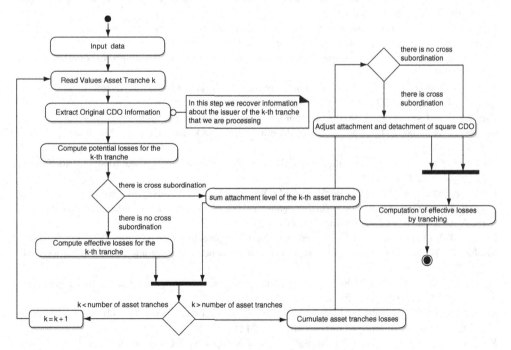

Figure 8.9 Squared CDO waterfall mechanism

Remark 8.1 From an OOP point of view, the most important thing is the capacity to build our application using a sort of iteration which permits us to consider each tranche either as a liability (for simple CDO) or an asset (for higher order CDO). In our example we have only partially developed this point of view. A very interesting alternative is the method proposed by Rott and Fries (2005). In their work they propose the design pattern of a stochastic iterator named "default time iterator". With this pattern it is possible to create a highly flexible product implementation framework in which any product may become the underlying of any other product. The interested reader will also find in this work an interesting discussion about efficient computation methods for the estimation of sensitivities.

REFERENCES AND FURTHER READING

Amato, J. & Remolona, E. (2003) The credit spread puzzle, *BIS Quarterly Review*, **10**, 51–63.

Andersen, L. & Sidenius, J. (2005) Extensions to the Gaussian copula: Random recovery and random factor loadings, *Journal of Credit Risk*, **1** (1), 29–70.

Andersen, L., Sidenius, J. & Basu, S. (2003) All your hedges in one basket, *Risk*, **10**, 67–72.

Banc of America Securities (2005) *Situation Room,* 9 May 2005.

Burtshell, X., Gregory, J. & Laurent, J.P. (2005) *A Comparative Analysis of CDO Pricing Models.* Working Paper, BNP Paribas.

Cherubini, U., Luciano, E. & Vecchiato, W. (2004) *Copula Methods in Finance.* John Wiley & Sons, Chichester.

Davis, M. & Lo, V. (2001) Infectious defaults, *Quantitative Finance*, **1**, 382–386.

Duffie, D. & Garleanu, N. (2001) Risk and valuation of collateralized debt obligations, *Financial Analysts Journal*, **57** (1), 41–59.

Esposito, M. (2001) Basic insight in pricing basket credit derivatives, in *Proceedings of the 2nd International Conference "Managing Credit and Market Risk"*, Verona.

Frey, R. & McNeil, A.J. (2003) Dependent defaults in models of portfolio credit risks, *Journal of Risk*, **6** (1), 59–92.

Friend, A. & Rogge, E. (2004) *Correlation at first sight.* Working Paper, ABN AMRO.

Gregory, J. & Laurent, J.P. (2003) I will survive, *Risk*, **6**, 103–107.

Gregory, J. & Laurent, J.P. (2004) In the core of correlation, *Risk*, **10**, 87–91.

Gregory, J. & Laurent, J.P. (2005) Basket default swaps, CDOs and factor copulas, *Journal of Risk*, **7** (4), 103–122.

Hull, J. & White, A. (2004) Valuation of a CDO and nth to default CDS without Monte Carlo, *Journal of Derivatives*, **12** (2), 8–23.

Hull, J. & White, A. (2006) *The perfect copula.* Working Paper, University of Toronto.

Laurent, J.P. & Gregory, J. (2003) *Basket default swaps, CDOs and factor copulas.* Working Paper, ISFA Actuarial School, University of Lion.

Li, D. (2000) On default correlation: A copula function approach, *Journal of Fixed Income*, **9**, 43–54.

Mashal, R., Naldi, M. & Zeevi, A. (2003) On the dependence of equity and asset returns, *Risk*, **10**, 83–87.

Marshall, A.W. & Olkin, I. (1967) A multivariate exponential distribution, *Journal of the American Statistical Association*, **62**, 30–44.

Meneguzzo, D. & Vecchiato, W. (2004) Copula sensitivity in collateralized debt obligations and basket default swaps, *The Journal of Futures Markets*, **24** (1), 37–70.

Rott, M.G. & Fries, C.P. (2005) *Fast and robust Monte Carlo CDO sensitivities and their efficient object oriented implementation.* Working Paper.

Schönbucher, P.J. (2003) *Credit Derivatives Pricing Models*. John Wiley & Sons, Chichester.

Schönbucher, P.J. & Schubert, D. (2001) *Copula dependent risks in intensity models*. Working Paper, University of Bonn.

Tavakoli, J. (2003) *Collateralized Debt Obligations and Structured Finance*. John Wiley & Sons, Chichester.

9

Risk Management

9.1 INTRODUCTION

In this chapter we conclude our analysis of the structured finance market by addressing the main issues that this line of business raises for the risk manager. We again assume that the reader is well acquainted with the general framework and the main topics involved in risk management. The reader without such a background is referred to excellent books such as Jorion (2001), Crouhy *et al.* (2000) and Embrechts *et al.* (2005) for in-depth treatments of the general framework of risk management.

The development of the structured finance market poses three main questions to risk managers:

- The first question is: Are the prices right? Since most of the derivative contracts embedded in structured products are not endowed with a sufficiently close replicating portfolio, the first problem is to select a price that may be representative of the cost of unbundling the position. The problem of liquidity, or its counterpart in financial mathematics – which is market incompleteness – has been rather overlooked in broad risk management applications, while it becomes a paramount feature in structured finance.
- The second question relates to nonlinearities in the portfolio: How is the value of the product likely to respond to changes in the risk factors? And what about changes in volatility and correlation? Nonlinearities make the task of measuring risk particularly complex. In the first place, it is more difficult to represent risk exposures: standard mapping techniques, designed to report the direction of the exposure to risk factors, must be supplemented by reports of *gamma* or *vega* exposures, to illustrate the sensitivity of the portfolio to changes in volatility and correlation. Beyond reporting, however, standard parametric risk measurement techniques are very difficult to apply. The presence of relevant second-order effects, *gamma* and *vega*, introduces chi-squared distributed sources of risk, so that the resulting overall distribution of profit and losses is no longer available in closed form. For this reason, *historical simulation* looks like a preferable strategy, and it is the technique that is mostly used: a set of scenarios is sorted from past history to simulate the distribution of future profits and losses. Furthermore, one would like to check what could happen to the distribution of profits and losses in particularly extreme market situations (*stress testing*).
- The third question refers to the management of risk. Which risk factors should be hedged and how should they be hedged? Notice that a prerequirement to this answer is to have a clear idea of the replicating portfolio of each structured product in the portfolio. As we saw previously, because of the incomplete market problem this is seldom an easy task. There is a trade-off, however, between two choices. A choice is to perform the hedging "in-house" by using liquid instruments. In this case, of course, the incomplete market problem materializes in the need to choose hedge ratios that are as close as possible to

the positions to be hedged. The alternative is to buy and/or sell the derivative products involved to a third party, which is a sort of re-insurance contract that raises the issue of the credit risk of the re-insurer. This problem is called *counterparty risk* and is one of the frontier issues in risk management practice.

9.2   OTC VERSUS FUTURES STYLE DERIVATIVES

A basic issue that is raised in the risk management analysis of a derivative contract is the kind of market in which the contract is exchanged. Typically, a contract can be exchanged in a bilateral transaction, in the so-called *over-the-counter* (OTC) market, or in a *futures style* market. A substantial trade-off is involved in the choice between these two kinds of markets.

In an OTC transaction, the contract is stipulated between two parties. Two disadvantages immediately come to mind. (1) If one of the parties defaults, the other party may remain with a net credit, in which case it would have lost money: this is what is called *counterparty risk*. (2) If one of the parties wants to get out of the contract before its maturity, he will have to write an offsetting contract, possibly with the same counterparty: this is what is called *liquidity risk*. These disadvantages have to be balanced against an advantage: one may write a contract on virtually any specific risk factor. So, in a structured finance application, one could buy from the re-insurer exactly the same derivative contract that is sold in the structured product.

Futures style markets are designed to reduce *counterparty risk* and *liquidity risk* as effectively as possible. This is accomplished by three provisions:

- *Marking-to-market*: Checking the position and making settlement of profits and losses every day.
- *Margin requirements*: Both parties deposit a percentage of the nominal value of the contract that is meant to absorb intraday losses: in case of substantial losses, the party losing money receives a *margin call* to reintegrate the margin.
- *Clearinghouse*: The relationship between buyer and seller is broken in two by the introduction of the clearinghouse. In case of substantial losses of one of the parties and failure to abide by the margin call, the margin is used by the *clearinghouse* to close the position with the counterparty.

Of course, the success to reduce credit risk is strictly linked to the ability to reduce liquidity risk. In fact, the possibility of closing a position at any time, following the default of one of the parties in the market, or for some other reasons, is linked to a feature that is called *contract standardization*. Both the features of the underlying asset and the delivery or exercise dates are determined in a *notional* contract. In case the contract required physical delivery, some price adjustments could be included to allow for the *delivery grade*. This structure makes sure that everyone interested in hedging or investing in a broad class of highly correlated risk factors could be interested in the same contract. The pros have to be balanced against the cons: the contract is not written on any specific underlying asset. So, in a structured finance example, hedging a derivative with a futures style contract should take into account that the underlying of the contract is generally different from the underlying asset in the structured product. This is known as *basis risk*. Furthermore, for some structured product a sufficiently close liquid market for the underlying may not exist at all, providing an extreme case of market incompleteness.

The choice to hedge on the OTC market rather than on *futures style* markets then hinges on a basic trade-off between credit and liquidity risk on the one hand and basis risk and market incompleteness on the other. In particular, *futures style* markets have proved highly effective in reducing counterparty risk, while *basis risk* may be completely erased in OTC transactions. The question is whether some intermediate arrangement could be made to strike a balance between these two advantages. It seems that financial intermediaries have addressed this issue since the 1990s. The way they have been doing so is by bringing some of the features of *futures style* markets into their operations process. This shows up clearly in two kinds of provisions that are nowadays largely diffused in the market, and will be discussed throughout this chapter:

- *Value-at-Risk limits*: Most intermediaries use a *Value-at-Risk* (VaR) requirement to allocate risk among the different desks and business units. It is easy to show that this concept is very close to that of margin requirement in futures markets.
- *Marking-to-market and collateral*: In derivative transactions, at least between intermediaries, there is an agreement to mark the value of the position to market every day or every week and to post the losses as collateral. This is also very close to the idea of *margin call* in the futures markets.

9.3 VALUE-AT-RISK & CO.

The *Value-at-Risk* (VaR) methodology has become the market standard of risk measurement since the last decade of the past century. The development has followed the increasing involvement of the financial intermediation system in the derivative markets. In a sense, this development has paralleled the growth of the structured finance business. As we noticed above, the concept of VaR can be traced back in some sense to that of *margin* requirement in the futures market: it is meant to measure the amount of capital that is likely to absorb losses for the time needed to unwind the position in front of adverse market movements or events. With respect to the traditional standard *asset and liability management* (ALM) techniques the innovative element is then that VaR is a probabilistic concept, just like the margin requirement, and has to do with the probability distribution of profits and losses. Beyond the traditional approach, the analysis is not limited to the evaluation of sensitivities of the position with respect to the risk factors (e.g. *duration gap*), but extends to the probability distribution of the risk factors themselves. The recent debate on alternative risk measures to be used in substitution of VaR has in no way diminished the relevance of this revolutionary feature. The argument actually builds on this innovation, and addresses the question of how to measure risk from a given distribution of profits and losses.

Designing a risk management process requires a set of strategic decisions that may be formalized in a sequence of steps

1. Analysis of the structure of products in the portfolio, identifying their replicating portfolios in terms of elementary products.
2. Evaluation of the risk factors and pricing of the products of the portfolio: *marking-to-market* of the position.
3. *Mapping* of each position into a set of exposures to the risk factors.

4. Evaluation of the statistical joint distribution of the risk factors and that of profit and losses.
5. Choice of a risk measure for the distribution of profit and losses.

As we focus in this chapter on peculiarities related to structured products, we will only touch upon some of the points above.

9.3.1 Market risk exposure mapping

A standard by-product of the risk measurement process is the so called *mapping* process of risk exposures. A set of risk factors is defined in such a way as to break down the exposures by

- country or issuer
- currency
- kind of security (equity, bond, commodity, etc.)
- maturity (a limited set of maturities is considered for every issuer).

The portfolio is *mapped* into exposures to the different risk factors. The *mapping* is performed taking into account each product in the portfolio and each cash flow in the product. Exposures are then collected in a set of *buckets*. In standard risk measurement analysis of linear products, attention is focused on the sensitivity of the position to movements in one direction or the other. With respect to this, positions are mapped in terms of exposures to the risk factors in such a way as to preserve their financial characteristics as closely as possible. For this purpose, the mapping procedure is performed, abiding by three requirements:

- The sign of the exposures resulting from the mapping should be the same as that of the original position.
- The *marking-to-market* value of the mapped exposure should be the same as that of the original position.
- The risk of the mapped exposure should be as close as possible to that of the original position.

The first two requirements are particularly easy to preserve, and imply that each cash flow be transformed into a linear combination of risk factor exposures. As for the third requirement, one has to make a further choice, particularly for positions that have to be mapped on several risk factors. The standard problem is to map a cash flow maturing at time τ in two exposures to the maturities t_{j-1} and t_j, with $t_{j-1} \leq \tau \leq t_j$. Three options are available:

- The mapped exposures must have the same *duration* (or PV01) as the original position: this choice preserves the sensitivity of the position with respect to a 1-bp shock in all the risk factors involved.
- The mapped exposures must have the same *volatility* as the original position. This choice was proposed in the first version of RiskMetrics™ and is meant to preserve the variance of the position, so taking into account both the volatilities and correlation between the risk factors.
- The mapped exposures must have the same *sensitivity* to each risk factor as in the original position. This is a latest proposal by RiskMetrics™. It strikes a compromise between the previous two choices. Allocation to the risk factors is determined in such a way as to preserve the sensitivity of the position with respect to a 1-bp shock in each of the risk

factors. In order to abide by the constraint that the marking-to-market value has to be preserved, however, part of the position has to be mapped in the cash bucket.

Let us now see what is different about the risk measurement of structured products. As we have shown throughout this book, risk analysis of a structured product must gauge two sensitivities:

- The sensitivity of the value of the product with respect to changes of risk factors in one direction or another. In this respect risk measurement calls for the same analysis as that of a linear product discussed above.
- The sensitivity of the value of the product with respect to volatility and correlation, or more generally changes in the distribution of the risk factors. This sort of higher moment dimension is what actually differentiates structured products from linear products.

In portfolios with substantial positions in structured products, the mapping procedure must be supplemented by reports of sensitivities to finite shocks (*gamma*) and to volatility changes (*vega*). As sensitivities are linear operators, they may be summed across all the positions and across all the risk factors, just as we do for linear products. So, in a risk management report each risk factor will be endowed with three buckets:

- The first bucket will collect the *delta* of the product with respect to the risk factors. This bucket will represent the sensitivity to *directional* changes in each risk factor.
- The second bucket will collect second-order sensitivity to changes in the risk factor in both directions, and will report the global *gamma* position of the portfolio with respect to each risk factor.
- The third bucket will collect the sensitivity with respect to volatility and correlation changes, and will report the global *vega* of the portfolio with respect to each risk factor.

Notice that representation of the exposure beyond first order is mandatory to ensure sound risk management decisions. The classical case it that of negative gamma and vega nightmares, well known to every trader and risk manager. In presence of a negative exposure to volatility changes, in fact, a *delta* hedging strategy would leave the position exposed to losses no matter which direction a risk factor moves.

9.3.2   The distribution of profits and losses

Once the portfolio of positions is mapped onto a set of exposures to risk factors, one is left with the problem of estimating the joint distribution of risk factor changes. The distribution would then be applied to the set of exposures to recover the profit and loss distribution of the portfolio as a whole.

In order to estimate the distribution of risk factor changes, three methodologies are available:

- Parametric method
- Monte Carlo simulation
- Historical simulation.

In the parametric method, a specific functional form for the distribution of factor shocks is assumed. The market standard, due to RiskMetrics™, is to assume that the shocks are conditional and normally distributed. Variances and correlations are updated with an exponentially weighted moving average scheme (EWMA). It may actually be proved that such an assumption corresponds to an integrated GARCH(1, 1) (IGARCH) model for the risk factors dynamics.

The parametric method is certainly to be recommended for portfolios in which nonlinearities are not substantial. This is not the case, of course, for portfolios of structured products. Sticking to the parametric approach in the presence of massive nonlinearities in the pay-offs would call for the extension of the model to the corresponding higher-order effect (*gamma*) and to volatility shocks (*vega*). There is a problem that this actually destroys the closed form solution that we postulated for the profit and loss distribution. As a matter of fact, even assuming conditional normality for the shocks, the second-order effect – that is, the squared shock – would be distributed according to a *chi-squared* law. Unfortunately, there is no closed form representation of mixtures of normal and *chi-squared* distributions. A more direct way to address the problem is then to move to simulation techniques. If one would like to stick to the assumption of conditional normality for the risk factors, Monte Carlo simulation could be a choice. Over the *unwinding* period, scenarios could be generated for the risk factors and the portfolio could be re-evaluated under each scenario. Sorting the scenarios by the associate profit and loss figures would then allow the profit and loss distribution to be designed. Of course, the reliability of the representation of the distribution would actually depend on the assumption of normality that we have imposed in the first place. A more radical choice is historical simulation: scenarios would be drawn from past experience of the markets, rather than from an assigned distribution. This method, which has become the market standard for nonlinear portfolios, will be covered in more detail in the next section.

9.3.3   Risk measures

Once the distribution of profit and losses has been properly estimated, a problem that has been debated for a very long time is which measure to use to represent the risk of losses. The measure that has been proposed since the 1990s, that is, *Value-at-Risk*, is actually the percentile of the distribution.

$$\text{VaR} \equiv F^{-1}(\alpha) \tag{9.1}$$

where $F(.)$ is the profit and loss distribution and α is a confidence level (typically 1% or 5%). The choice of VaR, which, as we saw previously, was inspired by the practice of *futures style* markets, has been questioned on several grounds. The most important arguments against it have been collected under the concept of *coherent risk measures* theory. The concept was first raised by Artzner *et al.* (1999) who addressed the question of a set of requirements that a measure has to fulfil to represent risk in a consistent way. Three axioms were considered

- Positive homogeneity: $\rho(\lambda X) = \lambda \rho(X)$
- Translation invariance: $\rho(X + \alpha/v(t, T)) = \rho(X) - \alpha$
- Subadditivity: $\rho(X_1 + X_2) \leq \rho(X_1) + \rho(X_2)$

The use of VaR was questioned on the grounds that it fails to abide by some of these requirements. Alternative measures, such as the so-called *expected shortfall* (ES), have been proposed. ES is the expected value of losses greater than the VaR. Formally,

$$ES \equiv E(X : X \le F^{-1}(\alpha)) \tag{9.2}$$

where X is the change in value of the portfolio. The choice of one measure or the other has been the subject of a long debate, and the issue cannot be considered to be definitely settled even today. Most of the argument has concentrated around subadditivity. On one hand, it is definitely true that the VaR measure could fail to be subadditive in some applications. This means that if one allocates 1 million dollars VaR to business A and 1 million dollars VaR to business B to ensure α probability of default of each business considered as a separate entity, one would have to allocate more than 2 million dollars to maintain the same probability α for the two businesses merged together. On the other hand, however, that would mean that merging the two businesses would actually increase the probability of default, and this is a piece of information that is no doubt particularly interesting for any risk manager: looking at the concrete risk management practice from this viewpoint it would seem that violation of the subadditivity axiom is an advantage, rather than a flaw of the VaR measure. And maybe the only one. There are in fact many other reasons why the ES measure would be expected to prevail in the long run. The most convincing of these is that it is almost straightforward to solve an asset allocation problem with a constraint on ES, but doing the same under a VaR constraint may be a very involved problem: this is not the case, of course, in the standard parametric approach for linear products, but it may become a hugely relevant problem if one allows for departures from normality and/or a substantial presence of payoff nonlinearities, which is the case of any structured product portfolio.

9.4 HISTORICAL SIMULATION

Historical simulation is the most straightforward and intuitive, and yet powerful, tool for the risk measurement of portfolios of structured finance products. The idea is very simple. We draw scenarios from past experience of the market and use them as possible future market conditions. The positions in the portfolio are evaluated using the risk factor realizations in each scenario and aggregated in the portfolio. The profit and losses are then sorted and reported in a histogram, in which the empirical percentile is recorded as the Value-at-Risk figure of the portfolio.

In further detail, a historical simulation algorithm is composed of three steps:

1. *Data compression*: As it is very hard to address non-Gaussian joint distributions, even with low dimensions, data is typically compressed into very few, possibly one, dimension. Standard data compression techniques provided by statistics include principal component or factor analysis. On economic grounds, an alternative would be to compress data into exposures to a similar risk factor, and to apply the analysis for each risk factor. The choice that is typically made in real applications is to use the current portfolio as a data compression criterion. The current portfolio composition is held fixed and revaluated under different scenarios.
2. *Choice of scenarios*: Scenarios are taken from past history. A period has to be selected subject to the typical trade-off that too long a period may include structural breaks, while too short a period may not be representative of the distribution of returns. Typically, in standard applications one year of data is selected. But, as we will describe below, most

of the problems with this method, as well as many of the advances proposed, refer to this point.

3. *Histogram*: The profits and losses of the current portfolio are evaluated under each and every scenario. Profits and losses are then ranked and represented in a histogram. The risk measure selected is finally computed on the empirical distribution.

The plain algorithm described, however (known as *classical historical simulation*), is exposed to some problems.

- The first argument that may be raised is that history never repeats itself, certainly not exactly in the same way. So, taking raw historical scenarios as they really occurred includes not only some systematic elements that are typical of the data-generating process of the risk factor, but also idiosyncratic features that belong to those specific days, and would not be likely to show up again in the future. As we are interested in simulating future distributions of profits and losses, trying to filter out idiosyncratic features would increase the reliability of the simulation. This trade-off actually shows up again and again in many instances and in the very strategic foundations of risk management. It closely recalls the concepts of *"generalization"* capability in artificial intelligence disciplines or that of *"parsimony"* in statistics: the idea is that increasing the number of parameters increases the ability of the model to fit the data *in-sample*, but beyond a reasonable dimension it reduces the ability of the model to describe the data *out-of-sample* (a phenomenon called *overfitting*).

- The second argument against classical historical simulation is that it is based on the assumption that the profit and loss variables are *identically and independently distributed* (i.i.d). This assumption ensures that when we draw scenarios from past history, we are actually drawing them from the same distribution as that of future history scenarios. There is overwhelming evidence that in financial markets this is not the case. The distribution of returns changes over time, particularly as far as variance and higher moments are concerned. More precisely, an empirical regularity that is very often observed in the market is the phenomenon of *"clustering"* of volatility and correlation – days of high (low) volatility tend to cluster in periods. It is not hard to understand that this phenomenon may have disruptive effects on the classical simulation technique. Consider, for example, what could happen if you draw scenarios from a period of low volatility when the market is moving to a high-volatility regime: the risk measure simulated from this data would prove to be looser than expected. On the contrary, if in the recent past the market has been through a high-volatility period, the risk measure could be more conservative than required.

In order to overcome these problems, the simulation technique widely used in the market relies on filtering the data. The idea was introduced by Barone-Adesi and Giannopoulos (1996, 1998). We are going to illustrate their procedure here below.

9.4.1 Filtered Historical Simulation

The main idea behind the procedure proposed by Barone-Adesi and Giannopoulos is to use a GARCH model to filter the data. Scenarios are constructed by drawing random samples from filtered data and using the estimated GARCH structure to simulate the dynamics of profits and losses over the *unwinding* period.

The innovation refers to Step 2 above – that is, the choice of scenarios. In detail, the step is described in the following algorithm: We assume that profits and losses on a position are computed for a set of $i = 1, 2, \ldots, T$ past scenarios and that we want to simulate losses from time T onwards over an unwinding period of n days.

Step 2.a   Specify and estimate a GARCH model on the series of portfolio returns.
Step 2.b   From the estimate, save the series of residuals ε_t and the series of fitted volatilities σ_t. Compute $z_t = \varepsilon_t / \sigma_t$, that is, divide the series of residuals by that of volatilities term by term. The series z_t is called *filtered residuals*.
Step 2.c   Randomly draw n filtered residuals from the series z_t.
Step 2.d   Set $i = 1$.
Step 2.e   Compute $\varepsilon_{T+i} = \sigma_{T+i} z_i$ Notice that for $i = 1$ we already know $\sigma_{T+1} = f(\sigma_T, \varepsilon_T)$
Step 2.f   Use the GARCH specification to compute $\sigma_{T+i} = f(\sigma_{T+i-1}, \varepsilon_{T+i-1})$.
Step 2.g   Set $i = i + 1$ and go back to Step 2.e unless $i > n$
Step 2.h   Compute $r_{T,\ T+n} == \varepsilon_{T+1} + \varepsilon_{T+2} + \cdots + \varepsilon_{T+n}$.
Step 2.i   Go back to Step 2.c until the number of number of scenarios is reached.

Once the generation of scenarios has been run, the algorithm proceeds as in standard historical simulation. The profits and losses are arranged in a histogram and the risk measures are computed on the empirical distribution.

9.4.2   A multivariate extension: a GARCH+DCC filter

One of the problems with historical simulation, in both the classical and filtered approaches is that the multivariate dimension of the risk exposure representation is somewhat lost. This was actually considered to be the price paid to address the problem of departures from Gaussianity in a multivariate setting. Nowadays, the diffusion of methods like copulas or dynamic conditional correlation (DCC) may actually make it possible to have a multivariate extension of the approach above.

As an example, we describe here a simple modification of the filtered simulation approach that uses Engle's DCC approach described in Chapter 3. Assume a number of $j = 1, 2, \ldots, k$ series of portfolio returns. We are still interested in simulating profits and losses over a n-day unwinding period, based on a set of past scenarios $i = 1, 2, \ldots, T$.

Step 2.a.1   Specify and estimate a GARCH model on each of the series of portfolio returns.
Step 2.a.2   Estimate a DCC model for the standardized residuals
Step 2.b   From the estimates, save the series of residuals ε_{jt} and the series of fitted volatilities σ_{jt} and the correlation matrices $\mathbf{R}_t$. Compute $\omega_{jt} = \varepsilon_{jt} / \sigma_{jt}$, that is divide the series of residuals by that of volatilities term by term, for each return. The vector series ω_t has correlation $\mathbf{R}_t$. Determines a sequence of matrices $\mathbf{A}_t$ such that $\mathbf{z}_t = \mathbf{A}_t \omega_t$ are independent. Say $\mathbf{A}_t$ is the matrix of orthonormalized eigenvectors of $\mathbf{R}_t$. The vector $\mathbf{z}_t$ contains the *filtered residuals*
Step 2.c   Randomly draw a set of n k-dimensional filtered residuals from the series $\mathbf{z}_t$.
Step 2.d   Set $i = 1$.
Step 2.e.1   Compute $\omega_i = \mathbf{A}'_{T+i} \mathbf{z}_i$.
Step 2.e.2   Compute $\varepsilon_{jT+i} = \sigma_{jT+i} \omega_{j,\ i}$ for all $j = 1, 2, \ldots, k$ for each return.
Step 2.f.1   Use the GARCH specification to compute $\sigma_{t+i} = f(\sigma_{t+i-1}, \varepsilon_{t+i-1})$ for each return.
Step 2.f.2   Use the DCC specification to compute $\mathbf{R}_{T+i} = f(\mathbf{R}_{T+i-1}, \varepsilon_{T+i-1})$, from which compute $\mathbf{A}_{T+i}$ what ε is the vector of returns.

Step 2.g   Set $i = i + 1$ and go back to Step 2.e unless $i > n$.
Step 2.h   Compute $\mathbf{r}_{T, \, T+n} = \boldsymbol{\varepsilon}_{T+1} + \boldsymbol{\varepsilon}_{T+2} + \cdots + \boldsymbol{\varepsilon}_{T+n}$.
Step 2.i   Go back to Step 2.c until the number of scenarios is reached.

This simple extension takes care of cleaning the data to i.i.d. even in the presence of a time-varying conditional correlation. Notice that if one were willing to rely on a constant conditional correlation (CCC) framework, Steps 2.a.2, 2.e.2 and 2.f.2 could be skipped. As conditional correlation is assumed constant, it would suffice to standardize the residuals by dividing them by the corresponding volatility. Samples could then be directly bootstrapped from these standardized residuals and iteratively used in the simulation: they would in fact carry their own realized value of correlation, which is assumed to be the same, apart from sampling errors, across the sample.

To summarize the main hypotheses behind the algorithms presented, and a guideline about the cases to which one or the other should be applied, we have the following recipe.

1. *Constant volatility and correlation*: Use *classical historical simulation*.
2. *Time-varying volatility and constant correlation*: Use *filtered historical simulation*, applying the GARCH filter series by series.
3. *Time-varying volatility and correlation*: Use *filtered historical simulation*, with a GARCH+DCC filter.

9.4.3   Copula filters

The above analysis was just a suggestion and an example, of course. Other models could be used to filter the data in Case 3, in which conditional and dynamic copula models are the most straightforward ideas that come to mind. For completeness, we report here a very broad description of a copula filter as an example.

Assume again a number of $j = 1, 2, \ldots, k$ series of portfolio returns. We are still interested in simulating profits and losses over a n-day unwinding period, based on a set of past scenarios $i = 1, 2, \ldots, T$.

Step 2.a   Transform the series of portfolio returns into probabilities, applying the probability integral transformations $u_{jt} = F_j(x_{jt})$. Such transformations can use conditional probabilities.
Step 2.b   Estimate a conditional copula model $C_t(u_{t1}, u_{t2}, \ldots, u_{tk})$, which is assumed to be a function of information available at time t.
Step 2.c   Randomly draw a set of n k-dimension vectors $\mathbf{u}_t = u_{t1}, u_{t2}, \ldots, u_{tk}$.
Step 2.d   Iteratively use the vectors to simulate marginals $\mathbf{u}_{T+i}$ as a function of the information set available, such as $\mathbf{u}_{T+i-1}$ and C_{T+i-1}.
Step 2.e   Having computed $\mathbf{u}_{T+n}$, compute $x_{j, \, T+n} = F_j^{-1}(u_{j, \, T+n})$.

9.5   STRESS TESTING

Nonlinear positions may react to changes in the market in ways that are difficult to predict. This is mainly due to the interplay of exposure to changes in risk factors, their volatility and correlation. For this reason it is essential to check the reaction of such positions to stress situations. In principle, stress testing looks like a straightforward technique: just reflect on what may go wrong with your position and create a scenario in which these worries materialize. Actually, performing such stress tests is easier said than done. First, it is not easy to neatly say what the worst scenario might be. Second, it is by no means easy to build meaningful scenarios. Actually, when performing stress tests one has to address three strategic problems:

- Choice of the information source to build scenarios.
- Make the scenarios globally consistent.
- Search for the worst possible scenarios.

In the following we will describe the main choices available to address these issues.

9.5.1   Sources of information

Scenarios can be built from three different sources:

- Historical information
- Implied information
- In-house information.

According to the first choice, one would just re-run history re-evaluating the positions with the prices of particular historical periods of severe financial crisis. So, for example, one could evaluate a position in a CDO tranche by using data from the crisis between the first two weeks of May 2005.

The choice of historical information is exposed to criticisms that are very similar to those discussed about historical simulation. If we may add something, it is that since we are examining extreme cases those arguments appear less clear-cut. Actually, on the one hand it is true that the worst possible scenario may not yet have taken place. "Diabolic Mrs Nature" may still have some trick in store for us, so we may try to work it out before it really happens and save capital for that event. On the other hand, being in the shoes of "Mrs Nature" is no easy task. Taking again the case of the credit market crisis of May 2005, not only did it come unexpectedly to all the players in the market, but as of today it is not even clear how that nasty scenario was created by Mrs Nature herself. By the same token, just imagine designing a scenario such as that of 19 October 1987 before it happened.

Beyond the fight between Mrs Nature and us, some insight on what could happen in the future could be backed out from the market as a whole. Implied information is then another important source for the construction of stress test scenarios. There is actually a third source of information that is very useful in stress tests: it is "in-house" information. Fundamental analysts and chartists produce a lot of such information to support investment ideas for clients and proprietary traders. This flow of information, which is a typical and valuable by-product of the investment and financial intermediation activities, is often overlooked by risk managers. It would represent instead precious matter on which to build realistic and sensible stress test scenarios.

9.5.2   Consistent scenarios

Once the source of information has been selected, the main problem is to build a consistent scenario for all the other risk factors. In fact, stress tests are typically focused on particular events which may occur to specific risk factors, e.g. a crisis in a particular credit sector, or a crash in the equity market. An important issue is what may happen in these cases to other risk factors. Evaluating the effect of a shock to a risk factor on the exposure to that risk factor is, of course, trivial: what instead is more problematic is how that shock would impact on other exposures, because of the co-movements with other risk factors. Historical scenarios provide a natural advantage with respect to this, as the dependence structure among the risk factors is built into the scenario itself. If one would like instead to stress test the portfolios to some scenario that has never occurred in history, he would have to be careful to model it by addressing two questions.

- How does the shock propagate from one risk factor to the others?
- How can the dependence structure possibly change in the presence of the shock?

The second question is particularly difficult to address. The main reason is that we do not have many models of the relationship between risk factors and dependence, particularly when extreme market movements are involved.

Cholesky decomposition

Let us address the problem of propagating a shock from one risk factor through the whole system. The first idea that would come to mind, particularly to econometricians, would be to resort to Cholesky decomposition. We should remember that by Cholesky decomposition we construct a lower triangular matrix $\mathbf{C}$ such that $\mathbf{CC'} = \mathbf{R}$. Remember also that $\mathbf{R}$ is the n-dimensional correlation matrix of the risk factors. Let us denote by $\mathbf{q}$ a k-dimensional vector of shocks, and denote by $\mathbf{e}_j$ an n-dimensional vector with all elements equal to zero, except the jth element, which is set equal to 1. Finally, construct $\mathbf{P}$ as an $n \times k$ matrix in which column j is the vector $\mathbf{e}_j$. This enables us to associate the ith shock in vector $\mathbf{q}$ to a risk factor j. In plain terms, $\mathbf{Pq}$ will be a n-dimensional vector with zeros at all places, except at positions corresponding to the stressed risk factor. A stress testing algorithm based on Cholesky decomposition would simply be as follows:

1. Arrange the shock to the risk factor in vector $\mathbf{q}$ and matrix $\mathbf{P}$.
2. Construct matrix $\mathbf{C}$.
3. Compute the vector of risk factor changes: $\varepsilon = \mathbf{CPq}$.
4. Re-evaluate the portfolio according to risk factor changes ε.

Cholesky decomposition has been largely used in econometrics, precisely in the simulation of dynamic *vector autoregression systems* (VAR). The technique is generally known as an *impulse–response* function: a shock is given to a variable in the system and the dynamic effects through the other variables are simulated using Cholesky decomposition. As econometricians know, however, Cholesky decomposition has a severe flaw: it is not unique. Intuitively, it is easy to check, even in a simple bivariate setting, that the decomposition is different if one shuffles the order of the variables in the system. A solution to this problem can be found among the techniques used in asset allocation.

Black and Litterman approach

Black and Litterman (1992) suggested a Bayesian approach to mix *"in-house"* views, provided by experts, with expected returns estimated on the market. This idea could be usefully borrowed in a risk management framework to design scenarios for stress-testing experiments.

Actually what in asset management is called a "view" is simply a description of an event. Scenarios are simply a collection of events. Sticking to the notation above, we may collect them in a k-dimensional vector $\mathbf{q}$. We may also endow these scenarios with a degree of precision and a dependence structure, represented by a covariance matrix Ω.

Note that we may design two kinds of events. The first refers to the *direction* of a risk factor. Assume, for example, that the change of the ith risk factor, r_i under the scenario may be represented as

$$r_i = \mathbf{e}_i'\mathbf{r} = q_1 + \omega_1 \tag{9.3}$$

where q_1 is the average change of the risk factor in the scenario and ω_1 is a zero mean normal variable. The vector $\mathbf{r}$ contains all of the changes in the risk factors, and vector $\mathbf{e}_i$ has the same meaning as before. The second kind of event refers to the spread between risk factors. We say that, on average, risk factor i would change by more than factor j by q_2 with uncertainty represented by the variable ω_2:

$$r_i - r_j = (\mathbf{e}_i' - \mathbf{e}_j')r = q_2 + \omega_2 \tag{9.4}$$

The views may be arranged in matrix form defining matrix $\mathbf{P}$. In our example above:

$$\mathbf{P}' \equiv \begin{bmatrix} \mathbf{e}_1' \\ \mathbf{e}_3' - \mathbf{e}_2' \end{bmatrix} = \begin{bmatrix} 1 & 0 & 0 \\ 0 & -1 & 1 \end{bmatrix} \mathbf{q} \equiv \begin{bmatrix} q_1 \\ q_2 \end{bmatrix} \omega \equiv \begin{bmatrix} \omega_1 \\ \omega_2 \end{bmatrix} \tag{9.5}$$

Assume that the unconditional distribution of the vector $\mathbf{r}$ is normal with mean μ and variance Σ. Consider the system of vectors $\mathbf{r}$ and $\mathbf{q}$. The unconditional distribution is given by

$$\begin{bmatrix} \mathbf{r} \\ \mathbf{q} \end{bmatrix} \sim \Phi\left(\begin{bmatrix} \mu \\ \mathbf{P}'\mu \end{bmatrix}, \begin{bmatrix} \Sigma & \Sigma\mathbf{P} \\ \mathbf{P}'\Sigma & \mathbf{P}'\Sigma\mathbf{P} + \Omega \end{bmatrix} \right) \tag{9.6}$$

Making a stress test scenario consistent amounts to computing the conditional distribution of $\mathbf{r}$ with respect to $\mathbf{q}$

$$\mathbf{r}|\mathbf{q} \sim \Phi(\mu + \Sigma\mathbf{P}(\mathbf{P}'\Sigma\mathbf{P} + \Omega)^{-1}(\mathbf{q} - \mathbf{P}'\mu); \Sigma - \Sigma\mathbf{P}(\mathbf{P}'\Sigma\mathbf{P} + \Omega)^{-1}\mathbf{P}'\Sigma) \tag{9.7}$$

Notice that all we have done is a *generalized least squares* (GLS) regression of the changes of risk factors vector $\mathbf{r}$ on the events vector $\mathbf{q}$. Notice in fact that $\text{cov}(\mathbf{r}, \mathbf{q}) = \Sigma\mathbf{P}$ and $\text{var}(\mathbf{q}) = \mathbf{P}'\Sigma\mathbf{P} + \Omega$. So, the unconditional mean of vector $\mathbf{r}$ is changed by the distance between events $\mathbf{q}$ and their unconditional means times a set of regression coefficients given by $\text{cov}(\mathbf{r}, \mathbf{q})/ \text{var}(\mathbf{q})$.

Using the same description as before, we may summarize the algorithm as follows:

1. Arrange the shock to the risk factor in vector $\mathbf{q}$ and matrix $\mathbf{P}$.
2. Define a matrix of scenario precision Ω.
3. Compute the vector of risk factor changes: $\varepsilon = \mathbf{r}|\mathbf{q}$.
4. Re-evaluate the portfolio according to risk factor changes ε.

Notice that the result of the algorithm is actually a distribution – namely, the conditional distribution with respect to the set of events (that is the scenario) that was simulated.

We may then choose to represent the risk associated to the scenario by any measure of such distribution. The measure that is usually presented is the average profit/loss under the scenario. However, one could also resort to other measures used in risk management such as Value at Risk or Expected Shortfall.

9.5.3   Murphy's machines

Up to this point, we have just seen how to build and "regularize" scenarios. A final problem, which is particularly relevant for complex portfolios of nonlinear positions, is that of searching the worst possible scenario. Let us assume that you start with a set of scenarios. Once we have decided a risk measure to rank the scenarios, we can of course easily decide which is the worst possible among those in that set. But we may ask the following question: "Could be worse?" The answer is not as easy as "could be raining" as in the *Frankenstein Junior* movie. It is immediately clear that it would be very difficult to answer this question by gradient methods. The reason is that this optimization problem may have many local minima. An idea would be to try to combine the initial scenarios in such a way as to generate others that are worse and worse. Taken to the extremes, this idea leads to *genetic algorithm* (GA) applications.

GA techniques differ from other optimization methods for some peculiar features:

- They use *encoding* of the parameters to be optimized, generally in binary notation. Every encoded parameter is called a *gene*. The set of strings identifying a parameter is called a *chromosome*. A chromosome is then a point in the optimization domain (a *scenario*, in our application).
- The search process uses the genetic material of the existing set of *chromosomes*, called a *population*, differently from other methods that instead at each iteration use a single member from the previous iteration. In our application, GAs allow to use all the views contained in all the scenarios, rather than only those in the worst scenario at the previous iteration.
- The model does not rely on gradients but only on the value of the function to be optimized (the *fitness* function) for the different *chromosomes* in the *population*. A new population is generated by a *cross-over* of the genetic material in the previous generation, plus a light random change of some of it (*mutation*). The *cross-over* process is organized in such a way that the fittest individuals have greater opportunities to produce offspring than the weaker individuals. Mutation allows instead an entirely new material to be added to the *population*.

GA represents the ideal tool to be used in an algorithm to search for the worst possible scenario. A general algorithm, that we may call *Murphy's machine* to remind us of Murphy's law, may be designed as follows:

1. Select a set of scenarios to start the process.
2. Regularize each scenario using the Black and Litterman procedure described above.
3. Compute a risk measure of the conditional distribution of profits and losses for each and every scenario in the population.
4. *Encode* the scenarios in the population in binary notation.
5. Randomly select couples of scenarios from the population. For that purpose, design a random device so that scenarios associated to a higher risk measure could be selected proportionally more often than those associated to lower risk.

6. Generate two new scenarios by the cross-over of two old scenarios. That is, for every couple of scenarios: (i) randomly generate an integer number, say j, smaller than the overall number of binary elements in the chromosomes; (ii) merge the first j binary elements of the first scenario with those to the right of the jth element of the second scenario; (iii) do the same using the first j elements of the second scenario and the remaining elements of the first.
7. Perform *mutation* – that is, randomly change a very small percentage of the binary elements of the chromosomes.
8. Transform back the binary elements to sets of parameters, that is, a new population of scenarios.
9. Go back to Step 2, unless the maximum number of iteration has been reached.

9.6 COUNTERPARTY RISK

When a financial intermediary issues a structured product, the risk manager has the choice between two alternatives:

- Hedge the derivative contract embedded in the product with liquid instruments, such as futures and the like.
- Offset the instrument bought or sold in the product with other counterparties in OTC transactions.

It is clear that the first choice calls for the availability of human resources with adequate education in quantitative finance. Besides this, of course, the strategy runs into objective problems: as most of the derivative contracts embedded in structured products are particularly complex, or exotic, it is often difficult to find a hedging strategy that could be satisfactorily close to the derivative. The second choice overcomes the problem, or rather transfers the problem to a specialized intermediary. The obvious shortcoming is that the counterparty has to be paid for that. A less obvious problem, which is all the more relevant nowadays, is that this strategy leaves the intermediary buying re-insurance exposed to the risk that the counterparty could go bankrupt before the re-insurance contract expires. If this happens, the intermediary would incur a loss equal to the value of transferring the re-insurance contract to another counterparty (*cost of substitution*). This kind of risk is called *counterparty risk*. In this section we will analyse that impact that counterparty risk may have on the risk and the price of derivative contract. We will also discuss the particular arrangements that the two parties may set up in order to mitigate this kind of risk. It will not come as a surprise that, again, the intermediaries will take inspiration from a *futures style* market organization.

9.6.1 Effects of counterparty risk

Curiously enough, it is more difficult to account for counterparty risk in the presence of linear products, rather than nonlinear ones. The very reason is that in linear contracts every counterparty provides insurance to the other, while in non linear contracts one of the two parties buys protection, while the other sells protection in exchange for a premium. It is clear that in the latter case it is only the protection buyer that is faced with a counterparty risk problem: if the protection seller defaults, the protection buyer would not be able to exercise her option. On the contrary, in linear contracts a party may be hurt by default only if two events occur:

- The counterparty defaults before the end of the contract.
- The contract has negative value for the counterparty in default.

To keep things simple, consider a plain forward contract, on an underlying asset S, for delivery at time T. Party A is assumed to be long in the contract, and party B is assumed to be short. Assume we consider that default may occur at time τ, $t \leq \tau \leq T$. If we look at the contract from the point of view of the long party A, we may break down the value of the contract at time τ into two parts depending on whether the contract has positive value (is *in the money*) for party A or has negative value (is *out of the money*) for her. We then introduce an indicator function $\mathbf{1}_B$ indicating default of counterparty B by time τ. Accordingly, we denote RR_B and LGD_B the recovery rate and the loss given default of counterparty B. Taking into account default of counterparty B, the value of the contract for party A would then be

$$
\begin{aligned}
CF_A(S, t : T) &= E_Q[v(t, \tau) \max(S(\tau) - v(\tau, T)F(0), 0)(1 - \mathbf{1}_B)] \\
&\quad + E_Q[v(t, \tau) \max(S(\tau) - v(\tau, T)F(0), 0)\mathbf{1}_B RR_B] \\
&\quad + E_Q[v(t, \tau) \max(F(0) - v(\tau, T)S(\tau), 0)] \\
&= CF(S, t : T) - E_Q[v(t, \tau) \max(S(\tau) - v(\tau, T)F(0), 0)\mathbf{1}_B LGD_B] \qquad (9.8)
\end{aligned}
$$

where $CF(.)$ is the value of the forward contract if it were free from counterparty risk. The equation is easy to explain. If by time τ the short counterparty in the contract is found to be in default, then the long counterparty would have to face the cost of substituting the contract with another counterparty by paying the marking-to-market value of the contract. At the same time she would join the other creditors to recover the percentage RR_B of it. Down the line, the long party would have lost LGD_B times the value of the contract at time τ. By the same token the value of the forward contract for the short party would be

$$
\begin{aligned}
CF_B(S, t : T) &= E_Q[v(t, \tau) \max(v(\tau, T)F(0) - S(\tau), 0)(1 - \mathbf{1}_A)] \\
&\quad + E_Q[v(t, \tau) \max(v(\tau, T)F(0) - S(\tau), 0)\mathbf{1}_A RR_A] \\
&\quad + E_Q[v(t, \tau) \max(v(\tau, T)F(0) - S(\tau), 0)] \\
&= -CF(S, t : T) - E_Q[v(t, \tau) \max(v(\tau, T)F(0) - S(\tau), 0)\mathbf{1}_A LGD_A] \qquad (9.9)
\end{aligned}
$$

where $\mathbf{1}_A$, RR_A and LGD_A denote the default indicator function, the recovery rate and the value of the loss given default figure for counterparty A.

Notice that the effect of counterparty risk is to modify the marking-to-market value of the contract. As a matter of fact, counterparty risk turns linear contracts into nonlinear ones by introducing a short position in an option. Namely, it is a short position in a call option from the point of view of the long end of the contract, and a short position in a put option for the short end of the contract.

To provide a general representation of counterparty risk for the linear contract, we could write

$$
E_Q[v(t, \tau) \max(\omega(S(\tau) - v(\tau, T)F(0)), 0)\mathbf{1}_i LGD_i] \qquad (9.10)
$$

where $i = A$, B and $\omega = 1$ for the long position and $\omega = -1$ for the short one.

Notice that the payoff of counterparty risk is not actually that of a plain vanilla option. In fact, exercise of the option is conditioned by default of the counterparty. Several risk factors could be actually identified in the value of counterparty risk, namely

- interest rate risk
- underlying asset risk
- counterparty default risk
- recovery risk.

All of these risks may be correlated, even though what is most relevant is the dependence structure between the underlying asset and the counterparty. We will address this issue below. For the time being we assume that underlying risk and counterparty risk be orthogonal and that the contract be monitored at a set of dates $\{t_1, t_2, \ldots, t_n\}$. Counterparty risk at time t_0 is then represented by the sum

$$\sum_{j-1}^{n} \text{LGD}_i[Q_i(t_{j-1}) - Q_i(t_j)]E_Q[v(t, t_j)\max(\omega(S(t_j) - v(t_j, T)F(0)), 0)] \qquad (9.11)$$

where $Q_i(t_j)$ is the survival probability of counterparty $i = \text{A}, \text{B}$ beyond time t_j.

Notice that in the representations above the options representing counterparty risk of the long and short counterparties have the peculiarity that the strike price is actually known only at the time of exercise t_j. In fact, it is represented by the delivery price of the contract (that is $F(0)$, the forward price at time 0) times the discount factor from time t_j to the delivery time T. If interest rates are stochastic, the latter variable is not known at time t. We know, however, that under the forward martingale measure the expected value is equal to the *forward price* at time t of an investment starting in t_j and delivering a unit of currency in T:

$$v(t, \tau, T) = \frac{v(t, T)}{v(t, \tau)} = E_{Q(T)}(v(\tau, T)) \qquad (9.12)$$

If we use $v(t, \tau, T)$ instead of $v(\tau, T)$ in the counterparty risk equation and we compute the expectation under the forward martingale measure we get

$$\sum_{j=1}^{n} \text{LGD}_i[Q_i(t_{j-1}) - Q_i(t_j)]v(t, t_j)E_{Q(T)}[\max(\omega(S(t_j) - v(t, t_j, T)F(t_j)), 0)] \qquad (9.13)$$

This kind of approach, assuming independence of the underlying and counterparty risk and representing default risk as a stream of options, was first introduced by Sorensen and Bollier (1994) for the case of swaps. Counterparty risk of a swap contract was represented as a stream of swaptions with strike equal to the swap rate at the origin of the contract, weighted by the probability of default of the counterparty in a given period. Here we have simply presented an extension of that idea to a generic linear payoff. Below, we will further extend the approach to the case of dependence among the risks and the adoption of risk-mitigating techniques. Let us just remark here that this representation is hugely useful since it provides a replicating portfolio for counterparty risk. As usual, a replicating portfolio immediately allows one to recover both the price and the hedging strategy for the corresponding risk factor, which in the case at hand is counterparty risk.

It is worth noting that counterparty risk has the effect of changing the very nature of linear contracts, by introducing nonlinearities and making them similar to the so-called *hybrid products* – that is, products that, by construction, mix credit risk with other risk factors. As a result, beyond the direct effect of introducing a new source of risk exposure, counterparty risk may bring about perverse indirect effects inasmuch as ignoring it may lead to inaccurate pricing and hedging decisions. More precisely, allowing for counterparty risk in linear products leads to

- lower prices of the contracts
- nonlinear hedges
- sensitivity to volatility and correlation.

Figure 9.1 shows the first effect for both long and short positions. Notice that, of course, the value for the long end of the contract is mostly affected by counterparty risk when the price is much higher than it was at the origin, while it is almost nil if the price is substantially lower than that. The reverse is obviously true for the short position, for which the impact of counterparty risk will increase in value following a decrease of the underlying asset.

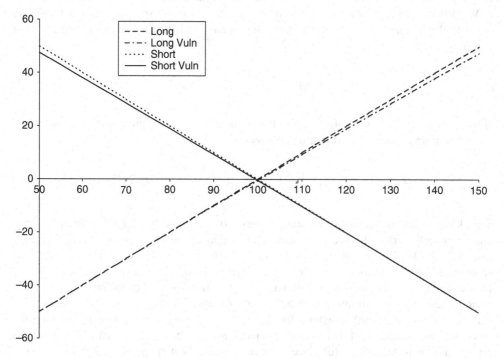

Figure 9.1   Counterparty risk for long and short positions

As counterparty risk amounts to a position in an option, this would actually induce non-linearity in the product, and in the hedge. The delta for the long and short positions would be

$$\Delta_A = 1 - \sum_{j=1}^{n}[Q_B(t_{j-1}) - Q_B(t_j)]\text{LGD}_B\Phi(\alpha)$$

$$\Delta_B = -1 + \sum_{j=1}^{n}[Q_A(t_{j-1}) - Q_A(t_j)]\text{LGD}_A\Phi(-\alpha) \qquad (9.14)$$

$$\alpha = \frac{\ln(S(t)/(F(0)v(t, T)) + 0.5\sigma^2(t_j - t)}{\sigma\sqrt{t_j - t}}$$

where we have used equation (9.13). Figures 9.2 and 9.3 depict nonlinearity for a single element of the sum. Notice that most of the nonlinearity is found to correspond to *at-the-money* values, while the product gets closer and closer to linearity when it gets more *in-the-money* or *out-of-the-money*. In the latter case it goes *to zero*, while in the former case it tends to the value of the expected loss of the counterparty.

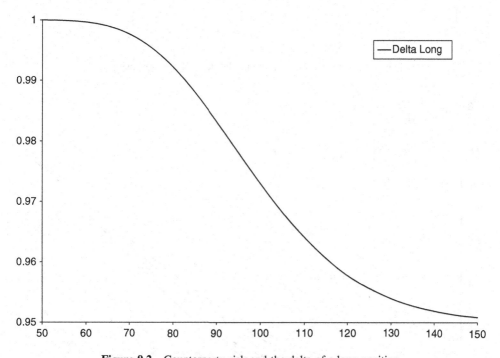

Figure 9.2   Counterparty risk and the delta of a long position

Nonlinearity also implies that the value of the product may be affected by changes in volatility, and this will be more so around the *at-the-money* value. Figures 9.4 and 9.5 show the effects of volatility changes on the counterparty risk for the long and short positions of the contract.

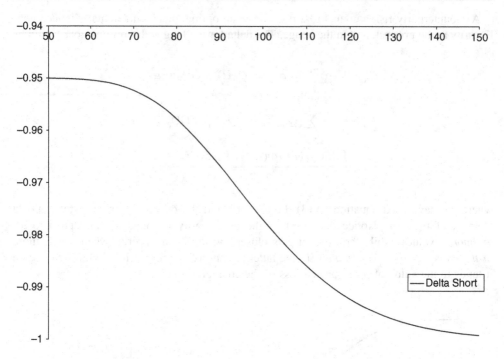

Figure 9.3   Counterparty risk and the delta of a short position

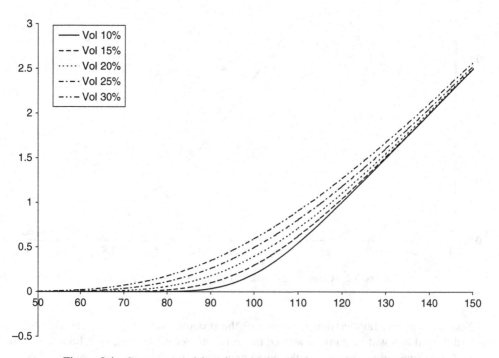

Figure 9.4   Counterparty risk and sensitivity of a long position to volatility

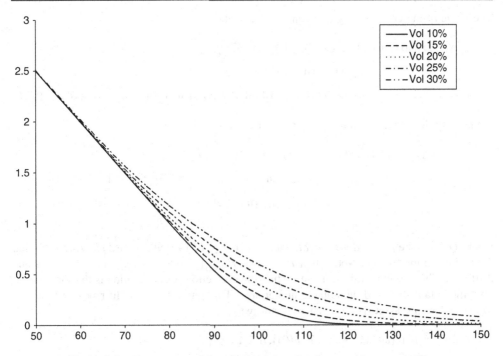

Figure 9.5   Counterparty risk and sensitivity of a short position to volatility

9.6.2   Dependence problems

We saw that counterparty risk is linked to the joint probability of two events: the positive value of the contract for one party and default of the other. Obviously the dependence between the two events may have a relevant impact on counterparty risk. More precisely, we may expect that dependence would have a positive impact on the value of counterparty risk, and therefore a negative impact on the value of the derivative. One would allow for more counterparty risk if one were to buy, for example, a put option on oil from an oil producer, simply because it is more likely that any decrease in the price of oil that triggered exercise of the option could also bring about default of the counterparty.

This dependence problem between underlying asset and counterparty risk can be addressed in two ways:

- change of numeraire
- use of copula functions.

The change in numeraire technique allows the probability measure to change in such a way as to make the two risks orthogonal. To decompose the risks, recall that the value of a defaultable zero-coupon bond issued by entity i is

$$D_i(t, \tau) = E_Q[v(t, \tau)(1 - \mathbf{1}_i \mathrm{LGD}_i)] \qquad (9.15)$$

The value of the counterparty risk can then be written as

$$E_Q[v(t,\tau)\max(\omega(S(\tau)-v(\tau,T)F(0)),0)\mathbf{1}_i\mathrm{LGD}_i]$$
$$= E_Q[v(t,\tau)\max(\omega(S(\tau)-v(\tau,T)F(0)),0)]$$
$$- E_Q[v(t,\tau)[1-\mathbf{1}_i\mathrm{LGD}_i]\max(\omega(S(\tau)-v(\tau,T)F(0)),0)] \quad (9.16)$$

and, using the change of numeraire technique, we get

$$E_Q[v(t,\tau)\max(\omega(S(\tau)-v(\tau,T)F(0)),0)\mathbf{1}_i\mathrm{LGD}_i]$$
$$= v(t,\tau)E_{Q(T)}[\max(\omega(S(\tau)-v(\tau,T)F(0)),0)]$$
$$- D_i(t,\tau)E_{Q^*(T)}[\max(\omega(S(\tau)-v(\tau,T)F(0)),0)] \quad (9.17)$$

where $Q(T)$ is the *forward martingale measure* and $Q_i^*(T)$ is the forward measure such that $D_i(t,T)$ be a martingale. Notice that $E_{Q(T)}(x)=E_{Q^*(T)}(x)$ would imply that x has the same drift under the two numeraires, meaning that the correction for correlation is the same under both the default-free and defaultable numeraires. This implies that credit risk is orthogonal to the underlying asset risk, so that we could write

$$E_Q[v(t,\tau)\max(\omega(S(\tau)-v(\tau,T)F(0)),0)\mathbf{1}_i\mathrm{LGD}_i]$$
$$= [v(t,\tau)-D_i(t,\tau)]E_{Q(T)}[\max(\omega(S(\tau)-v(\tau,T)F(0)),0)] \quad (9.18)$$

As for the second kind of approach, a copula function can be directly used to model the dependence between the two kinds of risk (Cherubini and Luciano, 2003). For the long position we have

$$E_Q[v(t,\tau)\max(S(\tau)-v(\tau,T)F(0),0)\mathbf{1}_B\,\mathrm{LGD}_B]$$
$$= v(t,T)\mathrm{LGD}_B \int_{v(\tau,T)F(0)}^{\infty} \tilde{C}[Q(S(T)>\eta),Q(t\le T)]\,\mathrm{d}\eta \quad (9.19)$$

and for the short position

$$E_Q[v(t,\tau)\max(F(0)-v(\tau,T)S(\tau),0)\mathbf{1}_A\,\mathrm{LGD}_A]$$
$$= v(t,T)\mathrm{LGD}_A \int_{0}^{v(\tau,T)F(0)} C[Q(S(T)\le\eta),Q(\tau\le T)]\,\mathrm{d}\eta \quad (9.20)$$

The dependence structure can then be directly accounted for by estimating it on a time series of the underlying asset and the default probability of the counterparty.

9.6.3 Risk mitigating agreements

Counterparty risk is one of the major concerns of the derivatives and structured finance business nowadays. This problem takes on different aspects, and calls for different solutions, depending on the kind of business relationship involved. On one side, the growing exposure between financial intermediaries and final investors raises concerns of risk and awareness of the final investor: in this case the only solution seems to be that of proper evaluation of the counterparty and determination of the appropriate premium for credit risk, along the lines described in the previous sections. On the other side, structured finance has led to a massive increase in OTC positions among the financial intermediaries for hedging purposes. Default of one of these intermediaries could actually trigger a worldwide systemic crisis. For this reason, financial institutions have reshaped the rules of their bilateral relationships in such a way as to mitigate the effect of counterparty default. Again, as with the VaR concept above, the main idea has been to try to internalize the rules of a *futures style* market in the bilateral relationship.

This process led to a set of "risk mitigating rules" codified in the ISDA protocol agreement. Just as in a futures style market, the main principles are:

- Periodic, daily or weekly, *marking-to-market* of the positions.
- Computation of the net exposure with respect to the counterparty.
- Posting of a collateral deposit for an amount corresponding to the loss.

In plain words, the main principle is that putting money on the table could actually reduce the loss in case of default of one of the two parties in the game. We are now going to see that these mitigating techniques may also be represented in terms of replicating portfolio.

Collateral

Let us now go back to our linear contract CF(.) and include a clause of collateral deposit at time τ when the contract is monitored.

$$\text{LGD}_B(1-Q_B(\tau))\text{Call}(S, t; v(\tau, T)F(0), \tau)$$
$$+ \text{LGD}_B(Q_B(\tau) - Q_B(T))\text{Call}(S, t; S(\tau), T)\text{Pr}(S(\tau) > v(\tau, T)F(0))$$
$$+ \text{LGD}_B(Q_B(\tau) - Q_B(T))\text{Call}(S, t; v(\tau, T)F(0), T)\text{Pr}(S(\tau) \leq v(\tau, T)F(0))$$
$$(9.21)$$

So, counterparty risk consists of three parts

- Default before the collateral is deposited, in which case counterparty risk is measured by a call option with strike equal to the forward price at the origin of the contract.
- Default after time τ if the collateral has been deposited, in which case counterparty risk is measured by a call option with strike equal to the value of the underlying asset at the monitoring date (a *forward start* option).
- Default after time τ if the collateral has not been deposited, in which case counterparty risk is measured by a call option with strike equal to the value of the forward price at the origin of the contract.

The model can be easily extended to cases in which the contract is monitored, and the collateral deposited, at a set of dates $\{t_1, t_2, \ldots, t_n\}$. Notice that the effect is similar to that of resetting the strike price in a futures contract. Conditional on the event that the market has moved in favour of the long end of the contract at the monitoring date, the value of counterparty risk in the next period is a *forward start* option, that is an option with strike reset at the monitoring date. If, instead, the market moves against the long end of the contract, the value of counterparty risk remains a stream of call options with strike equal to the forward price at the origin of the contract. If one looks at the contract from the point of view of the short end, the analysis is simply reversed and the counterparty risk is a put option that is activated only in the case in which the underlying asset has dropped below the discounted value of the forward price at the origin of the contract.

In Figure 9.6 we show the effect of collateral agreement on counterparty risk. The derivative product is assumed to be a forward contract for delivery in one year, and the position is assumed to be monitored on a weekly basis. The two lines represent counterparty risk for every week – that is, the stream of options with exercise date in each week. Overall counterparty risk of the position is then the integral below the two lines.

As we observed, the idea of posting collateral is somewhat mutuated from the organization of trading on *futures style* markets. Actually, this analogy is not perfect. First, in futures markets the margin is posted at the beginning of the transaction. Second, in futures markets the initial margin is deposited by both the long and the short party of the contract. However, the underlying basic intuition is roughly the same: ask the party who is losing money in the contract to pay for the loss before going ahead with the transaction. Furthermore, in analogy with the futures markets organization, this principle naturally rests on another: *mark-to-market* and monitor the value of the contract at short intervals of time. Figure 9.7 shows the reduction in counterparty risk that can obtained by marking-to-market the position over shorter and shorter intervals of time, and the reduction due to collateral agreements. As before, the position is on a forward contract for delivery in one year. Notice that the reduction of counterparty risk becomes substantial for the weekly and daily frequencies.

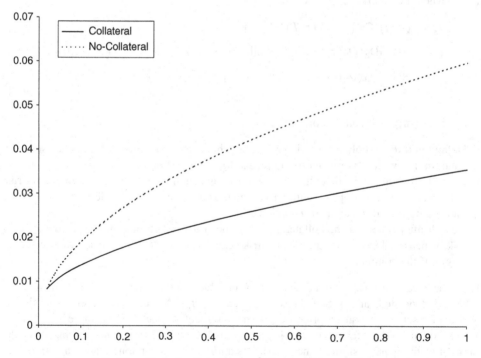

Figure 9.6   The effect of collateral on counterparty risk: weekly monitoring

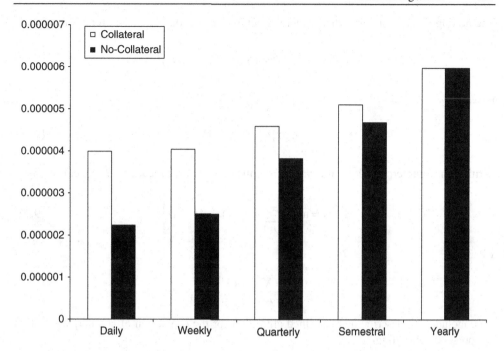

Figure 9.7   The effects of marking-to-market and collateral on counterparty risk

Furthermore, it is at these frequencies that the impact of the collateral agreement is highest, reducing counterparty risk by almost half.

Netting

Until this point we have considered the risk of a single transaction. For multiple positions, *netting* is an important provision that is added to collateral posting. The idea is that the value of all the contracts between two counterparties is marked-to-market over short time intervals (day or week). The value of all the contracts is consolidated and collateral is deposited only for the net value (if negative) of the overall position, rather than contract by contract. By the same token, in the case of default of one party, the counterparty would remain exposed only for the net value of all the positions that are open at the time of default. Application of netting agreement is often limited to derivative contract relationships between financial intermediaries, and for the set of countries whose bankruptcy regulations acknowledge the principle.

Netting applies to all the contracts between the parties, no matter whether linear or not and no matter what the underlying asset may be. From the point of view of evaluation, then, simulation is the only technique available. To illustrate the point in a simplified setting, however, assume that a financial intermediary has a portfolio of p forward contracts, written on a set of underlying assets with the same counterparty:

$$\mathrm{CF}_i(S_i, t, t_i) = \omega_i(S_i(t) - v(t, t_i)F_i) \tag{9.22}$$

The netting agreement states that if there is default of the counterparty at time τ the loss is

$$\text{Loss} = \max \sum_{i=1}^{p}[\omega_i(S_i(\tau) - v(\tau, t_i)F_i)] \tag{9.23}$$

instead of

$$\text{Loss} = \sum_{i=1}^{p}\max[\omega_i(S_i(\tau) - v(\tau, t_i)F_i)] \tag{9.24}$$

Writing the counterparty loss in terms of a replicating portfolio leads to a basket option

$$\text{Loss} = \max\left[\sum_{i=1}^{p}\omega_i S_i(\tau) - A(\tau), 0\right] \tag{9.25}$$

where

$$A(\tau) \equiv \sum_{i=1}^{p}\omega_i v(\tau, t_i)F_i \tag{9.26}$$

To conclude, we describe a streamlined algorithm for the evaluation of counterparty risk in the presence of netting.

- Define a set of monitoring dates $\{t_1, t_2, \ldots, t_n\}$.
- Run a Monte Carlo analysis to price a basket option for each and every date.
- In case of a collateral agreement, the Monte Carlo analysis should take care of collateral accrual.

9.6.4 Execution risk and FpML

There is a final feature that OTC markets would like to import from *futures style* markets. It is the velocity and safety of execution. This is in turn based on the two main features of futures markets: *liquidity* and *product standardization*. Liquidity is probably out of reach, since, as we stated above, it seems to be at odds with the very reason for the existence of OTC markets: increasing liquidity would only come at a cost of higher basis risk. The only response to the liquidity issue is then to ensure reasonable and robust pricing techniques. Much more can instead be done to improve the standardization of products, at least as far as the basic constituents – interest rate, equity and credit derivatives – are concerned. Further development of FpML standards across products and further diffusion of them across intermediaries would be the main driver of this standardization process. Use of the standard would ease the data transmission between counterparties and the automated execution of deals. That would in turn ensure the extension of the *delivery-versus-payment* (DVP) principle to these products, achieving a reduction of *execution risk* similar to that usually found in standard financial product trading.

Execution risk and the use of paper to finalize transaction is actually one of the main concerns of both public and private bodies in charge of designing sound risk management practices. For this reason, the best conclusion to this paragraph, this chapter and this book seems to lie in the following statement by Mario Draghi, Chairman of the Financial Stability Forum:

"The FSF welcomes progress by financial firms in improving the trading and settlement infrastructure for over-the-counter credit derivatives, particularly in reducing backlogs of outstanding confirmations, and in further strengthening counterparty risk management relating to complex products. The good cooperation between the private and public sectors provides a model for future work in other areas. The FSF noted that further work was needed to improve the infrastructure of these rapidly growing market segments, particularly in such areas as the automation of trade processing settlement, and they encouraged the extension of these efforts to equity derivatives and other types of OTC derivatives. The FSF also underscored the importance of reliable valuation practices for illiquid products."

REFERENCES AND FURTHER READING

Artzner, P., Delbaen, F., Eber, J.M. & Heath, D. (1999) Coherent measures of risk, *Mathematical Finance*, **9**, 203–228.

Barone-Adesi, G. & Giannopoulos, K. (1996) A simplified approach to the conditional estimation of value at risk, *Futures and Options World*, October, 68–72.

Barone-Adesi, G., Bourgoin, F. & Giannopoulos, K. (1998a) Don't look back, *RISK*, **11**, 100–104.

Barone-Adesi, G., Giannopoulos, K. & Vosper, L. (1998b) VaR without correlations for non-linear portfolios, *Journal of Futures Markets*, **19**, 583–602.

Cherubini, U. (2005) Counterparty risk in derivatives and collateral policies: The replicating portfolio approach, *Proceedings of the C.R.E.D.I.T Conference*, 22–23 September 2005, Venice.

Cherubini, U. & Della Lunga, G. (1999) Stress testing techniques and Value-at-Risk measures: A unified approach, *Rivista Italiana per le Scienze Economiche e Sociali*, **22**, 77–99.

Cherubini, U. & Luciano, E. (2003) Copula vulnerability, *RISK*, **10**, 83–86.

Crouhy, M., Galai, D. & Mark, R. (2000) *Risk Management*. McGraw-Hill, New York.

Duffie, D. & Huang, M. (1996) Swap rates and credit quality, *Journal of Finance*, **51**, 921–949.

Embrechts, P., Frey, R. & McNeil, A.J. (2005) *Quantitative Risk Management: Concept, Techniques and Tools*. Princeton University Press, Princeton.

Goldberg, D.E. (1989) *Genetic Algorithms in Search, Optimization and Machine Learning*. Addison-Wesley, Reading.

Hull, J. & White, A. (1995) The impact of default risk on the prices of options and other derivative securities, *Journal of Banking and Finance*, **19**, 299–322.

Johnson, H. & Stultz, R. (1987) The pricing of options with default risk, *Journal of Finance*, **42**, 267–280.

Jorion, P. (2001) *Value-at-Risk*. McGraw-Hill, New York.

Kupiec, P.H. (1998) Stress testing in a value at risk framework, *Journal of Derivatives*, Fall, 7–24.

Longin, F.M. (2000) From Value-at-Risk to stress testing: The extreme value approach, *Journal of Banking and Finance*, **24**, 1097–1130.

Mina, J. & Xiao, J.Y. (2001) *Return to RiskMetrics: The evolution of a standard*. Working Paper, RiskMetrics Group.

Sorensen, E.H. & Bollier, T.F. (1994) Pricing swap default risk, *Financial Analysts Journal*, **50**, 23–33.

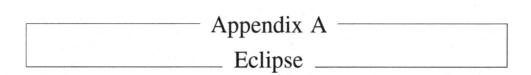

Appendix A
Eclipse

A.1   WHAT IS ECLIPSE?

Eclipse is an open, universal tool platform or tool base developed in recent years by IBM. Open means that Eclipse is an open-source project. Universal means that Eclipse uses an innovative plug-in architecture allowing near-infinite extensions to the base IDE. These plug-ins can do anything from syntax highlighting to interfacing with a source code control system. While the Eclipse project started with just a Java IDE, IBM and RedHat jointly released a C/C++ IDE earlier this year. (Other vendors have also built on the Eclipse platform.)

Unlike other open-source projects that do not allow proprietary derivative works, Eclipse can be extended with proprietary plug-ins, repackaged and sold commercially. In fact, there is a commercial IBM version of Eclipse called WebSphere Studio Workbench. The Eclipse platform itself consists of several major components: the platform runtime, the workspace, the workbench, the standard widget toolkit (SWT), the version and configuration management (VCM) and the help system. The platform runtime manages resources and plug-ins as well as provides bootstrapping code. At start-up, the platform runtime looks for plug-in manifest files – XML files that describe the plug-in – and loads this information into a registry. The platform runtime executes (activates) the plug-ins when they are first requested. The platform runtime itself is the only major component of Eclipse that is not a plug-in. The workspace is a platform-agnostic view of the file system. It provides resource management including low-level change tracking and virtual symbolic links (markers). As these capabilities are made available to the other plug-ins, they do not have to deal directly with varying platforms' file systems.

The user interface for Eclipse is known as the workbench. The workbench is made up of one or more main windows that display a collection of pages. Only one page can be active at a time. Pages can be thought of as a composite of workbench parts. A workbench part can either be a view or an editor. Further, these parts can be any combination of tiled or tabbed layouts. Finally, the workbench offers the concept of templates (perspectives). A template defines a page's parts and layout. Generally speaking, a perspective is tied to one or more workspace resources. Finally, the help component provides an easy way for plug-ins to supply HTML documentation that cannot be presented contextually from the workbench (see Figure A.1.1).

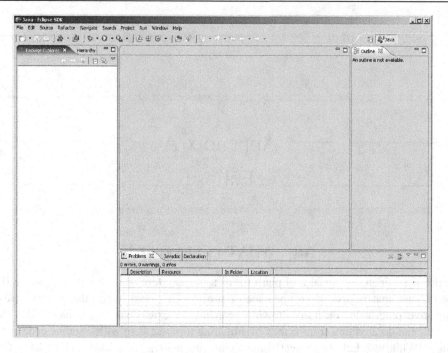

Figure A.1   Eclipse workbench

In addition to the above major components, Eclipse comes with some really useful plug-ins: the debugger, the content assist, ANT, compare, and a library of refactorings.

Eclipse's debugger is quite full-featured for an open-source project. It provides all the functionality you would expect from a commercial IDE, including the ability to set break-points, set values, inspect values, suspend and resume threads, and so on. Additionally, you can debug applications that are on a remote machine.

ANT is an open-source build tool that is part of Apache's Jakarta project. Eclipse provides a graphical front-end to ANT, which allows you to execute any option defined in your ANT build file.

Eclipse also provides two great features, "compare with" and "replace with", that allow you to compare differences between local and remote copies of your source code. This comparison feature goes beyond the standard diff by providing a more contextually aware presentation of the variances.

Finally, Eclipse comes with a library of refactorings. From extract method, to pull-up method, to self-encapsulate field, these refactorings can save you the headache of excessive copying and pasting.

A.2   UML PLUG-INS FOR ECLIPSE

In the great ensemble of Eclipse plug-ins there are a lot of resources for UML design. Among these there are also some free resources like the Poseidon Project and Omondo plug-in. You can download a trial version for free of both at the following sites

Poseidon: http://www.gentlesoftware.com/
Omondo: http://www.omondo.com/

FURTHER READING

http://www.eclipse.org/ is the home page of the Eclipse Consortium and contains detailed information about the code and the project, plus downloads, articles, and links to newsgroups and mailing lists. A synthetic and very useful manual is Steve Holzner's *Eclipse*, published by O'Reilly (2004).

Appendix B
XML

B.1 INTRODUCTION

The "Extensible Mark-up Language" (XML) is a World Wide Web Consortium|W3C-recommended general-purpose mark-up language for creating special-purpose mark-up languages, capable of describing many different kinds of data. In other words: XML is a way of describing data and an XML file can also contain the data, as in a database. It is a simplified subset of Standard Generalized Mark-up Language (SGML). Its primary purpose is to facilitate the sharing of data across different systems, particularly systems connected via the Internet.

XML provides a text-based means of describing and applying a tree-based structure to information. At its base level, all information manifests as text, interspersed with mark-up that indicates the information's separation into a hierarchy of "character data", container-like "elements" and "attributes" of those elements.

In this chapter we will give a brief, general introduction to XML. In the last paragraph we will present FpML, which is a set of financial specification developed by ISDA in order to facilitate OTC transactions. This is a rather technical chapter that the reader interested only in financial aspects can skip to a first reading.

B.2 WHAT IS A MARK-UP LANGUAGE?

Mark-up is a term for metadata, that is, information about information. It originated long before computers, in the field of publishing, where ***publishing mark-up*** referred to the tags inserted into an edited text to tell a processor (human or machine) what to do with the information. In this sense HTML is a classic mark-up language. The following is a simple fragment of an HTML page. Try to copy this in a text file, save it with HTML extension and open it with a browser. What you should get is reported in Figure B.1.

```
<html>
<head>
<title>This is an HTML very simple test</title>
</head>
<body>
My first HTML sentence is: <b>Hello World!</b>
</body>
</html>
```

In the phrase `"My first HTML sentence is: <b>Hello World! </b>"`, for example, the HTML `<b>` tags tell the browser how to display the information between them. Note that each HTML element starts with a start tag `<b>`and ends with an end tag `</b>`. This is also an HTML element:

```
<body>
This is my first homepage. <b>This text is bold</b>
</body>
```

This HTML element starts with the start tag `<body>`, and ends with the end tag `</body>`. The purpose of the `<body>` tag is to define the HTML element that contains the body of the HTML document. Finally the element `<title>This is an HTML very simple test</title>` write the string "This is an HTML very simple test" as the title of the window.

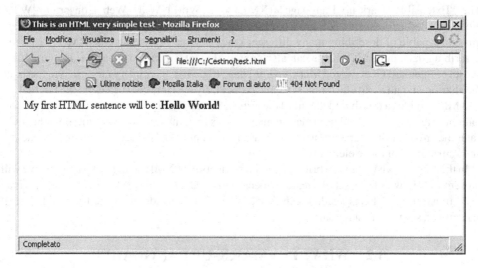

Figure B.1   A simple example of HTML

B.3   WHAT IS XML?

XML is not a mark-up language like HTML. Unlike HTML, XML tags *identify* the data, rather than specifying how to display it. Where an HTML tag says something like "display this data in bold font" (`<b>` ... `</b>`), an XML tag acts like a field name in your program. It puts a label on a piece of data that identifies it (for example: `<message>` ... `</message>`). XML was created to structure, store and to send information. The primary uses of XML are:

- **Exchanging information** between heterogeneous applications, enterprises, databases, etc.
- **Enabling styling and presentation** of the same information on multiple output devices and/or for different purposes and audiences
- As a **storage format** for long-lived or structurally rigorous document-centric information, such as aircraft manuals or enterprise information models.

Let us explain just a bit more on these points. With XML, data can be exchanged between incompatible systems. In the real world, computer systems and databases contain data in incompatible formats. One of the most time-consuming challenges for developers has been to exchange data between such systems over the Internet. Converting the data to XML can greatly reduce this complexity and create data that can be read by many different types of applications. With XML, plain text files can be used to share data. Since XML data is stored in plain text format, XML provides a software- and hardware-independent way of sharing data. This makes it much easier to create data that different applications can work with. It also makes it easier to expand or upgrade a system to new operating systems, servers, applications and new browsers.

B.4 XML SYNTAX IN A NUTSHELL

B.4.1 Mark-up building blocks

The syntax rules of XML are simple and very strict. The rules are easy to learn, and very easy to use. Let's take a look at a simple instance, in this case a fragment of data from a financial database:

```
<?xml version="1.0" encoding="UTF-8" ?>
<ASSET Type = "Equity Index">
  <DESCRIPTION>"MILAN STOCK EXCHANGE INDEX"</DESCRIPTION>
  <ISIN>"IT000MIB30"</ISIN>
  <LEVEL>"33.456,78"</LEVEL>
  <VOLATILITY>"22.3"</VOLATILITY>
</ASSET>
```

An XML file always starts with a prologue. The minimal prologue contains a declaration that identifies the document as an XML document, like this:

```
<?xml version="1.0"?>
```

The declaration may also contain additional information, like this:

```
<?xml version="1.0" encoding="ISO-8859-1" standalone="yes"?>
```

The XML declaration is essentially the same as the HTML header, <html>, except that it uses <?...?> and it may contain the following attributes:

- *version*: Identifies the version of the XML mark-up language used in the data. This attribute is not optional.
- *encoding*: Identifies the character set used to encode the data. "ISO-8859-1" is "Latin-1" the Western European and English language character set. (The default is compressed Unicode: UTF-8.)
- *standalone*: Tells whether or not this document references an external entity or an external data type specification (see below). If there are no external references, then "yes" is appropriate.

In the example above the document conforms to the 1.0 specification of XML and uses the ISO-8859-1 (Latin-1/West European) character set.

The prologue can also contain definitions of entities (items that are inserted when you reference them from within the document) and specifications that tell which tags are valid in the document, both declared in a Document Type Definition (DTD, more on this subject below) that can be defined directly within the prologue, as well as with pointers to external specification files.

This fragment illustrates several of the key building blocks of XML:

- The document consists of **elements** (the <tags> in brackets), which are roughly analogous to fields in a relational database. An element begins with the opening bracket of its start tag, ends with the closing bracket of its end tag, and includes everything in between. For instance, <DESCRIPTION> and <ISIN> are elements.
- An element can have **content**, which is the text between the opening and closing tags. For example, "MILAN STOCK EXCHANGE INDEX" and "33.456,78" are both element contents.
- Some elements contain **attributes**, which are additional information stored inside the opening tag of the element in the form of name = value pairs. Type in this example is an attribute, and its contents ("Equity Index") is referred to as **attribute value**.
- Elements can contain other elements. This is referred to as **nesting** or **containership**. Containership can be used to represent serialized collections of objects or rows of data, or for any other appropriate information. In this example the element ASSET contains the other elements (DESCRIPTION, ISIN, LEVEL and VOLATILITY).

  - *All XML elements must have a closing tag*: The closing tag contains a "/" (e.g. <ASSET> and </ASSET>). You might have noticed from the previous example that the XML declaration did not have a closing tag. This is not an error. The declaration is not a part of the XML document itself. It is not an XML element, and it should not have a closing tag.
  - *XML tags are case sensitive*: With XML, the tag <Letter> is different from the tag <letter>. Opening and closing tags must therefore be written with the same case.
  - *All XML elements must be properly nested*: Improper nesting of tags makes no sense to XML, in particular all XML documents must contain a single tag pair to define a root element and all other elements must be within this root element. All elements can have sub-elements (child elements). Sub-elements must be correctly nested within their parent element:

```
<root>
  <child>
    <subchild>.....</subchild>
  </child>
</root>
```

B.4.2   Well-formed and valid

XML allows you to work formally or informally. For small projects or when prototyping, you can quickly develop **well-formed** documents. On larger projects or projects involving multiple systems, you will usually go further and create **valid** documents.

- *Well-formed* XML conforms to a set of built-in structural rules, including:

  - one unique "root" element
  - every non-empty element has matching start and end tags
  - all elements neatly nested, with no overlaps
  - various character and name restrictions.

- *Valid* XML is well-formed *and*:

  - references or includes a schema or DTD (Document Type Definition)
  - conforms to the rules in that schema.

B.4.3   Schemas Provide Validity

The word "schema" refers to the rules applying to a set of similarly structured documents. In the case of XML, these rules include:

- What elements and attributes may occur?
- In what sequences and nesting?
- What kind of data can they contain (e.g., data types, ranges, character masks, etc.)?

XML provides two schema languages: DTD and XML-Schema.

- DTD (or Document Type Definition) is the schema mechanism invented originally for SGML and inherited by XML. DTDs are relatively document-centric, so they do not include a lot of useful features such as data typing, ranges and picture masks. Also, they are written in a syntax all their own, and there are relatively few tools that can process them.
- XML-Schema is a new schema standard that has been designed specifically for XML. It uses XML syntax, it addresses most of the shortcomings of the DTD format, and the major tools vendors are already shipping technology to support it. As a result, people just arriving in the XML world are advised to ignore the DTD syntax if possible and adopt the XML-Schema standard for their work.

B.5   DTD

A Document Type Definition defines the legal building blocks of an XML document. It defines the document structure with a list of legal elements. A DTD can be declared inline in your XML document, or as an external reference. If the DTD is included in your XML source file, it should be wrapped in a DOCTYPE definition with the following syntax:

```
<!DOCTYPE root-element [element-declarations]>
```

Example XML document with a DTD:

```
<?xml version="1.0"?>
<!DOCTYPE asset [
  <!ELEMENT asset (description, isin, level, volatility)>
  <!ELEMENT description (#PCDATA)>
  <!ELEMENT isin (#PCDATA)>
```

```
  <!ELEMENT level (#PCDATA)>
  <!ELEMENT volatility (#PCDATA)>
]>
<asset>
  <description>"MILAN STOCK EXCHANGE INDEX"</description>
  <isin>"IT00000"</isin>
  <level>"32000"</level>
  <volatility>"15%"</volatility>
</asset>
```

This DTD is interpreted as:

- !DOCTYPE asset (in line 2) defines that this is a document of the type asset.
- !ELEMENT asset (in line 3) defines the asset element as having four elements: "description,isin,level,volatility".
- !ELEMENT description (in line 4) defines the to element to be of the type "#PCDATA".
- !ELEMENT isin (in line 5) defines the from element to be of the type "#PCDATA"
- and so on.

If the DTD is external to your XML source file, it should be wrapped in a DOCTYPE definition with the following syntax:

```
<!DOCTYPE root-element SYSTEM "filename">
```

This is the same XML document as above, but with an external DTD:

```
<?xml version="1.0"?>
<!DOCTYPE asset SYSTEM "example_ch03_02.dtd">
<asset>
  <description>"MILAN STOCK EXCHANGE INDEX"</description>
  <isin>"IT00000"</isin>
  d<level>"32000"</level>
  <volatility>"15%"</volatility>
</asset>
```

And this is a copy of the file "example_ch03_02.dtd" containing the DTD:

```
<!ELEMENT asset (description, isin, level, volatility)>
<!ELEMENT description (#PCDATA)>
<!ELEMENT isin (#PCDATA)>
<!ELEMENT level (#PCDATA)>
<!ELEMENT volatility (#PCDATA)>
```

With DTD, each of your XML files can carry a description of its own format with it and, more importantly, independent groups of people can agree to use a common DTD for interchanging data. Moreover, your application can use a standard DTD to verify that the data you receive from the outside world is valid and you can also use a DTD to verify your own data.

B.6   NAMESPACE

Since element names in XML are not predefined, a name conflict will occur when two different documents use the same element names. This XML document carries information about a single point of an interest rate curve, and each point has two inner elements: TERM and LEVEL.

```
<CPOINT>
  <TERM>"01/01/2005"</TERM>
  <LEVEL>2.1</LEVEL>
</CPOINT>
```

This XML document carries information about an asset in which we have again an element called LEVEL:

```
<ASSET>
  <DESCRIPTION>"MILAN STOCK EXCHANGE INDEX"</DESCRIPTION>
  <ISIN>IT000MIB30</ISIN>
  <LEVEL>33.456,78</LEVEL>
  <VOLATILITY>22.3</VOLATILITY>
</ASSET>
```

If these two XML documents were added together, there would be an element name conflict because both documents contain a <LEVEL> element with different content and definition. To solve the problem, first of all, let us introduce a prefix in this way:

```
<xc:CPOINT>
  <xc:TERM>"01/01/2005"</xc:TERM>
  <xc:LEVEL>2.1</xc:LEVEL>
</xc:CPOINT>
```

and

```
<xa:ASSET>
  <xa:DESCRIPTION>"MILAN STOCK EXCHANGE INDEX"
    </xa:DESCRIPTION>
  <xa:ISIN>IT000MIB30</xa:ISIN>
  <xa:LEVEL>33.456,78</xa:LEVEL>
  <xa:VOLATILITY>22.3</xa:VOLATILITY>
</xa:ASSET>
```

Now there will be no name conflict because the two documents use a different name for their <LEVEL> element (<xc:LEVEL> and <xa:LEVEL>). By using a prefix, we have created two different types of <LEVEL> elements. Instead of using only prefixes, we can add an xmlns attribute to the <LEVEL> tag to give the prefix a qualified name associated with a namespace.

```
<xc:CPOINT xmlns:xc="http://www.w3.org/2001/XMLSchema">
  <xc:TERM>"01/01/2005"</xc:TERM>
```

```
<xc:LEVEL>2.1</xc:LEVEL>
</xc:CPOINT>
```

and

```
<xa:ASSET xmlns:xa="http://www.polyhedron.it">
  <xa:DESCRIPTION>"MILAN STOCK EXCHANGE INDEX"
   </xa:DESCRIPTION>
  <xa:ISIN>IT000MIB30</xa:ISIN>
  <xa:LEVEL>33.456,78</xa:LEVEL>
  <xa:VOLATILITY>22.3</xa:VOLATILITY>
</xa:ASSET>
```

The XML namespace attribute is placed in the start tag of an element and has the following syntax:

```
xmlns:namespace-prefix="namespaceURI"
```

When a namespace is defined in the start tag of an element, all child elements with the same prefix are associated with the same namespace. Note that the address used to identify the namespace is not used by the parser to look up information. The only purpose is to give the namespace a unique name. However, very often companies use the namespace as a pointer to a real Web page containing information about the namespace (see, e.g., http://www.w3.org/TR/html4/). A Uniform Resource Identifier (URI) is a string of characters which identifies an Internet Resource. The most common URI is the Uniform Resource Locator (URL) which identifies an Internet domain address. Another, not so common type of URI, is the Universal Resource Name (URN). In our examples we will only use URLs.

B.7   XML SCHEMA

The XML schema serves the same purpose as DTD, namely to define the allowed structure and value types for specific XML documents, but offers more functionality than DTD.

- XML schemas are the future for XML. DTDs are a dead-end technology, in terms of both vendor support and ongoing work in the W3C. While DTDs support will never completely vanish, the majority of technological advances and all new W3C specifications will be done in alignment with XML schemas, not DTDs.
- XML schemas have better support for defining reusable structures in an object-oriented fashion. These features had to be coerced into the DTD-based specifications, as there is no direct support for such notions in DTDs.
- XML schemas provide direct support for extensions: again, DTDs lack such support.
- XML schemas have facilities that make adding attachments and other addenda to a instance document more straightforward than possible with DTDs.
- XML schemas are fundamentally better designed to allow for independent, decoupled development groups to work on different parts of a specification, with minimal cross-group interaction required, and without necessitating a new revision of the entire specification if only

one of the parts changes. DTD support in this area is minimal, and requires a new overall release if only one "part" changes.

- XML schemas are expressed in XML, unlike DTDs which are written in their own language. This simplifies training for developers who will work with the standards generated.
- Going forward, XML schemas will enjoy better tools support from vendors and the Open Source community than will DTDs.

One of the greatest strengths of XML schemas is the support for data types.

With the support for data types it is easier to describe permissible document content and to validate the correctness of data. For example, when a calendar data is sent from a sender to a receiver it is essential that both parts have the same "expectations" about the content. With XML Schemas, the sender can describe the data in a way that the receiver will understand. A date like this: "03-11-2004" will, in some countries, be interpreted as 3 November and in other countries as 11 March, but an XML element with a data type like this:

```
<date type="date">2004-03-11</date>
```

ensures a mutual understanding of the content because the XML data type date requires the format YYYY-MM-DD.

There are also deeper technical advantages, such as namespace support, that we do not discuss considering the introductory nature of this chapter.

B.7.1   A simple XML schema

This is a simple XML schema file called "example_ch03_02.xsd" that defines the elements of the XML document above:

```
<?xml version="1.0"?>
<xs:schema xmlns:xs="http://www.w3.org/2001/XMLSchema"
targetNamespace="http://www.polyhedron.it"
xmlns="http://www.polyhedron.it"
elementFormDefault="qualified">

<xs:element name="asset">
  <xs:complexType>
  <xs:sequence>
    <xs:element name="description" type="xs:string"/>
    <xs:element name="isin" type="xs:string"/>
    <xs:element name="level" type="xs:decimal"/>
    <xs:element name="volatility" type="xs:decimal"/>
  </xs:sequence>
  </xs:complexType>
</xs:element>

</xs:schema>
```

The asset element is said to be of a complex type because it contains other elements. The other elements (description, isin, level, volatility) are said to be simple types because they do not contain other elements. The syntax for defining a simple element is:

```
<xs:element name="xxx" type="yyy"/>
```

where **xxx** is the name of the element and **yyy** is the data type of the element. XML schema has a lot of built-in data types. Here is a list of the most common types:

```
xs:string
xs:decimal
xs:integer
xs:boolean
xs:date
xs:time
```

The <schema> element is the root element of every XML schema:

```
<?xml version="1.0"?>
<xs:schema>
...

...

</xs:schema>
```

The <schema> element may contain some attributes. A schema declaration often looks something like this:

```
<?xml version="1.0"?>
<xs:schema
xmlns:xs="http://www.w3.org/2001/XMLSchema"
targetNamespace="http://www.polyhedron.it"
xmlns="http://www.polyhedron.it"
elementFormDefault="qualified">
...
...
</xs:schema>
```

The following fragment

```
xmlns:xs="http://www.w3.org/2001/XMLSchema"
```

indicates that the elements and data types used in the schema (schema, element, complexType, sequence, string, boolean, etc.) come from the "http://www.w3.org/2001/XMLSchema" namespace. It also specifies that the elements and data types that come from the "http://www.w3.org/2001/XMLSchema" namespace should be prefixed with "xs:". The fragment

```
targetNamespace="http://www.polyhedron.it"
```

indicates that the elements defined by this schema (`description`, `isin`, `level`, `volatility`.) come from the "`http://www.polyhedron.it`" namespace. The fragment

```
xmlns="http://www.polyhedron.it"
```

indicates that the default namespace is "`http://www.polyhedron.it`" and, finally, the fragment

```
elementFormDefault="qualified"
```

indicates that any elements used by the XML instance document that were declared in this schema must be namespace qualified.

This XML document has a reference to the above XML schema:

```
<?xml version="1.0"?>

<asset
xmlns="http://www.polyhedron.it"
xmlns:xsi="http://www.w3.org/2001/XMLSchema-instance"
xsi:schemaLocation="http://www.polyhedron.
 it example_ch03_02.xsd">

 <description>"MILAN STOCK EXCHANGE INDEX"</description>
 <isin>"IT0000"</isin>
 <level>32456.23</level>
 <volatility>.1567</volatility>
</asset>
```

The following fragment

```
xmlns="http://www.polyhedron.it"
```

specifies the default namespace declaration. This declaration tells the schema-validator that all the elements used in this XML document are declared in the "`http://www.polyhedron.it`" namespace. Once you have the XML schema Instance namespace available:

```
xmlns:xsi="http://www.w3.org/2001/XMLSchema-instance"
```

you can use the `schemaLocation` attribute. This attribute has two values. The first value is the namespace to use. The second value is the location of the XML schema to use for that namespace:

```
xsi:schemaLocation="http:// www.polyhedron.it
 example_ch03_02.xsd"
```

B.8   XML IN FINANCE

There are a number of areas in which the finance community is looking at XML to improve business. Within companies XML is used to integrate legacy systems, some of which implement complex financial models developed over many years and remain mission critical. This integration XML is sometimes internally developed and sometimes build using a selection of third-party mark-up language. In this case the use of XML for integration is not fundamentally different to what is done outside the financial world.

Perhaps the most compelling financial use of XML it is in financial transaction. In the context of structured finance XML is particularly appropriate to deal with the complexity of financial instruments. even with standard contracts, a lot of time is still required to confirm that both parties are actually agreeing to the same deal, to say nothing of OTC derivatives. This, in turn, greatly impacts on the overall cost of transaction. The main applications of XML to finance are, among others: FpML, XBRL and MDDL.

B.8.1   FpML

Financial products Mark-up Language (FpML) is a set of financial specifications which is initially focusing on transactions of over-the-counter financial instruments. FpML messages each have a known and predefined set of defaults which are be overridden explicitly by either party as required. This makes the process of not specifying something explicitly a well-defined one, and allows the confirmation to be done in a fast semi-automatic fashion where only mismatched information is brought to the attention of humans. We include a discussion of FpML in this appendix because of its relevance to financial engineering in general and because it is a good example of a structured approach to the management of information.

B.8.2   XBRL

The eXtensible Business Reporting Language (XBRL) is a financial specification which is initially focusing on company filings and reports. On an international level, the major complexity with company reports at present is that each country has its own accounting standard. In the United States of America (USA), the generally accepted accounting principles (GAAP) is used, while in the united kingdom (UK) it is the UK GAAP, Australia has an Australian GAAP, etc. Each accounting standard requires a different XBRL "taxonomy".

B.8.3   MDDL

Market Data Definition Language (MDDL) is a financial information specification produced by the Financial Information Services Division (FISD), part of the Software and Information Industry Association (SIIA). MDDL 1.0 was released at the start of November 2001, and supports the publication of snapshots and historical time-series of equity prices, financial indexes, and mutual fund data. Many of the world's major financial companies have contributed to the development of the MDDL 1.0 vocabulary, which guarantees that MDDL contains the items that are really used every day. A goal of MDDL is to stimulate the development of new and innovative applications of financial information by providing a common and flexible language that can be used to pass information between applications.

B.9   WHAT IS FpML

FpML (Financial products Mark-up Language) is a protocol for complex financial products based on XML (eXtensible Mark-up Language). FpML has been designed to be modular, easy-to-use and in particular intelligible to practitioners in the financial industry. The FpML standard was first published by J.P. Morgan and PricewaterhouseCoopers on 9 June 1999 in a paper titled "Introducing FpML: A new standard for E-commerce". As a result, the FpML standards committee was founded. The development of the standard, controlled by ISDA (the International Swap and Derivatives Association) will ultimately allow the electronic integration of a large range of services, from electronic trading and confirmation to risk management. It is expected to become the standard for the derivatives industry in the rapidly growing field of electronic commerce. The standard, which will be freely licensed, is intended to automate the flow of information across the entire derivatives partner and client network, independent of the underlying software or hardware infrastructure supporting the activities related to these transactions.

The description in this chapter is based on documentation for the 4.0 version which is freely downloadable from internet (www.fpml.org). FpML 4.0 covers FX, interest rates, equity and credit derivatives though the goal is, over time, to incorporate all types of OTC products. The FpML community is currently working on version 4.2, which already includes additional product support for inflation swaps, asset swaps, credit default swap baskets, and tranches on credit default swap indexes. New processes included are allocations, position reporting, cash flow matching, as well as a formal definition of party roles.

FpML adopts a structured approach by grouping related elements into so-called components. Each component may contain other components and may be contained into other components. Components serve as the building blocks for a flexible and extensible model. The main idea of structured finance which we are describing in this book is that, generally speaking, the complexity of financial products is a result of combining a few simple ideas in a variety of different ways. The component structure supports type definitions that are flexible enough to represent the wide variation of features found in traded financial instruments. There is a symmetrical view of the trade, such that the trade is counterparty neutral and will look identical to either the buyer or the seller of the trade. FpML separates the elements describing a feature of a financial product or trade into separate components, where each component serves a particular semantic purpose. Components are expressed using an XML schema. The definition are organized into small building blocks in order to improve maintainability. FpML makes use of a number of primitive entity components that describe the basic building blocks for financial products:

- FpML_Money
- FpML_AdjustableDate
- FpML_BusinessCenters
- FpML_Interval
- FpML_BusinessDayAdjustment
- etc.

These primitive components are reused in different business contexts.

In the next section we will give a short overview of FpML structure based on the original documentation that is freely available on www.fpml.org, to which the interested reader is referred for any further information.

B.9.1   An overview of FpML structure

Starting from version 4.0, FpML type definitions are expressed using XML schema. FpML is divided into several schema files, which organize the definitions into smaller and more maintainable building blocks. These building blocks include:

- *fpml-main-4-0.xsd*: Root definitions.
- *fpml-doc-4-0.xsd*: Trade definitions and definitions relating to validation.
- *fpml-shared-4-0.xsd*: Shared definitions used widely throughout the specification. These include items such as base types, shared financial structures, etc.
- *fpml-enum-4-0.xsd*: Shared enumeration definitions. These definitions list the values that enumerated types may take.
- *fpml-asset-4-0.xsd*: Underlying definitions plus some types used by these (e.g. ones relating to commissions or dividend payouts).
- *fpml-msg-4-0.xsd*: Definitions related to messaging and workflow.
- *fpml-ird-4-0.xsd*: Interest rate derivative product definitions.
- *fpml-fx-4-0.xsd*: Foreign exchange product definitions.
- *fpml-cd-4-0.xsd*: Credit derivative product definitions.
- *fpml-eqd-4-0.xsd*: Equity derivative option product definitions.
- *fpml-eqs-4-0.xsd*: Equity derivative swap product definitions.

An FpML 4.0 document can be either of two categories:

- A **DataDocument** is a document that contains only data, such as trades, parties and portfolios. The DataDocument type is provided for compatibility with previous version and for those who do not wish to use FpML 4.0 messaging features. When using a DataDocument, none of the FpML messaging features need be used.
- A **Message** is a document that contains a message header and data elements specific to that message. In fact, an FpML message will always be of a more specific type derived from Message, such as "RequestTradeStatus". Thought a very important part of the global FpML architecture, we will not refer further to this part of the standard.

The FpML root element

The FpML element forms the root for an FpML instance document. The structure of the FpML document depends on the `"xsi:type"` attribute. The simplest FpML document is a `"DataDocument"` (`xsi:type="DataDocument"`). This is described in the next section. The FpML root element contains attributes that specify the FpML version ("4-0" for FpML 4.0), the schema name and location, the namespace, and related properties, as well as the `xsi:type`. A fragment of this definition is shown as:

```
<xsd:element name="FpML" type="Document">
  <xsd:annotation>
    <xsd:documentation xml:lang="en">
      The FpML element forms the root for any
      conforming FpML instance document.The
      actual structure of the document is determined
      by setting the 'type' attribute
      to an appropriate derived subtype of the complex
```

```
      type Document.
    </xsd:documentation>
  </xsd:annotation>
</xsd:element>
```

The DataDocument

The DataDocument type contains three elements: trades, portfolios and parties. Portfolios contain only trade references, if the trades themselves need to be included in the document then the trades can be included within the root element (Figure B.2).

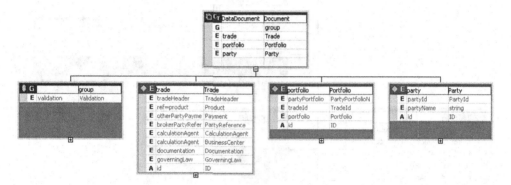

Figure B.2   The Data Document type

The Trade Component

The trade is the top-level component within the root element FpML. A trade is an agreement between two parties to enter into a financial contract and the trade component in FpML contains the information necessary to execute and confirm that trade (Figure B.3).

- **tradeHeader**   The information within tradeHeader is common across all types of trade regardless of product. In FpML 4.0 this element contains the trade date and party trade identifiers, as well as party-specific trade information.
- **product**   Product is an abstract concept in FpML and an actual product element is not used. Instead, one of the FpML products will appear directly under trade.
- **otherPartyPayment**   This component contains additional payments such as brokerage paid to third parties which are not part of the FpML Financial product Markup Language Recommendation 2 April 2004, economics of a trade itself.
- **brokerPartyReference**   The brokerPartyReference identifies the party or parties that arranged the trade.
- **calculationAgent**   The calculation agent identifies the party or parties responsible for performing calculation duties, such as cash settlement calculations.
- **documentation**   The documentation element defines where the legal definitions used for the trade are documented.
- **governingLaw**   The governingLaw element identifies which legal system will be used to enforce the contract.

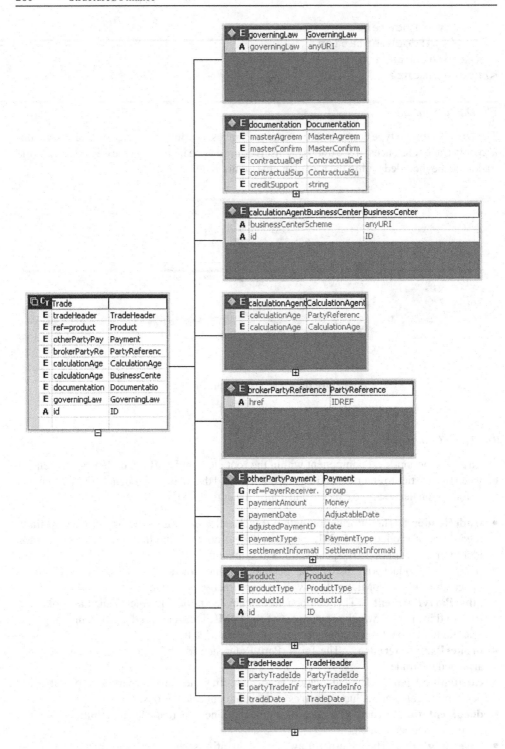

Figure B.3   The Trade Component

The portfolio component

The portfolio component specifies a set of trades as a list of tradeIds and a list of sub-portfolios. Portfolios can be composed of other portfolios using a composition pattern. By using the tradeId to identify the trade, the standard allows for portfolios to be sent around without the full trade record.

The party component

The party component holds information about a party involved any of the trades or portfolios included in the document. The parties involved will be the principals to a trade and potentially additional third parties such as a broker. For this release, this component is restricted to party identification. It should be noted that an FpML document is not "written" from the perspective of one particular party, i.e. it is symmetrical with respect to the principal parties. The particular role that a party plays in the trade, e.g. buyer, seller, stream payer/receiver, fee payer/receiver, is modelled via the use of references from the component where the role is identified to the party component.

The product component

The product component specifies the financial instrument being traded. This component captures the economic details of the trade. It is modelled as a substitution group; each asset class may create one or more product definitions. Some examples of products that different working groups have defined include:

- Interest rate swaps
- FRAs
- caps/floors
- swaptions
- FX spot/forwards
- FX swaps
- FX options
- Equity options
- Equity swaps
- Credit default swaps.

The strategy component

This component defines a special kind of product that allows the structuring of trade by combining any number of products within a strategy. A trade can be of a strategy rather than of a base product; this strategy can then in turn contain other products, such as multiple options. For example, you could define a strategy consisting of an FX call and an FX put to create a straddle or strangle, and then create a trade of that strategy. The strategy component makes use of a composition pattern since strategy itself is a product. This means that strategies can themselves contain strategies.

REFERENCES AND FURTHER READING

About XLM from a general point of view on the web

The main page of the World Wide Web Consortium (W3C) dedicated to XML activity and information is:

www.w3.org/XML/.

A very interesting site with community resources and solutions is:

www.xml.com.

At this site you can find a well-organized and easy-to-understand free tutorial with lots of examples and source code:

www.w3schools.com/xml/.

Books

The XML literature is almost infinite, we report only some manuals that authors have found useful in their daily work:

Van Der Vlist, E. (2002) *XML Schema*. O'Reilly.
St Laurent, S. & Fitzgerald, M. (2002) *XML Pocket Reference*. O'Reilly.
Harold, E.R. & Means, W.S. (2004) *XML in a Nutshell*. O'Reilly.

There are also some interesting chapters in:

Duffy, D.J. (2004) *Financial Instrument Pricing Using C++*. John Wiley & Sons, Ltd, Chichester.

As far as FpML is concerned, the best thing to do is to make a visit to the internet site:

http://www.fpml.org/.

Here you can find everything you need to known about FpML. In particular you'll find important updates with respect to the version discussed in this book.

Index

Printed in the United States
By Bookmasters